The Law of
Local Government

JAMES K. CANNY

DUBLIN
ROUND HALL SWEET & MAXWELL
2000

Published in 2000 by
Round Hall Ltd
43 Fitzwilliam Place
Dublin 2

Typeset by
Gough Typesetting Services
Dublin

Printed by
MPG Books, Cornwall

ISBN 1-85800-167-6

A catalogue record for this book
is available from the British Library.

Table of Contents

Table of Cases

Table of Statutes

Introduction

This book was written partly as a result of the passing of the twentieth Amendment to the Constitution in June 1999, and partly because more and more legislation and government policy are directed to local authorities. Local authorities have been given roles in the planning process, in health and safety, in the provision of essential services, in the provision of amenities, in the provision of housing and in pollution control.

The government of local authorities is addressed in Chapter 1 and outlines the legislative framework under which existing local authorities are based. The structure and the duties of local authorities are examined as well as the powers of local authorities to make bye-laws as well as the duties and powers of elected officials and loan authority officials.

The recent Local Government Bill 2000 is specifically addressed in Chapter 14. Naturally, only a brief outline of each of the sections is given while an attempt is also made to explain the way in which local authorities will operate should the Bill be passed in its present form. Although the Bill was said to be an attempt to modernise the legislation underpinning local government and to use ordinary language, some of its provisions may not be welcome, particularly the re-classification of some of Ireland's oldest boroughs, particularly Kilkenny, as mere towns. Other areas, especially in the greater Dublin region and its hinterland, will welcome the ability to become townships. A new feature of the Bill for local authorities will be the election of the chair of the local authority to be known as the Cathaoirleach, although whether or not this will be a welcome development remains to be seen. However, it will create extra interest in local government and may increase the participation of electors in local government.

The area of local elections is addressed in Chapter 11 and for local authority members may be the most interesting part of the text. The Bill will change the way in which local authority areas are established and may also increase the number of local authorities in the country. One criticism of the Bill may be that is has not done enough to address such specific issues as housing needs and pollution by providing for a unified approach to these problems. The Bill has attempted to create inter-authority co-operation, but problems such as the provision of housing in one local authority area for residents of another local authority area would need to be specifically addressed. This could have been achieved by the creation of a regional housing authority that could also have taken advantage of economies of scale.

Local authorities play a major role in the provision of housing in Ireland and in the control of housing, and the legislative background to this role is examined in Chapter 4. Local authorities add to the national housing stock both by directly building houses and through the shared ownership scheme. This is in addition to their role in preventing overcrowding and unfit housing, although the role of overseeing landlords has of late been passed to the health boards through landlord registration.

Local authorities also have a role in the environment, through powers given to them by the Derelict Sites Act 1990 and the Waste Management Act 1997, and these are examined in Chapters 5 and 10. This area of local government law is sure to increase in importance given the way in which the Irish economy is developing and the ever-increasing load of waste generated by it.

The other roles of local authorities are considered in the remaining chapters including street and casual trading and the control of animals. The chapter on Health Boards was written with a view to showing that these boards are themselves local government bodies and their role is being extended, practically with every administration. The chapter is brief, however, and cannot do justice to the impact that health boards have made on everyday life in Ireland since their establishment by the Health Act 1947.

The Planning and Development Bill 1999 was not considered in this book because, at the time of writing, the Supreme Court had not made a decision on the constitutionality of one part of it and the Bill had yet to become law. A decision is expected early in the Michaelmas term and the Bill itself is important in that it attempts to address the housing shortage in Ireland through the purchase of development land and also attempts to curtail the large profits generated through the sale of development land and the hoarding of land from development.

Finally, a personal note of thanks to all at Round Hall for their support and professionalism, and to my family and friends who continue to support my modest endeavors, and to my "proof reader", Berni O'Neill, who can spot a misspelling at 50 yards. However, mistakes remain mine and readers must note that this book is my interpretation of the law as it stood on February 28, 2000. Anyone who wishes to rely on any reference should examine the legislation and case law on that point carefully as several important issues have not been treated in great detail and are themselves worthy of separate study.

CHAPTER 1

The government of local authorities

A. STRUCTURE OF LOCAL GOVERNMENT

1. Introduction

1–01　The Local Government (Ireland) Act 1898 provided the model for the system of local government in Ireland establishing in each county a body entrusted with the management of the administrative and financial business of that county. The Local Government Act 1898 rationalised the system of local authorities and established a representative system of local government.

1–02　Section 4 of the 1898 Act transferred to each of the county councils all of the business of the grand juries. The county council were given the powers and duties of the grand juries and were conferred with additional powers as were necessary for conducting business within the county.[1] The county councils were also given the power of levying, collecting and recovering the poor rate in each part of the county which was not comprised in an urban district area and which was formerly carried out by the boards of guardians.[2]

2. County boroughs

1–03　The 1898 Act provided that the boroughs of Dublin, Cork, Limerick and Waterford were each to be an administrative county called a "county borough" with a mayor, aldermen and burgesses for each county borough exer-

---

[1]　s.4(1).
[2]　s.6.

cising the powers and duties of county councils.[3] The 1898 Act also transferred the business of the grand jury to district councils as well as the business
of the boards of guardians in so far as they relate to the district council area.
Section 33 of the 1898 Act also transferred the business of the rural sanitary
authority to the district council.

1–04 The Local Government (Dublin) Act 1993[4] divided the administrative
county of Dublin into three administrative counties of South Dublin, Fingal
and Dun-Laoghaire-Rathdown.[5] The Local Government Act of 1991[6] had
already reorganised the various Dublin authorities (Dublin Corporation, Corporation of Dun Laoghaire, Dean's Grange Joint Burial Board and the
Balbriggan Town Commissioners) into the present areas of South County
Dublin, Dun Laoghaire-Rathdown and Fingal as well as retaining the administrative area of Dublin Corporation. The Corporation of Dun Laoghaire, the
Borough Corporation was transferred to the Dun Laoghaire-Rathdown County
Council while the remaining area of the old County Dublin was divided into
the remaining two councils.

1–05 Section 21 of the 1991 Act provided for the creation of three assistant
county managers one each for the three councils, while section 22 provided
for the appointment of county managers for the council areas.

1–06 Section 32(1) of the 1993 Act provides that each of the local authorities in the Dublin area have a duty, when formulating their policies and carrying out their functional programmes, to have regard to the overall interests of
the combined administrative areas. The local authorities must also take all
appropriate steps to ensure proper co-ordination of all policies and programmes
including development plans which are likely to have a material effect on the
interests of their combined areas.

3. Towns and urban districts

1–07 Urban district councils were generally made up of boroughs which
became urban sanitary authorities under the Public Health Act 1878 and were
towns with a population of 6,000 or more, or towns having commissioners
under various local acts, or towns which were confirmed as urban districts
under the Public Health Act 1878. The Local Government (Ireland) Act 1878[7]

---

[3] s.21.
[4] No. 31 of 1993.
[5] Brought into effect under the Local Government (Dublin) Act 1993 (Commencement)
     Order 1993 (S.I. No. 400 of 1993).
[6] No. 11 of 1991.
[7] s.22.

also provided that all urban sanitary authorities were to be called urban district councils. Town commissioners are similar to urban district councils in the way in which meetings are held and the way in which business is conducted but have their statutory base in the Commissioners Clauses Act of 1847.

1–08 There are forty nine towns which have urban district councils: Arklow, Athlone, Athy, Ballina, Ballinasloe, Birr, Bray, Buncrana, Bundoran, Carlow, Carrickmacross, Carrick-on-Suir, Cashel, Castlebar, Castleblaney, Cavan, Ceannus Mor (Kells), Clonakility, Clones, Cobh, Dundalk, Dungarvan, Ennis, Enniscorthy, Fermoy, Killarney, Kilrush, Kinsale, Letterkenny, Listowel, Longford, Macroom, Mallow, Midleton, Monaghan, Naas, Navan, Nenagh, New Ross, Skibereen, Templemore, Thurles, Tipperary, Tralee, Trim, Tullamore, Westport, Wicklow and Youghal. There are five county boroughs, namely Cork, Dublin, Galway, Limerick and Waterford, and five borough corporations, Clonmel, Drogheda, Kilkenny, Sligo, and Wexford all of which had ancient charters founding them.

1–09 The words "city" or "town" mean the "the corporate or quasi corporate entity established by law as a community for municipal or legal administration"[8] and do not refer to the common use of those words. Towns mean those with Commissioners set up under the Towns Improvement (Ireland) Act 1854 namely Ardee, Balbriggan, Ballybay, Ballyshannon, Bandon, Bantry, Belturbet, Boyle, Cootehill, Droichead Nua (Newbridge), Edenderry, Gorey, Granard, Greystones, Kilkee, Leixlip, Lismore, Loughrea, Mountmellick, Muine Beag (Bagenalstown), Mullingar, Passage West, Portlaoise, Shannon, Tramore, and Tuam. The towns of Callan, Fethard, Newcastle West, Rathkeale, Roscommon and Tullow and the successor for all purposes of those town commissioners in each case is the council of the county which includes the particular area.

1–10 The boundaries of all of the towns are subject to change and alteration and the current Ordnance Survey maps for the relevant towns should be examined for the precise extent of their boundaries.

B.   DUTIES OF LOCAL AUTHORITIES

1–11 Section 82(1) of the Local Government (Ireland) Act 1898 imposed a duty on every county and district council to keep all public works maintained at the cost of the county or district in good condition and repair and to take all steps necessary for that purpose.

---

[8] In *Re McCann* [1953] I.R. 118, see also *State (Wyer) v. O'Sullivan* [1953] I.R. 109; (1955) 89 I.L.T.R. 81.

1–12   The Cork City Management Act of 1929 was the first of the post independence pieces of legalisation which addressed the management, administrative and financial business of a local authority. The Act provided that the council for the County Borough of Cork was to directly exercise and perform all and every of the powers, functions and duties of the Corporation in relation to the making of any rate or the borrowing of any moneys, the making, amending or revoking of any bye-law, the making of any order and the passing of any resolution by virtue of which any enactment is brought into operation in or made to apply to the Borough and the revoking of any such order and the rescinding of any such resolution.

1–13   The Corporation also had the reserved function to exercise the powers conferred by section 5 of the Borough Funds (Ireland) Act 1888, in relation to the promotion or the opposing of legislation, the prosecution and defence of legal proceedings, and the application for those purposes of the borough fund, borough rate or other public funds and rates under the control of the corporation, together with the appointment or election of any person to be a member of any public body. Parliamentary and local elections also were placed wholly within the sphere of the corporation of the borough. The power to admit persons to the freedom of the City of Cork, is under the sole preview of the council. The Cork City Management (Amendment) Act 1941 made further provision for the management of the administrative and financial business of the county borough of Cork. Section 7 added to the list of reserved functions of the corporation including the nomination of a person to be a candidate at an election of a person to the office of President of Ireland.

1–14   The Cork City Management (Amendment) Act provides that the City Manager shall attend any meeting of the Council or of any committee of the Council at which he is requested by the Council to attend, and shall give to the Council or a committee advice and assistance as may be reasonably be required.[9] The Manager is also obliged to arrange for the attendance at a meeting of the officers of the Corporation as may be necessary, having regard to the business to be transacted at such meeting.

1–15   Section 9 of the 1929 Act made provision for the appointment of a city manager who was to perform and exercise for and on behalf of the Corporation the powers, functions and duties of the Corporation in relation to the appointment and removal of officers and servants of the Corporation (including the Town Clerk, but not including the Manager) and shall also exercise

---

[9]   For the rules relating to meetings of local authorities, see Maloney and Spellman, *"The Law of Meetings"* (Dublin,1999).

and perform all other powers, functions and duties of the Corporation other than the reserved functions.

1–16 The 1929 Act was followed by the Local Government (Dublin) Act of 1930[10] which merged the areas of Blackrock, Dun Laoghaire, Dalkey, Killiney and Ballybrack into the borough of the Corporation of Dun Laoghaire while the urban areas of Pembroke, Rathmines and Rathgar were merged into the Corporation of Dublin City. All powers, functions, and duties vested by statute in the Lord Mayor in relation to any market, whether as clerk of the markets or otherwise became merged with the powers, functions, and duties of the City Corporation. All of the powers, functions, and duties of the City Corporation shall be exercised and performed for and on behalf of the City Corporation by the City Council or the City Manager.

1–17 The 1930 Act provided for new elections for the City and Borough Corporations including the provision for the election of commercial members of the City Council, a provision which was later repealed by the Local Government (Dublin) Act of 1935,[11] while it was also provided that the first ordinary member of the City Council elected at a city election for each borough electoral area was to be an alderman while every member of the City Council who is not an alderman was to be referred to as a councillor, a practice which still remains. The 1930 Act replaced the then existing committees which were established under the Tuberculosis Prevention (Ireland) Acts,[12] the Diseases of Animals Act of 1894 and the waterworks committee established under the Dublin Corporation Waterworks Act of 1861.[13]

1–18 The 1930 Act, in a mirror image of the 1929 Act, also established reserved functions which could only be performed by the City Council or by the Corporation and which were similar to the provisions contained in the 1930 Act. The Act, likewise, gave the power to the manager to carry out the functions and powers not reserved to the elected officials. It also imposed a duty on the manager to advise the elected members on the exercise of their reserved functions and in the preparation of plans for the elected members consideration.

1–19 Similar provisions were contained in the Limerick City Management Act of 1934 including the abolition of existing bodies,[14] who were concerned

---

[10] No. 27 of 1930.
[11] No. 10 of 1935.
[12] 1908 and 1913.
[13] s.41.
[14] Namely the Board of Health, the committee established under the Tuberculosis Prevention (Ireland) Acts 1908 and 1913 and the gas committee, together with the Board of Guardians of the Limerick Union.

with for the extension of the boundaries of the city by the making of an application to the Minister for Local Government. Like the two acts which preceded it, the 1934 Act gave the county manager the right, or rather the responsibility to oversee the employees and officials of the local authority. It provided that the officers and servants of the Corporation were to perform their duties in accordance with such directions as the manager may from time to time give, either generally or in regard to the performance of any particular duty or any particular class or classes of duties or by any particular officer or servant of the Corporation, and the manager shall have and exercise control and full supervision of and over officers and servants and any and every act or thing done or to be done by them in their capacity as officers and servants of the Corporation.[15]

1–20   The Waterford City Management Act of 1939[16] transferred the duties and powers of the then county borough of Waterford to the City Corporation and reserved to the council of the Corporation the functions regarding the making of any rate or the borrowing of any moneys, the making, amending, or revoking, of any bye-law. It also transferred the making of any order and the passing of any resolution by virtue of which any enactment is brought into operation in or made to apply to the City and the revoking of any such order and the rescinding of any such resolution, the application to be made to any authority in respect of the making or revoking of any such order, the nomination of a person to be a candidate at an election of a person to the office of President of Ireland, the powers in relation to the promotion or the opposing of legislation, and the application for those purposes of the public funds and rates under the control of the Corporation, the appointment or election of any person to be a member of any public body,   parliamentary and local elections. The Waterford Corporation retains the reserved function of the admission of persons to the freedom of the City, the appointment, suspension and the removal of the manager and the granting of an allowance or gratuity to the manager on his ceasing to be the manager, the determination of the amount of the salary and remuneration of the Mayor, applications to the Minister for a provisional order under this Act extending the boundary of the City, together with the doing under an Act passed before the 1939 Act of anything which is declared by that Act to be, in the case of the county borough of Dublin, a reserved function within the meaning of the Local Government (Dublin) Act 1930.

---

[15] s.21.
[16] No. 25 of 1939.

C . COUNTY MANAGER

1–21 The system of the appointment of county managers was extended to the remainder of the country through the passing of the County Management Act of 1940.[17] The Act provided that there shall be in every county a county manager for such county who shall be called and known as the ". . . County Manager", with the name of the county prefixed before it.[18] Section 3 of the Act provided that the office of the Dublin City Manager and the office of Dublin County Manager shall always be held by one and the same person, a position which has since changed with the passing of the Local Government Act of 1991.[19] The county manager is also the manager for each of the elected local authorities within whose functional area the elective body is situate, that is of a county borough, an urban district council, and town commissioners as well as for any board, committee or other body.

1–22 Section 5(1) provided that every person appointed to be the county manager for a county shall hold office until he dies, resigns, or is removed from office or resigns, while the retirement age for managers has been set at the usual age of 65. The county manager for a county cannot be removed by the council of that county without the sanction of the Minister.[20] The county manager for a county cannot be suspended or removed by the council save by a resolution passed by the council seeking the suspension or removal of the manager. Such a resolution requires not less than two-thirds of the members of such council voted and that the intention to propose the resolution giving not less than seven days' notice was given to every person who is a member of such council.[21]

1–23 Where a county has an assistant county manager the county manager for a county may delegate to such assistant county manager or to any of the assistant county managers such of his powers, functions and duties as the county manager shall think proper.[22] A county manager may revoke a delegation made by him.[23]

1–24 Where there is no assistant county manager appointed and whenever the county manager is on vacation or is, through illness, absent from his county, or suspended from performance of his duties, temporarily incapable of ex-

---

[17] No. 12 of 1940.
[18] s.3(1).
[19] No. 11 of 1991.
[20] s.6(1).
[21] s.6(2).
[22] s.16(1).
[23] s.16(2).

ecuting the functions of his office, a deputy county manager may be appointed for the duration of such vacation or incapacity, but may be removed at any time during such vacation or incapacity.[24] Where a county manager is on vacation and where a county manager is incapable or is absent from his county, the power of appointing a deputy county manager may be exercised by the county manager before a vacation or incapacity, after consultation with the chairman of the county council. In every other case, namely due to or owing to illness or suspension and also where a county manager is on vacation or is so incapable owing to absence from his county and a deputy county manager has not been appointed, the power of appointing a deputy county manager shall vest in the chairman of the county council.[25] A deputy county manager shall have all the powers and shall execute and perform all the functions and duties of a county manager, except for the appointment of a deputy county manager, which remains with the chairman of the county council.[26]

D.   FUNCTIONS OF LOCAL AUTHORITIES

1–25   Local authorities may take such measures, or engage in such activities or do such things in accordance with law, including the incurring of expenditure, as it considers necessary or desirable to promote the interests of the local community.[27] These measures are defined as a measure, or activity or thing which are intended to promote the interests of the local community provided such a measure promotes, directly or indirectly, the social, economic, environmental, recreational, cultural, community or general development of the functional area of the local authority concerned or of the local community or of any group consisting of members of the community.[28] Under the Local Government Act of 1994 a local authority may take measures in relation to amenities, facilities and services related to artistic and cultural activities, sports, games and similar activities, as well as general recreational and leisure activities, civic improvements, environmental and heritage protection and improvement, and the public use of amenities.[29]

1–26   Local authorities may also take appropriate measures in relation to the provision of allotments, fairs and markets and amenities, facilities and services related thereto, and facilities and services related to the promotion of public safety, including fire safety, road safety, as well as in connection with

---

[24] s.15(1).
[25] s.15(2).
[26] s.15(4).
[27] Local Government Act 1991, s.6.
[28] s.6(1), 1991 Act.
[29] s.31(2).

water safety and rescue and mountain and cave safety and rescue. The fifth schedule to the 1994 Act contains a list of amenities, or facilities or services which a local authority may provide for the benefit of the community and are listed under the headings of artistic and cultural activities, sports, games and related activities, general recreational and leisure activities, civic improvements, general environmental and heritage protection improvement, and the public use of amenities, natural and man made.

1–27 Under the heading of artistic and cultural actives the local authority may provide measures in relation to the provision of art galleries, arts centres, concert halls, museums, theatres, opera houses and the holding of artistic and cultural performances, exhibitions and events. Under sports and games the local authority may take measures including the provision of both indoor and outdoor playing fields, athletic tracks, swimming pools and other bathing places, sports centres, gymnasia and other facilities and the holding of sporting events.

1–28 Under civic improvements the local authority may arrange for the provision of street furniture, paving, clocks, statues, monuments and other features, such as illumination and decoration and other measures designed to upgrade the urban environment. To improve the general environment and provide heritage protection and improvement the local authority may make provision for the landscaping, the planting of trees and other flora, measures for the conservation, preservation and protection of landscapes and habitats, of buildings and other features of artistic, amenity, architectural, historic, heritage or natural interest. The local authority also may, for the public use of amenities, both natural and man made, arrange for the provision of access, signs, vehicle parks, safety equipment, information and refreshment facilities, sanitary accommodation, utilities, seating, shelter and any other apparatus, equipment or anything else necessary to facilitate such use.

1–29 In all cases the local authority may make charges for the use of or admission to amenities, facilitates or services which are provided by the authority and as maybe appropriate.[30] With respect to the provision of libraries, the library authorities are the county councils and the corporation of county boroughs.[31] Library authorities are able to take such measures and activities in relation to the provision of library services as it considers necessary or desirable. A library authority may in particular arrange for the provision of suitable premises and facilities, including mobile facilities, for the borrowing of and reference to books, other printed matters, tapes, discs, slides, videos and such other material as is considered appropriate. Library authorities may also arrange activities and events of educational, cultural, recreational or simi-

---

[30] s.31(3).
[31] s.32(1).

lar interest and provide such information services as can in its opinion be
supplied in conjunction with its functions as a library authority.[32] Library authorities may also make arrangements with other library authorities or public
authorities or other bodies including schools. However, a library authority
may not undertake any activity which would unnecessarily duplicate an activity arising from the performance of a function by any other public authority or
person. Library authorities also have the power to acquire land by agreement
or by compulsory purchase.[33]

1–30   Library authorities are obliged, from time to time, to prepare and adopt
a programme for the operation and development of the library service. In making or preparing a development programme the authority must include an outline of the existing service, the development objectives and priorities of the
authority, the measures which are to be taken and the financial implications of
the programme. The adoption of a library development programme is a reserved function.[34]

E.   GENERAL COMPETENCIES

1. Local Government Act of 1991

1–31   The Local Government Act of 1991 states that a local authority may
represent the interest of the local community in such a manners as it thinks
appropriate.[35] A local authority may, in order to give effect to their representative role, ascertain and communicate to other local authorities and public
authorities the views of the local community in relation to matters as respects
which those other authorities perform functions and which affect the interests
of the functional area of the authority and the local community. The local
authority may also facilitate and promote interest and involvement in local
government affairs, and promote, organise or assist the carrying out of research, surveys or studies with respect to the local community.[36] The making
of a decision by a local authority in relation to the representation of the views
of the local community is a reserved function. However a local authority may
not be forced to either directly or indirectly perform any duty of liability enforceable by proceedings before any court to which the authority may not be
otherwise be subject.[37]

---

[32] s.33.
[33] s.33(8).
[34] s.33(7).
[35] Local Government Act 1991, s.5(1).
[36] s.5(2).
[37] s.5(4).

1–32   A local authority may take measures or engage in such activities or do such things in accordance with law[38] as it considers necessary or desirable to promote the interests of the local community.[39] A measure or activity or thing is deemed to be a measure, activity or thing which promotes the interests of the local community if it promotes, directly or indirectly, the social, economic, environmental, recreational, cultural, community or general development of the functional area of the local authority concerned or of the local community. A local authority may, in order to pursue its role in the community, carry out and maintain works of any kind, it may provide, maintain, preserve or restore land or structures of any kind or facilities, or provide any service which in the opinion of the local authority is likely to benefit the local community.[40] Local authorities are also empowered to provide assistance in money or in kind upon such terms and conditions as the authority considers appropriate to persons engaging in any activity which in the opinion of the local authority would benefit the community. The local authority may also provide assistance in money or in kind, including the provision of prizes and other such incentives, and upon terms and conditions which the authority considers necessary in respect of the organisation or promotion or competitions, seminars, exhibitions, displays, festivals or other events. The local authority may also organise or promote such events.[41] The term "in kind" includes grants, loans, guarantees, or land and structures of any kind and services, as well as plant and machinery or the carrying out of works, as well as the provision of the services of the staff of the local authority, the provision of financial aid in relation to the employment of staff and the provision of professional or technical assistance. A decision by a local authority to provide assistance in money or kind is a reserved function.[42] Local authorities may not undertake or provide assistance which would prejudice or duplicate an activity which stems from the performance of a statutory function by any person within the functional area of the authority or which would involve wasteful or unnecessary expenditure by the authority.[43]

1–33   A local authority, in performing its functions are to have regard to the resources which are available or likely to be available to it for the purpose of such performance and the need to secure the most beneficial, effective and efficient use of such resources. The local authority is also to have regard to the need to maintain adequately those services provided by it which it considers to be essential and, in so far as practicable, to ensure that a reasonable balance

---

[38] Including the incurring of expenditure.
[39] s.6(1).
[40] s.6(2).
[41] s.6(2).
[42] s.6(4).
[43] s.6(6).

is achieved, taking account of all relevant factors. Local authorities are also to have regard to the need for co-operation and co-ordination of its activities with those of other local authorities and public authorities so as to ensure efficiency and economy in the performance of its functions. Where appropriate the local authority is to have regard to the need for consultation with other local authorities and public authorities in appropriate cases, and to the policies and objectives of the Government or any Minister of the Government in so far as they may affect or relate to its functions.[44]

1–34 Local authorities have a general power under section 8 of the Local Government Act of 1991 to provide ancillary functions and that the authority may do anything which is ancillary, supplementary or incidental to or consequential on or necessary to give full effect or which will facilitate or which is conducive to the performance of a function conferred on the authority. Local authorities are required under section 8 to decide by resolution the allocation of a grant between projects or services which has been allocated by the Minister to a local authority, however, this does not refer to a grant which was given in respect of a specific project or service of a local authority.[45]

1–35 Section 9 of the 1991 Act allows the Government, by provisional order, to transfer a function of a Minister of the Government[46] that, in the opinion of the Government, could be performed effectively by local authorities of a specified class or classes and is a function relating to the provision of a public service. The Minister may also transfer a function of a local authority to another local authority where in the opinion of the Minister, the function could be performed more effectively by local authorities of another class.[47]

1–36 Section 35 of the Local Government Act of 1994 makes it clear that the powers which are conferred on a local authority by section 8(1) of the Act of 1991 extend to anything which is related to the general administration or operation of the authority. It is also stated that a reference to a function conferred on a local authority in section 8(1) is to be construed as referring to all such functions as may at any material time stand conferred on the local authority by or under any Act.

---

[44] s.7(1).
[45] s.8(4).
[46] Other than a function that is required by the Constitution to be performed by a Minister of the Government.
[47] s.9(2)(a).

2. Local government liability[48]

1–37   All local authorities are capable of suing and being sued, and are similar to other corporate entities. Local authorities are therefore liable for the actions and negligence or torts which are committed by the servants or agents of the authority. Local authorities may, therefore, be sued for negligence, nuisance, trespass as well as to other wrongs.[49] The courts have over the past treated local authorities, or rather public authorities, in much the same manner as a private citizen.[50] As with all cases involving principles of tort, certain items need to be proved or shown, essential proofs, the most important of which is negligence or an examination of the standard of care. In defending a case of negligence involving a local authority the plaintiff must show not only that the local authority was in some way negligent but that the authority also owed a duty of care to the plaintiff, and that this duty was not in some way mitigated by a defence or exemption, such as remoteness, or prohibitive cost or social utility.[51]

1–38   In *Ward v. McMaster*[52] liability was imposed on the County Council on the basis that there had been a sufficient relationship of proximity or neighbourhood between the plaintiff and the County Council to such an extent that in the reasonable contemplation of the council carelessness on their part in the carrying out of their actions might likely cause the plaintiff damage. The Supreme Court found that the County Council had a duty of care to the plaintiff, and McCarthy, J.'s judgement refers to the principles contained in the cases of *Donoghue v. Stevenson*,[53] *Siney v. Dublin Corp.*[54] and *Anns v. Merton London Borough Council*[55] and that it was a simple extension of those principles of negligence to find that there was a relationship between the plaintiff and the County Council and that this relationship created the duty to take reasonable care which in turn had arisen from the public duty of the County Council under statute.[56] It has been suggested that this judgement means that local authorities have a general duty of care to all applicants arising from the public duties of the authority under statute.[57] In effect this means that the law of negligence can overcome the principle that where a statutory provision is en-

---

[48] This paragraph merely touches on the issue of local government or public authority liability for a more in deep examination see McMahon and Binchy, Hogan and Morgan.
[49] See Keane, p.51.
[50] McMahon and Binchy, p.341, misfeasance of public office being a notable exception.
[51] *ibid.*, p.340.
[52] [1988] I.R. 337.
[53] [1932] A.C. 56.
[54] [1980] I.R. 400.
[55] [1978] A.C. 728.
[56] In this case the Housing Act 1966.
[57] McMahon & Binchy, p.342.

acted for the common good rather than for private individuals that it does not create civil liability.[58]

1–39 But it is not only the law relating to negligence which concerns local authorities. Since local authorities are also statutory authorities they are open to cases involving breaches of statutory duty. In many cases both negligence and breach of statutory duty are pleaded. Whether or not a breach of a statutory duty gives rise to civil liability is in itself a difficult question to answer but the statutory provision itself may be a guide as to whether civil liability does or does not apply. Where the legislation is silent as to civil liability, courts have generally tended to examine the effect or nature of the legislation, for example whether the provision was enacted for the benefit of a particular class of persons rather than for the general public, and if so that that class of persons should be able to maintain an action for civil liability if the public authority is guilty of negligence and owes a duty of care to the claimant.[59]

F.   MAKING OF BYE-LAWS

1–40 Local authorities have the power to make bye-laws in relation to the use, operation, protection, regulation or management of any land or services which are under the control or the management of the local authority.[60] A local authority may also make bye-laws, where in its opinion it is desirable in the interests of the common good of the community that an activity or other matter should be regulated or controlled or that any nuisance should be controlled or should be suppressed.[61] Local authorities continue to have a power to make bye-laws in connection with other matters such as the control of litter, parking, and the control of dogs. Other authorities have their own independent authority to make bye-laws in connection with their activities in particular such as harbour authorities or the Dublin Docklands Authority.[62] The approval of any draft bye-laws which are to be made by a local authority is a reserved function.[63]

1–41 Before making a bye-law a local authority is obliged to, not less than two months before making a bye-law, publish a notice in one or more newspapers circulating in the area to which the bye-laws relate indicating that it is

---

[58] *ibid.*, p.343.
[59] McMahon and Binchy, p.377.
[60] s.37(1).
[61] s.37(2)
[62] Harbours Act 1996, No. 11 of 1996, and the Dublin Docklands Development Authority Act 1997.
[63] s.37(6).
[64] s.38(1).

proposed to make certain bye-laws and stating their general purpose, and indicating the times at which a copy of the draft bye-laws are available for public inspection. Copies of the draft are also to be provided to any person on payment of a reasonable sum. The notice which is published must also state that the local authority will consider any submissions in relation to the draft which may be submitted to the local authority in writing before a specified date, not being less than seven days after the end of the period for inspection of the draft.[64]

1–42 For a period of not less than one month, and as specified in the published notice, the local authority are obliged to keep a copy of the draft bye-law open for public inspection, free of charge, during ordinary office hours.[65] Following consideration of any submissions made to it the local authority may then make the bye-laws either by adopting the bye-laws without any changes or the authority may make such changes as the authority may, at its discretion determine.[66] Bye-laws then come into effect within thirty days after the date of their adoption. Bye-laws are then published in Iris Oifigiuil and the local authority must also place a notice in one or more newspapers circulating in the area to which the bye-law relates.[67] However, failure to publish a notice of the making or the approval of the making of bye-laws does not invalidate the bye-law.[68] After making bye-laws local authorities must keep a copy of the bye-laws for inspection at their offices and make available copies of the bye-laws for purchase at a reasonable fee.[69] Local authorities are obliged to maintain a register of bye-laws which are made and to keep the register available for inspection at the principal officers of the local authority during normal office hours.[70]

1–43 Where bye-laws are made in relation to the use, regulation or management of land which is provided by a local authority, the local authority are obliged to endeavour to keep a notice that a bye-law applies displayed at or near the lands. However, failure to display a notice is not a defence to a prosecution for a contravention of a provision of a bye-law.

1–44 However, in certain cases a slightly different procedure applies in that a Minister may by regulations designate a matter or a class of matters which before a local authority can make a bye-law must first seek the approval of the Minister.[71]

---

[65] s.38(2).
[66] s.38(3).
[67] s.42.
[68] s.42(4).
[69] s.42(3).
[70] s.42(6).
[71] s.39.

1–45 Persons who contravene a provision of a bye-law may be guilty of an offence and can on summary conviction be subject to a fine of not over £1,500[72] or such lesser amount as may be specified in the bye-laws. If the contravention of a provision of a bye-law continues after a conviction the person who has caused the contravention may be liable to a further fine of not over £100.[73] Further offences are provided for in respect of obstructing or impeding an authorised officer or refusing to comply with a request of an authorised officer. An offence is also committed when a person refuses to give their name and address when demanded by an authorised officer.[74] Offences may be prosecuted by the local authority or by members of the Garda Síochána.

1–46 Bye-laws may provide for a person to be served with a notice and to specify a fixed payment in respect of a contravention of a bye-law.[75] A notice which is served in respect of a contravention of a bye-law must specify the name and address of the alleged offender, the notice must also state in general terms the nature of the contravention alleged to have been committed, the date and place of the alleged contravention, the amount of the payment, the period within which and the place where the fixed payment may be made, and that the alleged offender is entitled to disregard the notice and defend a prosecution of the alleged contravention in court.[76]

G. EXECUTIVE FUNCTIONS OF LOCAL AUTHORITIES

1–47 Every power, function, or duty of the council of a county or of an elective body which is not a reserved function is deemed to be an executive function of the local authority.[77] Every county manager has the power to exercise and perform all the executive functions of the council and, in particular all powers, other than a power which is vested by law in the council and which are expressly made exercisable by resolution of such council, functions, and duties of such council in relation to the officers and servants of such council and the control, supervision, service, remuneration, privileges, and superannuation, of the officers and servants.[78] Likewise the county manager exercises, for the several elective bodies for which he is the manager, the executive functions of those bodies and, in particular, all powers, functions

---

[72] Amended from £1,000 by s.35 of the Litter Pollution Act 1997.
[73] s.40(2).
[74] s.40(4).
[75] s.41.
[76] s.41(2).
[77] s.17(1).
[78] s.17(2).

and duties of the elective bodies in relation to the officers and servants of such body and the control, supervision, service, remuneration, privileges of the officers and servants.[79]

1–48   The county manager is also responsible for all other matters, including the making of contracts and the affixing of the official seal, as are necessary or which are incidental to the exercise or performance of the executive functions of the local authority. However, a county manager is precluded from affixing the official seal of the local authority to any document except in the presence of the chairman of the local authority or in the presence of a member or members nominated by the local authority.[80]

H. RESERVED FUNCTIONS

1–49   Reserved functions are carried out by way of resolution of the council, while an executive function is performed by the manger through the signing of an order in writing, containing a statement of the time and date at which it was signed.[81] Under section 19 of the 1955 Act any function which a resolution is required by the Act is declared to be a reserved function.

1–50   Section 41 of the Local Government Act of 1991 now provides that it shall be a general function of the members of a local authority to determine by resolution the policy of the local authority in accordance with, and subject to, the provisions of the enactments relating to the authority. In addition, the Minister may by order declare that a specified function or specified functions of local authorities shall be performed by resolution of the members of the authority. However functions which cannot be classed as being reserved by the Minister or by resolution includes, functions relating to the officers or servants of a local authority or the control, supervision, service, remuneration, privileges or superannuation of the officers or servants.

1–51   The 1940 Act specified certain functions to be reserved functions in the second schedule to the Act. These functions include the making of a rate, that is the rate in the pound not a rate on individuals, the borrowing of money, the demanding under any enactment of the whole or a part of the expenses of the council of a county or of an elective body from any other local authority, the making, amending, or revoking bye-laws, the making or revocation of any order or the passing or recision of a resolution by virtue of which a particular

---

[79] s.17(3).
[80] s.17(5), 1940 Act.
[81] s.19(1), 1940 Act.

enactment is brought into operation within the functional area of the authority, the making of an application or an order or the causing of an inquiry to be made relating to the alteration of boundaries of the authority. Any proposal or an application for alteration of a local authority boundary is now governed by section 29 of the Local Government Act of 1991[82] and such a proposal or application remains a reserved function as a resolution of the council is required.

1–52   The second schedule also included parliamentary and local elections as being reserved functions, and these functions are still reserved under local elections legislation, as are the powers which were previously conferred on local authorities by the Borough Funds (Ireland) Act of 1888[83] which was repealed by the Local Government Act of 1994.[84] Other functions which are declared in the second schedule to be reserved functions are the admission of persons to the freedom of a borough, the suspension or removal of a county manager, the granting of a superannuation allowance or a gratuity to a county manager who has ceased being a county manager. The Minister for the Environment and Local Government may by order direct that other powers, functions and duties are also reserved functions.

1–53   The appointment of rate collectors was a reserved function, however, the County Management (Amendment) Act of 1972[85] amended section 16 of the 1940 Act and has made the appointment of rate collectors an executive function, namely one carried out by the manager. The appointment of a manager is a reserved function in that section 5(4) of the 1955 Act states that an appointment of a person as manager shall be by resolution.

1–54   Other reserved functions include: the making, review, amendment or replacement of a litter management plan under section 10 or 12 of the Litter Act;[86] the fixing of the rate for car tax under the Local Government (Financial Provisions) Act of 1997;[87] the making, review, variation or replacement of a waste management plan under the Waste Management Act of 1996[88] together with similar plans under the Local Government (Water Pollution) Act of 1977;[89] the making of bye-laws and making an exemption within the terms of section 19, the making of a scheme under section 20 of the Control of Horses Act of

[82] No. 11 of 1991.
[83] 51 & 52 Vict. c. 53.
[84] No. 8 of 1994.
[85] No. 32 of 1972.
[86] No. 12 of 1997.
[87] No. 29 of 1997, ss.9(2) and (3).
[88] No. 10 of 1996, s. 22(10).
[89] No. 1 of 1977, s.15(8).

1996;[90] the making of bye-laws and the extinguishment of a market right under section 8(7) of the Casual Trading Act of 1995;[91] the making of regulations for the general control of traffic and of pedestrians and of the parking of vehicles on public roads, the erection of a special category sign under the Road Traffic Act of 1994;[92] the issue of polling cards, the adoption of a library development programme, the adoption of bye-laws under section 37(6) and decision to hold or to cease to hold membership of an association of local authorities under section 64(8) of the Local Government Act of 1994 together with the powers to make bye-laws in part seven;[93] the sending of a draft plan to the National Roads Authority and the making and revocation of a toll scheme as well as the making of bye-laws in relation to toll schemes, the entering into an agreement in relation to the maintenance or construction of roads with other parties under the Roads Act of 1993;[94] the nomination of candidates under the Presidential Elections Act of 1993;[95] the establishment or the alterations of boundaries under the Local Government (Dublin) Act of 1993;[96] agreements between the Environmental Protection Agency and local authorities under the Act of 1993;[97] the giving of assistance to housing bodies under section 6 of the Housing (Misc. Provisions) Act of 1992 together with other functions under the Housing Acts 1966 to 1998; together with the powers or functions under sections 9(6), 14(4), 28,[98] the making of a scheme dividing a county into polling districts under section 28 of the Electoral Act of 1992;[99] the making of a decision by a local authority in relation to the representation of the views of the local community under 5(3) of the Local Government Act 1991, together with a decision under section 6 regarding the general competence of local authorities.[100]

Other reserved functions include the making of allowances to the chairman of a local authority under section 42, a decision to incur entertainment expenses and the holding of special events, the conferring of civic honours, the twinning of local authority areas, the adoption of the annual report regarding the functions of the local authority, the attendance of local authority representatives at conferences; the providing of assistance to housing bodies, the adoption of the housing estimates under the Housing Act of 1988;[101] the car-

---

90 No. 37 of 1996.
91 No. 19 of 1995.
92 No. 7 of 1994.
93 No. 8 of 1994.
94 No. 14 of 1993.
95 No. 28 of 1993.
96 No. 28 of 1993.
97 No. 7 of 1993.
98 No. 18 of 1992.
99 No. 23 of 1992.
100 No. 10 of 1991.
101 No. 28 of 1988.

rying out of research into air pollution, the making of special control areas, the making, review or replacement of an air pollution management plan under the Air Pollution Act of 1987;[102] various functions under the Canals Act of 1986;[103] a request to make documents part of the archive of the Department of An Taoiseach under the National Archives Act of 1986;[104] certain functions under the Fire Services Act of 1981;[105] designation of casual trading areas and the extinguishment of market rights under the Casual Trading Act of 1980;[106] the granting of assistance or the making of grants in the promotion of the arts under the Arts Act of 1973;[107] the consideration or a report and the making of a declaration by a county council that the promotion of a coast protection scheme is required under the Coast Protection Act of 1963;[108] various functions under the Local Government (Planning and Development) Act 1963 in particular the declaration by a county council of an area to be a town, the making of a development plan and any variations of the plan, the revocation and modification of a permission to develop land, and the making of a special amenity order;[109] the closing of roads to vehicles under section 94 of the Road Traffic Act of 1961;[110] and the adoption of part three of the Gaming and Lotteries Act of 1956 in relation to the licensing of amusement halls and funfairs.[111]

1–55   The Local Government Act 1991 (Reserved Functions) Order 1993[112] declares that various local authority functions, listed in the Schedule to the Order, shall be performed by resolution of the elected members of the authority and these functions thus become reserved functions for the purposes of the City and County Management Acts. These are the making of a contribution under section 40 of the Local Government (Sanitary Services) Act 1948, the making of arrangements under section 96 (1) of the Road Traffic Act 1961, the making of a request to the Minister to extend the period during which a planning authority may comply with the requirements of section 20 (1) of the Local Government (Planning and Development) Act 1963, entry into an agreement under section 7 of the Local Authorities (Traffic Wardens) Act 1975, the making of a contribution under section 29 of the Local Government (Water Pollution) Act 1977, the making of a plan under article 4 of The European

---

[102] No. 6 of 1987.
[103] No. 3 of 1986.
[104] No. 11 of 1996.
[105] No. 30 of 1981.
[106] No. 43 of 1980.
[107] No. 33 of 1973, s.12.
[108] No. 12 of 1963, s.2.
[109] No. 28 of 1963.
[110] No. 24 of 1961.
[111] No. 2 of 1956, s. 13.
[112] No. 37 of 1993.

Communities (Waste) Regulations 1979, the making of a scheme under section 279 (5) of the Social Welfare (Consolidation) Act 1981, the making of a special waste plan or of any variation in such plan under article 4 of the European Communities (Toxic and Dangerous Waste) Regulations 1982, entry into arrangements under section 15 (2) of the Control of Dogs Act 1986 and the granting of assistance (other than the provision of services of staff) under section 15 (4) of that Act, the making of a decision to provide a public abattoir under section 19 (1) of the Abattoirs Act 1988, the consideration of a request made under section 30 (3) of the Local Government Act 1991.

1–56   A further reserved function, which had been of some considerable interest in the past, is the ability of a local authority to license gaming machines. The local authority must pass a resolution under section 13 of Part III of the Gaming and Lotteries Act 1956.[113] A local authority may also decide to by resolution adopt Part III over all of its administrative area or a part of it, and the authority may also by resolution rescind the adoption. A resolution shall not have effect unless not less than one month's notice of the intention to propose it has been given in writing to every member of the local authority and has been published by advertisement in at least two newspapers circulating in the area to which the proposal relates.[114]

I. SECTION 2 REQUEST

1–57   Section 2 of the 1955 Act allows that a local authority may by resolution direct that, before the manager performs any specified executive function of the local authority, the manager shall inform the members of the local authority of the manner in which the manager proposes to perform that function, and the manager is bound to comply with the resolution made by the local authority. A resolution does not apply or extend to the performance of any function of the manager in relation to the officers or servants of a local authority or the control, supervision, service, remuneration, privileges or superannuation of such officers or servants and any resolution which has been passed in connection with these matters has no effect and shall be void.[115] Every dispute which arises between a local authority and the manager as to whether a resolution touches on matters outside the scope of section 2 shall be referred for decision to the Minister.

1–58   The manager is obliged to inform the members of a local authority

---

[113] See *Camillo v. O'Reilly*, unreported, Supreme Court, March 23, 1988 and *Dublin Corp. v. O'Hanrahan*, unreported, High Court, December 15, 1987.
[114] See *Application of Murphy*, unreported, High Court, December 21, 1987.
[115] s.2(3).

before any works, other than general maintenance or repair, of the local authority are undertaken or before committing the local authority to any expenditure in connection with proposed works, other than works of general maintenance or repair.[116] However, the manager cannot be prevented from carrying out any works or from dealing with any situation which the manager considers an emergency. Where the members of a local authority are informed of any works which are not works which the local authority are required by or under statute or by order of a Court to undertake, the local authority may by resolution direct that the works shall not be proceeded with, and the manager is obliged to comply with the resolution.[117]

1–59 In *East Wicklow Conservation v. Wicklow Co. Co.*[118] the Supreme Court held that the general scheme of local government distinguishes between those functions exercised by a local authority under an express statutory duty and other duties carried out in pursuance of a discretion.[119] The word "required" used in section 3 of the City and County Management (Amendment) Act 1955 referred to a mandatory requirement imposed on a local authority in relation to any type of works. The case resulted from a decision by Wicklow County Council to reject a proposal for a new landfill site, which was made subject to public consultation and the preparation of an environmental impact statement and the Ministers consent, by resolution under section 3 of the 1955 Act, even though there was an urgent need for a new landfill site. The county manager refused to comply with this resolution and the applicants were granted leave to apply for an order of *certiorari*. The High Court refused the relief sought on the basis that the works were required by or under statute and therefore fell within the exception to section 3 of the 1955 Act.[120] Section 55 of the Public Health (Ireland) Act 1878 provides that a sanitary authority are obliged to provide fit buildings or places for the deposit of any matters collected by them pursuant to that Act.

1–60 The Supreme Court on appeal found that to fulfil the duty under section 55 of the 1878 Act to provide a fit place for the deposit of waste material, firstly a decision on a place that would appear suitable and secondly that the carrying out of works necessary to make it a fit place for the deposit of waste material. Section 55 of the 1878 Act necessarily requires a local authority to choose where it will place the landfill site. Therefore the choice of the landfill site was authorised by statute and once that choice was made the works which

---

[116] s.2(7).
[117] s.3.
[118] *East Wicklow Conservation Community Ltd. v. Wicklow Co. Co. and Blaise Treacy* [1997] 2 I.L.R.M. 72.
[119] at p. 79.
[120] [1995] 2 ILRM 16, *per* Costello J.

were to be carried out there were works which the local authority were required by or under statute to undertake within the meaning of section 3 of the City and County Management (Amendment) Act 1955. The fact that the obligation to provide a fit place for the disposal of waste material could be discharged at a different location was not enough to grant the relief sought. The exception under section 3 of the 1955 Act with respect to "works required by or under statute" must be understood as referring to "any works" as used in section 2(7) and section 3, and was a general term and was not to be interpreted as meaning only specific clearly identified works.

J.   SECTION 4 RESOLUTIONS

1–61   Section 29 of the County Management Act of 1940 provided that a council could by resolution require any particular act to be done in exercise or performance of the executive functions of the council. This was replaced by section 4 of the City and County Management Act of 1955 which states that a local authority may by resolution require any particular act, matter or thing specifically mentioned in the resolution and which the local authority or the manager can lawfully do or effect to be done or effected in performance of the executive functions of the local authority.

1–62   The intention to propose a resolution under section 4 must be given in writing, signed by at least three members of the local authority. The notice to the county manager should also contain a copy of the resolution and the fact that the resolution shall be considered at a special meeting and shall then specify a day, not less than seven days after the day on which the notice is received by the manager, for the holding of the special meeting. A section 4 resolution cannot be considered at a meeting of the local authority which is held less than seven days after the day on which the manager received the notice.[121]

1–63   For the resolution to succeed it must be passed by majority, and the majority must exceed one-third of the total number of the members of the local authority.[122] Once the resolution has been passed the manager must carry out the matter, act or thing which was specified in the resolution, if and when and so far as money has or is been provided for. A resolution under section 4 must be specifically addressed to a particular act or thing, the resolution does not apply or extend to the performance of any function of a local authority generally. Nor does it extend to every case or occasion of the performance of

---

[121] s.4(3).
[122] s.4(6).

any such function. A resolution under section 4 cannot apply or extend to the performance of any executive function in relation to the officers or servants of a local authority or the control, supervision, service, remuneration, privileges or superannuation of such officers or servants. Any dispute which may arise between the manager and the members of the local authority must be referred to the Minister for decision whose decision is final and conclusive.[123]

1–64 However, where a resolution under section 4 would involve the authority in an illegal payment out of the funds of the local authority or which would involve a deficiency or loss from funds, the manager must object to the proposal and must state the grounds of the objection.

K . ORDERS OF MANAGERS

1–65 Every order shall, until the contrary is proved, be deemed to have been signed at the time stated in the signed order.[124] Every county manager is obliged to keep a register in which shall be entered a copy of every order made by the county manager. Every county manager is obliged, at every meeting of the council, to produce for the inspection of the members of the council that part of the register which contains any orders made since the previous meeting of the council.[125] Any member of the council is entitled on demand to be furnished by the county manager with a copy of any particular order which has been made by the county manager.

1–66 Where under any Act a public notice is required to be given by the council of a county of the passing of a particular resolution by which any particular act or thing is done or any particular decision is taken by the council, or before the holding of a meeting of the council at which is passed a resolution by which any particular act or thing is done or any particular decision is taken by the council, the public notice is to be given by the county manager before the manager makes the order by which the manager does a particular act or thing or takes a particular decision.[126]

1–67 Section 20 of the County Management Act specifies that the officers and servants of the county council are to perform their duties in accordance with the direction as the county manager may from time to time, either generally or in regard to the performance of any particular duty.[127] Every county

---

[123] s.4(10).
[124] s.19(3).
[125] s.19(5).
[126] s.19(2).
[127] s.20(1).

manager exercises control and full supervision of and over such officers and servants and any and every act or thing done or to be done by them in their capacity as officers and servants of such council or of any other body which the county manager is manager of. With respect to the remuneration, privileges or superannuation of the officers and servants of a local authority the county manager has the duty, and power, to consider and decide all questions as may from time to time arise in relation to the service, remuneration, privileges and superannuation of the officers and servants of the council. With respect to payments and the authorisation of payments the county manager considers and decides all questions relating to any payment as may from time to time arise in relation to the service, remuneration, privileges and superannuation of the officers and servants of the council.[128] The county manager also has the role of countersigning with the nominated officer of the local authority any payment out of funds in respect of any liability or expenses which has been incurred by the council.[129]

1–68   Every county manager has the right to attend meetings of the council of the county and of every other elective body, and to take part in discussions at such meetings as if he were a member of such council or body, but the manager is not entitled to vote on any question which is decided by a vote of the members of such council or the elective body.[130] A county manager is obliged, in so far as is not inconsistent with the due performance of the managers' duties, attend any meeting of the council which he is requested by the council to attend, and any meeting of a committee of the council which the manager is requested by the council to attend, and any meeting of an elective body for which the county manager is manager and which the manager is requested by the body to attend, and any meeting of a committee of such elective body which the manager is requested by the body to attend.[131]

1–69   Whenever the county manager attends a meeting of the county or other council, the manager is obliged to give such advice and assistance as be reasonably required and shall arrange for the attendance of any relevant officers to attend the meeting of the council.[132] In addition it is the duty of the county manager to advice and assist the county council, and other elective bodies, with regard to the exercise or performance by the local authority of their reserved functions in addition to anything which the council requests. It is also the duty of every county manager to carry into effect all lawful orders of the

---

[128] s.20(2).
[129] The Minister, by order nominates an officer of each council to be the nominated officer of the council.
[130] County Management Act 1940, s.30(1).
[131] s.30(2).
[132] s.30(3).

council in relation to the exercise and performance of the reserved functions of the council.[133]

1–70   In every action or in any legal proceeding, whether civil or criminal, which are instituted in any court of law or equity by or against the council of a county, the county manager acts for and on behalf of the council. In that regard the county manager may do all such acts, matters, and things as the manager may consider necessary for the preparation and prosecution or defence of an action or other proceeding in the same manner and in all respects as if the manager were the plaintiff or prosecutor or the defendant. Where the action or other proceeding relates to the exercise or performance by such council of a reserved function of the council, the county manager shall act with the express authority of the council, and such an authority is deemed to have been given, unless or until the contrary is shown.[134]

1–71   The City and County Management (Amendment) Act of 1955[135] amended the provisions of the 1940 Act in that it provides that the manager shall not submit any proposal to vary the number of permanent officers under a local authority for the sanction of the Minister except with the consent by resolution of the local authority. The 1955 Act also provides that the manager shall not submit any proposal to fix an increased or reduced rate of remuneration as regards any class, description or grade of office or employment for the sanction of the Minister again except with the consent by resolution of the local authority.[136] The manager shall also not submit any proposal to vary the number of permanent offices under a local authority for the sanction of such Minister as may be empowered to sanction the proposal save with the consent by resolution of the local authority.

L.   ESTIMATES

1–72   A local authority may by resolution appoint a committee, known as the estimates committee. An estimates committee of a local authority, other than the council of a county, consists of so many members of the local authority, immediately before electing the committee, shall decide by resolution, however, the number cannot exceed one third of the membership of the authority. The number of the estimates committee of a county council is twice the number of the county electoral areas in the county and with respect to each electoral

---

[133] s.31.
[134] s.32.
[135] S.I. No. 12 of 1955.
[136] s.6.

area two members of the council who were elected for that area shall be appointed to the committee.[137]

1–73 A local authority may by resolution require the preparation and submission to their members of statements of the financial position of the local authority, in other words preparation of a financial statement. The estimates are to be in such detail and shall be prepared and submitted at such intervals as may be specified in the resolution, and they shall be prepared and submitted in the case of a local authority having an estimates committee, by the committee with the assistance of the manager, and in any other case, by the manager.[138]

1–74 For each financial year there shall be prepared an estimate of expenses showing the amounts estimated as necessary to meet the expenses and provide for the liabilities and requirements of a local authority during the forthcoming local financial year and the preparation of the estimates are carried out in the case of a local authority having an estimates committee, by the committee, and in any other case, by the manager.[139]

1–75 The manager is obliged, in so far as is not inconsistent with the due performance of other duties, to attend every meeting of the estimates committee of a local authority and is obliged to furnish information, assistance and advice to the committee as is required by them in the performance of their functions.[140] The manager is obliged to afford all information which may be in the manager's possession or procurement to the chairman of the local authority when requested if that information concerns any business or transaction of the council[141] It is not necessary for the request to be made in writing so that a verbal request made by the chairman will suffice and can be made through the county secretary to the county manager as was held by the High Court in the case of *Cullen v. Wicklow County Manager*.[142] The term "information" is to be given a very wide and general meaning since section 27 does not give any express limitation and is not confined to written documents but also to any knowledge however gained or held.

1–76 In that case the Court also held that the law agent's files containing information concerning a transaction of the county council was within the

---

[137] s.7(3).
[138] s.8(2).
[139] s.9(1).
[140] s.9(2).
[141] County Management Act 1940, s.27.
[142] *Cullen v. Wicklow County Manager* [1997] 1 I.L.R.M. 41, McCracken J., approved the New Zealand case of case *of Commissioners of Police v. Ombudsman* [1985] 1 N.Z.L.R. 578.

possession or procurement of the county manager, and the purpose of section 27 was to allow the administration of a local authority without interference from individual councillors while also ensuring that the executive of the authority may be overseen by the elected members of the authority.

1–77   Where the manager considers that an estimate of expenses which has been prepared by the estimates committee of a local authority, either relating to the whole of the estimate or to a part of the estimates, would, if adopted, seriously prejudice the efficient or economical performance of the functions of the local authority, the manager shall prepare a separate report specifying the provision which in his opinion is necessary.[143] In the case where the estimate committee of the local authority have not prepared an estimate the manager is obliged to prepare the estimates.

1–78   An estimate of expenses shall be considered by the local authority at a meeting (in this Act referred to as an estimates meeting) of the local authority at which the manager shall be present and which shall be held during the prescribed period and of which not less than seven days' notice shall have been given to every person who is a member of the local authority when such notice is given.[144] In a situation where a manger cannot attend an estimates meeting, due to the performance of other duties, the manager may designate an officer of the local authority to attend the meeting on the manager's behalf.

M. ESTIMATES MEETING

1–79   An estimate of expenses shall be considered by the local authority at an estimates meeting of the local authority, at which the manager shall be present, and which shall be held during the relevant period[145] and of which not less than seven days' notice shall have been given to every person who is a member of the local authority when the notice is given.[146]

1–80   Not less than seven days before the holding of the estimates meeting of a local authority, the manager shall deposit in the offices of the local authority a copy of the estimate of expenses, and send a copy of the estimate of expenses, together with a copy of any separate report from the manager on the estimates, to every person who is, on the day before the commencement of the

---

[143] s.9(3).

[144] s.10(1).

[145] Between October 1 and December 21 in each year, Public Bodies (Amendment) Order 1992 (S.I. No. 327 of 1992).

[146] s.10(1).

said seven days, a member of the local authority. The manager is also obliged to give public notice in the prescribed manner of the fact that the estimate of expenses has been made and that a copy of the estimates and the managers report, if made, has been deposited.[147] A copy of an estimate of expenses which is deposited in the offices of a local authority may be inspected free of charge by any member of the public at any time during office hours, and the manager is obliged to supply to any person who requests a copy of the estimate of expenses.

1–81 At an estimates meeting of a local authority or at any adjournment of the meeting, the local authority may by resolution amend, either by addition, omission or variation, the estimate of expenses, and the local authority shall by resolution adopt the estimate of expenses either without amendment or with the amendments made. The local authority determines by resolution, in accordance with the estimate of expenses as adopted, the rates in the pound to be levied or in the case non rateable income by other instruments whereby the money to meet the expenses of the elective body in the local financial year is to be obtained.

1–82 Where the estimates are not adopted at the first meeting of the authority the local authority may adjourn an estimates meeting as often as the authority wishes, subject to the limitation that no adjournment shall be to a day not within the period of twenty-one days beginning on the day on which the estimates meeting begins.[148]

1–83 The holding of an estimate meeting and the subsequent adoption of the estimates and the simultaneous fixing of the rate were discussed in *Ahern v. Kerry Co. Co.*[149] which involved an application for judicial review by a member of Kerry County Council against the adoption of the estimates furnished by the county manager without a full discussion and debate on each of the groups or headings of the estimates. The councillors spoke on one particular group of estimates and were asked by the chairman not to discuss the other groups as these would be dealt with later. At the end of the discussion on one group of estimates a motion was put forward that the rate proposed by the county manager should be adopted and this motion was approved by the meeting. The applicant sought judicial review of the decision to adopt the estimates on the grounds that the meeting had not only not complied with the requirements of section 10 of the 1955 Act but that the meeting had also been conducted in breach of the rules of natural and constitutional justice and that

---

[147] s.10(2).
[148] s.10(5).
[149] [1988] I.L.R.M. 392.

the applicant as a councillor had a legitimate expectation that he would be given the opportunity to discuss and attempt to vary the estimates.

1–84   Blayney J. held that the applicant had the requisite *locus standi* to bring the application because as a member of the County Council he had a special interest in ensuring that the work and resolutions of the council were lawful and carried out in accordance with statutory requirements. The Court also held that since section 10(1) of the 1955 Act provides that an 'estimate of expenses shall be considered by the local authority at . . . an estimates meeting', that it could not be said that the Council had complied with this provision as only one group of estimates had been considered.[150] It was not sufficient that each councillor had been supplied, in advance with a copy of the estimates as there was a substantial difference between a councillor considering the estimates on his own and at a meeting, as section 10 required. It was not necessary that every single page of the estimates had to be considered, but that at least each group of estimates should be considered even though there may be very little discussion on some of the groups. The effect of not complying with the requirements of section 10(1) was that the resolution approving the estimates was invalid. The resolution fixing of the rate in the pound would also have to be reconsidered as it was clear from section 10(4) that it was impossible for a local authority to fix the rate in the pound without having first considered the estimates. Blayney J. was also of the view that since the adoption of the estimate and the determination of the rate in the pound are dealt with in separate paragraphs in section 10(1) of the 1955 Act that it would be appear to be more correct that there should be separate resolutions for each matter.

1–85   However, the Court held that since the applicant had attended the meeting, that the meeting would have not breached constitutional or natural justice. The Court also found that there was a legitimate expectation to be afforded the opportunity to discuss the estimates was in fact a reliance on the statutory requirements of the 1955 Act and was therefore not properly a legitimate expectation. The Court ordered that the matter be remitted back to Kerry County Council.

N. LIMITATION ON EXPENDITURE

1–86   At any time after the authority has adopted an estimate of expenses, a local authority may, authorise by resolution the expenditure of money or the incurring of a liability in excess of the expenditure for any particular purpose

---

[150] at p.395.

specified in the estimates.[151] Except where such a resolution is passed by the local authority the total amount of money which is expended and the amount of liability which is incurred by a local authority in any financial year for any particular purpose which has been specified in the estimate of expenses for that year cannot exceed the total amount specified in that estimated for that purpose.[152]

1–87 Where the manager is of the opinion that the proper performance of the functions of the local authority requires that the expenditure of money or the incurring of any particular liability in respect of any purpose which is in excess of the expenditure for that purpose already specified in the estimate of expenses, the manager may prepare an application for the authorisation by the local authority of the excess expenditure. The manager may submit the application for additional expenditure or the incurring of additional liability on the part of the local authority in the case of a local authority having an estimates committee, to the committee, and in any other case, to the members of the local authority.[153] Where an application is submitted to an estimates committee the committee considers the application and shall then submit it, with their recommendation to the members of the local authority at the next meeting of the local authority.

1–88 Where a proposal is made at a meeting of a local authority to do or effect any act, matter or thing which constitutes a reserved function or is mentioned in a resolution under section 4 of this Act, and in consequence of which an illegal payment is to be made out of the funds of the local authority, or a deficiency or loss is likely to result in the funds of the local authority, the manager shall object and stating the grounds of objection, and, if a decision is taken on the proposal, the names of the members present and voting for and against the decision and abstaining from voting on the decision shall be recorded in the minutes of the meeting.[154]

1–89 Where the names of the persons voting for a decision to do or effect any act, matter or thing are recorded in the minutes of the meeting of a local authority, those persons shall be surcharged on any surcharge or charged on any charge that may subsequently be made as a result of the decision as if they had made or authorised the making of the payment, loss or deficiency and no other person is to be surcharged or charged.[155]

1–90 Section 20 of the Local Government Act 1902 empowers a local gov-

---

[151] s.11(1).
[152] s.11(2).
[153] s.11(3).
[154] s.16(1), see also Application of Enactments Order 1898.
[155] s.16(3).

ernment auditor to charge against any member or officer of a local authority the amount of any deficiency or loss which is incurred through the negligence or misconduct of any member or officer of a local authority.

1–91   Section 61 of the Local Government Act 1925 provides that whenever a proposal is made at a meeting of a local authority to do any act, matter, or thing in consequence of which an illegal payment is to be made out of the funds of the local authority, or a deficiency or loss is likely to result in or to such funds, it is the duty of the responsible officer of the local authority to make an objection and to state the grounds of the objection. If the decision is taken on the proposal, the names of the members present and voting for and against such decision and abstaining from voting on such decision is recorded on the minutes of the meeting.

1–92   In the case of *Maurice Downey v. John O Brien*[156] the High Court held that there does not have to be any element of moral culpability or gross negligence on the part of the person against whom the charge is made and the ordinary principles or the law of negligence apply to the making of the charge under section 20 of the 1902 Act. In that case an appeal was made against a charge raised by the local government auditor under section 20 of the 1902 Act by the chairman of the Waterford Harbour Commissioners. Section 12 of the Local Government (Ireland) Act 1871 provides that a local government auditor may examine every account of a local authority and empowers the local government auditor to disallow any payments which the auditor decides are unfounded and to surcharge the person who made or who authorised the payments. The auditor is required to certify the amount due by the person surcharged and to state in writing the reasons for the decision. Section 12 also gives the person charged the right of appeal to the High Court by applying for a writ of *certiorari*. However the *certiorari* proceedings do not allow an appeal by way of rehearing but the High Court may come to a different conclusion from that reached by the local government auditor and the Court is not confined to merely considering whether there was evidence to support the findings of fact made by the auditor.[157]   The Court found that the Court was required to consider whether the chairman of the Waterford Harbour Commissioners owed a duty of care to the harbour commissioners the nature of that duty if it existed and whether that duty was breached and if so whether the commissioners suffered any loss.[158] The chairman of the commissioners submitted, which submission was rejected by the court, that the local government auditor had failed to comply with the rules of natural justice in arriving at the

---

[156] [1994] 2 I.L.R.M. 130.
[157] *ibid.* at 135.
[158] *ibid.* at 136.

decision to impose a charge on him, however, the Court did accept, albeit *obiter* that a local government auditor was bound to conduct his investigation under the principles of natural justice.

O. DELEGATION AND DEPUTY MANAGERS

1–93 The manager may delegate any function performable by the manager to any officer of the authority.[159] The manager must firstly consult with an appropriate person.

1–94 The officer to whom functions have been delegated shall perform the delegated functions under the general direction and control of the manager, and the officer shall perform the delegated function in accordance with any limitations as may be specified in the delegation, in particular as regards to the area or period in which or the extent to which the officer is to perform the delegated function.

1–95 The manager may revoke a delegation which has been made by the manager, the delegation or revocation being made by means of an order in writing signed by the manager.[160] Any document purporting to be an order of delegation and signed, or purporting to be certified in writing by the manager to be a true copy of an order, shall be received, without proof, as prima facie evidence of the order.[161] The making of a delegation or the revocation of an order is to be notified to the local authority at the next meeting of the local authority.

1–96 The manager may appoint a deputy manager to act temporarily for any reason, however, the manager may not do so if he is suspended. However, the manger must first consult the appropriate person, who in this case means the cathaoirleach of the relevant county council or county borough council.[162] Where a manager has for any reason become temporarily unable to act and either has not made an appointment or an appointment made has now ended or on account of the death or resignation of the appointee, the appropriate person may appoint a person to be deputy manager for the remainder of the duration of such inability. The appropriate person may at any time terminate the appointment of a deputy manager.

---

[159] s.17(1) of the 1955 Act as amended by s.52 of the Local Government Act of 1994, which removed the requirement that a Minister approve the delegation of functions.
[160] s.17(5).
[161] s.17(7).
[162] See s. 51 of the Local Government Act of 1994.

1–97   The Minister may authorise a person to be appointed from time to time to be a specified deputy manager if a manager is for any reason temporarily unable to act and a person has not already been appointed a deputy manager, and the Minister may at any time revoke the authorisation.[163] The 1955 Act states that every confirmation or revocation of the appointment of a deputy manager must be also sent to every member of the local authority or authorities concerned, and this provision was not repealed by the Local Government Act of 1994 and remains in force.

P. ORGANISATION AND REORGANISATION OF LOCAL GOVERNMENT FOR COUNTY DUBLIN

1–98   The Dublin Corporation Act 1890[164] gave Dublin Corporation power to make and repeal bye-laws for regulating all alterations and repairs of buildings which were erected before 1890 other than necessary repairs not affecting the construction of any external party wall or the stability of the premises.[165] The Corporation was also given the power to vary the direction of new streets and to control the height of buildings erected in any new street.

1–99   The 1890 Act also makes it an offence to place or fix a crane or scaffold against or in front of any building or land which projects over the main building line of the street without the written consent of the Corporation.[166] Section 42 of the Act also allows the Dublin Corporation to name any street or any part of a street which is already named or which requires a street name. Excavation under any street or public highway or to lay any pipes or wires under any street of footway may not be carried out without the consent of the Corporation.

1–100   The 1890 Act also imposed a duty on the owners and occupiers of every building which is used as a place of public resort to ensure that the means of entry and exit is safe and convenient.[167] A building is regarded as being used as a place of public resort where the building is used or constructed or adapted to be used as a church, chapel, or other place of worship or as a college or school or theatre, public hall, concert room, ballroom, public lecture room or exhibition room or a place of assembly for persons who are ad-

---

[163] Local Government Act 1994, s.51(2).
[164] 53 & 54 Vic., ch. 246.
[165] ss.33, 34.
[166] s.43.
[167] s.53, otherwise the owner may be guilty of an offence, however a penalty cannot be imposed unless a reasonable time has been allowed to alter the building.

mitted by ticket or payment. Notices may be issued by Dublin Corporation if it believes that a public building is not provided with a safe means of entrance and exit or is so defective that a danger from fire may result to the public requiring alterations to be made to the premises.[168] The Corporation must give the occupier or owner a reasonable time in which to make these alterations provided that the structural defects can be remedied at a reasonable or moderate expenditure.[169] The Corporation may make bye-laws with regard to the need to protect theatres and places of public resort within city from the risk of fire.[170]

1–101 The 1890 Act also deals with certain sanitary matters connected with the city, and specifically deals with refuse and with sewerage or surface or storm waters.[171]

Q. POWERS OF LOCAL AUTHORITIES UNDER PLANNING ACTS

1–102 Local authorities through their role as planning authorities have general powers to develop or secure the development of property within their functional areas. Section 77 of the Local Government (Planning and Development) Act 1963 also gives the planning authority specific powers to secure, facilitate, and control the improvement of the road frontage by either widening the road or by opening or enlarging the road. The planning authority may also develop any land in the vicinity of any road or bridge which the authority wishes to improve or construct. Local authorities have also specific powers under section 77 to provide lands within their functional areas with roads and other services in order to facilitate orderly and proper development. The authority may also develop or renew areas which have become run down and in need of development, this is distinct from their powers under the Derelict Sites Acts.

---

[168] A similar provision exists for the rest of the country under s.36(1) Public Health Amendment Act 1890, s.36(1).
[169] The owner may appeal against the notice to an arbitrator appointed by the Minister for the Environment and Local Government.
[170] s.55(1).
[171] ss.57, 58.

CHAPTER 2

Planning and development

A. LOCAL AUTHORITIES AS PLANNING AUTHORITIES

1. Duties of planning authorities

2–01 Upon the coming into operation of the Local Government (Planning and Development) Act of 1963 on October 1, 1964 each of the local authorities became, in addition to their existing functions as sanitary authorities, planning authorities. Each of the urban district councils, the borough corporations and the county councils are also the planning authority.[1] The main functions of the planning authorities consists of strategic planning and development, development control, enforcement of planning legislation and decisions,[2] involvement in planning appeals, the provision of access to information, as well as the ability to acquire and develop property. The main theme of the Local Government (Planning and Development) Act of 1963 has been said to give a citizen notice of a development which might affect him in a substantial way and have the opportunity of stating his case.[3]

2–02 Planning authorities are responsible for strategic planning of development within their functional areas, which is carried out through the adoption

---

[1] s.2(2)

[2] s.27 of the 1963 Act, see *MCD Management Services Ltd. v. Kildare Co. Co.* [1995] 2 I.L.R.M. 352, *South Dublin Co. Co. v. Balfe*, unreported, November 3, 1995, *Dublin Co. Co. v. O'Riordan* [1986] I.L.R.M. 104, *Cork Corp. v. O'Connell* [1982] I.L.R.M. 505, *Morris v. Garvey* [1983] I.R. 319.

[3] Carney J. in *Keogh v. Galway Co. Co.* [1995] 1 I.L.R.M. 141.

of development plans, which will be dealt with further in this chapter. Planning authorities are also responsible, under planning legislation, as the enforcer of the planning code, generally exercised to ensure compliance with the terms and conditions of planning permissions issued by the authority.[4]

2–03 Planning authorities are obliged to maintain a register which should be available to the public and which should contain details of all planning applications, planning decisions, planning correspondence, copies of any drawings or maps as well as any submissions or observations which were made in writing to the planning authorities.[5] Details of any appeals made and the decision of the appeal are also entered into the planning register, which in any event are required to be entered into the register within seven days of the date of the decision. The planning register also contains details of any enforcement notices which are made under the relevant provisions of the planning legislation.[6] The planning register also contains details of any notices made requiring the removal or alteration of a hedge, the making of any tree preservation orders, any conservation orders, rights of way agreements made or rights of way created by order of the planning authority under section 48 of the 1963 Act, or any agreements made in relation to the planting of plants and trees. The planning register should also contain details of any notices made in connection with the acquisition of property, as well as details of appeals made in connection with acquisitions.

2. Planning authorities and development plans

(a) Preparation

2–04 Planning authorities are given a number of roles under the Local Government (Planning and Development) Acts including the preparation and revision of development plans,[7] the capacity to make decisions in relation to individual planning applications,[8] the most frequently used power under the planning acts, as well as the role of enforcer of planning legislation and policy.

---

[4] On the power to attach conditions see *Bord na Mona v. An Bord Pleanála* [1985] I.R. 205.

[5] For the importance of the register see *Readymix (Éire) Ltd. v. Dublin Co. Co.*, unreported, Supreme Court, July 30, 1974. The register has on occasion been altered, see *Blessington Heritage Trust Ltd. v. Wicklow Co. Co.*, unreported, High Court, January 21, 1998.

[6] Enforcement notices must only deal with events occurring in the present or which have occurred in the past and not to future events, see O'Donnell, *Planning Law* (Butterworths, Dublin, 1999), p.10.

[7] Part II of the 1963 Act. See *Tennyson v. Dun Laogharie Corp.* [1991] 2 I.R. 527 on the definition of a development plan and the interpretation of development plans, see also *Huntsgrove Developments v. Meath Co. Co.* [1994] 2 I.L.R.M. 36.

[8] ss.26 and 27 of the 1963 Act.

Planning authorities are also given further powers in relation to ensuring that the development plan is effective as well as the power to protect specific amenities which are not included in development plans and the development of community amenities and facilities.[9]

2–05   Development plans are essentially statements of planning objectives for the functional area of the planning authority and the key element of a development plan is that once it has been adopted by the planning authority, the planning authority itself is bound by the provisions contained in the plan, which was reiterated in *Blessington & District Community Council v. Wicklow Co. Co.*[10] where the High Court stated that the local authority was bound to have regard to the development plan before making a decision on an application for planning permission.[11] Local authorities must therefore have regard to the development plan before any major developments are carried out by the local authority within its functional area.

2–06   The constitutionality of the making of a development plan was dealt with in *Central Dublin Development Association v. Attorney General*[12] where Kenny J. held that development plans were consistent with the Constitution and were not inconsistent with the right to hold property under Article 40.3 of the Constitution.

2–07   Each authority is bound to make a development plan indicating the objectives for its area and to review the plan at least once in every five years, and from time to time as required. The development plan itself is a formal written document, with maps attached if required, and the intention to make a development plan is notified by the placing of a notice in *Iris Oifigiúil* and at least one newspaper circulating in the area, together with placing the draft plan on public display at the offices of the planning authority and forwarding copies to prescribed authorities. The prescribed authorities include the Bord Fáilte, An Taisce, various government ministers, An Bord Pleanála, as well as every planning authority whose area is contiguous to the planning authorities area as well as to every local authority in the area to which the draft plan relates. Each local authority is bound to indicate zoning objectives in urban areas but not in rural areas.[13] If the draft development plan includes in it a proposal in relation to a structure or an internal fixture which is proposed to be preserved, because of artistic, historical or architectural interest, notice of the plan must also be given to the owner and to the occupier of that structure or

---

[9]   Part VII of the 1963 Act.
[10]   Unreported, High Court, July 19, 1996.
[11]   s.26 of the 1963 Act, see also *State (Pine Valley Properties Ltd.) v. Dublin Corporation*.
[12]   109 I.L.T.R. 69.
[13]   See *O'Connor v. Clare Co. Co.*, unreported, High Court, February 11, 1994.

building. If there is a reference to a public right of way which is to be preserved, notice must be given to the owner and occupier of the land over which it is situated.[14]

(b) Objections to Development Plans

2–08 Any representations or objections may be made to the planning authority in relation to the draft development plan, and these objections or representations must be taken into consideration by the planning authority before the development plan, or a variation of the plan is made.[15] The notice which is published by the planning authority must, not only indicate that a draft of the proposed plan is available for inspection at specified times and places, but also that any ratepayer[16] who wishes to make an objection has a right to make a case before a person appointed by the planning authority. With respect to the consideration of any objections or representations, the planning authority is bound to make a new draft and to again follow the usual procedures with respect to the publication of a notice and so on, if the authority accepts or introduces an objection or representation into the development plan.[17] This rule had resulted in the planning authorities declining to introduce any changes in the development plan,[18] but the introduction of section 21A by the 1976 Act[19] provides that where it is proposed to make a material alteration to the draft development plan that the authority again places a notice in Iris Oifigiuil and in a newspaper advertising the fact that an alteration has been proposed and the notice follows the same format as a notice under section 21, a resolution having been passed by the planning authority requiring that a decision to grant a permission, which if granted would contravene the development plan, be made by a majority of over one third of the total number of the membership of the authority.[20] Copies of the notice are to be given to an applicant, in the case of an application for planning permission under section 26 which if granted would contravene the development plan, and to any person who has submitted

---

[14] The notice shall also state that the draft includes provision relating to the preservation of the public right of way and that there is a right of appeal to the Circuit Court in relation to such provision.

[15] With regard to the considerations which must be taken with regard to objections or representations being made see *Malahide Community Council Ltd. v. Dublin Co. Co.*

[16] Ratepayer includes the owner of a dwelling which had been rated, Local Government (Financial Provisions) Act 1978, see Walsh, *Planning and Development Law* (2nd ed., 1984).

[17] In *State (Abenglen Property Ltd.) v. Dublin Corp.* [1984] I.R. 381; [1982] I.L.R.M. 590, the court held that the current development plan for Dublin was a new plan, and not a review of the earlier one, therefore development plans are new plans rather than reviews.

[18] See *Finn v. Bray Urban District Council* [1969] I.R. 169.

[19] Local Government (Planning and Development) Act 1976.

[20] s.26(3)(a) and (b) of the 1963 Act as amended.

an objection in writing to the proposed development. The authority may then, as they shall think fit, make the proposed plan or proposed variation, as the case may be, with or without the proposed amendment or with such other amendment as, having regard to the particular circumstances, they consider appropriate.[21]

(c) Contents

2–09   The contents of development plans has been the subject of some case law. In *Glencar Explorations plc and another v. Mayo Co. Co.* it was held that a blanket mining ban on one seventh of the county stating that no development should take place in relation to the extraction of minerals was an improper objective of the planning authority. The Court felt that the word "development" had a positive connotation and that the objectives of a development plan should also have a positive content, a mining ban essentially having a negative content. However, there is nothing to stop a planning authority from including in a development plan a specification that in relation to a limited area certain objectives would be pursued which would include not allowing certain activities to take place.[22]

2–10   Under section 22 of the 1963 Act planning authorities have a duty to take such steps as may be necessary for securing the objectives which are contained in the provisions of the development plan.[23] The Minister may also require the development plans of two or more planning authorities to be co-ordinated in respect of matters specified by the Minister and the authorities are obliged to comply with the requisition. Any dispute between them arising out of any matters inserted or which are to be inserted in a development plan shall be determined by the Minister.[24] The Minister may also require a planning authority to vary the development plan in respect of matters and in a manner specified by the Minister and the local authority are bound to comply with the request.[25] This provision is distinct from the provision contained in section 7 of the 1982 Act which allows the Minister, from time to time, issue such general directives as to policy in relation to planning and development as he considers necessary,[26] and the planning authority and An Bord Pleanála

---

[21] The plan cannot be amended by a simple resolution see *Ferris v. Dublin Co. Co.*, unreported, Supreme Court, November 7, 1990, see *also Grange Developments Ltd. v. Dublin Co. Co.* [1986] I.R. 146 where it was held that the council could not delegate to the County Manager the power to grant permission in contravention of the development plan.

[22] See *O'Connor v. Clare Co. Co.*, unreported, High Court, February 11, 1994.

[23] s.22(1) of the 1963 Act.

[24] s. 22(2) of the 1963 Act.

[25] s. 22(3) of the 1963 Act.

[26] See, for example, Local Government (Planning and Development) General Policy Di-

are obliged in performing its functions under the planning acts to have regard to any directive issued by the Minister.[27]

(d) Material contravention of development plans

2–11 Besides the duty to ensure compliance with the development plan planning authorities are prevented from carrying out development which is a material contravention of the development plan adopted for their functional area. In *O'Leary and others v. Dublin Co. Co.*[28] it was emphasised that planning authorities must comply with the requirements of the planning law with the same stringency as they would be enforced against a private developer.[29] With respect to material contravention's of the development plan, the cases which involved travellers' halting sites in Galway,[30] reiterated the fact that planning authorities must correctly follow the procedures laid down under section 21 and 21A of the 1963 Act. In *Keogh v. Galway Corporation*[31] the Corporation had attempted to change the development plan by permitting halting sites in all ten of the planning zones which the plan covered. Submissions were made on the draft variations and the Corporation proceeded to adopt their own proposed variations having altered the proposed changes to only include seven of the ten zones. The Court held that the Corporation had failed to consider that their change of the proposed variation amounted to a material alteration within the meaning of section 21A, and since they clearly did amount to a material alteration that the publication procedures under section 21A had to be followed.[32]

(e) Development Plans and Their Objectives

2–12 Certain mandatory objectives must appear in a development plan which is to be adopted by the planning authority with respect to areas classed as urban areas, being boroughs, urban districts and towns listed under the First Schedule to the 1963 Act. The mandatory objectives with respect to urban areas are the indication of the uses which particular areas are to be put, that is zoning, objectives regarding the safety of road users including pedestrians, and the preservation, improvement and extension of amenities.

2–13 Other objectives may be included in the development plan and these

---

rective (Shopping) Regulation 1998, S.I. 193/1998 regarding developments of supermarkets and other retail developments.
[27] Local Government (Planning and Development) Act 1982, s.27.
[28] [1988] I.R. 150.
[29] See O'Sullivan and Shepherd, para. 1.10.
[30] *McCann v. Galway Corporation*, unrep., HC, 20 June 1996 and *Keogh v. Galway Corporation*, unreported, High Court, March 3, 1995.
[31] Unreported, High Court, March 3, 1995.
[32] See O'Sullivan and Shepherd, para. 1.10.

are listed in the Third Schedule to the 1963 Act and are listed under the headings of roads and traffic, community planning, structures and amenities. Under part one of the third schedule which deals with roads and traffic the objectives which are listed are: securing the greater convenience and safety of road users and pedestrians, reservation of land for roads and parking places, establishment of public rights of way, construction of new roads and alteration of existing roads, the closing or diverting of existing roads, the extinguishment of public and private rights of way, establishing the line, width, level and construction of, the means of access to and egress from, and the general dimensions and character of roads, whether new or existing, the providing for works incidental to the making, improvement or landscaping of any road, including the erection of bridges, tunnels and subways and shelters, the provision of artificial lighting and seats and the planting or protecting of grass, trees and shrubs on or adjoining such road.

2–14   The second part to the third schedule deals with structures within the functional area of the planning authority and are, regulating and controlling, either generally or in particular areas, all or any of the following matters, (a) the size, height, floor area and character of structures, (b) building lines, coverage and the space about dwellings and other structures, (c) the extent of parking places required in, on or under structures of a particular class or size or services or facilities for the parking, loading, unloading or fuelling of vehicles, (d) the objects which may be affixed to structures, (e) the purposes for and the manner in which structures may be used or occupied, including, in the case of dwellings, the letting thereof in separate tenements; the regulating and controlling the design, colour and materials of structures, the reserving or allocating any particular land, or all land in any particular area, for structures of a specified class or classes, or prohibiting or restricting either permanently or temporarily, the erection, construction or making of any particular class or classes of structures on any specified land, the limiting the number of structures or the number of structures of a specified class which may be constructed, erected or made, on, in or under any area, the removal or alteration of structures which are inconsistent with the development plan, the regulating and controlling (a) the disposition or layout of structures or structures of any specified class (including the reservation of reasonable open space in relation to the number, class and character of structures in any particular development proposal); (b) the manner in which any land is to be laid out for the purpose of development, including requirements as to road layout, landscaping, planting; (c) the provision of water supplies, sewers, drains and public lighting; (d) the provision of service roads and the location and design of means of access to roads; (e) the provision of facilities for parking, unloading, loading and fuelling of vehicles on any land.

2–15   Community planning comes within the third area of objectives which may be included and are, regulating the layout of areas, including density, spacing, grouping and orientation of structures in relation to roads, open spaces[33] and other structures, determining the provision and siting of schools, churches, meeting halls and other community facilities, determining the provision and siting of sanitary services and recreational facilities.

2–16 The objectives regarding amenities include the reserving of lands as open spaces, whether public or private (other than open spaces), caravan or camping sites, the reserving, as a public park, public garden or public recreation space, land normally used for recreation, reserving of land for burial grounds, reserving of lands for game and bird sanctuaries, and the preservation of buildings of artistic, architectural or historical interest, together with the reservation of caves, sites, features and other objects of archaeological, geological or historical interest, and the preservation of views and prospects and of amenities of places and features of natural beauty or interest the preservation and protection of woods. Other objectives include the preservation and protection of trees, shrubs, plants and flowers,[34] prohibiting, restricting or controlling, either generally or in particular places or within a specified distance of the centre line of all roads or any specified road, the erection of an or any particular forms of advertisement structure or the exhibition of all or any particular forms of advertisement, preventing, remedying or removing injury to amenities arising from the ruinous or neglected condition of any structure, or from the objectionable or neglected condition of any land attached to a structure or abutting on a public road or situate in a residential area, prohibiting, regulating or controlling the deposit or disposal of waste materials and refuse, the disposal of sewage and the pollution of rivers. The planning authority may also consider using derelict sites or other land facilities such as car parks, seating, playing facilities, tennis-courts, shelters, toilets and playgrounds, the preservation of any existing public right of way giving access to seashore, mountain, lakeshore, riverbank, or other place of natural beauty or recreational utility.

2. Additional powers of planning authorities

(a) Special orders

2–17 Planning authorities have the power to declare certain areas within their functional area as being under a "special amenity area" order, a power derived under section 42 of the 1963 Act, and which must be confirmed by the

---

[33] See *Smeltzer v. Fingal Co. Co.* [1998] 1 I.R. 279 for dicussion on the law relating to open spaces and the non applicability of the Open Spaces Act 1906 to county councils.
[34] See *Boyne Grove Farms Ltd. v. J Murphy Developments Ltd.*, Laffoy, J., *ex tempore*.

Minister.[35] Before an order is made it must appear to the planning authority that the area is an area of special amenity by reason of its natural beauty, or its scenic or other amenities, including recreational utility, having regard to the open character of the area and its position in relation to centres of population or industrial or commercial development.

2–18   The order may then provide that in relation to development, other than development which is exempted, no such development or certain specified developments may take place. The order could also provide for the maximum number of structures of any specified class which may be erected, constructed or made in any specified part of the area.[36] One of the effects of the making of a special amenity can be seen with Article 10 of the 1994 Regulations which restricts the classes of exempted development which apply to special amenity areas.[37] Confirmation of the making of a special amenity area order is made using the procedure under section 43 of the 1963 Act.

2–19   Planning authorities may also make orders protecting hedges, trees, plants, and may also make orders under the planning acts controlling noise,[38] litter[39] and advertisements, although most of the situations relating to noise and litter are now dealt with under separate acts. In relation to advertisements section 53 of the 1963 Act provides for a limited power to the planning authority to prevent the exhibition or any advertisement on any structure or other land, door, gate, window, tree or post is in or fronts any public place, by any person who is not the owner, occupier or person in charge, unless he is authorised so to do by such owner, occupier or person in charge or by any enactment.

2–20   Section 54 allows the planning authority to serve on the person having control of the advertisement structure or advertisement a notice requiring that person to repair or tidy the advertisement structure or advertisement within a specified period, if it appears to the planning authority that, having regard to the interests of public safety or amenity, an advertisement structure or advertisement in their area should be repaired or tidied. If the notice is not complied with the authority may enter on the land on which the structure is situate or the advertisement is exhibited and repair or tidy the structure or advertisement and may recover as a simple contract debt in any court.[40]

2–21   Section 44 of the 1963 Act provides that if it appears to the planning authority, that it is expedient in the interests of amenity, that any hedge should

---

[35] Such as in the case of the *Liffey Valley*.
[36] s.42(1) of the 1963 Act, a review of the order must be made every five years, s.42(5).
[37] Art. 10(1)(b).
[38] s.51 of the 1963 Act.
[39] s.52 of the 1963 Act.
[40] s.54(2) of the 1963 Act.

be removed or altered, the planning authority may serve on the owner or on the occupier of the land on which the hedge is situate, a notice requiring the removal of the hedge or its alteration and, in the case of a removal, the notice may specify the type of replacement which the planning authority deems to be suitable.

2–22 In the case of trees section if it appears to the planning authority that it is expedient in the interests of amenity to make provision for the preservation of any tree or of a group of trees or woodlands, the planning authority may make an order with respect to any such tree, or group of trees or woodlands as may be specified in the order. The order may prohibit the cutting down, topping, lopping or wilful destruction of trees except with the consent of the planning authority, and for enabling that authority to give their consent subject to conditions. Compensation is allowable under section 45(2) for any person who has suffered damage in consequence of any refusal of consent required under an order provide that the claim is made to the planning authority within the time and in the manner specified by the order. However, where the order declares "that, as respects any tree, trees or group of trees not comprised in woodlands, the tree, trees or group is or are of special amenity value or special interest no compensation shall be payable in relation to the tree, trees or group", or where the order declares "that, as respects any trees comprised in woodlands, a condition comprising a requirement to replant is an essential condition for attachment in the interests of amenity to any consent given under the order no compensation shall be payable in relation to such a condition attached to any such consent."

2–23 In relation to conservation orders, which are made under section 46, where it appears to the planning authority, that it is expedient in the interests of amenity, to make provision for the protection of any rare species of flora or fauna of any area or to preserve from extinction any species of flora or fauna of any area, the planning authority may make an order with respect to such flora or fauna; and, in particular, prohibit the taking, killing, or destroying of flora or fauna except with the consent of the planning authority.[41]

2–24 Section 47 of the 1963 Act allows the planning authority to enter into an agreement with any person having the necessary power in that behalf for the creation, by dedication by that person, of a public right of way over land, commonly know as "taking in charge", more of a reference to taking over roads provided in housing estates by developers. While section 48 provides that where it appears to the planning authority that there is need for a public right of way over any land, the planning authority may by order create a public right of way over the land, this order may be similar to the "taking in charge"

---

[41] Such as is in the case of the Burren in Co. Clare.

of roads in housing estates and so on, but is an infrequently used power. The section makes provision for the service of notices on the owner and occupier of the lands and provides for an appeal process, supplemental provisions are provided for under section 49, including the placing of a duty on the planning authority to maintain the public right of way created under section 48, and provides for the punishment and prosecution against persons who interfere with the public right of way or who damage or obstruct the way, or hinder or interfere with the exercise of the right of way.[42]

2–25 For the purpose of preserving or enhancing the amenities or natural beauty of any land, the planning authority may plant trees, shrubs or other plants on the land, and assist any person or body proposing to plant trees, shrubs or other plants on the land by providing trees, shrubs or other plants or by through the grant of money to persons who provide such plants and trees, e.g. for the purposes of the Bord Fáilte "Tidy Towns" competition.[43]

2–26 Planning authorities may also, with the consent of the owner and of the occupier of any land which does not form part of a public road, place, erect or construct cables, wires and pipelines, other than waterpipes, sewers and drains, wires and pipelines, on, under or over such land, and may from time to time inspect, repair, alter or renew, or may at any time remove, any cables, wires or pipelines placed, erected or constructed under this section.[44] A planning authority may also, provided it has the consent of the owner and of the occupier of any structure, attach to such structure any bracket or other fixture required for the carrying or support of any cable, wire or pipeline placed, erected or constructed under this section.[45]

(b) Ancillary powers of planning authorities

2–27 The Planning Acts give planning authorities certain additional or ancillary powers, some of which are rarely used and others commonplace. Under section 15 of the 1963 Act, for instance, a planning authority may contribute to the funds of any body which provides for training and research in relation to town and regional planning. The ancillary power to enter lands given to them under section 83 is often used, but is restricted to use by authorised persons entering on any land at all reasonable times between the hours of 9 a.m. and 6 p.m.[46] In addition to the power to enter the lands, an authorised person entering on land may do all things reasonably necessary for the purpose for which the entry is made and, in particular, may survey, make plans, take levels, make

---

[42] s.48(2) of the 1963 Act.
[43] s.50(1) of the 1963 Act.
[44] s.85(1) of the 1963 Act.
[45] s.85(2) of the 1963 Act.
[46] s.83(1) of the 1963 Act.

excavations, and examine the depth and nature of the subsoil. However, before an authorised person enters under this section on any land, the authority shall either obtain the consent of the occupier or of the owner or shall give to the owner or occupier not less than fourteen days' notice in writing of the intention to make the entry.[47] In the case where the entry of the lands by an authorised officer is opposed or if the occupier or the owner refuses entry, the entry shall not be effected unless it has been authorised by an order of the District Court, having jurisdiction in which the land or part of the land is situate and, in the case of occupied land, save after at least twenty-four hours' notice of the intended entry, and of the object of the entry, has been given to the occupier.[48] Every person who, by act or omission, obstructs an authorised person in the lawful exercise of the powers conferred by this section may be guilty of an offence.[49]

3. Powers of elected officials – section 4 motions

2–28 Section 4[50] of the City and County Management (Amendment) Act of 1955[51] provides that a local authority may by resolution require any particular act, matter or thing specifically which is mentioned in the resolution and which the local authority or the manager can do lawfully or cause to be done or effected in performance of the executive functions of the local authority. Before passing such a resolution, subsection 2 provides that a notice of the intention to propose a resolution under section 4 must be given in writing to the city of county manager and that the notice shall be signed by three members of the local authority, the notice must also contain a copy of the resolution, and the notice may require that the resolution shall be considered at a special meeting. The notice must specify a day, which is not less than seven days after the day on which the notice is received by the manager, for the holding of the special meeting at which the resolution will be considered.

2–29 The Supreme Court has held that the procedure under section 4 does apply to the area of planning and that the elected members of the local authority have the power to give a direction to the manager in regard to planning permission.[52] Once a section 4 resolution has been validly exercised the Manager is not entitled to exercise any separate or independent discretion as to whether or not he should obey the resolution. Once the elected members of the local authority decide to use the section 4 procedure, the members must

---

[47] s.83(3) of the 1963 Act.
[48] s.83(6) of the 1963 Act.
[49] s.83(7) of the 1963 Act.
[50] Amended by s.44(1) of the Local Government Act 1991.
[51] No. 12 of 1955.
[52] *P. & F. Sharpe Ltd and another v. Dublin City and County Manager* [1989] I.R. 701.

act judicially, that is having regard to all relevant and legitimate factors and disregarding any irrelevant or misleading or illegitimate factors. The elected members of the local authority are still bound to follow the provisions of the planning legislation in particular the provisions of section 26 of the 1963 Act. In the case of *Flanagan v. Galway City and County Manager*[53] a section 4 motion was held to be invalid as the members of the local authority had considered matters which were irrelevant to planning considerations. This is because the provisions of section 26 clearly provide that in dealing with any planning application the planning authority is restricted to considering the proper planning and development of the area of the authority. The 1991 Local Government Act amended the provisions of section 4 of the 1955 Act by providing that a resolution under section 4 which is proposed and which relates to a planning function must be signed by not less than three members of the local authority and supported by not less than three-quarters of the local authority, while the resolution can only pass if it is supported by not less than three-quarters of the total number of members of the authority.[54]

2–30 A planning function within the meaning of the 1991 provision means a function of a planning authority with respect to a decision of the authority under part four of the Local Government (Planning and Development) Act 1963, on an application for permission or approval for the development land, or a condition attached to a permission or approval granted or a decision under section 4 of the Local Government (Planning and Development) Act 1982. Section 4 of the 1982 Act relates to the power of a local authority to extend the appropriate period of a planning permission, by such additional period as the authority consider requisite to enable the development to which the permission relates to be completed. An extension may only be granted if the appropriate planning regulations have been complied with and the development to which such permission relates commenced before the expiration of the appropriate period sought to be extended, and substantial works were carried out pursuant to such permission during such period, and further that the development will be completed within a reasonable time.[55]

2–31 The judgement of O'Hanlon J. in the High Court in *P. & F. Sharp Ltd. v. Dublin City and County Manager* is an interesting one in that he made two essential points regarding the latitude which must be allowed to an administrative authority in the exercise of any discretion conferred on them by statute. It must be possible for a planning authority to make a decision which conflicts with the advice which they have received from their professional advisers or

---

[53] [1980] 2 I.R. 66.
[54] Local Government Act 1991, s.44.
[55] See *Littondale Ltd. V. Wicklow Co. Co.* [1996] 2 I.L.R.M. 519, for matters to be cosidered in determining whether extension of a planning permission should be granted.

staff, otherwise it would mean that the power to make decisions would be taken away from the planning authorities and transferred to the planning officials. Where a planning authority is advised by its legal advisers that a motion or the granting of a particular permission would be illegal, the advice should not replace the ability of the planning authority to make a decision albeit risking a legal challenge.

2–32 However, local authorities must be careful to ensure that when proposing to make a resolution under section 4 that sufficient time and preparation is given. In the case of *Griffin v. Galway City and County Manager*[56] an engineers report had not been circulated to each of the members of the planning authority. The members of the planning authority had also neglected, in Blaney J.'s opinion, to pay sufficient attention to the fact that the development which was being discussed at the meeting of the authority was in contravention of the County Development Plan. The Court held that in considering the case for the applicant the planning authority, in particular two members of the authority, had not acted judicially and failed to comply with the provisions of section 26 of the 1963 Act. It was also held that the planning authority had taken into irrelevant considerations, in that members referred to the agricultural business which the applicant was engaged in entitling him to planning permission, and that as the applicant was engaged in the breeding of horses that it was important for him to live nearby. The Court held that these were considerations which were personal to the applicant and had nothing to do with the proper planning and development of the area, and therefore the members of the planning authority were precluded from considering them.

4. Development and material change

(a) Works

2–33 The Local Government (Planning and Development) Act 1963,[57] places development into two categories, works and material change. Works are defined in section 2 as including "any act or operation of construction, excavation, demolition, extension, alteration, repair or renewal". Alteration is defined as including plastering or painting which materially alters the external appearance of a structure so as to change its appearance and render it inconsistent with the character of neighbouring buildings or structures. The Principal Act gives a wide definition to the term "structure" as "any building, erection, structure, excavation, or other thing constructed, erected, or made on, in, or under any land, or any part of a structure so defined, and, where the context so admits, includes the land on, in, or under which the structure is situate."

---

[56] Unreported, High Court, October 31, 1990.
[57] No. 28 of 1963, referred to as the Principal Act.

2–34 The term "development" is defined in section 3 of the Principal Act as the carrying out of any works on, in, or under land or the making of any material change in the use of any structures or other land. Subsection 2 goes on to state that development also includes the case where any structure or other land or any tree or other object on land becomes used for the exhibition of advertisements. Development also takes place where land becomes used for the placing or keeping of any vans, tents or other objects, whether or not moveable and whether or not collapsible, for the purpose of caravanning or camping or the sale of goods, for the storage of caravans or tents, for the deposit of, or parts of, vehicles, old metal, mining or industrial waste, builders' waste, rubble or debris, and it is declared that the use of the land shall be taken as having materially changed.

(b) Change of use and material change

2–35 For the avoidance of doubt subsection 3 of section 2 states that for the use as two or more dwellings of any structure which had been previously used as a single dwelling involves a material change in the use of the structure and of each part of the structure which is so used. In the case of *The Rehabilitation Institute v. Dublin Corporation*[58] it was held that a change of use of a first floor of a three storey building from a workshop to an office was not a material change of use having regard to the general use of the premises as a whole. The building was used generally for administration and therefore an office was consistent with the overall use of the premises.

2–36 The 1994 Regulations provide for the change of use of certain developments without the need for obtaining planning permission.[59] Class 13 of the second schedule, part one, of the regulations provided that development consisting of a change of use from the sale of hot food off the premises, or the sale of leasing or display for sale or leasing of motor vehicles to the use as a shop is exempted development, as is the change of use from a public house to a shop, a funeral parlour to a shop, an amusement arcade or a restaurant to a shop. Certain other developments are also classed as being exempt, such as the change of use from two or more dwellings to a single dwelling which had been previously used as a single dwelling.

2–37 Uses which are ancillary to the use of existing structures are not defined as either being a development or a material change of use, such as the use of a room in a dwelling as a private office to which members of the public do not have access.

2–38 The Principal act did not define what the term a "material change"

---

[58] Unreported, January 14, 1988.
[59] Art. 11.

meant, but that it can come about through the intensification of an existing use by either increasing the amount of traffic into a site or by increasing the amount of visitors and the opening hours to a particular undertaking.[60] There has been some discussion regarding the different types of approaches which have been taken with respect to whether a development or works can be described as material.[61] In particular there has been a difference in approach taken in Ireland than that taken in England. The English approach stems from a decision to ignore the planning implications of a change of use in determining its materiality.[62] A qualitative approach was adopted in English decisions whereby the courts focused on determining whether the use involved a change in the "character" of the use or whether the change of use would affect a definable character of the use. A change in the identity of the person carrying out the use on the property or a change in the type of goods sold or service provided did not, of themselves, bring about a material change of use.[63]

2–39 In the Irish courts the term "material" has been held to mean "material for planning purposes,"[64] there must be sufficient planning considerations raised by the change in the activity being carried out or the development which has taken place in order to justify control being exercised under the planning code.[65] In fact the entire planning code and the statutes enforcing it must be strictly construed, and that planning considerations are also to be restricted to matters which are in the planning code itself, that is to matters expressed in the legislation and are usually contained in the relevant development plan.

2–40 A material change of use can also arise where different methods are being used in an undertaking which employ different machinery with differing effects on the general environment, such as the use of heavy crushing equipment in a quarry.[66] A material change of use can also arise where the amount of goods being produced at a site is increased to such an extent that the whole nature of the undertaking changes such as in the case of *Lee v. O'Riordan*[67] where the undertaking which had been engaged in the extraction of sand and gravel was further developed to include limestone excavation and a rate greater than the previous level of extraction and represented a complete departure from the normal type of operation carried on in a gravel pit.

2–41 However, it must be established that, where it is alleged that a material

---

[60] See *Stafford and Bates v. Roadstone Ltd.* [1980] I.L.R.M. 1.
[61] See Irish Planning Law and Procedure, p. 59.
[62] *ibid.* at p. 58.
[63] *ibid.* at p.590.
[64] *per* Keane, J. in *Monaghan Co. Co. v. Brogan* [1987] I.R. 333.
[65] See *Dublin Corporation v. Moore* [1984] I.L.R.M. 339.
[66] See *Patterson v. Murphy Trading Services Ltd* [1978] I.L.R.M. 85.
[67] Unreported, High Court, February 10, 1995.

change of use has occurred, that the change which has taken place has affected the proper planning and development of the area having regards to the methods employed and attitude taken by the relevant planning authority on the appointed day.[68] Items which are taken into consideration when deciding as to whether an operation could be classed as being a material change of use include any additional demands which the operation or activity has placed on the local authority services, whether any change has taken place in respect of the flow and nature or type of traffic,[69] whether any additional pollution has been caused over and above that previously associated with the site of operations,[70] whether the change of use has had or will have any impact on residential amenities,[71] and whether any complaints had been made to the planning authority regarding the change in operations or activities.[72]

2–42   Where a previous use of a premises or site has been recommenced the recommencement could amount to a material change of use if the operation or activity had not be carried out for some time.[73] The abandonment of the use of a property will also constitute a material change in use, especially if it is the case that the previous use of the land was not merely suspended for a temporary and determined period but was ceased for a considerable time and there was no evidence of an intention to resume the activity.[74] The use of only a small portion of a site or area for the carrying out of different operations or the carrying on of a different activity from that already established may not be regarded as a material change of use provided the main activity continues and the other, newer, activity does not have any consequences for the proper planning and development of the area.[75]

2–43   It can also be held that where a building for which planning permission was granted is destroyed, either by fire or otherwise, and is no longer structurally sound that the permitted use has expired and that any further development would constitute a material change of use and would require planning permission. This was the case in *Galway Co. Co. v. Connacht Proteins Ltd*[76] where a building which had the benefit of planning permission for use as an animal by-products processing was destroyed by fire. It was also held that it was not permissible to use outbuildings or construct a new building without first obtaining planning permission.

---

[68] *Galway County Council v. Lackagh Rock Ltd* [1985] I.R. 20. The appointed day is October 1, 1964.
[69] See *Cork Corporation v. O'Connell* [1982] I.L.R.M. 505.
[70] See *Dublin Co. Co. v. Macken*, unreported, May 13, 1994.
[71] See *Carrickhall Holdings v. Dublin Corporartion* [1983] I.L.R.M. 268.
[72] See *Galway Co. Co. v. Lackagh Rock Ltd*.
[73] See *Cork Co. Co. v. Ardfert Quarries Ltd*, unreported, December 2, 1982.
[74] See *Hartley v. Minister for Housing and Local Government*.
[75] See *McGrath Limestone Works Ltd. v. Galway Co. Co.* [1989] I.L.R.M. 602.
[76] Unreported, March 28, 1980.

2–44 Where a building is divided into a number of units a material change of use of any of the units may constitute a development for which planning permission may be necessary. However, if it can be said that in the case of a unit being in single occupation and where there are two or more physically distinct areas occupied by different and unrelated activities then it could be argued that each unit ought to be regarded as a separate enterprise for planning purposes.[77]

5. Exempted development[78]

(a) Categories

2–45 Section 4 of the Principal Act makes provision for certain developments to be exempted from the requirement to obtain planning permission. In all there are eight categories of works or development which are classed as "exempted development". The first relates to development consisting of the use of any land for the purposes of agriculture or forestry, including afforestation, and development consisting of the use for any of those purposes of any building occupied together with land which is used for agriculture or forestry. Agriculture is defined as including horticulture, fruit growing, seed growing, dairy farming, the breeding and keeping of livestock, including any creature kept for the production of food, wool, skins or fur, or for the purpose of its use in the farming of land, the use of land as grazing land, meadow land, land market gardens and nursery grounds, the use of land for turbary, and the use of land for woodlands where that use is ancillary to the farming of land for other agricultural purposes.[79] The exemption relates to the use of lands for agricultural use, it is still necessary to obtain planning permission for the construction or erection of buildings used for agricultural purposes.

2–46 The Local Government (Planning and Development) Regulations of 1994[80] specifies within part three the classes of exempted development in rural areas.[81] Rural areas are defined in article 9 of the Regulations as being

---

[77] See *Burdle v. Secretary of State for the Environment* [1972] 3 All E.R. 240, and Keane, *Planning and Development Law*, p.21.

[78] If any question arises as to what is or is not exempted development it shall be referred to the Board, s.5 of the 1963 Act. See also *McGoldrick v. An Bord Pleanála* [1997] IR 497, for a consideration of some legal principles in a s.5 reference, Barron J. quashed a decision of the board as it was contrary to fair procedures. The board may also be completted to decide on such issues, see *Palmerlane Ltd. v. An Bord Pleanála*, unreported, High Court, January 28, 1999.

[79] s. 2.

[80] S.I. 86 of 1994, as amended by the Local Government (Planning and Development) Regulations (No. 1) of 1995, S.I. No. 69 of 1995.

[81] Regarding the interpretation of regulations see *Dillion v. Irish Cement Ltd.*, unreported, Supreme Court, November 26, 1986, which requires that planning regulations are to be

areas other than county boroughs, boroughs, urban districts, towns which are specified in the First Schedule to the Principal Act and the excluded areas referred to in the Local Government (Reorganisation) Act of 1985.[82] Class 6 relates to the carrying out of works in respect of the provision of a roofed structure for the housing of pigs, cattle, sheep, goats, poultry, donkeys, horses, deer or rabbits and which have a floor area of not over three hundred square metres together with ancillary storage facilities for effluent.[83]

2–47 Class seven allows the carrying out of works consisting of the provision of roofless cubicles, open loose yards, self-feed silo or silage areas, feeding aprons, assembly yards, milking parlours, sheep dipping units, effluent storage facilities or structures for the making or storage of silage or other similar structures not having a floor area of over three hundred square metres, together with ancillary effluent storage facilities.[84] Class eight relates to the carrying out of works consisting of the provision of any store, barn, shed, glasshouse or other structure not specified in either classes six or seven and again not having a floor area of over three hundred square metres.[85] Class nine relates to the carrying out of development on land used for the purposes, only, of forestry or agriculture of field drainage, land reclamation, removal of fences, improvement of existing fences, improvement of hill grazing, or the reclamation of estuarine marsh land[86] or of callows, where the preservation of such land or callows is not an objective of a development plan.

2–48 Classes ten and eleven make provision for the exemption of works relating to the provision of roofed structures for the housing of horses or ponies which have floor area of less than one hundred square metres, together with ancillary storage facilities for effluent.[87] Class eleven relates to the development or the carrying out of works for the provision of roofed structures for the housing of greyhounds which have a floor area of less than fifty square metres.[88] Class twelve relates to the carrying out of works relating to the pro-

---

strictly construed. See also *Murray v. Buckley*, unreported, High Court, December 5, 1990.

[82] No. 7 of 1985, s. 9.

[83] Provided these structures are used only for the purposes of agriculture and the entire complex of structures does not exceed 450 sq. m. together with other provisions relating to the siting of the effluent, and that any structure must be over 100 m. from any dwellinghouse.

[84] Provided the conditions and limitations of column two of the schedule are complied with, which are similar to those for class six.

[85] Similar restrictions and limitations apply as for classes six and seven.

[86] The reclamation of marshland was held not to have been exempted in *Irish Wild Bird Conservancy v. Clonakility Golf and Country Club*, unreported, High Court, July 23, 1993.

[87] Subject to the conditions and limitations contained in the second column of the schedule.

[88] Again subject to the conditions and limitations in the second column.

vision of roofless hard-surfaced yards or enclosed areas which have an area not over one hundred square metres, provided these yards or enclosed areas are not used for any other purpose other than in connection with the keeping of horses, ponies or greyhounds. In addition a further condition is stipulated in that effluent storage facilities must be adequate to serve the yard or enclosed area having regard to its size, use, location and the need to avoid water pollution, mainly due to the fact that the run off surface water will consist of an effluent which is highly toxic.[89]

2–49 A further category of exempted development is provided for in section 4 of the Principal Act in the case of development by the council of a county in the county health district and development by the corporation of a county or other borough in that borough. This is distinct from the provisions of section 39 of the Principal Act which provides that a local authority cannot contravene the provisions of the development plan for the area. Section 39 states that the council of a county shall not effect any development in their county health district which contravenes materially the development plan, nor shall the corporation of a county or other borough effect any development in such borough which contravenes materially the development plan, nor can the council of an urban district effect any development in that district which contravenes materially the development plan.

2–50 The development consisting of the carrying out by the corporation of a county borough or borough or the council of a county or an urban district of any works which are required for the construction of a new road or the maintenance or improvement of an existing road and development consisting of the carrying out by any local authority or other statutory undertaker of any works for the purpose of inspecting, repairing, renewing, altering or removing any sewers, mains, pipes, cables, overhead wires, or other apparatus, including the breaking open of any street or other land for that purpose are also classed as being exempted development within the terms of section 4 of the Principal Act. It is not necessary that the local authority carry out these works within their own function area, any statutory undertaking, including planning authorities may carry out these kind of works.

2–51 Development which consists of the carrying out of works for the maintenance, improvement or alteration of any structure, which are works which affect only the interior of the structure or which do not materially affect the external appearance of the structure so as to render the structure inconsistent with the character of the structure or of neighbouring structures is also classed as an exempt development by section 4. However, a development plan can

---

[89] Other conditions and limitations also apply in relating to the overall size of the complex which cannot exceed 150 sq. m.

indicate whether certain interior fixtures or features are to be retained and those which are of artistic, historic or of architectural interest. The development plan may also specify that works may not be carried out which involve the alteration or removal or the causing of injury or damage to any such fixtures or features.[90]

2–52 Development consisting of the carrying out of any of the works referred to in the Land Reclamation Act, 1949 and not being works which relate to the fencing or the enclosure of land which has been open to or which has been used by the public within a period of ten years from the carrying out of the works,[91] is also stated to be exempt development. The Land Reclamation Act of 1949 relates to the reclamation of lands and provided for the carrying out of works which now forms class nine of the classes of exempted development relating to agricultural development in the 1994 Regulations.

2–53 The last class of development which was exempted by the Principal Act relates to development consisting of the use of any structure or other land within the curtilage of a dwellinghouse for any purpose incidental to the enjoyment of the dwellinghouse. The 1994 Regulations also make provision for the further exemption of works or development relating to development within the curtilage of a dwellinghouse.

2–54 Class one of the second schedule, part one, relates to the carrying out of an extension of a dwellinghouse by the construction or erection of an extension, including a conservatory, to the rear of the dwellinghouse, or the conversion for use as part of the dwelling of any garage, store, shed or other similar structure which is attached to the rear or to the side of the dwellinghouse. However, any extension must not exceed twenty three square metres, including conservatories and the size of any previous extension is aggregated with the new extension and together must not exceed twenty three square metres. The private open space to the rear of a dwelling must not be reduced to less than twenty five square metres, and the regulations provide that the height of the extension must be limited to the height of the existing dwellings' eaves or parapit. Furthermore the height of the highest part of the roof of the extension must not exceed the height of the highest part of the roof of the dwellinghouse.

2–55 Class two relates to the exemption of the carrying out of works relating to the provision of a chimney, boiler house or oil storage tank as part of a central heating system of a dwellinghouse. The capacity of the oil storage tank which accompanies the central heating system must not have a capacity of over 3,500 litres of home heating oil.

---

[90] s.43(1) of the Local Government (Planning and Development) Act 1976.
[91] Inserted by s.34(1) of the 1976 Act.

2–56 Class three provides that the construction, erection or placing within the curtilage of a dwellinghouse of any tent, awning, shade or other object, or of a greenhouse, garage, store, shed or other similar structure is also an exempted development. The use of these structures is limited to a purpose incidental to the enjoyment of the dwellinghouse and cannot be used for human habitation, the keeping of pigs, poultry, horses, ponies or pigeons.

2–57 Under class three no structure must be constructed, erected or placed forward of the front wall of the dwellinghouse, and the total area of the structures must not when aggregated with other similar structures exceed twenty five square metres in area. The erection or construction of any type of structure listed in class three must not cause the private open spaces of the dwellinghouse to be reduced to less than twenty five square metres. The regulations further provide that the external finishes and roof of any structure in class three must be of a similar finish and type to the external finish and roof size and type of the dwellinghouse. The height of the structure must not exceed, in the case of a building with a tiled or slated pitched roof four metres, and in any other case three metres.

2–58 With respect to the erection of a wireless or television antenna the height of the antenna above the roof of the dwellinghouse must not exceed six metres,[92] and in the case of the erection of a satellite television antenna the antenna must not have a diameter of over one metre, be erected on or forward of the front wall of the dwellinghouse, not be erected on the front roof slope of the dwelling or higher than the highest part of the roof. Not more than one satellite antenna can be erected on, or within the curtilage of a dwellinghouse.[93]

2–59 The construction, erection or alteration within or bounding the curtilage of a dwellinghouse, of a gate, gateway, railing or wooden fence or of a wall constructed of brick, stone, blocks with decorative finishes, either using concrete blocks or mass concrete is exempted under class five. However, the height of any of these structures must not exceed two metres and in the case of a wall or fence which is within or bounds any garden or other space in front of the house the height of same cannot exceed 1.2 metres. Every wall other than a dry stone wall is to be capped and the external surface of every wall of mass concrete or of concrete blocks, other than those with a decorative finish, which bound any garden or other space between a dwellinghouse and a road is to be plastered.[94]

2–60 The construction of any path, drain or pond or the carrying out of any

---

[92] Class 4.
[93] Class 4(b).
[94] Class 5.

landscaping works within the curtilage of a dwellinghouse is also classed as being exempt, as are works within the curtilage of a dwellinghouse for the provision of a hard surface for any purpose incidental to the enjoyment of the dwelling, and the provision to the front or side of a hard surface for the parking of not more than two motor vehicles and used for the purpose which is incidental to the enjoyment of the dwelling. However, the level of the ground shall not be altered by more than one metre above or below the level of the adjoining ground.[95]

2–61   The construction or the erection of a porch outside any external door of a dwellinghouse is allowed without permission, provided that any such porch is not less than two metres from any road, and its floor area does not exceed two square metres. The height of a porch is also restricted to four metres in the case of a structure with a tiled or slated pitched roof, and in any other case three metres.[96]

2–62   Classes eight to twelve deal with the carrying out of sundry minor works, and deal with gateways, fences and the improvement or repair of private streets, road or pavements. Class eleven exempts any alteration which consists of the painting of any external part of any building or other structure, provided that the painting does not consist of works which involve the creation of a mural. Article 10 of the regulations does not allow for exempted development for painting which is to be carried out on a building or structure which has been preserved under the development plan or in a draft development plan.

2–63   Class fourteen allows the occasional use for social or recreational purposes of any school, hall, club, art gallery, museum, library, reading room, gym, or any structure which is normally used for public worship or religious instruction. It is arguable as to whether such a provision need apply as any such premises could and would be used for occasional social or recreational uses as being ancillary to the main activity which would have been granted planning permission, or which predates the appointed day. Class thirty allows for development consisting of the laying out and use of land as a park, private open space or ornamental garden, or the erection of a roadside shrine,[97] or development for athletics or sports, other than a golf course, pitch and putt or sports involving the use of motor vehicles, aircraft or firearms, and where there is no charge made to the public for admission to the land.

---

[95] Class 6.
[96] Class 7, the previous regulation dealing with porches stipulated that the porch had to be two metres from a public road, now it is any road.
[97] Although exempt a roadside shrine cannot be illuminated, must be lower than two metres in height. A shrine cannot interfere with traffic or cause a danger to traffic under s.98(1) of the Road Traffic Act 1961.

2–64 Class thirty three relates to the exemption of development of the use of land for any fair, funfair, bazaar or circus or any local event of a religious, cultural, educational , political, social, recreational or sporting character and the placing or maintenance of tents, vans or other temporary or movable structures or objects in connection with those activities. The lands so used cannot be used for any purposes continuously for a period of fifteen days or occasionally for periods exceeding in aggregate thirty days in any year, and the lands must be reinstated to the original condition following these events.

2–65 Class thirty seven allows for development works which are incidental to the use or maintenance of any burial ground, churchyard, monument, fairgreen, market, school yard or showground except for the erection or the construction of any wall, fence or gate bounding or abutting on a public road, or the erection or construction of any building other than a stall or store which is wholly enclosed within a market building, or the reconstruction or alteration of any building other than such a stall or store.

2–66 Classes fifteen to sixteen dealt with the erection of temporary structures in the course of the construction of a structure which has been granted planning permission, and for the use of a premises as an election office during elections and referenda.

2–67 Development for industrial purposes comes within the confines of class nineteen to twenty and exempted development is restricted to the provision of private ways or private railways, sidings or conveyors, mains pipes, cables or other apparatus, or the installation or erection by way of addition or replacement of plant or machinery, or structures of the nature or plant or machinery, provided the industrial undertaking already has planning permission for the main activity, and that any development cannot materially alter the external appearance of the premises, and the height of any plant or machinery cannot exceed fifteen metres in height or the height of the existing structure, whichever is the greater.

2–68 Class twenty allows the storage within the curtilage of an industrial building, in connection with the industrial process which is carried on in the building, of raw materials, products, packing materials or fuel, or the deposit of waste which has arose from the industrial process. However, the raw materials, or products or packing materials, fuel or waste which is stored cannot be visible from any public road which is contiguous or which is adjacent to the curtilage of the industrial building.

2–69 Classes twenty one to twenty nine relate to the carrying out of development in connection with statutory undertakings such as works in relation to watercourses, canals, rivers, lakes, and in connection the development of public parks or certain works relating to the carrying out of works by the Commissioner of Public Works in Ireland in relation to nature reserves established under the Wildlife Act of 1976.[98] Class forty two allows the Commissioners of Public Works or the Environmental Protection Agency or a local authority which is outside of the relevant functional area to carry out development which consists of the provision, construction or erection of any equipment or structure for or in connection with the collection of information on the levels, volumes and flows of water in rivers or other watercourses, lakes or groundwaters provided the floor area of any building or other structure does not exceed eight square metres and the height of any building does not exceed four metres. Regional Fisheries Boards are allowed under class forty nine to erect footbridges, fish passes, fish screens, or barriers or a walkway or fishing stand, provided the footbridge does not exceed 1.2 metres in width or 8 metres in length, and any walkway does not exceed 1.2 metres in width. Fishing stands cannot exceed ten square metres in area.

2–70 Class thirty five concerns development relating to temporary structures or other facilities required for the visit of a foreign dignitary or delegation, and allows for such development providing that the temporary structures and facilities are removed after the conclusion of the visit and the land reinstated. Classes thirty six allows for the development involving the erection of lighthouses, beacons, buoys or other navigational aid, provided the same does not exceed forty metres in height. Class forty eight allows development consisting of the carrying out of works by the Gardaí for security reasons in respect of works within, or bounding the curtilage of the residence of a person in receipt of protection from the Gardaí.

2–71 Class thirty eight allows for the carrying out of works which are of or are incidental to the carrying out of works which are done in accordance with any licence to allow land to be used for camping granted under section 34 of the Local Government (Sanitary Services) Act 1948,[99] but not for the erection of any building, hut or chalet or the construction of any road or hard standing. This class also allows for the carrying out of works which are carried out in order to comply with a notice issued under section 26 of the Air Pollution Act of 1987,[100] or of a notice issued under section 12 of the Local Government (Water Pollution) Act of 1977.[101] Class thirty eight also allows for the carrying out of development in compliance with a condition or of conditions which are attached to a fire safety certificate granted in accordance with part three of

---

[98] No. 39 of 1976.
[99] No. 3 of 1948.
[100] No. 6 of 1987.
[101] No. 1 of 1977.

the Building Control Regulations of 1991[102] other than the construction or the erection of an external fire escape or water tank.

2–72 Class forty allows for the sinking of a well, the drilling of a borehole, the erection of a pump, or the construction of a pumphouse or other works which are necessary for the purpose of providing a domestic water supply. The class also allows for works connected with a group water scheme in accordance with a plan or proposal which has been approved by the Minister or by a local authority for the purpose of making a grant towards the scheme. Class forty one allows for any drilling or excavation for the purpose of surveying land or examining the depth and nature of the subsoil except for drilling or excavation for the purposes of minerals prospecting.

2–73 Class forty three allows for the connection of any premises to a wired broadcast, replay service, sewer, watermain, gas main or electricity supply, including the breaking open of any street or other land for those purposes. Class forty four allows for the construction or erection by a licensed person under the Wireless telegraphy (Wired Broadcast Replay Service) regulations of 1974 of a cabinet as part of a wired broadcast replay service provided the cabinet does not exceed one cubic metre, measured externally, above ground level.

2–74 The demolition of a building or other structure, other than a habitable house or a building which forms part of a terrace of buildings or a building which abuts on another building in separate ownership is allowed as exempted development under class forty five. The demolition of part of a habitable house due to the erection of an extension or of a porch under classes one or seven or in accordance with a planning permission granted for an extension or porch is also classed as exempted development.

2–75 Advertisements are covered in part two of the exempted development regulations and include advertisements exhibited on business premises relating to the business carried on in the premises. Article 10 of the regulations does not allow development to take place on a structure or building which is the subject of a restriction or preservation under the development plan or in a draft development plan.[103]

2–76 The total area of advertisements which are exhibited or attached to the front of any building may not exceed 0.3 square metres for every metre of length of the front of the premises and may not in total exceed five square metres. The total area of advertisements which are exhibited on or attached or

---

[102] S.I. No. 305 of 1991.
[103] Art. 10(1)(a)(x).

affixed to any face of a building other than the front of the building cannot exceed 1.2 square metres and the total area of the advertisement which is illuminated cannot exceed 0.3 square metres. In respect of the total area of advertisements which are not exhibited on or attached to a building cannot exceed three square metres and of this not more than 1.5 square metres can be illuminated. Advertisements cannot be more than 2.5 metres in height nor any part of the advertisement which is attached to the building can be more than four metres in height above the ground level, otherwise planning permission will be required.

2–77   In the case of advertisements which projects more than five centimetres over any public road, the diameter of the sign cannot exceed one metre and no other advertisement can be exhibited which projects more than five centimetres over the road. Where any of the advertisements used are on a swinging or a fixed sign and which projects over five centimetres from the external face of the building, the total area of the advertisements cannot exceed 1.2 metres and the area of any face of any of the advertisements cannot exceed 0.4 metres. An advertisement cannot contain or consist of any symbol, emblem, model, logo or device which exceed 0.6 metres in height or any letter exceeding 0.3 metres in height. An advertisement cannot cover any part of any window or door of any building to which it is attached.

2–78   Advertisements which are exhibited within a business premises and which are not visible from the outside of the premises are exempted under class three, as are illuminated advertisements affixed in a window display or inside the glass surface of a window, provided the total area of the advertisement does not exceed one quarter of the area of the window through which the advertisements are exhibited.[104] Classes seven and eight allow for the exhibition of advertisements on lands which are enclosed and where the advertisements are not visible to the public, and advertisements within railway stations, bus stations, airports and ferry terminals are also allowed, again provided the advertisements cannot be viewed from outside the premises.

2–79   A flag may be attached to a single flagstaff fixed in an upright position on the roof of a premises and which only bears an emblem, device or logo relating to the business or activity carried out on the premises. Not more than one flag may be exhibited on a business premises.[105] Advertisements which are exhibited at an entrance to a premises relating to the business or activity carried on in the premises are also exempted provided the advertisement does not exceed 0.3 square metres, and not more than one advertisement is exhibited at each entrance. A similar exemption is allowed for advertisements relat-

---

[104] Class 2, Part II.
[105] Class 4, Part II.

ing to religious, educational, cultural, recreational or medical institutions except that the advertisement may be up to 0.6 square metres in area and cannot be more than 2.5 metres in height. Premises providing overnight guest accommodation or public houses, flats, clubs, boarding houses or hostels may also provide similar signs to educational institutions and the like.

2–80 The advertising of the sale or letting of property or land is also allowed under class nine, provided the area of the advertisements do not exceed 0.6 square metres in the case of advertisements for the sale or letting of a dwelling and 1.2 square metres in the case of the sale or letting of other types of property. Not more than one advertisement for the letting or sale of the property is allowed and no advertisement can remain on the property for more than seven days after the sale or letting has taken place. Similar restrictions as to the sale or letting of dwellings is applied to the selling of goods or livestock on lands or at premises which is not normally used for the selling of goods or of livestock.[106]

2–81 With respect of the carrying out of building or other works on lands, and for the purposes of identification, direction or warning, advertisements may be erected which in the case of advertising the carrying out of works or building must not exceed 3.5 square metres, and in respect of direction and warning signs must not exceed 0.3 square metres.[107]

2–82 Statutory undertakers are allowed to erect advertisements for the purposes of announcement or direction or warning, while advertisements relating to elections are also allowed provided they are taken down within seven days after the date of the election or referendum.[108]

2–83 Classes 16 and 17 make provision for the advertising of religious, cultural, educational, political, social, recreational or sporting events which are temporary in nature as well as advertisements relating to circuses, funfairs, carnivals, shows, musicians, players or other travelling entertainment. The restrictions are that these advertisements cannot exceed 1.2 metres in area and cannot be over 2.5 metres above the ground, and the advertisements must be removed within seven days after the events have been completed. Advertisements relating to any demonstration of agricultural methods or processes on land are allowed under class eighteen provided the advertisement does not

---

[106] Class 10, Part II.
[107] Class 11 and 13, Part II, other conditions are applied in relation to class 11, mainly in relation to the taking down of the signs after works have been completed and the restriction on height and area, 4m and 3.5 sq. m.
[108] Class 12 and 14 Part II, see also class 15 relating to advertisements relating to statutory enactments.

exceed 0.6 square metres in area and not more than one advertisement is exhibited on the land, and the advertisement must be removed within seven days of the demonstration.

2–84 The exempted development classes contained in part three of the regulations relate to minor works and structures and the temporary use of land for camping together with provisions relating to mineral prospecting and agricultural structures. The temporary use of lands for camping and for caravaning and for mooring any boat or barge or vessel is allowed provided not more than one tent or caravan is placed within one hundred metres of another tent or caravan at a time, and that the tent or caravan does not remain on the same site for longer than ten days. Additionally, the tent or caravan cannot be used to store, display, advertise, or sell any goods or for the purposes of any business. Tents or caravans cannot be place on land within fifty metres of any public road unless the land is enclosed by a wall, bank or hedge having an average height of not less than 1.5 metres. Scouting organisations may use land for a period of not over thirty days in any year.[109]

2–85 All exemptions which are listed in the schedule to the 1994 Regulations, as amended, are subject to the general provisions of article 10 in that development cannot be exempted development if the carrying out of the proposed development would contravene a condition attached to a planning permission, consist or comprise of the formation, laying out or material widening an access route to a public road the surfaced carriageway of which exceeds four metres in width, and which endangers public safety by creating a traffic hazard or obstruction of road users. Additionally, if the development consists of the carrying out under a public road of works other than a connection to a wired broadcast relay service, sewer, water main, gas main, or electricity supply or other works specifically provided for, then the development will not be exempted. Any works which bring forward a building or any part of a building beyond the front wall of the building on either side or beyond a line which has been determined as the building line in a development plan or the draft of a new development plan are also not exempt from the necessity of obtaining planning permission. Development which will interfere with a view or prospect of a special amenity value or of a special interest the preservation of which is an objective of a development plan or of a draft development plan is also not classed as being exempt from the requirements of applying for planning permission.

2–86 The regulations also do not allow the carrying out of excavation, alteration or demolition of caves, sites, features, or objects of archaeological, geological or historical interest the preservation of which is an objective of a

---

[109]Class 2, Part III.

development plan or of a draft development plan, [110] or of the demolition or alteration of a building or structure which has been specified as being available for use under a development plan.[111] Any works or development which consist of or comprise of the extension, alteration, repair or renewal or an unauthorised structure or a structure the use of which is an unauthorised use is also not allowed under the exempted classes.[112]

2–87 Article 10 also does not allow the carrying out of development or works which consist of the fencing or the enclosure of any land which is habitually open to or used by the public during the ten years preceding the fencing for recreational purposes or as means of access to any seashore, mountain, lakeside, riverbank or other place of natural beauty or recreational amenity,[113] or which obstructs any public right of way.[114]

(b) Internal and external works and incidental use

2–88 Works which are carried out only to the interiors of a structure are exempted unless the works involved the alteration or the removal of a feature or fixture which forms part of a structure listed for preservation. External works are also exempted provided they do not materially affect the external appearance of the structure or of the neighbouring structures.[115] In *Dublin Corporation v. Bentam*[116] it was held that the replacement of Georgian windows with aluminium windows was not an exempted development as the works which were carried out affected the external appearance of the structure which made the building inconsistent with the character of the premises.[117]

2–89 Developments consisting of the use of any structure of other land within the curtilage of a dwellinghouse for any purpose which is incidental to the enjoyment of the dwellinghouse are regarded as exempted development.[118] The commonly accepted definition of "curtilage" is that it is the ground which is used for the comfortable enjoyment of house or other building and that the ground serves the purpose of the house or building in some necessary or reasonably useful way.[119]

---

[110] Art. 10(1)(a)(vii).
[111] Art. 10(1)(a)(xi).
[112] Art. 10(1)(a)(viii).
[113] Art. 10(1)(a)(xii).
[114] Art. 10(1)(a)(xiii).
[115] For the meaning of character see *Cairnduff v. O'Connell* [1986] I.R. 73.
[116] Unreported, High Court, July 22, 1992.
[117] See art. 10(1)(a)(ix) of the 1994 Regulations.
[118] s.4 Principal Act.
[119] See *Sinclair Lockhart's Trustees v. Central Land Board.*

6. Applying for planning permission[120]

(a) Application

2–90   Applying for planning permission involves four sections, pre-application publicity requirements, the particulars which need to accompany planning applications, the procedure and receipt of planning applications and the notification of planning decisions.

2–91   Article 14 of the 1994 Regulations provide that an applicant must give notice of an intention to apply for planning permission by publishing a notice in a newspaper and by erecting a notice on the relevant site. The newspaper notice should be placed within a period of two weeks before making a planning application and not later than the making of the application by the erection or fixing of a site notice. The newspaper notice must conform with the provisions of Article 15 of the regulations which provide that the notice must be published in a newspaper circulating in the district in which the land or structure is situated, and the notice must contain as a heading the name of the relevant planning authority, it must also contain the name of the applicant, the nature of the application, that is whether it is for a permission, an outline permission or an approval, the location of the land or the address of the structure to which the application relates to. The notice must also contain details of the nature and extent of the development including how may dwellings the application includes, whether the application relates to the retention of a structure, the nature of the proposed structure, and the period for which it is proposed to retain the structure or relating to the continuance of a use, the nature of the use and of the previous use. If the application is to be accompanied by an environmental impact statement (EIS) the notice must state that the EIS will be submitted to the planning authority with the application and that the EIS and any further information in relation to the development which is proposed will be available at the offices of the planning authority. If the application relates to an activity which requires a licence under part four of the Environmental Protection Agency Act of 1992,[121] that fact must also be stated in the notice.[122] An application can be made to the Minister for the Environment and Local Government for an exemption from the requirement of submitting an environmental impact statement under section 25(3) of the 1963 Act.[123]

---

[120] See s.40, 1963 Act which created the general obligation to obtain planning permission, see *Howard v. Commissioners of Public Works*, unreported, High Court, February 17, 1993, Supreme Court, May 26, 1993 and *Byrne v. Commissioners of Public Works*, unreported, High Court, November 27, 1992.

[121] No. 7 of 1992.

[122] See s.82 of the Environmental Protection Agency Act of 1992.

[123] Inserted by EIA Regulations and the E.C. (EIA) (Amendment) Regulations 1994, the

2–92 Article 16 provides that a site notice which is erected or fixed on any land or structure must be painted or inscribed, or printed and affixed on a durable material and is to be securely erected or fixed in a conspicuous position on or near the main entrance to the land or structure concerned from a public road, or on any part of the land or structure adjoining a public road so as to be easily visible and legible by persons using the public road. Where the land or structure does not adjoin a public road, a site notice is to be erected or fixed in a conspicuous position on the land or structure so as to be easily visible and legible by persons outside the land or structure.[124] The position of the site notice on the land or structure is to be indicated on a plan which accompanies the planning application.[125]

2–93 The site notice is headed as "Application to Planning Authority" in block letters and is to state the name of the applicant, the nature of the application, the nature and extent of the development, including the number of dwellings if any, or whether the application relates to the retention of any structure or the continuance of any use, and that the planning application may be inspected at the offices of the planning authority. The site notice is to be maintained in position on the land or structure for a period of at least one month after the making of the planning application and is to be renewed or replaced if it is removed or becomes defaced or illegible within that one month period.[126]

2–94 It may be necessary for further notices to be made under Article 17 of the Regulations where an applicant proposes to submit an EIS to the planning authority. Before submitting the statement the applicant must publish in a newspaper circulating in the district in which the land or structure is situated notice of intention to submit the statement. The notice which is published is to contain as a heading the name of the relevant planning authority, the name of the applicant, the date on which the planning application was made and its reference number in the planning register, the location of the land or the address of the structure to which the application relates, and the fact that an EIS will be submitted to the planning authority and that the EIS and any other or further information will be available for inspection at the offices of the planning authority.

2–95 Where a planning application relates to development which includes an activity which requires a licence under the Environmental Protection Agency Act of 1992 then this fact should also be included in the newspaper advertise-

---

period of determining an application is held in abeyance from the making of the application to the Minister until the Minister makes a decision.
[124] Art. 16(2).
[125] Art. 16(3).
[126] Art. 16(5).

ment. Once the newspaper notice has been published two copies of it should be submitted with an EIS.

2–96   If the planning authority are of the opinion that any notice which has been published in a newspaper which does not have a sufficiently large circulation in the district in which the land or structure is situate, or that the notice does not comply with the requirement of article 15, or if the notice which is erected or fixed on the land or structure does not comply with the provisions of article 16, or that the content of the notices does not comply with the requirements of the Regulation or is misleading or inadequate, the planning authority are obliged to require the applicant to further notice in such manner and in such terms as the planning authority may specify and to re-submit the application. The planning authority are obliged to order the resubmission of the application if a period or more than two weeks has elapsed between the publication of the notice in the newspaper, or where the site notice has not been erected or fixed on the land or structure in accordance with the provisions of article 16 or that the notice has not been maintained in position or has been defaced or has become illegible and was not replaced or renewed.

2–97   Where plans, drawings or other particulars of the application have been submitted to the planning authority following a request under article 35 of the regulations or where further information has been received following the request more than three months after the request for such information, the planning authority may require the applicant to give a further notice or notices in such manner and in such terms as it may specify and to submit to the authority such evidence as may be specified in relation to complying with any requirement.[127]

2–98   Each planning application must state the name, address, and telephone number of the applicant and of the person who is acting on behalf of the applicant, and must indicate the address to which any correspondence relating to the application should be sent. The application should clearly state whether the application is for a permission, an outline permission or an approval, and give particulars of the land or structure which is the subject matter of the application, including the location or address.[128]

2–99   The application must also give particulars of the interest in the land or structure which is held by the applicant and if the applicant is not the owner, the application must state the name and address of the owner. The application must be accompanied by at least two copies of the page of the newspaper which contains the notice and two copies of the text of the site notice which

---

[127] Art. 17(3).
[128] Art. 18(1).

was erected. Four copies of the location map, which is to be of a scale of not less than 1:10,560 and which is marked or coloured so as to identify clearly the land or structure must also be enclosed with the application. The application must also state the area of the land, the number of dwellings, if any, and where applicable the gross floor space of the building or buildings.[129] If the development consists of an industrial activity or contains an isolated storage area which come within the terms of Regulations 12 to 18 of the European Communities (Major Accident Hazards of Certain Industrial Activities) (Amendment) Regulations of 1989[130] or of the 1992 Regulations,[131] or comprises of an activity which requires a licence under the Environmental Protection Act of 1992, then this should be stated in the application.

2–100 The planning application must include four copies of any plans, including a site or layout plan and drawings of floor plans, elevations and sections, and other particulars as are necessary to describe the works or structure.[132] In the case of a planning permission relating to or partly relating to a material change in an existing use or the continuance of a use, the application shall also be accompanied by a statement of the existing and of the proposed use, together with particulars of the nature and extent of any proposed use.

2–101 An outline planning application may be accompanied only by plans and particulars which are only required to enable the planning authority to make a decision in relation to the siting, layout or other proposals for development.[133] An outline planning application cannot be made in respect of the retention on land of any structure or the continuance of any use of any structure or other land, or for development which is of a class specified under Article 24 of the Environmental Impact Assessment Regulations, or development which is of the type of class under Article 24, but for that fact that it does not exceed the quantity, area or other limits proscribed and which is an activity to which a licence is required under the Environmental Protection Agency act of 1992.

2–102 An outline planning permission does not operate so as to authorise the carrying out of any development until an approval has been granted, or until approval has been granted for a specified part of the application and a further approval has been granted, where required, where the terms of an ap-

---

[129] For the meaning of "gross floor space" see Art. 18(2).
[130] S.I. No. 194 of 1989, see also S.I. No. 292 of 1986.
[131] S.I. No. 21 of 1992.
[132] Art. 19. Art. 19(a) does not apply to an application relating to overhead or distribution lines for electricity, art. 19 A deals separately with these applications.
[133] Art. 20.

proval granted consequent on an application under Article 22(1) of the Regulations , or the terms of the outline planning permission.[134]

2–103 Article 22(1) specifies that an application for an approval following an outline planning permission is to be accompanied by whatever further plans and particulars are required under Article 19 dealing with an application for permission, i.e. full planning permission. An application for an approval may be related to a specific part of the development which has the benefit of an outline planning permission, and further separate applications may be made in respect of the development which first received outline planning permission. An application for an approval is to be accompanied by whatever plans and particulars as are necessary to enable the planning authority to make a decision in relation to the application.

2–104 Article 23 specifies the requirements for plans, drawings, and maps which have to accompany a planning application. The site or layout plans are to be drawn to a scale of not less than 1:500, and the site boundary is to be clearly delineated in colour. Buildings, roads, boundaries, septic tanks and percolation areas, bored wells, and other features within the vicinity of the land or structure are also to be shown on the map. Other plans, elevations of any proposed structure are to show the main features of the buildings which are contiguous to the proposed structure, and plans relating to works involving reconstruction, alteration or extension of an existing structure are to be marked or coloured so as to distinguish between the existing structure and the works which are proposed. Plans and drawings of floor plans, elevations and sections are to include an indication of the principal dimensions, including the overall height of the proposed structure and the distances between the structure and the boundaries of the site. All maps must indicate its northerly point, and any map which is based on the Ordnance survey must indicate the O.S. sheet number. All plans and drawings must indicate the name and address of the person by whom they were prepared. A planning authority may require an applicant to provide an additional two copies of any maps or drawings.[135]

2–105 Articles 24 and 25 deal with planning applications which are to be accompanied by environmental impact statements, and changed the 1990 regulations by providing that all applications for development which is subject to the requirement of obtaining an integrated licence from the Environmental Protection Agency must be accompanied by an impact statement, even though the development may not reach the thresholds provided for the E.C. (Environ-

---

[134] On approvals see *Irish Asphalt Ltd. v. An Bord Pleanála*, unreported, High Court, July 28, 1995.
[135] Art. 23(2).

mental Impact Assessment) Regulations of 1989.[136] Article 25 deals with, in particular, the procedure where a planning application is not accompanied by an environmental impact statement, and allows the planning authority to consider parts of the application while awaiting the receipt of a validly completed environmental impact statement.

2–106 Article 26 gives a planning authority a discretion in certain circumstances to require the submission of an environmental impact statement where the authority considers that the development is likely to have a significant effect on the environment. Article 27 allows an applicant to lodge an environmental impact statement even though there was no requirement so to do. The planning authority then treats the application as if the submission of such a statement was required. Article 28 of the regulation specifies the content of an environmental impact statement as requiring the statement to comply with the provisions of Article 25 of the Regulations, or of any amendment to those provisions. Where the EIS does not comply with the provisions of the 1989 Regulation the planning authority are obliged to inform the applicant in writing, and require that further information or particulars are provided to the authority.[137]

7. Planning procedures

2–107 Following receipt of any application the planning authority stamps the documents lodged with the date of their receipt and then considers whether the application meets with the relevant requirements of the Regulation, in particular with the requirements under Articles 18 and 23. Following this examination the planning authority forwards an acknowledgement to the applicant stating the date of receipt of the application.[138] The term receipt may refer to receiving the final part of an application if the application was lodged in stages,[139] alternatively where the planning authority consider that the application does not comply with the provisions of the Regulation, the authority may by notice in writing inform the applicant that the application is invalid and cannot be considered by the planning authority or may require the applicant to furnish further particulars, plans, drawings or maps as may be necessary.[140] If the application is invalid all of the documents submitted are returned to the applicant.

2–108 Every notification which is given by the planning authority in rela-

---

[136] S.I. No. 349 of 1989.
[137] See Art. 25(2) and Art. 3 of the 1994 Regulations.
[138] Art. 29(1).
[139] See *Grenport Ltd. v. Dublin Corporation.*
[140] Art. 29(2)(b).

tion to an application or of a decision shall specify the reference number of the application in the planning register, the development or retention or continuance of use to which the decision relates to, the nature of the decision made by the authority, the date of the decision, and any conditions which may be attached to the permission or approval.[141] A planning authority is also obliged to give their reasons for refusing an application, and are also obliged to specify the purposes for which a structure may or may not be used, whether or not any further approval is required in the case of the carrying out of works, the period of expiration required before a permission or approval will issue, and that an appeal against the decision of the planning authority may be made to An Bord Pleanála by any person within a period of one month from the date of the making of a decision.

2–109 Article 30 of the Regulations provide that a planning authority make available a list of planning applications which are received by the planning authority, and this list should be drawn up not later than the third working day of the following week. This list is to display the name and address of the applicant, the nature of the application, the location of the land or structure, the nature and extent of the development and the date of receipt of the application. The list is also to indicate planning applications which have been submitted with an EIS or which relate to a development which requires a licence under the Environmental Protection Agency Act of 1992. The list is also to refer to whether an EIS has been received under the requirements of articles 25 or 26, or if further particulars, maps, drawings and plans have been received following a request by the authority or whether revised plans or drawings have been received following an invitation under article 25.

2–110 The list is to be displayed for a period of not less than two months beginning on the day it was made and is to be displayed in or at the offices of the planning authority so as to be convenient for public inspection during office hours, and is also to be displayed for public inspection in each public library or mobile public library which is situated or operating within the functional area of the planning authority, and may also be displayed at any other place which the planning authority considers appropriate. Copies of the list may be purchased or forwarded at a reasonable cost to any person who requests it.[142] A similar requirement exists for the determination of planning applications under Article 42 of the Regulation which provides that a weekly list is to be provided detailing the determinations on planning applications which were made by the planning authority.

2–111 Planning authorities are required to notify the Minister of any plan-

---

[141] Art. 41.
[142] Art. 30(5).

ning application which has been accompanied by an EIS or which requires the submission of an EIS. The planning authority must also inform the Minister of any planning applications which relates to development likely to have significant effects on the environment of another Member State of the E.U.[143] The notification to the Minister must include the usual details, name, address of the applicant, nature and extent of the development and so on, and must include whether the application relates to development which comprises or is for the purposes of an activity which requires a licence under the Environmental Protection Agency Act of 1992. The planning authority is obliged to furnish a copy of any environmental impact statement which it has received in respect of a planning application which requires such a licence, and the Minister, in any case, may require a planning authority to forward an EIS and further details and particulars if the Minister is of the opinion that the proposed development is likely to have a significant impact on the environment of another Member State.[144] The Minister also has the power to extend the period for the determination of a planning application in these circumstances.[145] Where the Minister extends the period the planning authority are obliged to publish notice of the extension in a newspaper circulating in the district in which the relevant structure is situated.

2–112 If it appears to the planning authority that a planning application relates to an area which has been declared to be a special amenity area under section 42 of the Local Government (Planning and Development) Act of 1963, or that the development or retention of an existing structure, would obstruct any view or prospect of a special amenity value or special interest it is obliged to inform the An Chomhairle Ealaíon, Bord Fáilte Éireann and An Taisce. If the application appears to the planning authority to involve a development which would obstruct or detract from the value of any tourist amenity or tourist amenity works the planning authority must inform Bord Fáilte Éireann. If the planning authority believe that the proposed development would be unduly close to any cave, site, feature or other object of archaeological, geological, scientific or historical interest, or would detract from the appearance of any building of artistic, architectural or historical interest or which would obstruct any scheme for improvement of the entrance or surroundings of such a place the authority are obliged to inform An Chomhairle Ealaíon, Bord Fáilte Éireann (or the Shannon Free Airport Development Company Ltd.), the Commissioners of Public Works in Ireland, the National Monuments Advisory Council and An Taisce.

2–113 Where it appears to the authority that a proposed development would

---

[143] Art. 31(1)(a).
[144] Art. 31(3).
[145] See art. 45.

obstruct or detract from the value of any existing or any proposed development by a local authority, the planning authority is obliged to so inform the local authority. Where an application indicates that the development might give rise to discharges of polluting matters to waters or is likely to cause serious water pollution or the danger of water pollution the planning authority is obliged to inform the relevant Regional Fisheries Board. If the development consists of an industrial activity or of an isolated storage area to which the E.C. (Major Accident Hazards of Certain Industrial Activities) (Amendment) Regulations, 1986,[146] the authority must inform the National Authority for Occupational Safety and Health.

2–114   If the proposed development has consequences for the safety of aircraft or the safe and efficient navigation of aircraft the planning authority must inform the Irish Aviation Authority. Where the development consists of or involves the formation, laying out of a widening of an access to a national road, which is not a national road within a built up area, or where it appears to the planning authority that the development might give rise to a significant increase in the volume of traffic using a national road, the planning authority must inform the National Roads Authority.[147] If the development comprises of or relates to an activity to which a licence under the Environmental Protection Agency Act of 1992 is required the planning authority must inform the Environmental Protection Agency of that fact. A failure on the part of the planning authority to send any of the above notices may invalidate any resulting planning permission.[148]

2–115   If an application includes an environmental impact statement the planning authority are obliged to forward a copy of the statement to the relevant body. Additionally, a copy of a statement should also be forwarded to the Minister for the Marine where the planning application relates to the breeding of salmonid fish, to the Minister for Agriculture, Food and Forestry where the application relates to the replacement of broadleaf high forest by conifer species, or which relates to initial afforestation of land. If an application appears to include a significant risk or effects on public health the planning authority are obliged to forward a copy of the impact statement to the Minister for Health. If the application has or might have significant effects in relation to nature conservation the planning authority are required to forward a copy of the impact statement to the Commissioners of Public Works in Ireland, while if the application relates to the extraction of minerals, within the meaning of the

---

[146] S.I. No. 292 of 1986, as amended by S.I. No. 194 of 1989, and S.I. No. 21 of 1992.
[147] Within the meaning of s.2 of the Roads Act 1993 (No. 14 of 1993). Built up areas are defined in s.45 of the Road Traffic Act 1961.
[148] See *Nolan v. Dublin Corporation.*

Minerals Development Acts, 1940 to 1979, then a copy should be sent to the relevant government minister.

(b) Further information

2–116 Where a planning authority believe that further information is required from the applicant, the authority may require the applicant to submit further information, including plans, maps and drawings or any information as to the estate or interest in or right over land, which the authority believes is required in order to enable them to deal with the application.[149] The planning authority may also require an applicant to produce any evidence which the planning authority might reasonably require in order to verify any of the particulars contained in the planning application. The request for further information must be genuine.[150]

2–117 A planning authority is not entitled to require an applicant, who has complied with a notice to submit further information or particulars or evidence, to submit further information, particulars or evidence except in order to clarify matters dealt with in the applicant's response to the previous notice or requirement. In addition, the two month period during which the planning authority have to make a decision on an application for planning permission is extended or recommences on the date of compliance with a requirement under Article 33(1). Where the applicant refuses to comply with a request for additional information, the planning authority may proceed and determine the application even in the absence of the information or evidence, although the likelihood is that the application will be refused.

2–118 Article 35 gives the planning authority an avenue whereby revised plans or drawings may be submitted where the planning authority intends to allow development to take place having first made modifications in the original application. A request for revised plans or drawings under this article does not extend the two month period under section 26, and the power is a discretionary one, the planning authority is not obliged to exercised the power even though they may consider that a modified development is acceptable.[151] Article 35 is generally used by planning authorities where a proposal is acceptable subject to modifications, but the request will not have the effect of extending the appropriate period so that an extension of time should be sought, furthermore the power to request modifications on a planning application is discretionary.[152]

---

[149] Art. 33(1).

[150] *State (Conlon Construction Ltd.) v. Cork Co. Co.*, unreported, High Court, July 31, 1975 and *O'Connor's Downtown Properties Ltd. v. Nenagh UDC*, unreported, High Court, September 22, 1992.

[151] See *State (Abenglen Properties Ltd) v. Dublin Corporation.*

[152] *ibid.*

2–119   Where the planning authority receive information from the applicant which contains significant additional information in relation to the potential effects on the environment, the planning authority must forward a copy of this information to any of the relevant bodies to which notices of the planning application was given under Article 32. Article 38 specifies the type of form which must be used by the planning authority where the planning authority intends to consider an application which would contravene materially the development plan or any special amenity order.[153]

(c) Third party involvement

2–120   Article 34 allows any person or body to make submissions or observations in writing to the planning authority in relation to a planning application. However, a person or a body is not entitled to make submissions or observations in relation to an activity to which a licence under the Environmental Protection Agency Act of 1992 is required as they may relate to the risk of environmental pollution from that activity.

2–121   Article 36 provides that all documents which are received or obtained by a planning authority in relation to a planning application are to be made available for inspection by members of the public during office hours until the application is withdrawn or a decision is made. Any submission or observations made in writing which are received by the planning authority are to be made available for inspection, during office hours, by members of the public, until the application is withdrawn or after a period of one month beginning on the day of the giving of the decision of the authority or after the determination of an appeal if one is made.

2–122   Copies of an environmental impact statement which are submitted with a planning application, and extracts of a statement are to be made available during office hours for inspection by members of the public and copies or extracts may be purchased for a price not exceeding the reasonable cost of making the copy.[154]

(d) Minimum period for determining an application

2–123   Article 39 prevents a planning authority from deciding on granting or refusing an application for planning permission or an approval until after the expiration of twenty eight days beginning on the day on which the requirement to submit an environmental impact statement, under articles 24(1), 25(1)

---

[153] Form No. 1, Third Schedule.
[154] Art. 37.
[155] See *Ardoyne House Management Co. Ltd. v. Dublin Corp.*, unreported, High Court, February 6, 1998.

or 26(1) has been complied with or twenty eight days following the requirement of an application to give further notice of the application under article
17. In any other case the time period is fourteen days following compliance
with a requirement under article 17 to give further notice of the application,
and where the applicant has not been required to give further notice, the expiration of fourteen days beginning on the day of receipt by the planning authority of the application.[155]

2–124 A planning application can be withdrawn at any time, by the service
of a notice in writing, at any time to the planning authority before the authority
makes a decision.[156]

Planning authorities are obliged to make available a list, similar to the list
giving details of planning applications under Article 30, and this list must be
displayed in or at the offices of the planning authority for a period of not less
than two months beginning on the day on which it was made available. The
list is also to be displayed in the public libraries within the functional area of
the planning authority.

2–125 Where a planning authority has given notice of a planning application under article 32 to various bodies or to the Minister, the planning authority is under an obligation to send notice of the making of a decision in relation
to that application within three working days of the giving of the decision.
Where any person or body has made submission or observations on the application, the planning authorities are obliged to send notice of the decision to
those persons or bodies, unless a notice of the decision is published in a newspaper within a list of recent decisions published under article 41. Where a
planning authority does not publish a list in a newspaper the authority is obliged
to, within seven days of giving their decision on an application which related
to the submission of an environmental impact statement, publish a notice of
their decision in a newspaper circulating in the district in which the land or
structure is situate. Publication of a notice of the making of a decision can
only be used where the list is published in accordance with the provisions of
Article 42(3), otherwise the decision will be invalid.[157]

8. Extension of planning permission

2–126 Section 4 of the Local Government (Planning and Development) Act
of 1982 provides that an application may be made to a planning authority to
extend the appropriate period of the planning permission. Section 2 of the Act
outlines the appropriate period into four categories, (i) planning permissions

---

[156] Art. 40.
[157] See *Nolan v. Dublin Corporation*, Barron, J. 19/5/1989.

in relation to any permission which was granted before November 1, 1976, (ii) permissions granted before October 31, 1983, (iii) before October 31, 1987, and in any other case, the period of five years beginning on the date of the grant.

2–127 The planning authority shall extend the appropriate period in order to enable the development to which the permission relates, to be completed, if, and only if, the application is in accordance with such regulations as may apply to it, any requirements of, or made under, such regulations are complied with as regards the application, and the authority are satisfied in relation to the permission that the development to which such permission relates commenced before the expiration of the appropriate period sought to be extended, and substantial works were carried out pursuant to such permission during such period. The development must be completed within a reasonable time. The section does not provide that the appropriate period cannot be extended because the period of the planning permission has expired.[158]

2–128 Where the planning authority has already extended the period of a planning permission the planning authority are not allowed to further extend the appropriate period, unless an application in that behalf is made to them in accordance with such regulations under this Act as apply to it, any requirements of, or made under, such regulations are complied with as regards the application, and the authority are satisfied that the relevant development has not been completed due to circumstances beyond the control of the person carrying out the development. An appropriate period can only be extended by the authority if the relevant planning authority consider requisite to enable the relevant development to be completed. Where a decision to extend, or to further extend, has been given the decision is construed and is to have effect subject to and in accordance with the terms of the original decision, *i.e.* the original conditions and plans could still apply.[159]

2–129 An application which is made under section 4 of the 1982 Act to extend or further extend the period of duration of planning permission not earlier than one year before the expiration of the appropriate period which is sought to be extended or further extended.[160]

2–130 An application to extend the appropriate period is to be made in writing and shall contain the name and address and telephone number of the person acting on behalf of the applicant or of the applicant and the address to

---

[158] s.(6).
[159] s.(5).
[160] Art.80, 1994 Regulations.

which any correspondence should be sent.[161] The application should also give the location of the land or the address of the structure, the development to which the application relates, the particulars of the interest held in the structure or land, the date of the permission and the relevant reference number, the date of any approval or subsequent approvals, the date on which the permission will cease or cease to have effect, the date of the commencement of the development, the particulars of the substantial works[162] which were carried out or which will be carried out before the expiration of the appropriate period, the additional period which is sought and the date on which the development is expected to be completed. It should be noted that works which are carried out in breach of the planning permission granted will not satisfy the requirements of section 4 relating to the requirement of having substantial works completed.[163] The term "substantial works" was examined in *Garden Village Construction Co. Ltd. v. Wicklow Co. Co.*[164] where the Supreme Court held that the term works must be referable to the permission sought to be extended, but that works which are necessary to facilitate the permission to be extended but not carried out under that permission could not amount to substantial works.

2–131 Following receipt of an application for an extension or further extension of the appropriate period of a planning permission, a planning authority shall, after stamping the application, consider whether the application complies with the requirements of article 81 or 82. Where a planning authority considers that an application complies with the relevant article the planning authority shall send to the applicant an acknowledgement stating the date of receipt of the application. If the application does not comply with the requirements of the relevant article the authority must notify the applicant in writing and give the applicant details of the particulars which are necessary in order to comply with the requirements.[165]

2–132 A planning authority may require further information in order to consider the application, including information regarding any estate or interest in or right over the land, or to produce any evidence which the authority may reasonably require in order to verify any particulars or information given in

---

[161] There is no provision for appeal against a decision not to extend the lifetime of a planning permission, but the decision may be subject to judicial review, see *Littondale Ltd. v. Wicklow Co. Co.* [1996] 2 I.L.R.M. 519.

[162] See *Frenchurch Properties Ltd. v. Wexford Co. Co.* [1991] I.L.R.M. 769.

[163] See s.2 of the 1982 Act for requirements of applying for a further period of extension.

[164] Unreported, Supreme Court, July 1994, see also *State (McCoy) v. Dun Laoghaire*, unreported, High Court, June 1, 1984.

[165] Art. 83.

the application, and the authority may request such information by forwarding a notice in writing to the applicant. Once an applicant has responded to a request for further information or particulars by the planning authority, the planning authority may not request any further information except by way of clarification of information already supplied. If the applicant fails or refuses to comply with any requirement within one month the planning authority may refuse the application.[166]

2–133 Every notification which is given by a planning authority in relation to an application to extend or further extend the appropriate period shall specify the date of the permission and reference number in the register, the location of the land or the address of the structure, the development to which the decision relates, the date of the decision and the nature of the decision, and if applicable the additional period by which the period has been extended, if an additional period, and if an application has been refused, the reasons for the refusal.[167] There is no provision for an appeal against a decision to refuse to extend the appropriate period of a planning permission.[168]

(b) Fees

2–134 Article 89 of the Regulation provides that where an application relates in whole or in part to a development which, in the opinion of the planning authority, relates to development which is proposed to be carried out by or on behalf of a voluntary organisation and which is designed or intended to be used for social, recreational, educational or religious purposes by inhabitants of the locality generally or for the benefit of a particular group or religious denomination and is not to be used mainly for profit or gain, or is designed or intended to be used as a hostel, workshop or other accommodation for persons with a disability and is also not used for profit or gain, or is a development which is ancillary to any of these developments, a fee shall not be payable. If an application relates to a development which is to be carried out by an approved housing body[169] and which relates to the provision of accommodation for poor or homeless persons or person who would be likely to require housing accommodation provided by a housing authority and is not a development which is mainly for profit or gain, a fee shall also not be payable.

2–135 Articles 90 to 100 inclusive relate to the calculation of the relevant fees which are to be paid for planning applications and which also relate to the Fourth Schedule which details the relevant fees which are to be paid. Refunds

---

[166] Art. 84(3).
[167] Art. 85.
[168] See O'Sullivan, para. **S1 418**.
[169] Within the meaning of s.6 of the Housing (Miscellaneous Provisions) Act 1992.

of fees are provided for in Article 94 and which allows for a refund of the fees if the application is withdrawn or if the application is determined by the planning authority or by the Board and a subsequent planning application is made by or on behalf of the same applicant, the authority shall refund three quarters of the fee paid in respect of the subsequent application but only if the authority is satisfied that the subsequent application relates to development of the same character or description as the previous development, a fee in respect of the class or classes of development to which the subsequent application relates has been paid for the earlier application and the period between the withdrawal of the first application and the making of the subsequent application does not exceed twelve months and the planning authority are satisfied that the subsequent application relates to land substantially consisting of the site or part of the site to which the earlier application related and a previous refund had not been made at any time to the same applicant, and that the application does not relate to a refund under article 93.

2–136 Article 96 gives the planning authority an absolute discretion to refund a part of the fee payable in respect of a planning application where the authority is satisfied that the payment of the full fee would not be just and reasonable having regard to the limited extent of the development, the limited cost of the development and the fee payable in respect of an application for any other development of a similar character, extent or description.

9. Local Government (Planning and Development) Act 1999[170]

2–137 The Local Government (Planning and Development) Act of 1999 was enacted in order to make better provision for the protection of the architectural heritage. In order to protect structures which are, or which are part of structures which are of special architectural, historical, archaeological, artistic, cultural, scientific, social or technical interest every development plan is to include a separate record of those structures which are in the opinion of the local authority of such interest within their functional area.[171]

2–138 In making an addition to or a deletion from the record contained in the development plan the planning authority is obliged to serve on each person who is the owner or occupier of the structure which is proposed to be protected, publish a notice in *Iris Oifigiúil* and in at least one newspaper circulating in the area as well as to forward details of the proposal to the Minister for Arts, Heritage, Gaeltacht and the Islands. The notice is to state the particulars of the proposed addition or deletion and may be inspected at a particular

---

[170] No. 17 of 1999.
[171] s.2.

place during a period of not less than one month. The notice is also to state that within fourteen days from the end of the period of inspection that any person may make written objections or representations, that any person who makes an objection or representation may include a request for an opportunity to state their case before persons appointed by the planning authority, and whether or not the proposed addition or deletion was recommended by the Minister.[172]

2–139 Before making the proposed addition or deletion from the record the planning authority are obliged to consider any written objections or representations which have been received, as well as hear any representations which are made as well as to have regard to any observations received from the Minister, within one month after the receipt by the minister of the objections or representations. Following three months after the period allowed for inspection of the proposal the planning authority shall decide on whether to include the structure in the record contained in the development plan. Within fourteen days following the making of a decision the planning authority shall serve on the owner and on the occupier of the structure concerned a notice of the addition or deletion.

2–140 Where a structure or part of a structure is included in the record its inclusion may be registered under the Registration of Title Act of 1964 as a burden affecting registered land, within the meaning of that Act.

2–141 The 1999 Act amends the provisions of the 1963 Act, in particular section 4 by providing that the carrying out of works to a protected structure or even to a proposed protected structure can only be regarded as exempted development if the works which are to be carried out would not materially affect the character of the structure or any element of the structure which contributes to its special, architectural, historical, archaeological, artistic, cultural, scientific, social or technical interest.[173]

2–142 To help the owner or occupier of the protected structure section 8(2) provides that a declaration can be sought from the planning authority as to whether or not the type of works which are to be carried out would or would not materially affect the character of the structure or any element of that structure and the planning authority has three months in which to issue the declaration to the person who has requested it in writing before issuing the declaration. Before issuing any declaration a planning authority is obliged to have regard

---

[172] See also s.38 for transitional provisions relating to development plans in existence immediately before the commencement of that section.
[173] s. 8(1).

to any guidelines issued by the Minister under section 3 of the Act and any recommendations made to the planning authority under section 4.

2–143 If a declaration relates to a protected structure which is regularly used as a place of public worship the planning authority are obliged to respect any liturgical requirements of the relevant religion and shall also comply with any guidelines issued by the Minister or if there are no such guidelines the planning authority are obliged to consult any person or body as the planning authority considers appropriate. A planning authority may at any time review a declaration which is issued, however the review cannot affect any works carried out which had been previously covered by a declaration issued by the planning authority.[174]

2–144 Details of any declaration issued by the planning authority are entered into the register and a copy of the declaration is to be made available for inspection by members of the public during office hours at the office of the planning authority.

2–145 When an application is made for planning permission or approval for development relating to the interior of a protected structure and that structure is regularly used as a place of public worship the planning authority, or the Board, as well as regarding another requirements of the planning acts, are to have liturgical requirements.[175]

2–146 In considering any application for permission or approval under the Principal Act the planning authority are obliged to have regard to the protected status of the structure and a planning authority or the Board shall not grant permission for the demolition of a protected structure except in exceptional circumstances.

2–147 The Act imposes upon each owner and occupier of protected structures the duty to ensure that the structure or any part or element of it which contributes to its special architectural, historical, archaeological, artistic, cultural, scientific, social or technical interest is not endangered.[176] This duty becomes operative when the owner or occupier is notified under section 6 of the proposal to add the structure to the record of protected structures. Any person who causes damage to a protected structure or a proposed structure may be guilty of an offence, however it is a good defence in any proceedings to prove that the damage to the structure resulted from works which were

---

[174] s.8(7).
[175] s.8(6).
[176] s.9(1).

urgently required in order to secure the preservation of the structure or any part of it, were undertaken in good faith solely for the purpose of temporarily safeguarding the structure and the works were unlikely to permanently alter the structure or any part of it.[177]

B. POWER TO REQUIRE WORKS

2–148	A planning authority, if it believes that it is necessary for works to be carried out in order to prevent a protected structure from becoming or continuing to be endangered, may serve a notice requiring works to be carried out.[178] The planning authority serves on each person who is the owner or occupier of the protected structure a notice specifying the works which the authority considers necessary in order to prevent the protected structure from becoming endangered and requiring works to be carried out within a specified period of not less than two months from the date of the notice which comes into effect under section 13 of the Act.

2–149	A person who has been served with a notice may within one month from the date of service of the notice make written representations to the planning authority regarding the terms of the notice, the provision of an assistance which may be sought or required from the planning authority as well as any other material considerations. Following these representations the planning authority may confirm, amend, or revoke the notice and shall duly notify the person concerned.[179]

2–150	Following the service of a notice a planning authority may, at the authority's discretion, assist the person in carrying out the works required under the notice and may also provide assistance in any form which the authority considers appropriate including advice, financial aid, materials, equipment as well as the services of the planning authority's staff.

2–151	Section 11 allows a planning authority to serve a notice on the owner or occupier of a structure within the functional area of the authority if the structure is a protected structure the character of which ought to be restored. The planning authority may also serve a notice in respect of a structure which forms part of a place, an area, a group architectural, historical, archaeological, artistic, cultural, scientific, social or technical interest and in the opinion of the planning authority it is desirable to restore the character of that place, area,

---

[177] s.9(5).
[178] s.10(1).
[179] s.10(3).

group of structures or townscape. The notice specifies the works required to be carried out for the purposes of restoring the structure or element referred within the notice, the notice also states that the person on whom the notice is served may, within a period of not less than two months from the service of the notice, make representations to the planning authority. The notice must also invite the person on whom the notice is served to enter into discussions with the planning authority, again within two months. In particular discussions may be entered into regarding the provision by the planning authority of advice, materials, equipment, the services of the planning authority's staff or other assistance in carrying out the works which are specified in the notice, and the period in which the works are to be carried out.[180] Unless an agreement has been arrived following discussions, the notice must specify the period within which the works are to be carried out, and which must in any event be carried out within two months from the end of the period allowed for entering into discussions. The notice must also state that, to the extent that the works relate to an authorised structure or a structure which has been constructed erect or made five years or more prior to the notice being served, the planning authority shall pay any expenses that are reasonably incurred in the carrying out of the works in accordance with the notice.[181] Within section 11 the terms "works" includes the removal, alteration or replacement of any specified part of the structure or any element of it as well as the removal or alteration of any advertisement structure.[182] Works which are carried out under section 10(1) or under section 11(2) are classed as exempted development under section 19, and consequently do not require planning permission under the Principal Act.

2–152 Before deciding to whether or not to serve a notice under section 11 the planning authority are to have regard to any guidelines which are issued under section 3 of the Act and to any recommendations which are made under section 4.[183] After considering any representations which are made or any discussions which are held, the planning authority may confirm, amend or revoke the notice which was issued under section 11 and shall notify the person of the decision of the authority. Particulars of the notice which are severed are entered into the planning register which is kept under the 1963 Act.

2–153 Appeals may be made against notices concerning the endangerment or restoration of structures within fourteen days after notification of the confirmation or amendment of a notice. An appeal may be made to the District Court based on either that the person is not the owner or occupier of the structure in respect of which the notice has been served, or that compliance with

---

[180] s.11(3).
[181] s.11(3)(e).
[182] s.11.
[183] s.11(4).

the requirements of the notice would involve unreasonable expense and that the person had stated in representations made to the planning authority, under section 10(3), that the person did not have the means to pay. An appeal can also be based on the ground that the person on whom the notice has been served has already taken all reasonable steps to prevent the structure from becoming or continuing to be endangered, or that reasonable steps have been taken in relation to the restoration of the character of the structure or an element of the structure. An appeal may also be grounded in respect of a notice under section 11 that reasonable steps have been taken in relation to a structure that forms part of a place, area, group of structures or townscape to assist in restoring the character of that place, area, group of structures or townscape.[184]

2–154   A person who has been served with a notice under section 10(1) and who has already carried out the works which were required under the notice may apply to the court, of whichever appropriate jurisdiction, for an order directing that all or part of the costs of those works be paid by another person who has an interest in the protected structure.[185]

2–155   Section 13 states that a notice which is served shall not have effect until the expiry of one month from the date of the service of the notice except where representations are made and no appeal is taken within the period allowed under section 12(1) in which case the notice has effect on the expiry of the appeal period. In the case of an appeal which is taken under section 12(1) a notice comes in affect on the date on which the District Court makes a decision or the date on which the order is to have effect whichever is the later. If an application is made to the District Court for an order authorising the carrying out of works and if a person who is served with a notice is unable without the consent of another person to carry out the required works and that other person withholds consent to the carrying out of the works, then the notice takes effect on the date of the District Court decision or on the date on which the order is to take effect whichever is the later.

2–156   Any person who fails to comply with a notice which is served under section 10(1) may be guilty of an offence.[186] A person who is guilty of an offence under section 9(40) or under section 14 shall be liable on summary conviction to a fine not exceeding £1,500, and in the case of a continuing offence a fine not exceeding £150 for every day on which the offence is continued, or to a term of imprisonment of not over twelve months or to both a fine and imprisonment. In the case of a conviction on indictment a person is

---

[184] s.12(1).
[185] s.18(1).
[186] s.14.

liable to a fine of not over £1,000,000, and in the case of a continuing offence to a fine of not over £10,000 for every day on which the offence is committed, or to a term of imprisonment of not over five years or at the discretion of the court to both a fine and imprisonment.[187]

2–157 Where an offence is committed by a body corporate under section 9(4) or section 14 and is proved to have been committed with the consent of connivance of or are found to be attributable to any neglect on the part of any person, who is a director, manager, secretary or other officer of the body corporate or a person who was purporting to act in any similar capacity, then that person as well as the body corporate may be found guilty of an offence and may be liable to receive similar punishment as the body corporate.[188]

2–158 A planning authority is empowered to carry out works which are required under a notice which has been served under section 10(1) and section 11(2) and which were not carried out by the person on whom the notice has been served.[189] The planning authority may take such steps as the authority considers reasonable and necessary in order to give effect to the terms of the notice including entering onto land, and carrying out or arranging for the works to be carried out. The planning authority may then attempt to recover the expenses which have been reasonably incurred from the owner of the structure by recovering that amount as a simple contract debt in the relevant court. The planning authority may also secure the expenses incurred by charging the structure with a registered charge under the Registration of Title Act 1964. The planning authority may also secure the expenses incurred by vesting the ownership of the structure in the planning authority with the right of redemption by the owner, a type of judgement mortgage.[190]

2–159 Section 22 of the Act allows the planning authority to acquire by agreement or compulsory any structure protected under the Act within their functional area provided it appears to the planning authority that it is necessary or desirable to do so for the protection of the protected structure. In the case of compulsory acquisition the structure must not be lawfully occupied as a dwelling house by any person other than a person who is a person employed as a caretaker.[191]

2–160 A planning authority who intends to acquire any protected structure compulsorily shall first publish in one or more newspapers circulating in its

---

[187] s.40.
[188] s.40(2).
[189] s.20.
[190] s.21(b).
[191] s.22(1).

functional area a notice stating its intention to acquire the protected compulsorily, and describing the structure to which the notice relates, naming the place where a map showing the location of the protected structure is deposited and the times which it may be inspected as well as specifying the time within which, being not less than one month, and the manner in which the objections to the compulsorily acquisition may be made to the planning authority. The planning authority is also obliged to serve on every owner, lessee and occupier of the structure to which the notice relates, except in the case of tenants for one month or a period of less than one month. The term owner relates to a person, other than a mortgagee who is not in possession, who is for the time being entitled to dispose of the fee simple of the structure and a person who, under a lease or agreement which has an unexpired term of exceeding five years, holds or is entitled to the rents or profits of the structure.[192] A reference to a protected structure includes a reference to any land which forms part of the attendant ground of the structure and which is in the planing authority's opinion necessary to secure the protection of that structure whether or not the land lies within the curtilage of the structure or which is specified as a feature in the record of the structure.[193]

2–161 Any person who is served with a proposed compulsorily purchase notice may within the time specified within the notice submit to the planning authority an objection to the proposed acquisition which may be withdrawn at any stage by sending a notice in writing to the planning authority.[194] Where an objection has been submitted to the planning authority the authority may not acquire the structure without the consent of the Minister, and an application for the consent of the Minister is to be made within one month following the expiry of the time which was allowed for the submission of the objection. The application for the consent of the Minister is to be accompanied by a map of the structure, a copy of the objection which was made to the planning authority, the planning authority's comments regarding the objection, and whatever other documents as may be required. Following receipt of the planning authority's comments regarding the objection, the Minister is to send a notice on the person who has made the objection a copy of the authority's comments. Within twenty one days from the date of the service of this notice the person who has made the objection must make observations on those comments to the Minister.

2–162 The planning authority may acquire the structure by vesting order if no objection has been submitted to the authority or if the objection or objections have been withdrawn, the Minister consents to the acquisition of the

[192] s.23(2).
[193] s.22(2).
[194] s.24(1).

structure.[195] Within fourteen days after the making of a vesting order the planning authority must publish in one or more newspapers circulating within its functional area a notice stating that the order has been made, describing the protected structure which it relates and naming the place which a copy of the order and the map may be seen at reasonable times. The planning authority must also serve on every person who appears to the authority to have an interest in the protected structure stating that the order has been made and the effect of the order.[196]

2–163 The effect of the order is to vest in the planning authority the fee simple of the property free from any encumbrances and vests all estates, rights, titles and interest of whatsoever kind on a specified date not earlier than twenty one days after the making of the order, except that any annual sums owing to the Minister for Agriculture and Food or the Commissioners of Public Works in Ireland remain due and payable by the planning authority. The planning authority then forwards the vesting order to the relevant registering authority.[197] Following acquisition of the protected structure the planning authority may use the structure in connection with its functions and may sell, let, transfer or exchange all or a part of the structure.[198]

2–164 Section 28 provides for the right of compensation with respect to the making of a vesting order. Any person who, immediately before the making of the vesting order, has any estate or interest in, or any right in respect of the structure which has been acquired may apply to the planning authority within twelve months after the making of the order for compensation. The planning authority are required to pay to the application an amount equal to the value of that estate, interest or right, and the compensation which is to be paid by the planning authority is, in default of agreement to be determined by arbitration under the Acquisition of Land (Assessment of Compensation) Act, 1919.[199] The planning authority may deduct whatever sum which is due to it by an order of court or whether remaining due after deducting expenses reasonably incurred by the planning authority from the compensation which is to be paid.[200]

2–165 The remainder of the Act makes provision for amendment to the Principal Act in relation to the status of protected structures and their inclusion in

---

[195] s.25(1), planning authority must also ensure that any annuities or revenue charges are notified to the relevant authorities.
[196] s.25(3)(b).
[197] s.27(1).
[198] s.29.
[199] s.28(3).
[200] See also s.28(5) and (6) in relation to the provisions of the Lands Clauses Consolidation Act 1845, as amended.

draft development plans and development plans, as well as amending section 26(1) of the Principal Act by inserting a paragraph dealing with the preservation of protected structures and the architectural salvaging of elements of protected structures. Section 37 of the Act also amends the Local Government (Planning and Development) Act 1990 by inserting into the Second Schedule of that act a paragraph relating to developments which would materially affect a protected structure or a proposed protected structure as well as including an extra paragraph into the Fourth Schedule in relation to conditions concerning the protection of a protected structure or a proposed protected structure.

C. ARCHITECTURAL HERITAGE (NATIONAL INVENTORY AND HISTORIC MONUMENTS) (MISCELLANEOUS PROVISIONS) ACT 1999 [201]

2–166 The Architectural Heritage (National Inventory and Historic Monuments) (Miscellaneous Provisions) Act 1999 was passed in order to provide for the establishment of a national inventory of architectural heritage and for other related matters. The Act provides for the establishment and maintenance of an inventory known as the National Inventory of Architectural Heritage and the information contained in the National Inventory is to be made available by the Minister to planning authorities, solely for the purpose of the exercise of its statutory functions relating to architectural heritage.[202] The term "architectural heritage" refers to all structures and building together with their settings and attendant grounds, fixtures and fittings as well as groups of such structures and buildings and sites which are of architectural, historical, archaeological, artistic, cultural, scientific, social or technical interest.[203] The reference to "attendant grounds" seems to be a broader phrase than the term curtilage and clearly intends to cover a larger amount of property than the mere curtilage of a building or premises.

2–167 Section 3 of the Act provides for the appointment of authorised officers who may at reasonable times enter any premises for the purposes of the establishment and maintenance of the inventor, as well as to enter any premises and to do all things which are necessary for or which are incidental to the provisions or purposes of the Act. However, an authorised officer is not permitted to enter a private dwelling or any part of a premises which constitutes a private dwelling except where the authorised officer considers it necessary to

---

[201] No. 19 of 1999.
[202] s.2.
[203] s.1.

carry out the purposes of section 3 of the Act or in accordance with a warrant issued by a judge of the District Court.[204] An authorised officer may also apply for a warrant authorising the entry of any premises where the officer is prevented from carrying out the duties or functions under section 3.

2–168　A person commits an offence under the Act if that person obstructs or interferes with an authorised officer in the exercise of the officer's functions under section 3 or if that person without reasonable excuse, fails to comply with a requirement under section 3.[205] Any person found guilty may be liable to a fine, on summary conviction, of not over £1,500, and proceedings which are brought under section 4 may be brought and prosecuted by the Minister for Arts, Heritage, Gaeltacht and the Islands.

---

[204] s.3(5).
[205] s.4(1).

CHAPTER 3

Essential services and public health

A. ROADS AND BRIDGES

1. Roads

(a) Public roads

3–01 Section 81(1) of the Local Government (Ireland) Act of 1898[1] provides that is the duty of every county and district council according to their respective powers, to keep all public roads maintainable at the cost of their county or district in good condition and repair, and to take all steps necessary for that purpose, and the term "public works" includes roads.[2] Section 24 of the Local Government Act of 1925[3] provided that the maintenance and construction of all county and main roads in a county shall be the duty of the council of that county and this provision was repealed and replaced by section 13 of the Roads Act of 1993.[4]

3–02 Section 13 of the Roads Act 1993 provides that local authorities are responsible for the maintenance and construction of all national and regional roads in the relevant administrative county. In the performance of their functions under section 13 a local authority is obliged to consider the needs of all road users. Section 13 also allows a person or group of persons may, with the consent of a road authority, carry out maintenance works on a local road pro-

---

[1] 61 & 62 Vict., c.37.
[2] See s.109 of the 1898 Act.
[3] No. 5 of 1925.
[4] No. 14 of 1993.

vided the local authority gives its consent, which consent can be subject to such conditions, restrictions and requirements as it thinks fit.[5] A road authority may provide materials, plant, equipment and the services of its staff to a person or group carrying out works. Local authorities were, and are, able to seek from the owner of lands on which excavations or other works which adjoin a public street or footway costs in relation to damage to the footway or street as a result of those works or excavations.[6]

3–03 Provided these works have been carried out with the consent of the local authority and carried out in accordance with any conditions which the local authority attached to the consent, any person who carries out repairs or maintenance works on a local road receive the benefit of an indemnity against all actions and claims howsoever arising in respect of the works and the carrying out of works. The works must have been carried out in a bona fide manner and in accordance with every condition, restriction or requirement specified, the works are deemed to have been carried out by the road authority, and the person or group who carried out the works are indemnified by the local authority.[7]

3–04 Carroll J. in the case of *Brady v. Cavan County Council*[8] held that the general rule regarding the upkeep of roads is that the local authority must maintain the road in a condition adequate to meet ordinary traffic. In that case the applicants were residents of an area in Co. Cavan who alleged that the County Council were in breach of their statutory duties in failing to maintain in good condition and repair the roads between two areas in Cavan. The applicants sought judicial review by way of *mandamus* compelling the county Council to repair and maintain the road, the County Council maintained that it did not have an absolute duty to maintain public roads, and argued that they had limited resources which prevented it from maintaining and repairing the road. The Court held however that the Local Government (Ireland) Act of 1898 and section 13 of the Roads Act of 1993 did in fact not only give the local authority a power but also imposed a duty and obligation to repair and maintain roads. There were no statutory provisions which relieved a local authority of its obligations to maintain or repair roads within its functional area, and the court granted the relief sought by the applicants.

3–05 An order of *mandamus* is the most appropriate remedy where a local authority is guilty of nonfeasance as section 81 of the Local Government (Ireland) Act 1898 provides that where an order of *mandamus* is issued by the

---

[5] s.13(6).
[6] Public Health Amendment Act 1907, s.20.
[7] s.13(6)(c).
[8] [1997] 1 I.L.R.M. 390 at 394.

High Court to a council and the council fails to comply with the order, the Court may appoint an officer and may confer upon that officer all or any of the powers of the defaulting council which appear to the court necessary for the carrying into effect the *mandamus*.

(b) Non-maintained roads

3–06 The Local Government (Roads and Drainage) Act 1968[9] provides that if certain circumstances exist a county council may make and carry out an agreement for the construction of a road or the reconstruction or improvement of an entire road or part of a road which the council is not responsible to maintain. The road, or part of the road, must be or will be used as a means of access to parcels of land which are occupied or owned by at least two persons, or the road, or part of the road will be used by at least two persons as a means of access relating to the removal of turf or seaweed or the exercise of any other *profit a prendre* or the road or part of the road is or will be used by the general public.[10]

2. Bridges

3–07 A local authority may construct a bridge, viaduct or tunnel where the local authority is of the opinion that one should be provided in order to improve the road infrastructure in its area.[11] The authority must obtain the consent of the Minister for the Environment and Local Government for a bridge order to construct or to reconstruct a bridge. Before making the bridge order the Minister may direct the local authority to prepare a preliminary report in relation to the feasibility and probable cost of the work involved.[12] The Minister may also require the holding of a local inquiry before deciding whether to make or refuse to make a bridge order.[13]

3. Reclamation works

3–08 Local authorities are able to execute works giving relief or protection from flooding, landslide, subsidence and other occurrences. The local authority may carry out works on permanent constructions within the relevant functional area where it has sustained or is likely to sustain damage from flooding, landslide, subsidence or other similar occurrence.[14] The local authority may

---

[9] No. 6 of 1968.
[10] s.2(2) gives a similar power in relation to drainage works.See also s.2(3) in relation to making of contribution towards the expenses of carrying out the works.
[11] Local Government Act 1946, s.44.
[12] *ibid.*, s.46(1).
[13] s.47(1).
[14] Local Authorities (Works) Act 1949, s.2(2).

make drains, remove substances causing obstructions in watercourses, widen or deepen watercourses, make or repair walls or embankments, or divert water into watercourses. The Local Authorities (Works) Act 1949 also allows the local authority to deposit any substance or thing removed from a watercourse onto land adjacent to the watercourse.[15] The local authority may also use the waste taken from the watercourse or dispose of it otherwise as they think fit. The local authority is also given the power to enter onto lands in order to execute the relevant works. However, before entering on land for a purpose other than the execution of urgent works, a local authority executing the works shall either obtain the consent of the occupier, or of the owner or shall give not less than fourteen days' notice in writing of the intention to enter onto the lands.[16]

3–09 Any person who suffers damage by reason of any interference, caused by the execution of works by the local authority is entitled to compensation in respect of that damage.[17] Every claim for compensation is made in writing to the local authority before the expiration of the period beginning with the commencement of the works which caused the interference and ending either two years thereafter or one year after the completion of such works, whichever is the later.[18]

B. FIRE SERVICES

1. Fire Services Act

3–10 The Fire Services Act of 1981[19] repleaded the earlier Fire Brigades Act of 1940 which imposed a general duty on sanitary authorities to make reasonable provisions for fire fighting within their sanitary district and empowered the sanitary authority to establish and maintain a fire brigade. The 1981 Act provides that local authorities are the fire authority in particular the council of a county, the corporation of a county borough, the corporation of any other borough and the council of any urban district who had established and were maintaining a fire brigade.

---

[15] s.2(5).
[16] s.4(2).
[17] s.5(1).
[18] In default of agreement the claim for compensation is referred to arbitration under the Acquisition of Land (Assessment of Compensation) Act 1919.
[19] No. 30 of 1981.

2. General duties

3–11   Fire authorities are obliged to make provision for the prompt and efficient extinguishing of fires in buildings and other places of all kinds in its
functional area and for the protection and rescue of persons and property from
injury by fire, and to establish and maintain a fire brigade, provide premises
and make such other provision as it considers necessary or desirable for such
purpose, and make adequate provision for the reception of and response to
calls for the assistance of the fire brigade.[20] In performing their functions fire
authorities are to have regard to the nature of the fire hazards and the probable
incidence and extent of fires within its functional area, as well as to the character of the area and the value of the property liable to be damaged by fires.[21]

3–12   Fire authorities may send a fire brigade to any place outside its functional area, and where any such fire brigade is sent outside the functional area
of any fire authority, the person who is for the time being in charge thereof
shall have the powers available to the person in control at a fire or other emergency under section 28. A fire authority may carry out or assist in any operations of an emergency nature, whether or not a risk of fire is involved, and a
fire authority may make provision for the rescue or safeguarding of persons
and protection of property as it considers necessary.[22]

3. General powers

3–13   Section 28 provides that a person in control at a fire or other emergency may, either personally or by a member of a fire brigade present at the
incident or by a member of the Garda Síochána, or by other persons as, do, if
necessary, by force, all such things as are, necessary or expedient for the purpose of extinguishing the fire or for protecting or rescuing persons or property
and, in particular, may enter any land or building in which there is reason to
believe fire has broken out or the emergency exists at any other land or building. The person in charge of the emergency may cause any land or building to
be vacated by the occupants, or pull down or demolish any building or part of
a building, and may use any water supply, whether public or private, take
water from any watercourse, lake, pond or other source, whether natural or
artificial, and may remove anything from the vicinity of the fire or other emergency.[23]

3–14   Every fire authority is protected from an action against the person in

---

[20] s.10(2).
[21] s.10(3).
[22] s.25.
[23] For definition of person in charge see s.27.

control at the fire or other emergency or any person acting under powers in the Fire Services Act.[24] Where damage is caused to any property as a result of the fire services attending to an emergency the damage shall, for all purposes and in particular for the purpose of any contract of insurance, be deemed to have been caused by the fire or emergency.[25] Additionally, no action or other proceeding can lie or be maintained against the Minister, or against a fire authority, or person engaged by the fire authority for the recovery of damages in respect of injury to persons or property alleged to have been caused or contributed to by the failure to comply with any functions under the Act.[26] Each fire authority assumed the duties of the local authority in relation to the functions of a local authority, within its functional area, under the Dangerous Substances Act 1972, the Explosives Act 1875, and such other provisions of any other enactment as are specified by the Minister by order. The functions of a local authority under section 36 of the Public Health Acts Amendment Act 1890 are also now performed by the fire authority. The fire authority performs the functions relating to means of escape in case of fire which was given to sanitary authorities in under the Safety in Industry Acts, 1955 and 1980, and the Office Premises Act 1958. Fire authorities are also empowered to give the planning authority advice in relation to applications for planning permission and permission for retention made under the Local Government (Planning and Development) Act 1963.[27]

3–15 Fire authorities are under a duty to make arrangements for the efficient training of the personnel of its fire services and a fire authority may establish and maintain facilities for providing courses of instruction for personnel and for training other persons in fire-fighting techniques, fire drill procedure, fire safety and related matters.[28]

4. Offences

3–16 The Act provides that where any person wilfully obstructs or impedes the person in control at a fire or other emergency or by a person fighting a fire or attending to an emergency or by any member of the Garda Síochána may be guilty of an offence.[29] Section 30 of the Act makes it an offence for a person to knowingly give or cause a false alarm to be given to a fire brigade whether by telephone, message or otherwise.

---

[24] s.28(2).
[25] s.28(4).
[26] s.36.
[27] s.13.
[28] s.15.
[29] s.28(3).

3–17   Section 18 of the Act provides that every person having control over premises to which this section applies, have a duty to take all reasonable measures to guard against the outbreak of fire on the premises, and to ensure, as far as is reasonably practicable, the safety of persons on the premises in the event of an outbreak of fire. The section applies to a premises which is used for any purpose which involves the provision of sleeping accommodation, but excluding premises consisting of a dwelling house occupied as a single dwelling, or used as an institution providing treatment or care, or used for purposes of entertainment, recreation or instruction or for the purpose of any club, society or association, used for purposes of teaching, training or research, or any premises used for any purpose which involve access to the premises by members of the public, whether by payment or in any other way, comes within the terms of section 18.

5. Duties on other persons

3–18   Section 18(3) places a duty on any person who is on premises to which section 18 applies, to conduct themselves in such a way as to ensure that as far as is reasonably practicable any person on the premises is not exposed to danger from fire as a consequence of any act or omission on their part.[30] A fire authority may give advice in relation to fire safety to the owner or occupier of any premises or to any person having control over any premises.

6. Fire safety notice

3–19   A fire authority may serve a fire safety notice on the owner or on the occupier of any building which appears, to the fire authority, to be a potentially dangerous building.[31] A potentially dangerous building means any building which would, in the event of a fire occurring, constitute a serious danger to life. The fact that large numbers of person are accommodated in the building or are present in the building, or an absence of any adequate fire safety appliances of fittings for example fire extinguishes, fire exits, fire alarms, or emergency lighting could render a building dangerous.

3–20   The fire authority will also take note of the flammable nature of the materials of which the building is made including the flammable nature of the furniture, furnishings and fittings in the building. The fire authority will also examine as to whether a fire in a building would be likely to spread rapidly within the building or into other buildings.

3–21   Section 19(1) does not apply to premises which consist of a dwelling-

---

[30] s.18(4).
[31] s.19(1), s.21 allows an appeal from the service of a fire safety notice.

house which is occupied as a single dwelling, or to premises which consists of a store which is already subject to the licensing requirements of the Dangerous Substances Act 1972.[32]

3–22 A fire safety notice may prohibit the use of the building, or a specified part of the building, for the purpose or any of the purposes which may be specified in the notice. The fire safety notice may prohibit the use of the building, or a part of the building, unless or until specified precautions have been taken to the satisfaction of the fire authority whether by the provision in the building of specified appliances or fittings, or by the execution of specified structural alterations or additions to the building, or the removal from the building of furniture, furnishings, fittings or any other materials.[33]

3–23 A fire safety notice may impose on the owner or occupier of a building requirements as to the provision and maintenance of exit signs, emergency lighting and notices as to the procedure to be followed in the event of fire, the arrangements to be made for the provision and maintenance of equipment and fittings for fire detection, fire prevention, the extinguishing of fires, the giving of warning in case of fire, and for securing that the means of escape can be safely and effectively used at all material times. The fire safety notice may require works to be carried out in relation to the installation, maintenance and use of the existing power, lighting, heating and ventilating systems of the building in order to render them safe, and may order that certain arrangements be made for the safe storage of flammable, explosive or potentially explosive articles or materials which are used, stored or deposited in the building.

3–24 A fire safety notice may also specify the measures to be taken for ensuring that persons who are employed in a building receive appropriate instruction or training in fire safety, and that records are kept of such instruction or training, the holding of fire safety evacuation drills at specified intervals, and that records are kept of such drills, the nomination of an appropriate person or persons employed in the building to have responsibility for fire safety measures in the building, and limiting the number of persons who may be in the building at any one time. All fire safety notices may require that the specified works must be carried out within a specified time.

3–25 Where a fire authority is of the opinion that a flammable, or explosive or potentially explosive substance is used, stored or deposited in lands or buildings which are adjacent to buildings in such a manner as to represent a serious danger to life, the fire authority may serve a fire safety notice on the owner or

---

[32] s.19(2).
[33] s.20(2).

occupier of the land requiring the owner to take specified measures in order to reduce the danger to a reasonable level.

6. Power of entry

3–26   Section 22 of the Act allows a person authorised by the fire authority to enter at all reasonable times and inspect any land or building, other than a dwelling house occupied as a single dwelling, for any of the purposes of the Act. Any authorised person may inspect any water supply in a building or on any land, or inspect all records which are required to be kept by a fire safety notice or by any regulation, or require to be informed by the owner or occupier of any land or building or by any person in his employment as to the purposes for which the land or building is used, the number of persons who are habitually employed or accommodated on the land or building and the substance of which any building is made and the method of its construction and any other relevant matter.[34]

3–27   Fire authorities may by notice in writing require the owner or occupier of land or buildings to provide to the authority, plans, including line or simple dimensional drawings, of the land or buildings, and any additional information in writing which the fire authority may require.[35]

3–28   If a fire authority considers that the risk to persons in the event of fire is so serious that the use of particular land or a particular building, should be restricted, or should be immediately prohibited until specified measures have been taken so as to reduce the risk to a reasonable level, the fire authority may apply to the High Court for an order restricting or prohibiting the use of the land or building.[36] This amended the 1940 Act in that it gave the fire authority an additional means of enforcing a fire notice rather than the sole power of prohibiting the use of a potentially dangerous building.

8. Other functions

3–29   Fire authorities are given a role in section 24 in relation to applications for a certificate for the grant or renewal of a licence (other than an off-licence) under the Licensing Acts, 1833 to 1981, and for applications regarding the grant or renewal of a certificate of registration under the Registration of Clubs Acts, 1904 to 1981, and applications for a licence in respect of premises under the Public Dance Halls Act 1935, or Part IV of the Public Health Acts Amendment Act 1890, or a certificate in respect of premises under the Gaming and

---

[34] s.22(3).
[35] s.22(4).
[36] s.23(1).

Lotteries Acts, 1956 to 1979. An applicant for any of these certificates must give the fire authority one month's notice in writing, or a shorter period of notice as the fire authority may in the special circumstances of the case agree to accept. The application must go to the fire authority in the functional area of which the premises are situated, and the fire authority may appear, be heard and adduce evidence in respect of the application.

9. Fire plans

3–30 Every fire authority is obliged to prepare or revise plans for fire and emergency operations, showing the provisions made in respect of its organisation, its appliances, equipment, fire stations, water supplies and extinguishing agents, as well as regarding training, operational procedure and such other relevant matters, and in particular relating to operations assisting in any operations of an emergency nature.[37]

10. Offences

3–31 A person may commit an offence if that person refuses to allow an authorised person to enter any land or building, or obstructs or impedes an authorised person in the exercise of any of the powers conferred by statute, or fails or refuses to give to an authorised person on demand or to the fire authority under to a notice in writing any plan or information, or wilfully or recklessly gives to an authorised person or a fire authority information which is false or misleading in a material respect, or fails to comply with any requirement of this section.[38] Where an authorised person is refused entry to land or a building in the exercise of his powers, the fire authority may apply to the District Court for a warrant authorising such entry.[39]

3–32 A person who is found guilty of an offence under the Fire Services Act may be liable to a fine of £500 or to a term of imprisonment of six months of both at the discretion of the Court. The District Court has jurisdiction to try summarily an offence where the DPP consents to the prosecution and the District Court judge is of the opinion that the facts proved constitutes a minor offence fit to be tried summarily and the accused consent to the summary disposal of the matter.

---

[37] s.26.
[38] s.22(6).
[39] s.22(7).

C. OTHER LOCAL AUTHORITY SERVICES AND POWERS

1. Dangerous places

3–33   The Local Government (Sanitary Services) Act of 1964[40] gives a sanitary authority a number of powers in relation to the control of dangerous places and structures. A "dangerous place" is defined as including an excavation, quarry, pit, well, reservoir, pond, stream, dump, or land that is in the opinion of the sanitary authority in whose district it is situate or which is likely to be dangerous to any person.[41] A "dangerous structure" is defined as including any building, wall or other structure of any kind or anything attached to a building, wall or other structure of any kind which is in the opinion of the sanitary authority is or is likely to be dangerous to any person or property.[42]

3–34   It was held by the Supreme Court, dismissing an appeal by the Corporation from a High Court injunction, in *Treacy v. Dublin Corporation*[43] that the terms of section 1 of the Local Government (Sanitary Services) Act 1964 clearly indicate that they are statutory provisions expanding and developing the right of a sanitary authority to deal with the public risk and danger arising from dangerous places and buildings. The powers vested in the sanitary authority are not merely permissive but mandatory but involving a duty as well as a power, and where the sanitary authority intends to exercise the power of demolition of a building their overall obligation is to prevent the creation or development of dangerous structures. The case involved a premises at No. 87 Thomas Street, Dublin which was a dangerous structure and was about to be demolished by the Corporation. The plaintiff owned a premises adjoining the dangerous premises, No. 86, and was fearful that if the premises was demolished by the Corporation that his premises would become unstable as the building would not have any support. The High Court had made an order preventing the Corporation from demolishing No. 87 Thomas Street as the owner of No. 87 Thomas Street was under an obligation of an easement of support to the adjoining premises at No. 86. Costello J. in the High Court found that the Corporation could not enter the premises at No. 87 Thomas Street except in accordance with statutory powers and that no powers existed which authorised the Corporation to interfere with the easement enjoyed by the owner of No. 86. The Corporation had intended to restore the easement of support by putting some form of shoring, but this was found to leave a wall likely, in a very short time to become unstable due to wind and weather, having regard to the age and condition of the premises.

---

[40] No. 29 of 1964.
[41] s.1.
[42] s.1.
[43] [1992] I.L.R.M. 650.

3–35   The sanitary authority has the power to carry out any necessary works which will in its opinion prevent the place or structure from being dangerous. The sanitary authority may also carry out any works at the request of the owner who occupies the dangerous place. The sanitary authority may require the owner of the place or structure to make a contribution toward the cost of those works.[44] Before the sanitary authority begin to carry out any works the authority must give a notice to the owner and the notice must not only state that the place is dangerous but must also specify the works which are necessary to prevent the place from being dangerous, as well as an estimate of those works.

3–36   Once a notice has been served, the person on whom it is served has twenty one days in which to apply for the notice to be annulled to the District Court, whose decision is final and unappealable.[45]

3–37   Where the authority wishes to enter on any land for the purposes of carrying out works on a dangerous structure it must also serve a notice as soon as possible to the owner of the land, if the same can be ascertained by reasonable inquiry, or to the occupier of the structure, stating that the authority proposes to enter onto the land. The authority must also specify the works which it is proposed to be carried out.[46]

3–38   Failure to comply with a notice under section 3(1) is an offence and carries with it a fine on summary conviction of up to £1,000.[47] Where a person fails to comply with a notice served under section 3(1) in relation to a dangerous structure the District Court may, on the application of the authority, order that person to carry out the works described in the notice. The Court can also prohibit the use of the structure, or part of it, or it may also prohibit the use of the structure for a particular purpose or purposes.[48]

3–39   The sanitary authority may also require the vacation of a dangerous structure or its curtilage and may also require the removal of property from the dangerous structure. Failure to comply with the order of the authority will invariably mean that the authority makes an application to the District Court under section 3(9)(b). The sanitary authority may also decide to acquire either by agreement or compulsorily any land within its district which is dangerous. The authority may also decide to acquire the land, again either by agreement or compulsorily upon which the authority has carried out works.[49] The proce-

---

[44] s.2(5).
[45] s.5(3).
[46] s.3(2)(b).
[47] As amended by s.113 Environmental Protection Agency Act 1992.
[48] Failure to comply with such an order is an offence, s.3(6), max. fine £1,000.
[49] s.6.

dure whereby the authority may acquire land compulsorily under section 6 is that notice must be given to every occupier of the land and to every owner of the land where that person ordinarily reside as can be ascertained by the sanitary authority through reasonable enquiries.[50]

3–40   Objections to compulsory acquisition of the property must be made within one month of the date of the notice. These objections may be made by writing to the authority, and once an objection is received by the authority it may not proceed with the acquisition of the property without the consent of the Minister for the Environment and Local Government. Where an application is made to the Minister to a proposed compulsory acquisition of land, the Minister may not give his consent to the acquisition of the property if no part of the property is or is likely to be dangerous to any person.[51]

3–41   Where the sanitary authority has acquired any land under the Sanitary Services Act 1964 the authority must take whatever steps as may be necessary to prevent injury to health or to any amenities of neighbouring lands. Once the authority has acquired the property it may use the property for any purpose connected with its powers and duties.

2. Sewers

3–42   The 1878 Act vested then existing sewers in the various sanitary authorities and imposes a duty on the sanitary authority to keep all sewers in good repair and also obliges the sanitary authority to provide enough sewers as may be necessary for effectually draining the district.[52] The sanitary authority is given power under section 18 to carry any sewer across, or under any road or street following reasonable notice in writing to the owner or occupier of the property. The sanitary authority must ensure that the sewers in its functional area are kept clean so as not be to injurious to public health. In the case of *Merriman v. Dublin Corporation* the Supreme Court held[53] that not only was a grid or grating in a road used to drain off surface water a sewer within the meaning of the 1878 Act but also that the sanitary authority was under a duty to keep it in repair under section 17 of the 1878 Act. The judgement of the Court also examines what is and what may not be a sewer or a private drain.[54]

3–43   However, the sanitary authority is prohibited from allowing sewage or

---

[50] s.7.
[51] s.8(5)(a).
[52] See *Merriman v. Dublin Corporation* [1998] 2 I.R. 155.
[53] *per* Keane J. at p. 161.
[54] *ibid.*

filthy water into any natural stream, watercourse, canal, pond or lake until the sewage or filthy water has been purified.[55] This provision however does not prevent the sanitary authority from allowing sewage or filthy water into rivers or seas.

3–44 The owner or occupier of any premises within the district of the sanitary authority has the right to connect to the sewerage system of the sanitary authority on giving notice to the authority and subject to such requirements as the sanitary authority may require.[56]

3. Graveyards and burial grounds

3–45 Each of the county councils, being the relevant sanitary authorities, are responsible for the upkeep of graveyards and burial grounds within their functional areas. Section 160 of the Public Health (Ireland) Act of 1848[57] provided that the sanitary authority of each district was to be the "burial board" for the sanitary district. The Act provided that every burial ground which had been under the control and care of the Commissioners of Church Temporalities in Ireland were transferred to the burial boards.[58] This does not include burial grounds which are in the direct control and ownership of parishes or other bodies. The burial boards are empowered to provide a suitable and convenient burial ground where a burial ground has been closed within their district, and the boards may provide new burial grounds either within their own district or in other districts.[59] However, no burial ground can be opened within one hundred yards of any dwellinghouse without the consent in writing of the owner and occupier of the dwelling. Section 175 of the 1878 Act provides the burial board to purchase land for graveyards and section 178 of the Act allowed the burial board the right to sell plots within the graveyard.

3–46 In order to remove any doubt regarding the power of joint burial boards to purchase lands compulsorily section 2 of the Local Government (Sanitary Services) (Joint Burial Boards) Act of 1952[60] provided that the powers of a joint burial board include the powers of a sanitary authority acting as burial board for a sanitary district to acquire land compulsorily for the purposes of providing a new burial ground or making additions to an existing burial ground, and in particular to acquire land compulsorily. Some of the joint burial boards

---

[55] s.19.
[56] See chapter on waste and litter.
[57] 1878, 41 & 42 Vict. c. 52.
[58] See, Keane, *The Law of Local Government in the Republic of Ireland* (Incorporated Law Society of Ireland, 1982).
[59] ss.173 and 174.
[60] No. 22 of 1952.

have now been absorbed within the local authorities for their areas, such as the Deans Grange Joint Burial Board which was reorganised under the Local Government (Dublin) Act 1993,[61] or separate legislation has been introduced to deal with cemeteries established in Victorian times such as the Dublin Cemeteries Committee Act of 1970.[62]

3–47 Section 44 of Local Government Act of 1948 provides that a person cannot bury the body of a deceased person in a place which is not a burial ground. The section further provides that places which shall be burial grounds are a place which is in lawful use as a burial ground and which was in lawful use as a burial ground, a place as respects which the Minister has given his approval to its being used as a burial ground, and a burial ground provided by a burial board, that is the local authority. A person may not bury the body of a deceased person within the limits in which burials have by order, under section 162 of the 1878 Act, been ordered to be discontinued in violation of the provisions of that order. However, the Act does not prevent the burial of a clergyman in or adjacent to a church.

3–48 Section 45 of the Local Government Act of 1948 provides that where a person requests a burial board to maintain in proper order, either in perpetuity or for a limited period, a grave in a burial ground provided by the board, the board may, in consideration of a payment as the board may consider reasonable, make and carry out an agreement for that purpose. A person cannot exhume from a burial ground the body of a deceased person except by under a licence granted under section 45 of the 1948 Act or by an order of the Minister for Justice under section 15 of the Coroners (Amendment) Act 1927.[63]

3–49 Section 6 of the Local Government Act of 1994[64] provides for the general competence of the local authorities which is couched in such general terms as to include the provision of graveyards and cemeteries. Section 6 provides that a local authority may, take such measures, or engage in such activities or do such things in accordance with law, as it considers necessary or desirable to promote the interests of the local community, and for those purposes, a measure, activity or thing shall be deemed to promote the interests of the local community if it promotes, directly or indirectly, the social, economic, environmental, recreational, cultural, community or general development of the functional area of the local authority concerned or of the local community. To give effect to these activities the local authority may take such practical steps as it deems necessary to achieve their objective, including carrying out

---

[61] No. 31 of 1993.
[62] No. 1 of 1970.
[63] No. 1 of 1927.
[64] No. 8 of 1994.

and maintaining works of any kind, providing, maintaining, preserving or restoring land, structures of any kind or facilities, and so on. However, it is suggested that this section while allowing the local authority to certainly carrying out works to improve cemeteries and graveyards it does not provide the local authority with any additional powers to acquire land or to establish a burial ground without the requirement of planning permission.

3–50 Section 170 of the 1878 Act prohibits the burial in any grave, vault or place of interment which has been used as the burial place of any family unless that person is a member of that family or has the written consent of the family concerned. The 1878 Act also prohibits the grazing of animals in graveyards the maximum fine provided is £1,000.[65]

4. Water services

3–51 Sanitary authorities are enabled under section 61 of the 1898 Act to provide, within their districts, a supply of water which is proper and sufficient for public and private purposes.[66] The sanitary authorities may construct and maintain waterworks, dig wells, as well as to purchase waterworks or acquire any right to take or convey water within the sanitary district or outside of that district. Section 53 of the Waterworks Clauses Act of 1847 gave households the right to connect to a supply of water already provided by the local authority however, the Local Government (Planning and Development) Act 1990 limited section 53 of the Waterworks Clauses Act 1847 by providing that section 53 of the Waterworks Clauses Act 1847, and any other enactment which confers a right to a supply of water for domestic purposes shall not apply in relation to a dwelling house which is an unauthorised structure or the use of which constitutes an unauthorised use. Section 65A(5) of the Public Health (Ireland) Act allowed the sanitary authority to charge for the supply of water and to supply the water by meter where a charge for water is made by reference to the quantity supplied.[67] The sanitary authority had a discretionary power to disconnect water supply under section 65A of the 1878 Act but that the section did not empower a sanitary authority to exercise the power in order to enforce payment of sums that were not lawfully due and water rates become payable on the dates provided by statute and where one of the statutory dates has passed at the time of the making orders for the payment of water rates

---

[65] Increased to £1,000 by s.113(3) of the Environmental Protection Agency Act 1992.

[66] See also s.26 of the Local Government (Sanitary Services) Act 1948 which allows local authorities to contribute to private water supplies.

[67] s.69 of the 1898 Act provides that the water meter reading is prima facie evidence of the amount of water consumed.

payment becomes legally impossible and the order is ultra vires and consequently void.[68]

3–52   The Water Supplies Act 1942[69] provides for the taking of supplies of water by sanitary authorities. The sanitary authority must firstly make a proposal for so taking such supply of water from such source of water. Following the making of the proposal the sanitary authority shall take all reasonable steps to ascertain the persons to whom damage may be caused by the taking of water and estimate the amount of that damage. A water proposal is deemed to have been agreed to if either, no objection is made to the proposal or every objection which was made to the proposal is withdrawn. Confirmation of the water proposal is made by the Minister following which the local authority publishes the proposal.[70]

3–53   When the proposal has come into force it is lawful for the sanitary authority to take a supply of water from the source of water and to use such supply for the purpose of increasing, extending, or providing under the Public Health Acts, 1878 to 1931, a supply of water.

3–54   Contracts between private persons may also be undertaken for the supply of water within the district. Section 65 of the 1898 Act also provides that a sanitary authority is obliged to keep a supply of pure and wholesome water within the waterworks which have been constructed or purchased by them. Section 6(1) of the Local Government (Sanitary Services) Act 1962[71] further amended the 1898 Act[72] by allowing sanitary authorities for the purpose of drainage or sewage disposal, to purchase either within or without their district any sewerage undertaking, 'sewerage undertaking' including sewers, drains, pumps, tanks, sluices, culverts and engines, and machinery, lands, buildings and things for the purposes of drainage or sewage disposal.

3–55   Section 49 of the Local Government (Sanitary Services) Act 1948[73] permits a sanitary authority to take any steps which are reasonably necessary to prevent injury being caused to public health, or to the amenities of any locality as a result of obstructions in any river or watercourse.

---

[68] *O'Donnell v. Dun Laoghaire Corp.* [1991] I.L.R.M. 301, a defective order cannot be cured by a subsequent demand note from the manager, save by order of the sanitary authority.

[69] No. 1 of 1942.

[70] Compensation is also payable under s.14, s.15 provides for arbitration in default of agreement.

[71] No. 26 of 1962.

[72] In particular s.202 of the Act.

[73] No. 26 of 1948.

3–56 The Local Government (Financial Provisions) Act of 1997[74] provided for the removal from the local authorities the power to make charges for the provision of water supplies for domestic purposes, thereby amending section 65 A of the Public Health (Ireland) Act 1878[75] from December 31, 1996 onwards.[76] However, authorities were allowed to recover any charges for the supply of domestic water made on or before December 31, 1996, for a supply by them of water after that date.

3–57 Where water is supplied by a sanitary authority and involves or may involve a supply for domestic as well as for other purposes, the sanitary authority may estimate the proportion of the water supplied which is likely to be used for domestic purposes, and may accordingly charge for the supply of water for non-domestic purposes. Domestic supply refers to the supply of water to a 'dwelling house' which refers to a building or part of a building used by a person as their place of private residence, whether as his or her principal place or not and includes accommodation provided to one or more students to enable them to pursue their studies but does not include any part of a building used for the provision, for the purposes of reward, with a view to profit or otherwise in the course of business, of accommodation, including self-catering accommodation, unless the person to whom the accommodation is so provided uses the accommodation as his or her principal place of private residence.[77]

3–58 Section 2 of the Local Government (Financial Provisions) (No. 2) Act 1983[78] enabled local authorities to make certain charges in respect of an existing enactment which requires or enables a local authority to provide a service but which did not empower the local authority to charge for the provision of those services. That provision was amended by the 1997 Act to read that section 2 of the 1983 Act shall not apply to any service consisting of the supply by a local authority, after December 31, 1996, of water for domestic purposes or the disposal by it of domestic sewage, or which stands specified in an order made by the Minister. However this provision does not prevent the local authority from recovering a charge made by it, on or before December 31, 1996, for a disposal by it of domestic sewage after that date.

3–59 The Local Government (Delimitation of Water Supply Disconnection

---

[74] No. 29 of 1997.

[75] As inserted by s.7 of the Local Government (Sanitary Services) Act 1962, and amended by s.8 of the Local Government (Financial Provisions) (No. 2) Act 1983, and ss.2 and 3 of the Local Government (Delimitation of Water Supply Disconnection Powers) Act 1995.

[76] s.12.

[77] s.12(2) amending s.65A.

[78] No. 21 of 1983.

Powers) Act of 1995 still retains its relevance even with the passing of the 1997 Act as the local authorities are still empowered to seek charges made for water before December 31, 1997 and since the statute of limitations on the recovery of such charges is six years the provisions for the 1995 Act will retain some bearing in certain situations.

3–60   Section 3 of the 1995 Act provides that a sanitary authority may discontinue a supply of water for domestic purposes in respect of which a charge remains wholly or partly unpaid, or there has been default on payment due under an instalment order made pursuant to the Enforcement of Court Orders Acts 1926 and 1940, if it has been authorised to do so by order of the District Court.

3–61   Before an order can be granted the Court must be satisfied that in the case of default in payment all the conditions set out in the Schedule to the Act have been complied with, and the default in payment by the consumer was not due to hardship. In considering whether or not to grant an order the Court is obliged to have regard to the personal and household circumstances of the consumer. The Schedule to the Act provides that before a sanitary authority can make an application to the Court for a water discontinuance order, a sanitary authority shall send to the consumer an initial demand in writing in respect of a charge for the supply of water for domestic purposes. This initial demand must indicate the amount of the charge, and the date by which the charge is liable to be paid. Where, following the sending of the initial demand, a charge has not been paid in full after it has become payable, the sanitary authority must also send at least two further demands in writing, reminders, to the consumer and following, or in conjunction with, the sending of reminders, send a warning notice in writing to the consumer on at least two occasions, ensuring that a period of at least fourteen days has elapsed between the sending of the first warning notice and the second warning notice, stating that, where the charge remains unpaid, the sanitary authority may apply to the Court for a water discontinuance order. Following the sending of warning notices, secure the delivery to the consumer of, or send by post in a prepaid registered letter to the consumer, a final notice in writing that the sanitary authority intends to apply to the Court for a water discontinuance order.

3–62   The initial demand, reminders, warning notices and final notice shall be addressed to the consumer at the address in respect of which the supply of water is provided or, in a case in which an address for service has been furnished, at that address. Where the name of the consumer cannot be ascertained by reasonable inquiry, the initial demand, reminders, warning notices or the final notice may be addressed to "the consumer" without naming the consumer.

3–63   Where the Court grants a water discontinuance order, unless the Court is satisfied that there are special and substantial reasons for not so doing the costs and expenses of the order may be ordered to be paid by the consumer to the sanitary authority, measured by the Court, which have been incurred by the sanitary authority in, and incidental to, its application for a water discontinuance order.[79] Where a supply of water is disconnected pursuant to a water discontinuance order the cost of reconnection shall be payable by the consumer and such cost shall include the cost of discontinuance.[80]

5. Drainage

3–64   The Local Government (Sanitary Services) Act 1948[81] provides that a sanitary authority may open up and examine a drainage system of a premises where it is suspected that the drainage system is defective or foul or neglected. The sanitary authority is empowered to cause the system to be restored or cleared and the sanitary authority may recoup the costs from the owner of the relevant premises.[82]

3–65   Where it is found that a drainage system or part of the system is found to be defective, foul or neglected and the system is not drained satisfactorily the sanitary authority may serve a notice on the owner of the premises stating that it intends to make a provisional drainage order in respect of the premises.[83]

D.   PUBLIC HEALTH

1. Public Health (Ireland) Act 1878

3–66   The Public Health (Ireland) Act 1878[84] incredibly remains the principal Act dealing with public health in Ireland and deals with not only the provision of water supply and maintenance of sewers but also the control of certain offensive trades and the provision of burial grounds. The 1878 Act divided the country into urban and rural sanitary districts each governed by a separate authority. Urban sanitary areas included Dublin, corporate towns, towns with a population of over 6,000 where Commissioners have been appointed and towns or townships where Commissioners have been appointed.[85]

---

[79]   s.4(1).
[80]   s.4(2).
[81]   No. 26 of 1962.
[82]   s.18.
[83]   s.18(4).
[84]   41 & 42 Vict.,c.52.
[85]   s.4.

3–67   However, there have been some enactments which have been specifically addressed certain issues relating to public health such as the Sale of Food and Drugs Acts 1875 to 1936 and the Food Safety Authority of Ireland Act 1998.

2. Abattoirs

(a) Licences

3–68   The Abattoir Act of 1988 provided for the granting of licences to the operators and owners of abattoirs and knacker yards. The Act also made provision for the transfer of every function and duty of a sanitary authority in relation to abattoirs to the local authority in whose functional area the abattoir and knackery is situate.[86] The Act also made provision for the adoption of a health mark which is applied to meat by veterinary inspectors and provides that no meat which is intended for human consumption may be sold to the public which does not bear a health mark.[87]

3–69   The occupier of any premises shall not use such premises, or may permit such premises to be used, as an abattoir unless that person is the holder of an abattoir licence for the premises.[88] A person, who is not the occupier of a premises, also shall not use a premises as an abattoir unless the occupier of the premises is the holder of an abattoir licence for that premises. A person who uses any premises as an abattoir without first holding an abattoir licence and contravenes the provisions of this section may be guilty of an offence.

3–70   An abattoir, within the meaning of the Abattoir Act, means any premises used for or in connection with the slaughter of animals whose meat is intended for human consumption. An abattoir includes a slaughterhouse but does not include a place situate on a farm which is used for the occasional slaughter of a pig, or for the slaughter of an animal which has been injured by accident and the slaughter of which is necessary to prevent its suffering.[89] The Abattoir Act does not apply to premises which are licensed under the Pigs and Bacon Acts or which are registered under the Agricultural Produce (Fresh Meat) Acts and which is occupied by a person who holds a licence under the Acts.

(b) Duration and conditions

3–71   A licence for an abattoir is granted by the Minister and remains in force for a period of not over twelve months, or such less time as may be fixed

---

[86] s.38(1).
[87] ss.41 & 42.
[88] Abattoir Act 1988, s.8(1), No. 8 of 1988.
[89] s.2(1).

by the Minister, and may be renewed on expiry by application to the Minister. The functions of the Minister may be transferred to the local authorities who may then issue the abattoir licence for premises within their functional area. Every application must be accompanied by the relevant fee, which for a premises which slaughters less than five hundred animals is £10, for premises which slaughter between five hundred and one thousand animals the fee is £50, while in every other case the fee is £100.[90] A licence may be granted by the Minister or by a local authority if they are satisfied that the applicant is a fit and proper person to hold an abattoir licence and has complied with all of the provisions relating to the slaughter of animals and any other enactment relating to abattoirs. An abattoir licence may contain a condition limiting the class or the number of animals which may be slaughtered in the abattoir or a part of the abattoir.[91]

3–72   The holder of an abattoir licence may not transfer a licence to any other person and any transfer is null and void and of no effect.[92] If the holder of a licence dies, the licence continues in full force and effect for the benefit of the holder's personal representative or the deceased's spouse or any other member of the family for a period of four months, or for a lesser period if the licence has less than four months to run, and then expires.

3–73   The local authority, or Minister, may at any time, refuse an application for the granting or the renewal of an abattoir licence, and shall notify, in writing giving twenty one days notice, the applicant of the intention to refuse the application and setting out the reasons for the refusal to renew the licence.[93] Whenever the local authority or Minister decides to refuse an application for the grant or renewal of an abattoir licence, he shall, by notice in writing, notify the applicant of its decision and of the reasons for making the decision, and of the time limit within which, and of the manner in which, an appeal against such decision and if, at the date on which such application is made, the premises to which the application relates are used as an abattoir, whether such premises may continue to be so used.[94]

3–74   Holders of licences are obliged, under section 59, to keep and maintain records of all animals which are slaughtered or handled in the licensed premises. These records are to be kept for a period of at least three years.

3–75   A local authority or the Minister may, at any time, revoke an abattoir

---

[90] s.10(7).
[91] s.11(2).
[92] s.13(1).
[93] s.14.
[94] s.14(3).

licence if he is satisfied that the licence has been obtained by fraud or by misrepresentation, whether fraudulent or innocent, or where there has been any contravention of any provision of the Act or of any Regulation made under the Act, or where the holder of a licence has not, within a reasonable time, complied with the requirements of a notice served under section 18 of this Act. Before a local authority can revoke an abattoir licence, the local authority or the Minister, by at least twenty one days notice in writing, must notify the holder of the licence of his intention to revoke the licence and of the reasons for the revocation of the licence.[95] Whenever the local authority or the Minister decides to revoke an abattoir licence a notice in writing must be sent in order to notify the holder of the licence of the decision and of the reasons, and of the time limit within which, and of the manner in which, an appeal against such revocation may, pursuant to section 16 of this Act, be made, and whether the premises concerned may, in accordance with the provisions of this Act, continue to be used as an abattoir.

(c) Appeals

3–76   An appeal against the decision to refuse to grant or renew a licence, or the revocation of an abattoir licence may be made within twenty one days after the date of service of the relevant notice to the Circuit Court. Before the hearing of the appeal the abattoir may continue to be used provided there is no danger to public health. The Circuit Court may do whatever appears to be just and proper having regard to the provisions of the Abattoir Act and regulations made under the Act and may dismiss the appeal, with or without costs, or allow the appeal, with costs, and direct that the local authority or Minister to grant or renew the licence or to cancel the revocation. The onus of establishing that the provisions of the Act in relation to the granting, renewal or the continuing in force of a licence have been complied with lies with the person making the appeal. There is no appeal from a decision from the Circuit Court other than on a point of law to the Supreme Court.[96]

(d) Notices

3–77   A notice is served under section 18 whenever an authorised officer of the local authority or of the Minister is of the opinion that there is a grave and immediate danger to public health arising from the manner in which such abattoir is managed or maintained, or that meat, which is in such abattoir and is intended for sale for human consumption, is liable, if consumed, to cause serious illness, or that meat, which is in such abattoir and is intended for sale for human consumption, is, or may become, unfit for human consumption by virtue of non-compliance with the provisions of the Act or any regulations

---

[95] s.15(3).
[96] s.16(4).

made under the Act. The authorised officer may serve on the holder of the abattoir licence in relation to that abattoir or on the person who seems to him to be, for the time being, in charge of such abattoir, a notice in writing requiring the immediate closure of such abattoir or part thereof, or that the slaughtering of animals or the preparation of meat in that abattoir ceases.

3–78 The notice may specify the steps that ought to be taken, or the things that ought to be done, before such abattoir or part thereof, as the case may be, is reopened or before the slaughtering of animals or the preparation of meat is resumed in that abattoir.[97] A person who is served with a notice is obliged to comply with the terms of the notice, and any person who fails to comply with the terms of the notice may be guilty of an offence under the Act.[98] Any person who has been served with a notice may appeal to the District Court against the notice, and the District Court may, as it thinks proper, cancel or confirm the notice, and the decision of the District Court on such hearing shall be final save that, by leave of that Court, an appeal shall lie to the High Court on a point of law.[99]

(e) Authorised officers

3–79 Authorised officers may be appointed by the Minister or by local authorities to carry out the functions as specified under the Act. An authorised officer may enter, by force if necessary, and inspect any premises which is, or which he reasonably suspects is, being used as an abattoir or as a knackery, enter, by force if necessary, and inspect any vehicle or container which is, or which he reasonably suspects is, being used in connection with an abattoir or with a knackery, the authorised officer may also request the production of, or search for, and inspect any records kept in such premises, vehicle or container which relate to animals, fees, or the business of an abattoir or knackery.[100] Authorised officers may also take copies of, or remove any records found in an abattoir or a knackery or on any vehicle or container for examination or for any proceedings under the Act.

3–80 The holder of an abattoir licence or a knackery licence, or any person employed by the holder of a licence shall, upon request by an authorised officer or a member of the Garda Síochána, produce all records kept on the premises and shall permit the authorised officer or the member of the Garda Síochána, to inspect, copy or remove such records.[101] The same is the case for any person in charge of any vehicle or container, which is, or which an author-

---

[97] s.18(1).
[98] s.18(3).
[99] s.18(7).
[100] s.54(1).
[101] s.54(3).

ised officer or a member of the Garda Síochána reasonably suspects is being used in connection with an abattoir or a knackery.

3–81 In respect of meat which is intended for human consumption an authorised officer or a member of the Garda Síochána, may seize, detain and remove any meat intended for human consumption which he finds in an abattoir, knackery, vehicle or container and which does not bear a health mark, or bears an unapproved health mark, or has already been marked as unfit for human consumption, or is otherwise unfit, or he reasonably suspects is unfit, for human consumption. Where any meat is detained or removed the authorised officer or Garda shall cause the meat to be examined by a veterinary inspector and, if the veterinary inspector declares that such meat is unfit for human consumption, the meat shall be marked and be destroyed or be otherwise disposed of.[102] Any person who obstructs or unreasonably delays an authorised officer or a member of the Garda Síochána while in the exercise of his powers under this Act or who fails to facilitate an inspection of a premises, vehicle or container by an authorised officer or a member of the Garda Síochána may be guilty of an offence.[103]

(f) Offences

3–82 Offences under the Abattoir Act are punishable by a fine of not over £1,000 or to a term of imprisonment of not over six months or to both the fine and the imprisonment on a summary conviction, and in respect of a conviction on indictment to a fine of not over £10,000 or to a term of imprisonment of not over three years or to both the fine and term of imprisonment.[104] The prosecution of offences may be brought and prosecuted by a local authority or by the Minister for Agriculture and Food. Summary offences may be instituted within a period of one year from the date of the commission of an offence.[105]

3–83 In a prosecution for any offence under the Abattoir Act a person who claims that a licence exists in relation to a premises, the onus or proving the existence of the licence and of its validity lies with the person making the claim.[106] In a prosecution for any offence, it is presumed until the contrary is proved that any premises in which carcass or parts of carcass or offal or viscera of any animal, or dead animals or parts of dead animals, or slaughtering or dressing equipment or instruments are found is an abattoir or a knackery.[107]

---

[102] s.54(8).
[103] s.54(9).
[104] s.56.
[105] s.57(2).
[106] s.58(1).
[107] s.58(2).

3. Knackeries

3–84 Under section 22 of the Abattoir Act a person cannot sell, offer, expose for sale, or have in his possession for the purposes of sale, or of preparation for sale, for human consumption, any part of an animal, or any meat or other product derived wholly or partly from a knackery, or which has been slaughtered or cut-up in, or which has been delivered to, or originated in, a knackery. Any person who contravenes the provisions of this section may be guilty of an offence under the Act. An offence is also committed where a person who is the occupier of any premises permits the premises to be used as a knackery, nor may the occupier of a premises use the premises as a knackery unless the occupier holds a knackery licence.

3–85 A knackery licence may be granted under section 24 of the Abattoir Act and every application for the grant or renewal of a knackery licence is accompanied by a fee of £10. Every application for the grant or renewal of a knackery licence shall relate to one premises only. Where an application is made pursuant to this section for the grant or renewal of a knackery licence, the Minister shall, before considering the application, cause the premises to which the application relates to be inspected by an authorised officer of the Minister.[108] Renewals or the granting of a knackery licence are conditional on the local authority or the Minister being satisfied that the person is a fit and proper person to hold a knackery licence, and has, in relation to the knackery concerned, complied with the provisions of the Slaughter of Animals Act 1935, and of the Act and the Regulations made under the Act.[109]

3–86 Local authorities or the Minister are required to keep a register of knackery licences and abattoir licences. The register must give the full name, address and description of the holder of the licence, an exact description of the location and the limits and extent of the knackery to which the licence relates, the date on which the licence was issued and the expiry date.[110]

3–87 Knackery licences are, like the abattoir licences, not transferable and on the death of the holder of a knackery licence the same provisions apply as in the case of the death of the holder of an abattoir licence.[111] Similar provisions as to the revocation of knackery licences apply to abattoir licences in respect to appeals to the Circuit Court.[112]

---

[108] s.25.
[109] s.26.
[110] s.27(1).
[111] s.28(1).
[112] s.31.

3–88   Whenever an authorised officer is of opinion that there is grave and immediate danger to public health or to animal health, arising from the manner in which a knackery is managed or maintained, the authorised officer may serve on the holder of the knackery licence, or on the person who seems to be, for the time being, in charge of such knackery, a notice in writing requiring the immediate closure of the knackery.[113] Similar provisions as are contained in the Act relating to abattoirs are also contained in section 33 of the Act in relation to the imposition of a duty to obey the notice in respect of knackeries as well as in the provision of offences and appeals to the District Court.

3–89   In the sphere of veterinary control and hygiene each local authority is obliged to appoint one or more whole-time veterinary inspectors to carry out the functions conferred on a veterinary inspector under the Abattoir Act. The local authority may also appoint such other veterinary inspectors as may be required and as it considers necessary, and the authority may also appoint other servants and agents to assist the veterinary inspectors.[114]

3–90   Veterinary inspectors may be appointed to carry out duties in one or more abattoirs in the functional area of the local authority, and the veterinary inspector shall attend each abattoir at such times as the local authority may determine, after consultation with the holder of the licence, and the inspector may inspect all animals, carcasses, meat, offal and viscera contained on the premises. In particular, the veterinary inspector may inspect the conditions of hygiene and maintenance at each abattoir.[115] A local authority are obliged to make arrangements, as it considers necessary, for the inspection of knackeries within its functional area. A veterinary inspector may at all reasonable times enter and inspect any abattoir or knackery for the purpose of exercising his powers and duties under this Act and the Regulations made under the Act.

3–91   A veterinary inspector may examine, and carry out such tests as he considers necessary on any animal, or part thereof, or the carcass, meat, offal or viscera of any animal which he finds in an abattoir or in a knackery and he may take and remove, without payment, samples of the animal or part thereof, or the carcass, meat, offal or viscera of any animal he finds therein, or any materials used within the premises.[116] A person who obstructs or unreasonably delays a veterinary inspector in the exercise of the inspectors powers and duties under the Act may be guilty of an offence.

---

[113] s.33(1).
[114] In relation to the appointment of veterinary inspectors, the provisions of s.59 of the Local Government Act 1955 apply in respect of the entering into agreements with other statutory bodies to carrying out of some of the functions of the local authority.
[115] s.36.
[116] s.36(5).

CHAPTER 4

Housing

A. INTRODUCTION

4–01 In the nineteenth century housing legislation sought to provide new houses for certain classes and groups within society who were unable to obtain accommodation, such as the Housing of the Working Classes Act 1890, the Housing (Ireland) Act 1919. Legislation also sought to maintain, preserve and improve existing houses as well as removing old houses especially those which were a danger to public health and safety, such as slum clearance and redevelopment of inner cities.[1] The Housing Act of 1966 was the vehicle by which earlier legislation was repealed and replaced and was then the first serious attempt at addressing the housing crisis which had been troubling the State since its foundation in 1930. The 1966 Act still forms the bulk of social housing legislation and is referred to throughout the modern housing legislation as the Principal Act. Since the Principal Act was passed, it has given local authorities, in the form of housing authorities, a major role in the development of housing in the State, at times being the only housing developer in certain parts of the State.[2]

B. PROVISION OF DWELLINGS

4–02 Section 56 of the Housing Act 1966 gave housing authorities the power to erect, acquire, purchase, convert or reconstruct or lease dwellings, includ-

---

[1] See Wylie, *Irish Law Land* (2nd ed., Dublin, 1986), para. 1.62.
[2] Which can give rise to quite a deal of interesting litigation, for an example see *Felloni v. Dublin Corporation* [1988] I.L.R.M. 133.

ing houses, flats, maisonettes and hostels, and such dwellings may be temporary or permanent. A housing authority may also construct and maintain in good order and repair roads, shops, playgrounds, places of recreation, parks, allotments, open spaces, sites for places of worship, factories, schools, offices and other buildings or land and such other works or services, as will, in the opinion of the authority, serve a beneficial purpose either in connection with the requirements of the persons for whom the dwellings are provided or of other persons.[3] Section 57 of the 1966 Act allows the housing authority to provide sites for building purposes on land which is acquired or appropriated by the authority for the purposes of the Housing Act and the authority also has the power to construct roads and lay out open spaces on the land and provide such other services and carry out such other works as may be necessary for or incidental to the development of the land for building purposes, including works or services necessary for or incidental to the development of the land for places of worship, factories, schools, shops, offices, playgrounds, places of recreation, parks and open spaces.

4–03   The management and control of dwellings or buildings or other lands, are vested in and exercised by the housing authorities under section 58 of the Housing Act 1966. The Housing Act of 1966 transferred existing functions with regard to small dwellings and the housing of working classes and cottages to the relevant housing authorities.[4] A housing authority may reconstruct, enlarge or improve a dwelling of which they are the owner and the housing authorities are required to draw up and adopt a written statement of its policy in relation to the effective performance of their functions. The housing authority may, from time to time, review the policy and make any amendments to it, or draw up and adopt a new written statement of policy.[5] A housing authority may delegate to a designated body all or any one of their functions, including maintenance, in respect of the management and control of any dwellings of which the authority is the owner. [6] Housing authorities are also allowed to provide subsidies towards the rental of houses provided by bodies which are approved of in respect to the provision of housing.[7]

C.   SHARED OWNERSHIP SCHEMES, GRANTS AND SALES

4–04   Section 56 of the Housing Act 1966 allows housing authorities to ac-

---

[3] s.56(2).
[4] ss.119 and 120 and 93 of the Housing Act 1966.
[5] s.9, Housing (Miscellaneous Provisions) Act 1992.
[6] s.9(2) of the 1992 Act.
[7] s.7 of the 1992 Act.

quire and purchase or lease houses and section 2 of the Housing (Miscellaneous Provisions) Act 1992 allows a housing authority to grant a shared ownership lease of a house. This lease may be granted for a term of between twenty and one hundred years and is granted on payment to the housing authority of purchase monies of not less than 25% and not more than 75% of the market value of the house. The shared ownership scheme must also provide that the lessee has a right to purchase the remaining interest of the housing authority, in one or more payments.

4–05 Under a shared ownership scheme the tenant is the owner of part of the property and the housing authority retains the ownership of the remainder of the property and charges a rent to the tenant of that interest.[8] The interest owned by the housing authority is secured by way of a mortgage on the property. The mortgage agreement may include terms relating to insurance of the property from fire, requirements in relation to standards of construction, works and repair and the availability in a house of water, sewage and other services, the determination of the sum of money payable by the lessee in respect of the grant of a shared ownership lease and of the rent reserved under the lease and the purchase by the lessee of the interest of the housing authority in a house and the determination of the sums of money payable.

4–06 A housing authority may also pay a subsidy towards the rent of a house which has been leased to a person under a shared ownership lease.[9] A housing authority may also pay a subsidy towards the loan charges which are incurred by a person in respect of a loan made from a financial institution of a housing authority for the acquisition or construction of a house.[10]

4–07 Where a person or their spouse provides the authority with vacant possession of a house which was supplied by the housing authority, by surrendering the tenancy or by conveying the house without compensation to the authority, or where a member of the Defence Forces who now wishes to build a house, surrenders accommodation provided by the Minister for Defence, the housing authority may provide a grant to that person in order to assist in the construction of the new house and to enable the housing authority's house to return to the use of the authority.[11]

4–08 Section 90 of the Housing Act 1966[12] allows a housing authority to sell a dwelling house to a tenant who is in occupation of the house, or to another housing authority or to a body approved under the 1992 Act. The

---

[8] s.3(2) of the 1992 Act. Rent books must be provided as *per* s.17 of the 1992 Act.
[9] s.4(1) of the 1992 Act, s.4(1).
[10] Housing Act 1988, s.3.
[11] Housing Act 1988, s.4.
[12] As amended by s.26 of the 1992 Act.

housing authority is also allowed to sell a dwelling, which is not occupied by a tenant, to any person. The purchase scheme under which the dwellings are sold is made subject to the relevant regulations by the Minister, may be restricted to a specific period of time, and is adopted by the housing authority by resolution and subject to the Local Government Act 1946 in relation to the adoption of resolutions.[13] The sale is done by way of a transfer order and if applicable may include the provision of a periodic charge in relation to maintenance or improvement of common areas. However, when disposing of a dwelling no warranty is deemed to be implied as to the state of repair or condition or the fitness for human habitation of the dwelling which is to be sold.[14]

4–09 The housing authority may refuse to dispose of a dwelling if the authority is of the opinion that the intended purchasers is not a person in need of housing or that the intended sale would leave the seller or any person who might reside with the seller without adequate housing.[15] The housing authority may give retrospective permission or consent to the mortgaging or charging or alienation of a dwelling but where consent has not been given by the housing authority the purported mortgaging, charging or alienation is null and void against all persons.[16]

D. LOANS FOR REPAIR AND IMPROVEMENT

4–10 The 1966 Housing Act allowed housing authorities to make a loan for the carrying out of reconstruction, repair or improvement works on a house. The housing authority were to be firstly satisfied that after the proposed works are carried out the house will be fit for human habitation, that the proposed works are necessary for the purpose of providing suitable housing accommodation, as well as that the house is suitable for reconstruction, repair or improvement, as the case may be.[17]

4–11 Section 40 of the Housing Act 1966 is the principle provision which allows housing authorities to carry out reconstruction, repair or improvement works on a house, provided that the authority is satisfied that after the proposed works are carried out, the house will be fit for human habitation, and that the proposed works are necessary for the purpose of providing suitable housing accommodation, and that the house is firstly suitable for reconstruction, repair or improvement.[18]

---

[13] s.90(2).
[14] s.90(8).
[15] s.90(12)(a).
[16] s.90(12)(b).
[17] s.40(1).
[18] s.40(1).

4–12 Section 8 of the Housing (Miscellaneous Provisions) Act 1979[19] provided that housing authorities could make loans to persons who wished to carry out improvement works to a house. This provision was replaced by section 11 of the Housing (Miscellaneous Provisions) Act 1992[20] which allows housing authorities to make loans allowing for the acquisition of estates or interests in or the construction of houses, or for the carrying out of improvement works to houses, or the acquisition of buildings or other land for the purpose of providing housing or the development of sites for housing. The Act also allows the conversion of a building, in whole or in part, into one or more self-contained dwelling units, the provision of hostel accommodation, or the payment of deposits for any of the above. The main provision regarding the making of loans by housing authorities for reconstruction, repair and improvement of houses is section 40 of the Housing Act 1966.

4–13 Section 5 of the Housing (Miscellaneous Provisions) Act of 1992 allows a housing authority to, with the consent of the owner, carry out, or arrange to have carried out, works of improvement or adaptation to a house not owned by the authority for the purpose of rendering the house fit for human habitation, relieving overcrowding and rendering the house more suitable for the accommodation of occupants of the house.

4–14 The housing authority may carry out such works for houses occupied by persons who have been included in the most recent assessment made by the authority under the 1988 Act, or for persons who have been accepted by the authority as being qualified to be included in the next housing assessment which will be made by the housing authority. However, the authority must be satisfied that the person's need for accommodation will be addressed by the carrying out of works and that the person can then be removed from the assessment or that the person will not need to be included in the next assessment.

4–15 The housing authority can also carry out such works on houses which are owned or provided by the housing authority and the property has been or will be vacated either by the surrender of the tenancy or through a conveyance with or without compensation being paid.

4–16 Section 12 of the Housing Act 1988 provides that the Minister for the Environment, on the application of a housing authority, may consent to the carrying out of reconstruction or improvement works to a house which has been included in a group of houses, in the ownership of the housing authority, which are in need of reconstruction by reason of defects in either their design

[19] No. 27 of 1979.
[20] No. 18 of 1992.

or construction or due to deterioration caused by age. A group of houses may also be included for reconstruction or repair where the houses are in the opinion of the Minister are reasonably necessary for the purpose of making the houses more suitable for human habitation. Where works are carried out on a house which the housing authority have sold or leased the housing authority can require the owner or lessee of the house to make a contribution as the authority sees fit or which the Minister may direct towards the costs which have been incurred by the housing authority.[21]

4–17   Section 15 of the same act allows the provision of funds to a housing authority to allow a grant or subsidy for the provision of dwellings by the authority, the improvement or reconstruction of dwellings already provided for by the authority, and the acquisition of land for the provision of dwellings or sites. The section also allows the carrying out of ancillary works in connection with the provision or the improvement of dwellings or sites as well as the provision or the improvement of sites for caravans. Section 16 of the Act allows the housing authority to guarantee a loan which has been used for the purpose of acquiring, or constructing or carrying out of improvement works to a house.

E.   REPAYMENTS AND RECOVERY

4–18   Repayments of loans made for reconstruction, repair or improvement are secured by vesting the ownership of the house in the housing authority subject to the right of redemption by the person who has borrowed from the housing authority and by charging the house with the repayment of the loan, together with any interest, where the ownership of the property is vested in another person besides the borrower then an instrument of a further charge charging the repayment of the loan must be executed. In addition, the loan is also secured by the deposit of the land certificate with the local authority.[22] Where any sum is due to the housing authority the authority may recover the loan as a simple contract debt in the relevant court.[23]

4–19   Where the loan becomes outstanding section 11 of the 1992 Act allows an authority to enter into possession of property or other land in respect of which the loan is made or, in the case of the bankruptcy of the borrower of such a loan, subject to the rights of any prior mortgagee or chargee, recover possession of the house, property or other land either under sections 84 to 89 of the Landlord and Tenant Law Amendment Act, Ireland, 1860, as if the

---

[21] s.12(4).
[22] s.40(2), loans under £200 need not be secured, s.40(3).
[23] s.40(4).

authority were the landlord and the borrower were the tenant, or by order of possession by a court in accordance with the terms of a mortgage given as security for the loan.

4–20 Where a housing authority recovers possession of a house, property or other land the housing authority, at their discretion, may sell it at the best price reasonably obtainable, or retain and use it for the purposes of any of their functions.[24] Any sum due to a housing authority by any person in respect of a housing loan may, without prejudice to any other power in that behalf, be recovered by the authority from that person as a simple contract debt in any court of competent jurisdiction.[25]

4–21 The procedure under which a housing authority may reclaim possession of dwellings which they have let under the Housing Acts is contained in section 62 of the Principal Act. Where the occupier of a dwelling or building neglects or refuses to deliver up possession of a dwelling or of a building on a demand being made by a housing authority and a statement of demand of the intention of the authority to make an application to recovery possession of the property has been made, the authority may apply to the District Court for the issue of a warrant. Where rent has been outstanding or in arrears for a period of not less than one month, or where the dwelling has been abandoned or is not actually occupied by any person then notice to quit must be served, of not less than four weeks, as now provided for in section 16 of the 1992 Act or such longer period as may be provided for under the terms of the original agreement.

4–22 Local authorities, as housing authorities are obliged to consider their overall management of housing and to the obligation the authority has to all persons in need of housing as well as to any one individual, therefore it is reasonable that a housing authority seek possession of any one dwelling without having to give reasons for so doing.[26] This was held in the case of *Dublin Corporation v. Hamilton*[27] following a case stated from the District Court whereby the District Court judge sought the opinion of the High Court on whether he had a discretion to go outside the scheme contained in section 62 of the Housing Act 1966. The District Court judge also asked the High Court to consider the provisions of section 11 of the 1988 Act as well as the provisions of the Constitution. The district judge had come to the conclusion that the formal proofs set out in section 62 of the 1966 Act were complied with but it was argued that this alone was not sufficient to justify the granting of an

---

[24] s.11(7) of the 1992 Act.
[25] s.11(12) of the 1992 Act.
[26] "Reasons" in this case refers to the maintenance of confidentiality.
[27] [1998] 2 I.L.R.M. 524.

order for possession in favour of Dublin Corporation. It was argued that a consideration of whether a demand for possession could include a consideration of section 11 of the 1988 Act as well as the provisions Article 40.1 of the Constitution.

4–23 The High Court, Geoghegan J., found that it was both reasonable and constitutional that there be available a rapid means of recovering possession. The Court also decided that a housing authority must carry out its obligations in a proper manner and must not abuse its powers or discretions. If such abuses occur the appropriate remedy is an application for judicial review, it is not a matter for the district judge to consider during a hearing under section 62 of the 1966 Act.[28]

4–24 Section 62 of the Housing Act 1966 had been previously challenged in the *State (O'Rourke) v. Kelly*,[29] where it was argued before the Supreme Court that section 62 deprives the District Judge of any real discretion in deciding to issue a warrant for recovery. The Supreme Court rejected that contention, in the judgement of the court, O'Higgins C.J. stated that:

> ". . . It is only when the provisions of section 62(1) have been complied with and the demand duly made to the satisfaction of the District justice that he must issue the warrant. In other words, it is only following the establishment of specified matters that the subsection operates. This is no different to many of the statutory provisions which, on proof of certain matters, make it mandatory on a court to make a specified order."[30]

The High Court had previously held that the conditions precedent to the issue of a warrant under subsection 3 was proof that the dwelling was provided by the local authority under the Housing Act 1996, that there was no tenancy in the dwelling, that possession had been duly demanded, that the occupier failed to give possession, that the demand stated the authority's intention, in the event of non-compliance, to apply for a warrant. Therefore the District Court judge was required to make a judicial determination as to whether or not the necessary statutory preconditions existed.[31]

4–25 Geoghegan J. also decided in the Hamilton case that it would be inconsistent with the purpose of section 62 of the 1966 Act to interpret the sec-

---

[28] At p. 548.
[29] [1983] I.R. 58.
[30] Quoted at p. 585 in the judgment of Geoghegan J. in *Dublin Corporation v. Hamilton*.
[31] Casey, *Constitutional Law in Ireland* (1987), Dublin, p. 212, this case was distinguished, however, in *State (McEldowney) v. Kelleher* [1983] I.R. 289, involving the Street and House to House Collections Act 1962 where the Supreme Court held that s.13(4) of that Act was unconstitutional which removed all discretion from the District Court on an appeal from a refusal of the gardaí to issue a permit.

tion in any other way than that formal proofs set out in the alone are required and that the district judge is not entitled to enquire into anything else. It had been argued that subsection 3 required the district court judge to also decide as to whether the housing authority was carrying out its statutory obligations towards the defendant both in a substantive sense and in the sense of affording the defendant fair procedures, including the giving of reasons by the housing authority. It was also argued that the Housing Acts should be read together as a single code and that the obligations of the housing authority should be interpreted in that way. The latter argument was accepted by Geoghegan J. while the remaining arguments were not.[32]

4–26 Housing authorities must carry out their obligations in a proper manner and must not abuse its powers or discretions.[33] Geoghegan J. did concede that judicial review was a cumbersome and expensive procedure and that the ordinary person in need of housing might not even know of the procedure, or indeed if they did whether they could afford to proceed with it, but the Court could not import into section 62 requirements which were never there, it is for the Oireachtas to alter it.[34]

F. OVERCROWDING

4–27 With respect to overcrowding of houses a housing authority may serve on the owner of a house a notice in writing specifying the maximum number and categories of persons, the house or any room may at any time be occupied without causing overcrowding, and the authority may, as respects any notice served, require the owner on whom it is served to publish, in such manner as the authority may specify, the contents of the notice.[35]

4–28 The definition of overcrowding is contained in section 63 of the 1966 Act, and this section deems a house to be overcrowded at any time when the number of persons ordinarily sleeping in the house and the number of rooms therein either are such that any two of those persons, being persons of ten years of age or more of opposite sexes and not being persons living together as husband and wife, must sleep in the same room, or are such that the free air space in any room used as a sleeping apartment, for any person is less than four hundred cubic feet, the height of the room, if it exceeds eight feet, being taken to be eight feet, for the purpose of calculating free air space.

---

[32] p. 547.
[33] At p. 548.
[34] *ibid.*
[35] Housing Act 1966, s.65(1).

4–29 Where the owner of the house is causing or permitting the house to be overcrowded, the housing authority may also serve on the owner a notice in writing requiring the owner to desist from causing or permitting overcrowding and specifying the period, being not less than twenty-one days beginning on the date of the notice, within which, or the event after the occurrence of which, the requirements of the notice are to be complied with.[36] Any person who fails to comply with a requirement of a housing authority to publish the contents of the notice as required may be guilty of an offence and may be liable to a fine of not over £25.[37] A further offence may be committed if the person on whom the notice has been served , causes or permits the house to be overcrowded, and may be liable to a fine of not over £100 or to a term of imprisonment of not over one month or to both the fine and imprisonment.[38] The owner of a house which is overcrowded may not be guilty of an offence if the overcrowding relates solely to children of the person who occupies the house.

4–30 To assist the housing authority in the exercise of its functions a housing authority may by notice in writing require the owner or occupier of a house to state in writing to the authority, within a period specified in the notice, being not less than fourteen days beginning on the date of the notice, the total number and the dimensions of the rooms in the house, and the purpose for which each such room is currently used. Information must also be provided regarding the number of occupants in the house on a date specified in the notice, the sanitary and cooking facilities available to such occupants, and such other particulars relating to the house as the housing authority may require.[39] Housing authorities are in fact under an obligation to eliminate in a realistic manner over a period of time the local accommodation of persons within its functional area.[40]

G. UNFIT HOUSES

4–31 Under the Public Health (Ireland) Act 1878 a sanitary authority may apply for an order from the District Court prohibiting the use of a house or building which has been rendered unfit for human habitation until remedial work has been done.[41]

---

[36] Housing Act 1966, s.65(2).
[37] Housing Act 1966, s.65(3).
[38] Housing Act 1966, s.65(4).
[39] Housing Act 1966, s.65(1), failure to do so may result in a fine of £25.
[40] See *County Meath VEC v. Joyce* [1994] 2 I.L.R.M. 210.
[41] s.113.

4–32   Housing authorities are also given a role in relation to the unfit houses. Where a housing authority are of the opinion that a house is unfit for human habitation in any respect, the authority shall, unless they are also of the opinion that the house is not capable of being rendered fit at a reasonable expense, serve on the owner of the house and, on any other person having an interest in the house, a notice in writing (referred to as a repairs notice). A repair notice specifies the reasons why the house is unfit for human habitation and requires the owner to execute, within a period specified in the notice, being not less than twenty-eight days, such works as may be necessary to make the house fit for human habitation. A repairs notice may specify the repairs which are to be carried out in order to prevent the structure of the house deteriorating, the owner, his servants or agents are obliged to carry out the works which are necessary to comply with the requirements of the notice.[42]

4–33   In making a decision as to whether a house is unfit for human habitation, the housing authority is to have regard to the extent to which the house is deficient as regards to stability, resistance to spread of fire, safety of staircases and common passages including the state of paving in any yard or open space appurtenant to the house. Regard is also to be had to resistance to moisture, resistance to transmission of heat, resistance to transmission of sound, resistance to infestation, water supply, sanitary arrangements and drainage, air space and ventilation, natural and artificial lighting, facilities for preparing, storing and cooking food, and to the extent to which the house does not comply with any standard or requirement of building bye-laws.[43]

4–34   The authority is also to have regard to the estimated cost of the repairs to the house as well as to the increase in the value of the house which the authority estimates will be attributable to repairing the house or rendering the house fit for human habitation. Where the housing authority is of the opinion that a house is unfit for human habitation in any respect and is not capable of being made fit in such respect at a reasonable expense, the housing authority shall serve upon the owner of the house and on any other person having an interest in the house, notice of the time and place at which the condition of the house and any offer with respect to the carrying out of works, or the future use of the house, which the owner may wish to submit will be considered by the authority.[44]

4–35   After consultation with the owner the housing authority may take an undertaking from the owner to carry out such works as will, in the opinion of the authority, render the house fit for human habitation, or that the house shall

---

[42] s.66(1).
[43] Contained in the Second Schedule to the Act.
[44] Being some time not less than twenty-one days after the service of the notice.

not be used for human habitation until the authority, on being satisfied that it has been rendered fit for the purpose, cancel the undertaking.[45] After the specified period in the undertaking, and if the works have not been carried out, or if no undertaking has been given, the housing authority may make an order prohibiting the use of the house or any part of the house, known as a closing order.

4–36 The housing authority may make an order requiring the person who has given an undertaking or the owner of the house to vacate the house or ensure that the house is vacated and to secure the house in order to make sure that the house will remain unoccupied. Within six weeks, or such longer period as the housing authority may consider reasonable, or within six weeks after the house is vacated, the housing authority may demolish the house and clear and level the site and remove any debris and the authority may secure the site by erecting a wall or barrier.[46] Where a closing order has been made in relation to a house the authority may at any time, not less than six months, after the making of an order, determine the order and may make a demolition order.[47] The housing authority may also determine a closing order if the house has been rendered fit for human habitation.[48]

4–37 If, after a repairs notice has been served and which applies to a house and the notice has not been complied with, any person who uses the house for human habitation before the house was vacant, or permits the house to be used for human habitation may be guilty of an offence and liable to a fine and a term of imprisonment of not over one month or both a fine and the term of imprisonment. Any person who allows a house to be used in contravention of a closing or demolition order or permits the house to be used, may also be guilty of an offence and to a similar fine and term of imprisonment. If after having been convicted of any of the above two offences the person again uses the house or permits the house to be used in contravention of an order, then that person may be convicted of a continuing offence and to an increased fine (£500) and to a term of imprisonment of not over six months or to both the fine and imprisonment.[49]

4–38 Enforcement of a repair notice or of a demolition order may be carried out by the housing authority under section 69 of the Housing Act 1966. If it is the case that a repairs notice of a demolition order have not been complied with within the relevant period then the owner of the house to which the no-

---

[45] s.66(5).
[46] s.66(6).
[47] s.66(10).
[48] s.66(11).
[49] s.68(3).

tice or order relates may be guilty of an offence and shall be liable on summary conviction to a fine not exceeding £1,000,[50] and the housing authority may do anything required to be done by the notice or order, or by the notice or order as varied by a court, and for that purpose the authority, their servants or agents may enter any land. The housing authority may give notice of their intention to do so to the owner of the house and, at their discretion, to any other person having an interest in the house, and if at any time after the expiration of seven days from the service of the notice and while any workman or contractor employed by the authority is carrying out works in the house any person upon whom the notice was served or any workman employed by him, or by any contractor employed by him, is in the house for the purpose of carrying out any works, the person upon whom the notice was served shall be guilty of an offence and shall be liable on summary conviction to a fine, unless it is proven to the court that there was a urgent necessity to carry out works in order to protect against danger.[51]

4–39   Where the housing authority have incurred any expense in relation to repairing a dwelling or in relation to the demolition of a house the housing authority may demand in writing from the owner of the house for payment of the expenses.[52] After fourteen days the amount due may be recovered by the sale of any materials which have been salvaged from the works carried out by the authority. The housing authority may require the occupier of the house to pay to the authority any rent or payment in lieu of rent or if the house is vacant the authority may let the house until the amount due, with interest is paid. An order may be made charging the property and all other premises held under the same tenure or under the same tenancy with the amount of the expenses together with any interest, or by recovery as a simple contract debt.[53]

H.   ASSESSMENTS FOR HOUSING NEEDS

4–40   Housing authorities, meaning a county health district, the council of the county in which such county health district is situated, a county or other borough, the corporation of such county or other borough, an urban district, the council of the district, a town having commissioners, under the Towns Improvement (Ireland) Act 1854,[54] are required to make an estimate of the existing housing requirements as well as the prospective housing requirements in the relevant functional area of the authority.[55]

---

[50]   As amended by s.33 of the Housing (Miscellaneous Provisions) Act 1992.
[51]   Maximum fine is £1,000 as per s.33 of 1992 Act.
[52]   s.71(1).
[53]   s.71(1).
[54]   Housing Act 1966, s.2.
[55]   Housing Act 1988, s.8. A functional area of a county council also includes the areas

4–41   In making an estimate of housing requirements the housing authority
is to have regard to information, derived from surveys of housing in their
functional area, relating to housing conditions, including the number of houses
which are in any respect unfit or unsuitable for human habitation, are overcrowded, are shared involuntarily or are expected to be lost to the supply of
housing over the period to which the estimate relates. Regard is also to be had
to the extent to which there are persons who are homeless or living in temporary or movable accommodation, as well as the expected changes in the size
and structure of the population of the area, the prospective housing requirements of persons residing outside the functional area of the authority to such
extent as the authority consider appropriate, and any such other information
as the authority may consider relevant.[56]

4–42   In relation to temporary dwellings bye laws may be made by a sanitary
authority regulating the use of temporary dwellings within their functional
district and the bye-laws may, in particular, provide for the securing of the
habitable condition of temporary dwellings and the cleanliness of temporary
dwellings and their surroundings, the prevention of injury to the amenities of
any locality by reason of filth, refuse, litter or other débris or noise from temporary dwellings, the securing of orderly and decent behaviour by the inhabitants of temporary dwellings, and the prevention of nuisances in relation to
temporary dwellings.[57]

4–43   The Local Government (Sanitary Services) Act of 1948[58] also regulates the use of temporary dwellings in that section 32(1) deems a temporary
dwelling to be a nuisance[59] where the temporary dwelling is in such a state as
to be a nuisance or injurious to health or the use of the temporary dwelling
gives rise to a nuisance or conditions injurious to health. Such a use would
include the absence of proper sanitary conveniences, overcrowding or other
cause. Where a temporary dwelling is deemed to be a nuisance a notice requiring the abatement of the nuisance may be served under section 110 of the
Public Health (Ireland) Act 1878 on the occupier of the site of the dwelling.
Section 33 of the 1948 Act gives the District Court the power to make an order
prohibiting or restricting the erection or retention of a temporary dwelling or
vessel at a place or within a specified area.

4–44   Housing assessments are to be reviewed not less than every three years
and an assessment of the need for the provision by the authority of adequate

---

under town urban district councils, and a housing authority may act outside of their own
functional area, s.109 Housing Act 1966.
[56] s.8(2).
[57] Local Government Act 1948, s.30.
[58] No. 29 of 1948.
[59] Within the meaning of s.107 of the Public Health (Ireland) Act 1878 as amended.

and suitable housing accommodation for persons whom the authority have reason to believe require, or are likely to require, accommodation from the authority, and who are in need of such accommodation and are unable to provide it from their own resources.[60] A housing authority, in making an assessment, is also to have regard to the need for housing of persons who are homeless, or travellers,[61] persons who are living in accommodation that is unfit for human habitation or is materially unsuitable for their adequate housing, persons who are living in overcrowded accommodation, as well as persons who are sharing accommodation with another person or persons and who, in the opinion of the housing authority, have a reasonable requirement for separate accommodation. Other persons to take into account when making an assessment of the housing requirements of the functional area are young persons leaving institutional care or without family accommodation, and are in need of accommodation for medical or compassionate reasons, or who are elderly, disabled or handicapped, or persons who are not reasonably able to meet the cost of the accommodation which they are occupying or to obtain suitable alternative accommodation.[62] In making an assessment the housing authority may take into account the requirements of persons who are residing outside of the functional area of the authority.[63]

4–45 Before making an assessment a housing authority is obliged to give one month's notice to any housing authority whose functional area adjoins the functional area of the authority, to any health board whose functional area includes or adjoins the functional area of the health board, and other bodies, including voluntary or non-profit making organisations engaged in the provision of housing accommodation or other organisations whose purposes include the provision of accommodation, shelter or welfare.[64]

4–46 Section 20 of the Housing Act 1988 places an onus on the housing authority, in the making of an assessment, to have regard to the maintenance of a reasonable balance between the needs of the various classes of persons within the assessment. This section was amended by the 1992 Act [65] in that housing authorities must draw up and adopt a written statement of the housing authorities policy to counteract undue segregation in housing between people of different social backgrounds.

---

[60] s.9(1).
[61] See *O'Reilly v. O'Sullivan & Dun Laoghaire Rathdown Co. Co.*, unreported, High Court, July 25, 1996, and *Mongan v. South Dublin Co. Co.*, unreported, High Court, July 31, 1995.
[62] s.9(2).
[63] s.9(5).
[64] s.9(4).
[65] s.28 inserted s.20(1A).

4–47 Within a housing assessment a housing authority is obliged to make a scheme determining the order of priority which is to be accorded in the letting of dwellings, of which the housing authority is the owner, to persons in need of accommodation.[66]

A. Homeless persons

4–48 Under the Housing Act of 1988[67] a person is regarded as being homeless by a housing authority if there is no accommodation available which, in the opinion of the authority, the person, together with any other person who normally resides with him or her or who might reasonably be expected to reside with him, can reasonably occupy or remain in occupation. A person may also be regarded as being homeless if that person is living in a hospital, county home, night shelter or other such institution, and is so living because that person has no accommodation, and that person is, in the opinion of the authority, unable to provide accommodation out of the person's own resources.[68]

4–49 A request for accommodation may be made to a housing authority by or on behalf of a person who is homeless.[69] The housing authority may then make arrangements, including financial arrangements for the provision of accommodation for a person who is homeless, or may provide a person who is homeless with assistance, including financial assistance, or may rent accommodation, or arrange lodgings or contribute to the cost of such accommodation or lodgings. If the authority provide accommodation or lodgings they may impose a charge, having regard to the means of the person and the cost to the authority of the accommodation or lodgings and such other matters as the authority may consider appropriate.[70] However, a charge which is made in respect of accommodation or lodgings to a person who is homeless is not subject to the terms of any rent scheme for houses which are let by the housing authority.

4–50 The housing authority may require a person to vacate accommodation or lodgings provided for persons who are homeless if the person is now able to provide accommodation from their own resources, or if the accommodation or lodgings were no longer available the person would not be homeless. This last provision seems to have been drafted so as to include situations whereby a person who was classified as homeless now has a home arising from other resources other than personal resources, for example finding a home with rela-

---

[66] s.11(1).
[67] No. 28 of 1988.
[68] s.2.
[69] s.10(2).
[70] s.10(5).

tives. The housing authority may also require a person who has been provided with accommodation or lodgings to vacate if the person has failed to pay a charge for the accommodation.[71] Once a person who is homeless has been given accommodation that person may still be included in any assessment which is made under section 9 of the 1988 Act.

4–51 Housing authorities are under a statutory obligation to perform their functions under the Housing Acts in a rational and reasonable manner and to provide accommodation for persons defined as homeless.[72]

B. Provision for traveller accommodation

4–52 The Housing (Traveller Accommodation) Act of 1998[73] amended the Housing Acts 1966 to 1997 by making provision for the accommodation needs of travellers and to provide for the appointment of a national traveller accommodation consultative committee as well as local traveller accommodation consultative committees.[74]

4–53 The National Traveller Accommodation Consultative Committee is appointed by the Minister for the Environment and Local Government and advises the Minister in relation to any general matter concerning accommodation for travellers and any other matter which may be referred to it by the Minister.[75] The National Committee may advise the Minister on the most appropriate measures for improving, at local level, the consultation with and the participation of travellers regarding the provision and management of accommodation. The National Committee may also advise the Minister regarding general matters concerning the preparation, adequacy, implementation and co-ordination of traveller accommodation programmes.[76] The National Committee is to consist of not more than twelve members,[77] the chairman is appointed by the Minister and one person each is nominated by the Minister for Justice, Equality and Law Reform, the General Council of County Councils, the Association of Municipal Authorities of Ireland, two persons by the County and City Managers' Association, three persons nominated to the Minister by bodies representing travellers concerned with the accommodation for travellers as the Minister may determine, one civil servant from the Department of the En-

---

[71] s.10(8).
[72] *County Meath VEC v. Joyce* [1994] 2 I.L.R.M. 210.
[73] No. 33 of 1998.
[74] See *County Meath VEC v. Joyce* [1994] 2 I.L.R.M. 210, where the High Court held that one of the objectives of the Housing Acts was to solve a real housing problem in relation to traveller accommodation.
[75] s.19(1).
[76] s.19(2).
[77] Whose term is limited to not more than three years, s.20(4).

vironment and Local Government, and two persons who, in the opinion of the Minister, have experience in relation to accommodation for travellers or who are concerned with the general welfare of travellers.[78]

4–54   Local authorities appoint the local consultative committee to advise on the provision and management of accommodation for travellers.[79] The local committee may advise the local authority on the preparation and implementation of any accommodation programme for the functional area of the local authority, on the management of accommodation for travellers and may provide a liaison between travellers and members and officials of the local authority.[80] The composition of the local committee is made up of members of the local authority, officials of the local authority, representatives of local travellers and traveller bodies, and one member from each of the relevant housing authorities within the administrative county concerned. Local authority members may not exceed one half of the membership of the committee, while at least a quarter of the committee must be composed of representatives of local travellers and traveller bodies.[81]

4–55   When a housing authority is making a housing assessment under section 9 of the Housing Act 1988[82] the authority is obliged to make an assessment of the need for sites for traveller accommodation in their area.[83] The housing authority while making an assessment[84] are to have regard to the estimate of travellers families and households for whom accommodation will be required within their area as well as the need for sites with limited facilities referred to in section 13 of the 1988 Act as well as the views of the local consultative committee. Section 13 of the Housing Act 1988 related to the provision of sites for travellers and applies to persons belonging to the class of persons who traditionally pursue or have pursued a nomadic way of life. Under section 13 the housing authority may provide, improve, manage and control sites for caravans used by travellers and may carry out any works incidental to the provision, improvement, management or control, including the provision of services for these sites. Section 13 also provided that the housing authority may, in respect to the use of a site provided by it or of any services or facilities provided or made available in connection with the site, charge for same, being a simple contract debt recoverable in the usual manner.[85]

---

[78] s.20(2).
[79] Appointments to local committees is a reserved function, s.22(3).
[80] s.21(3).
[81] s.22(1).
[82] No. 28 of 1988.
[83] s.6(1).
[84] Assessments made by urban district are to forwarded to the county councils, except for the UDC of Bray and Dundalk, s.6(6).
[85] s.13(4).

4–56 Before the housing authority prepare an accommodation programme or a draft of an amendment or replacement accommodation plan, the authority is obliged to give notice in writing to any housing authority which adjoins the functional area of the housing authority making the plan or to the urban district council within the functional area of the housing authority. Notice is also required to be given to a health board within, or adjoining, the functional area, to the local consultative committee, any local community bodies which the housing authority consider appropriate and any other body, including voluntary or non-profit making bodies that are engaged in the provision of accommodation, shelter and welfare.[86]

4–57 The housing authority is obliged to publish a notice in not less than one newspaper circulating within the functional area of the authority.[87] The notice must state that the authority proposes to adopt, amend or replace an accommodation programme, that the draft of the programme will be available for inspection at the offices of the authority, and that submissions in writing may be made to the authority within two months of the publication of the notice. A submission from the manager of a housing authority is required as soon as may be after the date by which the submissions are to be received.[88] Within the report the manager is required to summarise the matters which are contained in submissions received by the authority, specifying the names of the persons who made the submissions, specifying the response of the housing authority and indicating whether it is proposed to proceed with the draft of the programme or modify or not proceed with the programme.[89]

4–58 Within the accommodation programme the housing authority shall include the most recent assessment made by the housing authority and any particulars concerning the accommodation needs of travellers, including a statement of the policy of the housing authority concerning meeting the accommodation needs of travellers and specifing the strategy of the relevant housing authority concerning the implementation of the accommodation programme. The programme must also include a statement of the measures implementing the provision of the range of accommodation required to meet accommodation needs which have been identified, the provision of assistance to travellers to provide accommodation for their own use, the provision of assistance to bodies specified under section 6 of the Housing (Miscellaneous Provisions) Act 1992,[90] and the proper management, including assistance towards the management of accommodation for travellers.

---

[86] s.8.

[87] s.9(1).

[88] s.11.

[89] Managers report is to be submitted to the members of the housing authority not late than three months before the date specified by the Minister under s.7.

[90] No. 18 of 1992.

4–59   In preparing an accommodation programme the housing authority shall have regard to the distinct needs and family circumstances of travellers, the provision of sites to address the accommodation needs of travellers other than as their normal place of residence and having regard to the annual patterns of movement by travellers.[91]

4–60   If a housing authority fails to adopt an accommodation programme by the date which has been specified by the Minister[92] the manager may by order adopt the draft accommodation programme which was submitted. As soon as the programme has been adopted the authority must publish a notice in at least one newspaper circulating in the area stating that the programme has been adopted and where it may be inspected and that copies may be obtained. The authority must then forward copies to the bodies mentioned under section 8 and to those to whom it gave notice of their intention to make a programme.[93]

4–61   Once the programme has been adopted the housing authority is to take any reasonable steps which are necessary for implementing the programme.[94] Other housing authorities are also to take such steps as are necessary for the implementation of proposals for the functional area of the housing authority especially as regards the provision of accommodation for travellers.[95]

4–62   A housing authority is obliged to review an accommodation programme at least once in each three year period, or at an earlier time which may be specified by the Minister or at any time during the period to which the programme relates.[96]

4–63   A housing authority may provide accommodation for travellers even if an accommodation programme has not been adopted under the Act.[97] The city or the county manager may exercise any of the powers granted to that office under the City and County Management (Amendment) Act 1955[98] in relation to housing in emergency situations.[99] Housing authorities are also allowed under section 25 to make a loan for the acquisition or repair of a caravan or for the acquisition of land for the purpose of providing a site and any construction works required for that purpose.

---

[91] s.10(3).
[92] Or within the period specified in ss.10 and 13(2).
[93] s.15.
[94] s.16(1).
[95] s.16(3).
[96] s.17.
[97] s.23.
[98] No. 12 of 1955.
[99] s.24.

4–64 Section 56(2) of the Housing Act of 1966[100] provided that a housing authority may erect, acquire, purchase, convert or reconstruct, lease or otherwise provide dwellings and these dwellings may be temporary or permanent and the 1988 Act applied this section to the needs of travellers. The Housing (Traveller Accommodation) Act amended the Housing Act of 1988 in providing that housing authorities may provide, improve, manage and control sites for caravans used by travellers or sites with limited facilities for travellers.[101]

4–65 The 1998 Act also amended section 10(1) of the Housing (Miscellaneous Provisions) Act of 1992 which deals with the removal of temporary dwellings from certain locations. Section 10 of the 1988 Act provides that where, without lawful authority, a person erects, places, occupies or otherwise retains a temporary dwelling in a public place and that the temporary dwelling is within a five mile radius of any site which is provided, managed or controlled by a housing authority under section 13 of the 1988 Act, relating to the provision of sites for travellers, or any site which is provided or managed through assistance under section 6 of the 1992 Act, and the temporary dwelling could, in the opinion of the housing authority, be accommodated on the existing site, the housing authority may serve a notice requiring the removal of the temporary dwelling to the provided site.

4–66 The housing authority may also serve a notice requiring the removal of a temporary dwelling where the place where the temporary dwelling is situated is unfit for human habitation due to the lack or inadequacy of water supply, sanitation or other essential services, or the temporary dwelling is likely to obstruct or interfere with the use of public or private amenities or facilities, or the maintenance of such amenities or facilities or is likely to constitute or constitutes a significant risk to personal health, public health or safety.

4–67 A notice may also be served requiring the removal of a temporary dwelling where there is within a one mile radius a site which is provided, managed or controlled by a housing authority for the use of travellers or any other traveller accommodation. A notice may also be served where the temporary dwelling is causing a nuisance or obstruction to the occupants of that site or traveller accommodation or other dwellings within the vicinity of that site or that traveller accommodation or that the temporary dwelling creates a risk to the quality of water, sanitary, electrical or other services associated with that site or traveller accommodation or other dwellings within the vicinity of that site or traveller accommodation.

4–68 The notice which is to be served under section 10 shall specify the

---

[100] No. 21 of 1966.
[101] s.13 of the Housing Act 1988 as amended.

location and description of the temporary dwelling to which it relates, the location of the site to which the temporary dwelling is required to be removed to or that the temporary dwelling is to be required to be removed to at least a distance of one mile from the specified site. The notice is also to include to specify the period, being not less than twenty four hours, from the time at which the notice is served, within which the requirements of the notice are to be complied with, and shall state the statutory consequences of failure to comply with the requirements of the notice.[102]

4–69 Any person who is served with a notice under section 10, and fails in any respect to comply with any requirement of the notice may be guilty of an offence. Where, in the opinion of the housing authority, the requirements of the notice have not been complied with in all or in any respects, then, the housing authority may, without further notice, remove or procure the removal of the temporary dwelling. The temporary dwelling may be removed to the site specified in the notice or to a location that is not less than one mile from the site referred to in subsection (1)(c), or where the housing authority is for any reason prevented from so doing, to another location for storage by or on behalf of the housing authority. If a temporary dwelling has been removed by the housing authority without the knowledge of any person claiming to own, occupy or retain it, or without that person or persons presence, the housing authority is obliged to serve upon such person or persons a notice stating where the temporary dwelling has been removed to or where it is being stored.[103]

4–70 Any person who obstructs or impedes or assists a person to obstruct or impede a housing authority in the exercise of their functions under section 10 may be guilty of an offence.[104]

I. SCHEMES FOR LETTING DWELLINGS

4–71 A housing authority is obliged to make a scheme determining the order of priority which is to be accorded in the letting of dwellings which are provided by the housing authority and of which they are the owner in the letting of dwellings to persons in need of accommodation. These persons must be, in the opinion of the housing authority, unable to provide accommodation from their own resources, and whose need for accommodation has been included in the most recent assessment made by the authority or that it has been accepted by the authority, after having already made an assessment, that the person should be included in the assessment.

---

[102] s.10(2) of the 1992 Act as amended.
[103] The Acts have not made a provision for any expenses to be charged for storage or removal of temporary dwellings.
[104] s.10(6).

4–72   A scheme made under section 11 must provide that the housing authority may, from time to time, determine, as they see fit, to set aside for persons of such category or categories as the authority may decide, a particular number or proportion of the dwellings becoming available to the authority for letting.[105] The scheme must also provide that the housing authority, in applying its terms to a person, may disregard the accommodation that person is occupying where it is the case that the authority have reason to believe that the person has deliberately or without good and sufficient reason done or failed to do anything (other than an action or omission in good faith) as a result of which the accommodation the person is so occupying is less suitable for his adequate housing than other accommodation which it would have been, or would be, reasonable for that person to occupy. Housing authorities are also obliged, when making a scheme to make particular provision for persons in need of accommodation arising from an emergency.[106]

4–73   In the making of a scheme for priority letting, the housing authority may obtain and when obtained, the authority shall, have regard to a report from a medical officer of the relevant health board.[107] Housing authorities may, from time to time, review a scheme and as they see fit make amendments to the scheme, and the making of a scheme as well as any amendments to the scheme are reserved functions.[108]

J.   HOUSING (MISCELLANEOUS PROVISIONS) ACT 1997[109]

4–74   The Housing (Miscellaneous Provisions) Act 1997[110] was enacted in order to amend the Housing Acts 1966 to 1992, as well as the Social Welfare Acts, and to make provision to redress the intimidation of certain persons. The Act provides for the application to the District Court for an order, known as an excluding order, by a tenant in respect of a house which is let to the tenant by the housing authority against a person, including a joint tenant, whom the tenant making the application believes to be engaging in anti-social behaviour.

4–75   Anti-social behaviour includes the manufacture, production, prepara-

---

[105] Schemes may be inspected during office hours by any person, s.11(12), see *County Meath VEC v. Joyce* [1994] 2 I.L.R.M. 210.
[106] s.11(2).
[107] s.11(4).
[108] s.11(6).
[109] Came into operation from 1 July, 1997.
[110] No. 21 of 1997.

tion, importation, exportation, sale, supply, possession for the purposes of sale or supply, or distribution of a controlled drug,[111] as well as any behaviour which causes or is likely to cause any significant or persistent danger, injury, damage, loss or fear to any person living, working or otherwise lawfully in or in the vicinity of a house provided by a housing authority under the Housing Acts, 1966 to 1997, or a housing estate in which the house is situated and, without prejudice to the foregoing, includes violence, threats, intimidation, coercion, harassment or serious obstruction of any person.[112]

4–76   A housing authority may apply to the District Court for an excluding order against a person whom the housing authority believes to be engaging in anti-social behaviour.[113] The housing authority must, having consulted the tenant and the health board for the area, believe that a tenant may be deterred or prevented by violence, threat or fear from pursing an application for an excluding order and the authority considers that, in the interest of good estate management, it is appropriate to apply for the excluding order.[114] The term good estate management includes the securing or promotion of the interests of any tenants, lessees, owners or occupiers, whether individually or generally, in the enjoyment of any house, building or land provided by a housing authority under the Housing Acts, 1966 to 1997, as well as the avoidance, prevention or abatement of anti-social behaviour in any housing estate in which is situate a house provided by a housing authority under the Housing Acts.[115]

4–77   On the hearing of an application for an excluding order, the court, if it is of the opinion that there are reasonable grounds for believing that the respondent has been engaged in anti-social behaviour, may direct the respondent to leave the dwelling, and may also prohibit the respondent for the period during which the order is in force from entering or being in the vicinity of the house or from the vicinity of a specified housing estate.[116]

4–78   An excluding order may, if the court thinks fit, prohibit the respondent from causing or attempting to cause any intimidation, coercion, harassment or obstruction of, threat to, or interference with the tenant or other occupant of any house concerned,[117] and where an excluding order has been made, the tenant or the housing authority, or the respondent, may apply to have the order varied, and the court may make whatever order as it considers appropriate in

---

[111] Within the meaning of the Misuse of Drugs Acts 1977 and 1984.
[112] s.1(1).
[113] See District Court (Housing (Miscellaneous Provisions) Act 1997) Rules 1999, S.I. No. 217 of 1999. Proceedings may be heard otherwise than in public.
[114] s.3(1).
[115] s.1(1).
[116] s.3(3).
[117] s.3(4).

the circumstances.[118] Excluding orders expire three years after the date of the making or the order, although an order can be made for a shorter time as the court may decide.[119]

4–79 On making an application for an excluding order or between the making of the application and the determination of the application, and the court is of the opinion that there are reasonable grounds for believing that there is an immediate risk of significant harm to the tenant or other occupant of the house if an order is not made immediately, the court may make an interim excluding order.[120] The interim excluding order may direct the respondent, if residing at the house in respect of which the application was made, to leave that house, and prohibit the respondent from entering or being in the vicinity of that house or any other specified house or being in or in the vicinity of any specified housing estate until further order of the court or until such other time as the court shall specify.[121] An interim excluding order may, if the court thinks fit, prohibit the respondent from causing or attempting to cause any intimidation, coercion, harassment or obstruction of, threat to, or interference with the tenant or other occupant of any house concerned. Interim excluding orders may be varied in the same manner as an excluding order made under section 3.

4–80 In exceptional cases where a court considers it necessary or expedient in the interests of justice, an interim excluding order may be made *ex parte*, notwithstanding the fact that the summons or other notice of the application is ordinarily required to be duly served on the respondent to the application for an excluding order has not been so served.[122] In the case where a Garda or a housing officer of a housing authority or a health board states to the court that he or she believes that a person is or has been engaged in anti-social behaviour, then, if the Court is satisfied that there are reasonable grounds for such belief and that another person would be deterred or prevented by violence, threat or fear from providing evidence in that regard, the statement shall be evidence of such anti-social behaviour.[123]

4–81 An excluding or interim excluding order shall take effect on notification of its making being given to the respondent and an oral communication to the respondent by or on behalf of the tenant or the housing authority, of the fact that an excluding order or interim excluding order has been made, together with production of a copy of the order, shall be taken to be sufficient

---

[118] s.3(6).
[119] s.3(7).
[120] s.4(1).
[121] s.4(1)(b).
[122] s.4(3).
[123] s.21.

notification to the respondent of the making of the order.[124] If it is the case that the respondent is present at the court at which the excluding or interim excluding order is made, the respondent shall be taken to have been notified of its making.[125] The effect of an appeal of the making of an excluding order, is to stay the operation of the order, unless the court determines otherwise, and an appeal from an interim excluding order does not stay the operation of the order.[126]

4–82   A respondent who contravenes an excluding or an interim excluding order may be guilty of an offence and may be liable on a summary conviction to a fine of not over £1,500 or, at the discretion of the court, to imprisonment for a term not exceeding 12 months, or to both the imprisonment and the fine. The imposition of a fine or a term of imprisonment by a court is made without prejudice to the law as to contempt of court or any other liability, whether civil or criminal, that may be incurred by the respondent.[127]

4–83   On the making or the varying or the discharge of an order a copy of the order is to be given, as soon as practicable, to the applicant, the respondent, the housing authority and health board, and the member in charge of the Garda station in which the house in relation to which the application for the order is situate, however, this does not affect the validity of any order made under the Act.[128]

4–84   Where the authority considers that a person who is being considered for a letting of a house by the housing authority and that person is or has been engaged in anti-social behaviour or that a letting to that person would not be in the interest of good estate management, or where the person fails to provide information, including information relating to persons residing or to reside with that person, which is requested by the housing authority and which the authority considers necessary in connection with an application for the letting, the authority may refuse or defer to make a letting of a dwelling to that person.[129] Likewise, where a tenant has applied to purchase a dwelling under section 90 of the Housing Act 1966 or through a purchase scheme, the housing authority may refuse to sell the dwelling to that tenant if the authority considers that the tenant is or has been engaged in anti-social behaviour or that the sale would not be in the interest of good estate management.[130] To

---

[124] s.6.
[125] s.6(3).
[126] s.8.
[127] s.5.
[128] s.7.
[129] s.14(1).
[130] s.14(2).

allow local authorities to acquire the necessary information as to whether a person is engaging in anti-social behaviour, section 15 allows a housing authority to request information from another housing authority or from the Criminal Assets Bureau, the Gardaí, the Minister for Social Welfare, a health board, or an approved body under the Housing (Miscellaneous Provisions) Act 1992.

4–85 The Act has also made provision for the removal of illegal occupiers of local authority housing. Where a house provided by a housing authority or any part of it is occupied, whether continuously or not, by a person, other than the tenant or a person who has failed to vacate a house on termination of a tenancy, the local authority may send notification to a Garda that the authority believes that the person is or has been engaged in anti-social behaviour and that it is necessary in the interest of good estate management that the said person be required to leave the house, the Garda may direct that the person leave the house immediately in a peaceable and orderly manner.[131] A Garda may arrest a person who does not comply with the direction to vacate, without warrant, and may enter the dwelling by the use of reasonable force and may search any place, including a dwelling where the person is or where the Garda believes that person to be.

4–86 If that person fails to comply with a direction from a Garda to vacate the dwelling then an offence may have been committed and the person may be liable to a fine of not over £1,500 on a summary conviction or to a term of imprisonment of not over twelve months or to both the fine and the term of imprisonment.[132] Under section 18 a person who causes or attempts to cause any threat, intimidation or harassment, coerces, obstructs, impedes, or interferes with, an officer or employee of a housing authority or of a health board or a member of the family of such officer or employee or any person who provides or is to provide evidence in any proceedings under the Housing Act 1966, or this Act, may be guilty of an offence.

---

[131] s.20(1).
[132] s.20(2).

CHAPTER 5

Derelict sites

A. DERELICT SITES ACT 1990[1]

5–01 The Derelict Sites Act of 1990, which replaced the 1961 Act, was enacted to enable local authorities to prevent land from being or becoming a derelict site, and to enable local authorities to require owners or occupiers to improve sites. The Act also allows local authorities to compulsorily acquire sites which have become or are likely to become derelict.

5–02 Under the 1990 Act a "derelict site" means any land which detracts, or which is likely to detract, to a material degree from the amenity, character or appearance of land in the neighbourhood of the land because of the existence of structures which are in a ruinous, derelict or dangerous condition, or there is neglected, unsightly or objectionable condition of the land or any structures on the land, or the site is derelict because of the presence of litter, rubbish or waste, otherwise than by right under law.[2] Section 9 of the Act places a duty on every owner and occupier of property to take all reasonable steps to ensure that land does not become or does not continue to be a derelict site. Section 10 of the Act obliged the local authority to take all reasonable steps to ensure that any land situate in their functional area does not become or continue to be a derelict site. This duty includes the exercise of any appropriate statutory power

---

[1] No. 14 of 1990 came into operation June 27, 1990, the Act may not be applied in relation to any rights or powers of the Minister for Finance, the Commissioners for Public Works in Ireland, any local authority, given under the National Monuments Acts in relation to national monuments or historic monuments.

[2] s.3.

by the local authority to ensure that a property does not become or continue to be a derelict site.

5–03 If the local authority are of the opinion that it is necessary to do so, and in order to prevent land from becoming or continuing to be derelict, the local authority shall serve a notice in writing on any person who appears to be the owner or occupier of the land.[3] The notice specifies the measures which the local authority or the Minister,[4] consider necessary in order to prevent the land from becoming or continuing to be a derelict site and shall direct the person on whom the notice is being served to take such measures as may be specified in the notice, and specifies a period, or not less than one month, within which such measures are to be taken. The notice is not to have effect until the expiration of fourteen days from the date of service of the notice or if any representations are made then the notice is not to have effect until the date on which the local authority notifies the person making the representations that they have been considered.[5] These representations on behalf of the owner or occupier, which must be in writing, may be made within fourteen days from the date of the service of the notice.

5–04 Where the owner or occupiers do not, within the specified period, comply with the requirements of the notice, the local authority may take such measures as they deem appropriate to give effect to the terms of the notice and any expense incurred may be recovered from the owner or occupier as a simple contract debt in the relevant court.[6]

B .   R E G I S T E R   O F   S I T E S

5–05 Derelict sites are also liable to be placed on a register, which every local authority are obliged to keep, but before such sites are placed on the register, the local authority are required to give any owner and occupier notice of their intention to place the property on the register.[7] As a preference local authorities hope that the service of the notice to carry out remedial works will ensure that the property is improved, but in the situation where works are not carried out, and where the local authority are unable to carry out the works themselves the property may be entered on the register of derelict sites.

---

[3] s.11.
[4] The Minister may direct the local authority to serve a notice or to carry out works on a site, s.12.
[5] s.11(2).
[6] s.11(5), under s.11(6) the carrying out of these works are "exempted developments" within the meaning of the Local Government (Planning and Development) Acts, 1963 to 1983.
[7] s.8.

5–06   The significance of placing a site on the register of derelict sites is that the owners or occupiers face derelict sites levy which can be charged on the property,[8] and further that the local authority can acquire the property compulsorily or by agreement.[9] Section 22 of the Derelict Sites Act, 1990 requires local authorities to determine the market value of derelict sites on urban land for the purposes of a derelict sites levy payable by the owners of such land. The section also allows appeals to the Valuation Tribunal against local authorities' determinations.[10]

5–07   Before entering the property onto the register the authority is obliged to ascertain, by reasonable enquiry, the ownership of the property and who the occupiers may be, and are obliged to consider any representations which any owner or occupier may make (in writing) and which is made within the period mentioned in the notice. However, it is up to the local authority to make a final decision as to whether the site is entered onto the register, and may remove the site from the register when it considers it no longer appropriate. Once the terms of the notice to place the site on the register have been complied with the local authority can then remove the property from the register.

C. ACQUISITION BY LOCAL AUTHORITY

5–08   In the case where the local authority wishes to acquire the site by compulsory purchase the local authority is required to firstly, publish their intention in one or more newspapers circulating in their functional area, describing the land, naming the place where a map of the site can be inspected and the manner in which the objections to the acquisition of the land may be made to the local authority. The local authority is also obliged to serve on every owner[11], and occupier and lessee[12] of the land a notice in the prescribed form stating their intention to acquire the derelict site and detailing similar information as the newspaper notices.

5–09   Objections to compulsory acquisition of a derelict site can be made under section 16 of the Act by any of the persons upon whom notices of the proposed compulsory acquisition of the derelict site have been served. Such

---

[8]   s.23(2), 1992 was prescribed as the year in which the derelict sites levy began, S.I. 286 of 1991.

[9]   s.14.

[10]   See Derelict Sites (Appeal Fees) Regulations, 1991, S.I. 149 of 1991.

[11]   Owner is defined in this section as being a person other than a mortgagee not in possession, who is entitled to dispose of the fee simple interest in the property and also includes a person entitled to the rents and profits of the land under a lease or agreement having an unexpired term of over three years, s.15(2).

[12]   Except tenants who have a tenancy for a month or a period of less than a month, s.15(1)(b).

objections are required to be made within the time period specified in the notice of acquisition, and where an objection is made against compulsory acquisition the site may not be compulsorily acquired by the local authority without consent of the Minister of the Environment.[13] Following an objection the local authority apply to the Minister for consent for the acquisition and such an application is to be accompanied with the objection, a copy of the relevant map, the comments of the authority. The comments of the local authority are then forwarded by the Minister to the person who objected to the acquisition and has the right to reply to the Minister regarding the application within twenty one days, after which the Minister may make a decision.[14]

5–10 When the provisions of section 15 have been complied with, or where no objection is received under section 16 or an objection is withdrawn or the Minister gives his consent to the compulsory acquisition, the local authority may by order acquire the derelict site by way of a vesting order.[15] Following the making of a vesting order the local authority are obliged to publish, within fourteen days after making the order, on one or more newspapers circulating in the area the fact of the making of the order and a description of the site to which it relates. The authority are also obliged to serve on every person appearing to the authority as having an interest notice of the fact that an order has been made.[16]

5–11 Following the making of a vesting order, and within twelve months, any person who has any estate or interest in or right in respect of the derelict site, that person may apply to the local authority for compensation in respect of that right, interest or estate.[17] The compensation which is to be paid in respect of the site shall, in default of agreement, be determined by arbitration under the Acquisition of Land (Assessment of Compensation) Act, 1919, and any sums due to the local authority on the site, whether derelict sites levy[18] or on foot of any court order may be deducted from the amount of compensation payable.

5–12 Section 20 of the Derelict Sites Act allows a local authority to use the site acquired for any purpose connected with its statutory functions.

---

[13] s.16(3).
[14] s.16(5).
[15] s.18 prescribes the form of the vesting order and the procedure for registration.
[16] s.17(3).
[17] s.19.
[18] Levies may be charged on derelict sites under part three of the Act.

D.   OTHER PROVISIONS

5–13   Part five of the Act imposes a duty on occupiers of any property or structure to give details of ownership of the site or structure within fourteen days after having been so required, and any person who fails to provide the information or who provides false or misleading information may be guilty of an offence and liable, on summary conviction, to a fine not exceeding £1,000.[19]

5–14   An authorised person, appointed by the local authority or the Minister, may enter on any land at all reasonable times between the hours of 9 am and 6 pm for any purpose within the terms of the Act, and this authorised person may do all things reasonably necessary for the purposes of the Act, such as surveying, making plans, take levels, make extractions and examine the depth and nature of the subsoil.[20] However, if the entry is opposed by the occupier or the owner refused to permit entry, any entry may not take place unless it has been authorised by an order of a judge of the District Court.[21] Where an owner or occupier is unable to carry out remedial works required by the local authority due to the fact that some other person refuses permission for the works to be carried out, the person who wishes to carry out the works may apply to the District Court for an order to authorise the carry out of any necessary works, and if the Court is of the view that such consent is being unreasonably withheld, the District Court may, at its sole discretion, deem the consent to have been given and direct the carrying out of the necessary measures.[22]

---

[19] s.30.
[20] s.30(2).
[21] s.30(3).
[22] s. 32.

CHAPTER 6

Compulsory purchase

A. INTRODUCTION[1]

6–01 The Public Health (Ireland) Act 1878 gave powers relating to public health and other matters, as well as imposed duties on urban and rural sanitary authorities. Section 203 of the Act of 1878 gave the sanitary authorities the power to acquire land compulsorily through a provisional order made by the Local Government Board. Modern legislation has now given local authorities, the power to acquire land through compulsory purchase orders for a variety of purposes all of which are geared toward the public interest.

B. COMPULSORY ACQUISITION OF PROPERTY

1. Acquisition of Land (Assessment of Compensation) Act of 1919

6–02 Section 1 of the Acquisition of Land (Assessment of Compensation) Act 1919[2] provides that where land is, under any statute, to be acquired compulsorily by a Government Department or by any local authority, any question relating to the figure for compensation and any question regarding the apportionment of any rent payable under a lease, if one exists, shall be

---

[1] For a more detailed examination see McDermott and Woulfe, *Complusory Purchase and Compensation: Law and Practice in Ireland* (Dublin, 1992).
[2] As amended by the Property Values (Arbitrations and Appeals) Act 1960.

referred to and be determined by the arbitration of one or a panel of official arbitrators.[3]

6–03   A Reference Committee, meaning the Reference Committee established by section 1 of the Act of 1919[4] may appoint one or more persons having special knowledge of the valuation of land or having such other qualifications as the Reference Committee considers suitable to be an arbitrator or arbitrators, and a person so appointed is known as a property arbitrator.[5] The Reference Committee consists of the Chief Justice, the President of the High Court, the Chairman of the Surveyors' Institution (Irish Branch), or a person nominated by the Chairman who is a member of the council of the institution and who has a special knowledge of the valuation of land in Ireland.

2. Assessment of value

6–04   In assessing compensation the official arbitrator acts in accordance with rules set down under section 2 of the 1919 Act. In assessing the relevant compensation no allowance is made in respect of the fact that the acquisition is being made by compulsory purchase. The value of the land is taken to be the amount which the land, if sold in the open market by a willing seller might be expected to realise, and the arbitrator is entitled to consider all returns and assessments of a capital value for taxation made by the claimant. However, this does not affect the assessment of compensation for disturbance or any other matter not directly based on the value of the land.

6–05   The suitability or the adaptability of the land for any purpose is not to be taken into account if that purpose is a purpose to which it could be applied only through statutory powers, or for which there is no market for apart from the special needs of a particular purchaser or the requirements of a local, public or government authority. Where the value of the land is increased through the use of the land, or of any premises on the land, in a manner which could be restrained by a court or which is contrary to law or which is detrimental to the health of the occupiers of the premises or to public health, then that increase in value cannot be taken into account in assessing the level of compensation.

6–06   Where land is devoted to a particular purpose and but for the compulsory acquisition would continue to be used for that purpose, and that purpose does not have a general demand within the market for land used for that purpose, the compensation may be assessed on the basis of the reasonable cost of

---

[3]   The Act does not apply to acquisition by the Land Commission.

[4]   1919 as amended by the Acquisition of Land (Reference Committee) Act 1925.

[5]   See Acquisition of Land (Assessment of Compensation) Fees Rules 1999, S.I. No. 115 of 1999 regarding the relevant fees charged on awards.

equivalent reinstatement. If the compulsory acquisition relates to buildings the reasonable cost of equivalent reinstatement is taken to be a reference to that cost not exceeding the estimated cost of buildings such as would be capable of serving an equivalent purpose over the same period of time as the buildings being acquired would have done while having regard to any structural depreciation of those buildings.

6–07 The value of land is to be calculated with due regard to any restrictive covenant which is to be entered into by the body acquiring the land once the land is compulsory acquired. Regard is also to be had in the assessing of compensation to any compensation which has already been paid under the Local Government (Planning and Development) Acts following a restriction on the development of land. The arbitrator is also to have regard to any restriction on the development of the land which could be imposed under any other statute or bye-law or other similar provision and which did not confer a right of compensation.

6–08 Any depreciation or increase in value which is attributable to the land or any land in the vicinity, being reserved for any particular purpose in a development plan or inclusion of the land in a special amenity order is to be disregarded. This follows rule 11 of the 1963 Act which was held to refer to land which is set apart from other land zoned for a particular purpose and in valuing the land no account is to be taken of the setting apart and to value the land at the value it would have been if it had not been reserved under the development plan. The intention being to protect the owner of the land from the detrimental effect on the value of the land due to its benefit to the community and to ensure that owners of other land do not profit.[6]

6–09 No account is to be taken of any value which is attributable to any unauthorised structure or unauthorised use, nor to the existence of proposals for development of the land or any other land by a local authority or the possibility or probability of the land or other land becoming subject to a scheme of development undertaken by a local authority. In making an assessment of compensation regard can be had to any contribution which a planning authority would have required as a condition to any development of the land. Where land is incapable of a reasonably beneficial use which is purchased by a planning authority under section 29 of the 1963 Act the compensation shall be the value of the land exclusive of any allowance for disturbance or severance. As and from June 10, 1990 the rules relating to planning compensation cases are governed by the rules contained in the First Schedule to the Local Government (Planning and Development) Act 1990.

---

[6] See *Shortt v. Dublin Co. Co.* [1983] I.L.R.M. 377.

3. Procedure

6–10   Section 3 of the 1919 Act details the procedures which are to be followed before the official arbitrators and it provides that not more than one
expert witness on either side shall be heard unless the official arbitrator decides otherwise, and one additional witness on either side is allowed to give
evidence in relation to compensation in respect of minerals, or the disturbance
of business, as well as in respect of land, or on the damage in relation to the
disturbance may be allowed. It is not necessary for an official arbitrator to
make any declaration before entering into the consideration of any matter referred for decision.[7] Proceedings under the 1919 Act are to be heard by the
official arbitrator sitting in public and the official arbitrator is entitled to enter
onto and inspect any land which is the subject of the proceedings. Section 3 of
the Property Values (Arbitrations and Appeals) Act of 1960 provides that where
there is an appeal in relation to the value of any minerals the appellant and the
Revenue Commissioners may each nominate one person having experience in
the valuation of minerals to consult with the property arbitrator.

6–11   The decision of an official arbitrator regarding any questions of fact is
final and binding on all parties, including the persons who are claiming under
the respective parties. The official arbitrator may state at any stage, a special
case to the High Court for its opinion regarding any question of law which has
arose in the course of the proceedings and the official arbitrator may state the
award either in whole or in part as a special case to the High Court. The decision of the High Court is final and conclusive and is not subject to any appeal
to any court.[8]

6–12   In the case of *In re Deansrath Investments Ltd*[9] the arbitrator had assessed compensation to include the development potential of the relevant lands
for housing purposes in place of agricultural values which had been assessed
at a lower rate. The pre compulsory purchase order contract price appeared to
include a value above the agricultural value and negotiations had been made
regarding possible planning permission, however no such permission existed,
but it was shown that there was a potential future use for the lands for housing
purposes, which in fact was the reason for the compulsory purchase. The local
authority, Dublin Co. Co., contended at arbitration that the effect of the rules
under the 1963 Act, which are largely reflected in the 1990 Act, with important additions, was to preclude the arbitrator from taking into account any
development potential or hope value of the lands including potential develop-

---

[7]   s.3(2).
[8]   s.6.
[9]   [1974] I.R. 228.

ment by a non-local authority and that the correct value of the lands was at agricultural value as this was the only use to which the lands could be put at the date of the service of the compulsory purchase notice.

6–13 The landowner put forward the view that the value of the land on the open market was the relevant criterion. The arbitrator agreed with the landowner's contention and assessed compensation on the development potential of the lands for housing purposes. In a case stated by the arbitrator the High Court confirmed the decision of the arbitrator and the local authority appealed the decision to the Supreme Court.

6–14 The Supreme Court found that the value which was to be taken as the value for compensation was the value to the owner before the date of the taking and not the value to the taker of the land, the value was to be the market value or full price of the land, and that every element of the value including present and future uses were to be taken into account in assessing the value of the property, and it is the present value of these elements which are to be considered when arriving at the full market value. However, no value was to be included in respect of the scheme which the local authority were to implement on the property and no value was to be taken into account in respect of work carried out by the local authority of other land or services which were to be provided by the local authority. It was also held that no reference was made within the rules under the 1963 Act with respect to proposals for development by any person other than a local authority and that the rules did not restrict the compensation to be paid to the value of the land as used on the date of the service of the notice and therefore it was correct in taking into account the hope value of the property.

6–15 It was suggested by the local authority that the arbitrator should have taken into account the fact that the development of the land could not be carried out without planning permission which might not have been forthcoming so that therefore the land would not have a development potential to be considered for valuation purposes. It was agreed that planning permission would have been granted in about five to seven years, the delay due to the lack of existing support services. The Supreme Court also dealt with the provision contained in Rule 3 referring to the provision that no account was to be taken of the special suitability or adaptability of the land if that purpose could only be applied in respect of statutory powers. The Court found that this provision only refers to purposes which actually require a particular purpose to be carried into effect such as the making of a railway, the development of land for housing does not specifically require statutory powers to enable houses to be built.

4. Statutory purposes

6–16   A good example of this type of purpose can be seen from the Transport (Dublin Light Rail) Act 1996.[10] Following the making of a light railway order under section 9 of the Act, CIÉ is entitled to acquire compulsorily any land or rights in, under or over land and the light railway order has the same effect as if it were a compulsory purchase made under section 10(1) of the Local Government (No. 2) Act 1960.[11] Where CIÉ proposes to acquire land for the benefit of the railway, and in the opinion of CIÉ, it is more efficient and economical to acquire additional adjoining land, CIÉ may acquire that land with the consent of the Minister and of any person having an interest in or right in, under or over the adjoining land notwithstanding the fact that the adjoining land is not specified in the light railway order.

6–17   However the Transport (Dublin Light Railway) Act provides that where an owner or occupier of land suffers loss, injury or damage or incurs expenditure as a result of the actions of CIÉ, during the course of construction CIÉ are obliged to pay compensation in respect of the loss, injury, damage or expenditure and the amount of the compensation shall, in default of agreement, be determined by arbitration under the Lands Clauses Acts,[12] as opposed to the 1991 Act.

5. Costs

6–18   Section 5 makes provision as regards costs of any proceeding before the official arbitrator. Where the acquiring authority has made an unconditional offer in writing of any sum as compensation to a claimant and the sum which is awarded by the arbitrator does not exceed that amount, the official arbitrator is obliged to order the claimant to bear their own costs as well as the costs of the acquiring authority in so far as the costs were incurred after the offer was made. If the official arbitrator is of the opinion that a claimant has failed to deliver to the acquiring authority a notice in writing of the amount which is claimed giving sufficient details and in sufficient time so as to enable the acquiring authority to make a proper offer, the official arbitrator may make a similar order regarding costs.

6–19   A notice of claim is to state the exact nature of the interest and give details of the compensation which is claimed, giving the amount under appro-

---

[10] No. 24 of 1996.

[11] As amended by s.86 of the Housing Act 1966.

[12] Lands Clauses Consolidation Act 1845, see also *Comyn v. Attorney General* [1950] I.R. 142, and Wylie, para. 6.102.

priate headings and showing how each is claimed. When such notice of a claim has been delivered the acquiring authority may at any time within six weeks after delivery withdraw any notice to treat which has been served on the claimant or any other person, but shall be liable to pay compensation for any loss or expenses which have arose. The acquiring authority may deduct the costs awarded from the compensation payable.

6–20 An acquiring authority may be ordered to pay the costs of the claimant, and their own costs, if the claimant has made an unconditional offer in writing to accept a sum as compensation and the sum awarded by the official arbitrator exceeds that sum accepted.

C. COMPULSORY PURCHASE OF LAND ROAD ACT 1993 [13]

1. Acquisition of land and implementation of scheme

6–21 Section 52(1) of the Roads Act 1993 provides that where the Minister approves a scheme, referring to a motorway scheme, a bus way scheme, a protected road scheme, a protected road scheme amending a protected road scheme, the road authority is authorised to compulsorily acquire any land or any rights in relation to that land and the scheme shall have the same effect as if it were a compulsory purchase order made by the road authority, pursuant to section 10 (1) of the Local Government (No. 2) Act 1960. However, a claim for compensation under the Roads Act 1993 is to be made not later than six months after the date on which the scheme to which it relates was approved by the Minister. The level of compensation shall, in default of agreement, be determined by arbitration under the Acquisition of Land (Assessment of Compensation) Act 1919, in the same manner in all respects as if such claim arose in relation to the compulsory acquisition of land, but that the arbitrator shall have jurisdiction to make a nil award.

6–22 A claim under the Roads Act 1993 for compensation may be made in relation to a planning permission which is revoked or modified under a scheme approved by the Minister as if the revocation or modification had been made by notice under section 30 of the Principal Act, the road authority being treated as being a planning authority for that purpose.

---

[13] No. 14 of 1993.

D. COMPENSATION AND PLANNING

1. Right to compensation

6–23 Section 55 of the 1963 Act (the Principal Act) laid down the principle that if as a result of a decision by the planning authority a refusal of a planning permission to develop land or where a permission has been granted by subject to conditions which adversely affect the value of an interest of any person to which the decision relates at the time of the decision is reduced, the person affected shall be entitled to be paid by the planning authority by way of compensation the amount of any reduction in value and, in the case of the occupier of the land, the damage done to the trade, business or profession being carried out on the land. This provision and Part VI along with it was repealed by the Local Government (Planning and Development) Act 1990.

6–24 Section 11 of the Act,[14] provides that if, as a result of the refusal of planning permission the value of an interest of any person existing in the land to which the decision relates at the time of the decision is reduced, that person shall, be entitled to be paid by the planning authority an amount, which represents the reduction in value determined in accordance with the First Schedule, and in the case of the occupier of the land, the damage to his trade, business or profession carried out on the land.

6–25 Section 12 of the 1990 Act provides that compensation cannot be paid in respect of the refusal of permission for any development of a class or description set out in the Second Schedule, or if the reason or one of the reasons for the refusal is a reason set out in the Third Schedule. Compensation is not payable in respect of the imposition, on the granting of permission to develop land, of any condition of a class or description set out in the Fourth Schedule.[15] Compensation is also not be payable in respect of the refusal of permission, or of the imposition of conditions on the granting of permission, for the retention on land of any structures to which section 28 of the Principal Act relates.[16] Section 28 of the Principal Act relates to the power to grant permission for the retention on land of any structures constructed, erected or made on, in, or under the land on or after the appointed day and before the date of the application, or for the continuance of any use of land instituted on or after the appointed day[17] and before the date of the application.

---

[14] Which more or less replicates s.55 of the 1963 Act.
[15] s.12(2).
[16] s.12(3).
[17] Referring to the appointed day under the 1963 Act, namely October 1,1964.

2. No compensation

6–26 If the planning authority are regarded as being under section 29 of the 1963 Act, a duty of a planning authority to acquire an interest in land, compensation is not payable. Section 29 of the 1963 Act provides that where, in a case determined on an appeal, permission to develop land has been refused or has been granted subject to conditions, then, the owner may serve on the planning authority a notice requiring them to purchase the property. However, the owner of the land must show that the land has become incapable of reasonably beneficial use in its existing state, and that the land cannot be rendered capable of reasonably beneficial use by the carrying out of any other development for which permission has been granted, and in a case where permission to develop the land was granted subject to conditions, that the land cannot be rendered capable of reasonably beneficial use by the carrying out of the permitted development in accordance with the conditions. The term "reasonable beneficial use" is rather vague and difficult to pin down in real terms and there are no regulations governing the section and its implementation.[18]

(ii) Second Schedule

6–27 The Second Schedule provides that compensation is not payable in respect to any development which consists of or includes the making of any material change in the use of any structures or other land, or the demolition of a habitable house, or the demolition of a building of artistic, architectural or of historical interest which it is a development objective of the development plan to preserve. Compensation is also not payable where planning permission is refused in respect of the erection of any advertisement structure, or the use of land for the exhibition of any advertisement.

6–28 Likewise compensation is not payable in respect of refusal of planning permission in relation to an application which involves the development in an area to which a special amenity area order relates. Compensation is not payable with respect to any development on land to which there is available, notwithstanding the refusal of permission, a grant of permission for any development of a residential, commercial or industrial character, if the development consists wholly or mainly of the construction of houses, flats, shops or office premises, hotels, garages and petrol filling stations, theatres or structures for the purpose of entertainment, or industrial buildings, or indeed any combination of these, subject to no conditions.[19] Compensation may also not be paid regarding any development on land to which compensation has al-

---

[18] See however, *Portland Estates Ltd. v. Limerick Corp.* [1980] I.L.R.M. 77, and *R. v. Minister for Housing and Local Government* [1960] 1 W.L.R. 587.

[19] Other than conditions of the kind referred to in the Fourth Schedule.

ready been paid in connection with a previous decision involving a refusal of permission.

(iii) Third Schedule

6–29   The Third Schedule to the Act lists the constraints which would prevent the granting of permission for development on the grounds that it would be premature to grant a planning permission due to any one or a combination of those constraints listed in paragraph one as well as the period within which the constraints involved may reasonably be expected to cease. These constraints relate to any existing deficiency in the provision of water supplies or sewerage facilities, or to the capacity of existing or prospective water supplies or sewerage facilities being required for prospective development as regards which a grant of a permission under the Principal Act. They also relate to an undertaking under the Principal Act or to a notice under section 13, as well as to the capacity of existing or prospective water supplies or sewerage facilities being required for the prospective development of another part of the functional area of the planning authority, as indicated in the development plan, the capacity of existing or prospective water supplies or sewerage facilities being required for any other prospective development or for any development objective.

6–30   The Third Schedule includes any existing deficiency in the road network serving the area of the proposed development, including considerations of the capacity of the road or its width, alignment, or the surface or structural condition of the pavement, which would render that network, or any part of it, unsuitable to carry the increased road traffic likely to result from the development. The Third Schedule also includes any prospective deficiency in the road network serving the area of the proposed development which would arise because of the increased road traffic likely to result from that development, as well as from other prospective developments, or would arise because of the increased road traffic likely to result from that development and from any other prospective development or from any development objective, as indicated in the development plan, and would render that road network, or any part of it, unsuitable to carry the increased road traffic likely to result from the proposed development.

(iv) Historic monuments

6–31   Compensation is also not allowed in respect of development of the kind which is proposed, which would be premature pending the determination by the planning authority or the road authority of a road layout for the area or any part thereof, development of the kind proposed, which would be premature by reference to the order of priority, if any, for development indicated in the development plan, the proposed development would endanger public safety

by reason of traffic hazard or obstruction of road users or otherwise, the proposed development, by itself or by the precedent which the grant of permission for it would set for other relevant development, would adversely affect
the use of a national road or other major road by traffic.

6–32   Where the proposed development would interfere with a view or prospect of special amenity value or special interest which it is necessary to preserve, or where the proposed development would cause serious air pollution,
water pollution, noise pollution or vibration or pollution connected with the
disposal of waste compensation is not payable.

6–33   Compensation is also not payable in the case of development including any structure or any addition to or extension of a structure, the structure,
addition or extension would infringe an existing building line or, where none
exists, a building line determined by the planning authority.[20] Compensation
is not payable in respect of planning permission refused for development involving development under a public road, or which would seriously injure the
amenities of, or depreciate the value of property in the vicinity, or tend to
create any serious traffic congestion, or endanger or interfere with the safety
of aircraft or the safe and efficient navigation thereof, endanger the health or
safety of persons occupying or employed in the structure or any adjoining
structure, or be prejudicial to public health.

6–34   Where an application for planning permission has been made in the
case of development including any structure or regarding any addition to or
extension of a structure, and has been refused, compensation is not payable
where the addition or extension which would infringe an existing building
line, or a building line determined by the planning authority, or be under a
public road, seriously injure the amenities, or depreciate the value of property
in the vicinity, tend to create any serious traffic congestion, endanger or interfere with the safety of aircraft or the safe and efficient navigation thereof,
endanger the health or safety of persons occupying or employed in the structure or any adjoining structure, or be prejudicial to public health.

6–35   Where the proposed development would contravene materially a condition attached to an existing permission for development compensation cannot be payable, which is also the case where the proposed development would
contravene materially a development objective which is indicated in the development plan for the use solely or primarily of particular areas for particular
purposes. However this restriction on compensation does not apply where a
development objective for the use applied to the land at any time within the

---

[20] Or by the An Bord Pleanála.

five years immediately prior to the date on which the relevant application for planning permission was made. However, the restriction on compensation applies in a case where a person acquired his interest in the land after the development objective has come into operation, or after notice has been published, in accordance with section 21 of the Principal Act, of a proposed new development plan or of proposed variations of a development plan. Nor can compensation be payable where the proposed development would injure or interfere with a historic monument, or is situated in an archaeological area.[21]

6–36   Compensation is also not payable if the development would contravene materially a condition attached to an existing permission for development or if the proposed development would injure or interfere with a historic monument which stands registered in the Register of Historic Monuments,[22] or is situated in an archaeological area which is also registered as a historic monument.

(v) Material contravention

6–37   Where the development would contravene materially a development objective indicated in the development plan for the use solely or primarily of particular areas for particular purposes, compensation will not be payable.[23] However, compensation may be allowable in a case where a development objective for the use applied to the land at any time within the five years immediately prior to the date on which the relevant application was made for permission to develop the land, and the development would not have contravened materially the objective development plan.

6–38   Where a claim for compensation has become payable, of an amount exceeding one hundred pounds, the planning authority are obliged to prepare and retain a statement specifying the refusal of permission or a grant of permission subject to conditions, or the revocation or modification of planning permission, the land to which the claim for compensation relates, and the amount of the compensation.[24] The planning authority enters these particulars in the planning register and every entry is to be made within the period of fourteen days beginning on the day of the preparation of the statement.[25] No development can take place on land in respect of which a statement relates, until the issue of compensation has been decided or has been paid or secured

---

[21] Registered in the Register of Historic Monuments under s.5 of the National Monuments (Amendment) Act 1987.

[22] Made under s.5 of the National Monuments (Amendment) Act 1987.

[23] para. 11.

[24] s.9.

[25] s.9 of the 1990 Act.

to the satisfaction of the planning authority, unless the property is the subject of a planning permission.

6–39 Where, regarding the development of any land, an amount becomes recoverable in respect of the compensation which is specified in a compensation statement, then no amount shall be recoverable, in so far as it is related to that land, in connection with any subsequent development of the same land or part of it.

3. Claims

(i) Time limits

6–40 Claims for compensation under the Local Government (Planning and Development) Act 1990[26] are generally required to be made within six months. For claims under section 11, which refers to a decision involving a refusal of permission to develop land or a grant of a permission subject to conditions, the value of an interest of any person existing in the land to which the decision relates at the time of the decision is reduced. The six months commences after the notification of the decision of the planning authority or following an appeal.

6–41 For claims made under section 18, which refers to a claim made to the planning authority, as a result of the removal or alteration of any structure consequent upon a notice under section 36 of the Principal Act, the six month period commences following the removal or alteration of the structure. Regarding claims made under section 19 referring to as a result of the discontinuance, or the compliance with conditions on the continuance, of any use of land following a notice under section 37 of the Principal Act, the six month period begins following the discontinuance or compliance.

6–42 The six month period begins following the removal or the alteration of a hedge which was removed following a notice made under section 20 of the Principal Act. For claims under section 21, referring to the making of a tree preservation order, which is where a permission to develop land has been revoked or modified by a notice under section 30 of the Principal Act, the six month period begins on the date on which the consent is refused or is granted subject to conditions.In the case of a claim under section 22, which refers to a claim made to the planning authority, the six months commences when the time the order creating the public right of way commences to have effect.

---

[26] No. 11 of 1990.

6–43   In the case of a claim under section 23, referring to the power of authorised person to enter on land and to carry out necessary acts on the land and by so doing causes damage, the six month limitation period begins when the damage is suffered, while a claim under section 24 which refers to the placing, renewing or removing any cable, wire or pipeline, attaching any bracket or fixture or affixing any notice, which affects the value of an interest of any person in the land or structure, the six month period begins when the planning authority causes the alleged damage.

(ii) Determination of a compensation claim

6–44   Section 5 of the 1990 Act sets out the procedure which is to be adopted in deciding on a claim for compensation made under the Act. A claim for compensation under the Act, where the parties are not in agreement, is to be determined by arbitration under the Acquisition of Land (Assessment of Compensation) Act, 1919. However in relation to these planning matters the 1919 Act is amended by the First Schedule of the 1990 in respect of a reduction in the value of an interest in land, and by adding the proviso that the arbitrator shall have jurisdiction to make a nil award, and the application of the First Schedule to a claim for compensation for claims of damages resulting from actions under section 36 (removal or alteration of a structure), section 37 (discontinuance, or compliance with conditions on the continuance of the use of land), section 44 (removal or alteration of a hedge), section 45 (refusal of consent following a tree preservation order), section 48 (creation of a right of way) and section 85 (laying of cables, wires or pipelines).

6–45   Section 7 prevents any person becoming entitled to double compensation in respect of the same matter or thing under different enactments. A claim for compensation, once determined is recoverable as a simple contract debt, under section 8, as are the costs and expenses payable by the planning authority.

6–46   Section 10(1) provides that a person cannot carry out any development on land where a compensation statement is registered, until the compensation which is recoverable has been paid or secured to the satisfaction of the planning authority. This inhibition applies to any development referred to in section 13 of the 1990 Act, provided that the inhibition does not apply to any development authorised by a permission referred to in section 13(5) where the permission granted was granted subject to conditions, other than conditions of a class or description set out in the Fourth Schedule. Section 10(1) also does not apply where the compensation which is to become payable is payable in respect of the imposition of conditions to a planning permission to develop land.

6–47 The rules for determining the level of compensation payable contained in the First Schedule differ somewhat from the provisions of the 1919 Act. The first rule states that the reduction in value is to be determined by reference to the difference between the antecedent and subsequent values of the land, the antecedent value of the land being the amount which the land, if sold in the open market by a willing seller might have been expected to realise, and the subsequent value of the land is the amount which the land, if sold in the open market by a willing seller immediately after the said decision, might be expected to realise.

6–48 The prior and subsequent values of the land are also calculated by reference to any contribution which a planning authority might have required or might require as a prior condition to the development of the land, as well as to any restriction on the development of the land which, without conferring a right to compensation, could have been imposed under any Act, together with the fact that exempted development might have been or may be carried out on the land, and the open market value of comparable land, if any, in the vicinity of the land whose values are being determined.

6–49 In ascertaining the value of any compensation no account shall be taken of any part of the value of the land which is attributable to subsidies or to grants available from public moneys, or to any tax or rating allowances in respect of development, from which development of the land might benefit, or to the special suitability or adaptability of the land for any purpose if that purpose is a purpose to which it could be applied only in pursuance of statutory powers. Regard cannot also be taken in with respect to any suitability or adaptability of the land, for which there is no market apart from the special needs of a particular purchaser or the requirements of any statutory body,[27] provided that any bona fide offer for the purchase of the land which may be brought to the notice of the arbitrator shall be taken into consideration.

6–50 No account, in deciding compensation can be taken in respect of any increase in the value of land attributable to the use of the land or of any structure in a manner which could be restrained by a court, or which is contrary to law, or which is detrimental to the health of the inmates of that structure or to public health or safety or to the environment, nor in respect of any depreciation or increase in value attributable to the land, or any land in the vicinity, being reserved for a particular purpose in a development plan, nor to any value attributable to any unauthorised structure or unauthorised use. Rule 2 also provides that no account is to be taken in respect of the existence of proposals for development of the land or any other land by a statutory body, or the pos-

---

[27] See r.5 for statutory bodies.

sibility or probability of the land or other land becoming subject to a scheme of development undertaken by such statutory body, and all returns and assessments of capital value for taxation made or acquiesced in by the claimant may be considered.

6–51 In assessing the possibilities, if any, for developing the land, for the purposes of determining its prior value, regard is to be had only to such reasonable possibilities as, having regard to all material considerations, could be judged to have existed immediately prior to the relevant decision which gave rise to the claim for compensation. The term material considerations, includes the nature and location of the land, the likelihood or unlikelihood, as the case may be, of obtaining permission, or further permission, to develop the land in the light of the provisions of the development plan, the assumption that, if any permission to develop the land were to be granted. The term also relates or refers to any conditions which might reasonably be imposed in relation to matters referred to in the Fourth Schedule, being conditions which may be imposed without compensation but no other conditions would be imposed, and any permission to develop the land, not being permission for development of a kind specified in section 13 (2), referring to the notice preventing compensation, already existing at the time.

6–52 In determining the subsequent value of the land where there has been a refusal of permission it shall be assumed, that, after the refusal, a permission for development would not be granted for any development of a kind specified in section 13(2),[28] regard is to be had to any conditions referred to in the Fourth Schedule which might reasonably be imposed in the granting of permission to develop the land.

6–53 Where there has been a refusal of permission in relation to land in respect of which there is in force an undertaking under the Principal Act, it is assumed in determining the subsequent value of the land that, after the refusal, permission for development would not be granted for any development other than development to which the said undertaking relates.

6–54 The Second Schedule specifies the type of development of which a refusal of permission does not attract compensation. A decision to refuse planning permission for any development which consists of or includes the making of any material change in the use of any structures or other land, or the demolition of a habitable house, the demolition of a building of artistic, archi-

---

[28] Development means development of a residential, commercial or industrial character, consisting wholly or mainly of the construction of houses, flats, shops or office premises, hotels, garages and petrol filling stations, theatres or structures for the purpose of entertainment, or industrial buildings (including warehouses), or any combination thereof.

tectural or historical interest which it is a development objective of the development plan to preserve, or the erection of any advertisement structure, of the use of land for the exhibition of any advertisement, or development in an area to which a special amenity area order relates, does not entitle the applicant to compensation.

6–55 Compensation is not allowed with regard to the refusal of a grant of planning permission in respect of any development on land with respect to which there is available a grant of permission for any development of a residential, commercial or industrial character, if the development consists wholly or mainly of the construction of houses, flats, shops or office premises, hotels, garages and petrol filling stations, theatres or structures for the purpose of entertainment, or industrial buildings, subject to no conditions other than conditions referred to in the Fourth Schedule or in respect of any development on land with respect to which compensation has already been paid.

6–56 The Third Schedule to the Act outlines the reasons for the refusal of permission which excludes compensation.[29] If a development is refused due to any existing deficiency in the provision of water supplies or sewerage facilities, the capacity of existing or prospective water supplies or sewerage facilities being required for prospective development as regards which a grant of a permission, an undertaking or a notice under section 13 exists.

6–57 Compensation is also not payable in respect of the refusal to grant a permission by reason of the capacity of existing or prospective water supplies or sewerage facilities which would be required for the prospective development of another part of the functional area of the planning authority, and as indicated in the development plan, or due to the capacity of existing or prospective water supplies or sewerage facilities being required for any other prospective development or for any development objective contained in the development plan. Nor can compensation be paid because of any existing deficiency in the road network which serves the area of the proposed development, including considerations of capacity, width, alignment, or the surface or structural condition of the pavement, which makes the road network unsuitable to carry the increased road traffic, including any prospective deficiency in the road network. Deficiency in the network includes the situation where a determination is pending by the planning authority or the road authority of a road layout for the area or any part thereof.

---

[29] The reasons used must be exact, see *XJS Ltd. v. Dun Laoghaire Corp.* [1986] I.R. 750; [1987] I.L.R.M. 659, and *Eighty Five Developments Ltd. v. Dublin Co. Co.*, unreported, High Court, January 31, 1992 and *J. Wood & Co. Ltd. v. Wicklow Co. Co.* [1995] 1 I.L.R.M. 51.

6–58   Compensation is not allowable where there is an order of priority, if any, for development indicated in the development plan and where proposed development would endanger public safety by reason of traffic hazard or obstruction of road users or otherwise as well as where a proposed development would adversely affect the use of a national road or other major road by traffic, or where the proposed development would interfere with a view or prospect of special amenity value or special interest which it is necessary to preserve. Where the proposed development would cause serious air, water or noise pollution, or vibration or pollution connected with the disposal of waste, compensation is not allowable where the planning authority refuses to grant planning permission. The onus is on a person to prove all relevant facts relating to their interest in the land to the satisfaction of the planning authority.

4. Conditions

6–59   The Fourth Schedule to the Act contains a list of the conditions which may be imposed on the grant of a planning permission and which do not entitle an applicant to compensation. The Act specifically provides that no compensation is payable in respect of a condition requiring the giving of security for satisfactory completion of the proposed development, including maintenance until taken in charge by the local authority concerned of roads, open spaces, car-parks, sewers, watermains or drains,[30] or a condition, requiring a contribution towards expenditure incurred by any local authority in respect of works, including the provision of open spaces, which have facilitated the proposed development.[31]

6–60   No compensation is payable in respect of the imposition of a condition, requiring a contribution towards expenditure, including expenditure on the acquisition of land, that is proposed to be incurred by any local authority in respect of works facilitating the proposed development,[32] nor in respect of a condition requiring the removal of an advertisement structure or any condition relating to an application for permission relates to a temporary structure.[33]

6–61   Conditions relating to the size, height, floor area and character of structures, building lines, site coverage and the space about dwellings and other structures, the extent of parking places required in, on or under structures of a particular class or size or services or facilities for the parking, loading, unloading or fuelling of vehicles, the objects which may be affixed to structures, the purposes for and the manner in which structures may be used or occupied,

---

[30]   s.26(2)(e) of the Principal Act.
[31]   s.26(2)(g).
[32]   s.26(2)(h).
[33]   s.26(2)(j).

including, in the case of dwellings, the letting thereof in separate tenements, either one of these or any combination of these conditions do not attract compensation. This is also the case in relation to the imposition of any condition relating to the design, colour and materials of structures, or any conditions reserving or allocating specified land for structures of a specified class, or conditions which prohibit or restrict either permanently or temporarily, the erection, construction or making of any particular classes of structures on any specified land, or any condition limiting the number of structures of a particular class which may be constructed, erected or made, on, in or under any specified land.

6–62 Compensation is not payable in relation to the inclusion in a grant of planning permission of any condition which relates to the disposition or layout of structures or structures of any specified class, including the reservation of reasonable open space in relation to the number, class and character of structures in any particular development proposal, the manner in which any land is to be laid out for the purpose of development, including requirements as to road layout, landscaping, planting, the provision of water supplies, sewers, drains and public lighting, and the provision of service roads and the location and design of means of access to roads, the provision of facilities for parking, unloading, loading and fuelling of vehicles on any land. Neither is compensation allowable in respect to any condition relating to the alteration or removal of unauthorised structures or conditions relating to the layout of the proposed development, including density, spacing, grouping and orientation of structures in relation to roads, open spaces, and other structures.[34] It is also reasonable to include any conditions relating to the provision and siting of sanitary services and recreational facilities, and conditions relating to the reserving, as a public park, public garden or public recreation space, land normally used as such in the interests of the community at large and for a development in particular that compensation is not allowable, and instead becomes part of the price of development.

6–63 Conditions relating to the preservation of buildings of artistic, architectural or historical interest, and any condition relating to the preservation of plasterwork, staircases, woodwork or other fixtures or features of artistic architectural or historical interest, together with any conditions relating to the preservation of plasterwork, staircases, woodwork or other fixtures or features of artistic, architectural or historical interest and forming part of the interior of structures, are also included within the fourth schedule as being conditions which do not attract compensation under the Act.

---

[34] For an interesting case on the law relating to open spaces see *Smeltzer v. Fingal Co. Co.* [1998] 1 I.R. 279.

6–64   The preservation of caves, sites, features and other objects of archaeological, geological or historical interest, and the preservation of views and prospects and of amenities or places and features of natural beauty or interest, conditions relating to the preservation and protection of trees, shrubs, plants and flowers, are deemed to be of sufficient importance to warrant inclusion in the fourth schedule as being exempt from compensation.

6–65   Several of the conditions which are included in the fourth schedule are matters which relate to the proper planning and development of an area and as such would come within the general terms of reference of the planning authority when making a decision on an application for permission, such as the prohibition or restriction or controlling development within a specified distance of the centre line of a specified road, or the erection of all or any particular forms of advertisement structure or the exhibition of all or any particular forms of advertisement. Conditions preventing, remedying or removing damage to amenities which arose from the ruinous or neglected condition of a structure, or from the objectionable or neglected condition of any land attached to a structure or abutting on a public road or situate in a residential area are also listed in the fourth schedule and come firmly within the proper planning and development of a functional area of a planning authority.

6–66   Conditions prohibiting, regulating or controlling the deposit or disposal of waste materials and refuse, the disposal of sewage and the pollution of rivers, lakes, ponds, gullies and the seashore, together with conditions regarding the preservation of any existing public right of way giving access to seashore, mountain, lakeshore, riverbank, or other place of natural beauty or recreational utility, together with conditions relating to measures to reduce or prevent the emission or the intrusion of noise or vibration, or a condition prohibiting the demolition of a habitable house being matters which are related to the proper planning and development of an area are also included in the schedule.

6–67   Conditions relating to a matter in respect of which a requirement could have been imposed under any provision or enactment without liability for compensation are obviously included within the fourth schedule although if the enactment provided for that no liability for compensation would arise it seems to be somewhat unnecessary to include a mention in the Act.

6–68   Lastly conditions relating to the safety of aircraft or the safe and efficient navigation, conditions determining the sequence in which works shall be carried out or specifying a period within which works shall be completed, together with conditions relating to the filling of land and any condition restricting the occupation of any structure included in a development until the completion of other works included in the development or until any other specified condition is complied with or until the planning authority consent to such occupation make up the remainder of the schedule.

5. Purchase notice

6–69 Where permission to develop any land has been refused or has been granted subject to any conditions, and if the owner claims that the land has become incapable of reasonably beneficial use in its existing state and the land cannot be rendered capable of reasonably beneficial use by the carrying out of any other development for which permission has been granted, or which the planning authority have undertaken to grant a permission and in a case where permission to develop the land was granted subject to conditions that the land cannot be capable of reasonably beneficial use by the carrying out of the permitted development in compliance with those conditions, the owner may within a period of six months after that decision, serve on the planning authority a purchase notice requiring the planning authority to purchase the owners' interest in the property.[35]

6–70 The planning authority who has been served with a purchase notice, before the end of three months, beginning on the date of the service of the notice, serve on the owner a notice, in writing, stating that the planning authority is either willing to comply with the notice or is unwilling to comply with the purchase notice. If the planning authority are unwilling to comply with the terms of the purchase notice it is obliged to forward a copy of the purchase notice and a copy of the authority's replying notice to An Bord Pleanala.[36] The Board must then decide whether to confirm the purchase notice. The Board in making its decision is restricted to considering whether or not the owner of the property has established a valid claim and that the property has become incapable of reasonably beneficial use in its existing state and cannot be rendered capable of reasonably beneficial use by the carrying out of any other development, or by carrying out of a permitted development, in accordance with any conditions which may be attached.

6–71 If the Board confirms the purchase notice the planning authority are obliged to acquire the interest of the owner and that planning authority serves on the owner a notice stating that the authority intends to comply with the notice and the notice has the same effect as if it were a compulsory purchase order.

6–72 If it appears to the Board that, if is expedient so to do, the Board may in lieu of confirming the purchase notice, instead grant permission for the

---

[35] s.29 of the Principal Act.
[36] s.29(2) of the Principal Act.

development in respect of which the application was made or, where permission for that development was granted subject to conditions, revoke or amend the conditions in order to enable the land to be rendered capable of reasonably beneficial use by the carrying out of the development. If it appears to the Board, that the land or a part of the land, could be made capable of reasonably beneficial use within a reasonable time by the carrying out of any other development for which permission ought to be granted, the Board may, in lieu of confirming the notice, direct that the permission shall be granted in the event of an application being made.

D. OTHER ENACTMENTS AUTHORISING COMPULSORY PURCHASE

(i) Various purposes

6–73   Local authorities also have the power to acquire land for other purposes including water supply and waste management under the Waste Management Act of 1997. Local authorities can also acquire derelict sites within their functional areas under the Derelict Sites Act 1990. Section 10 of the Local government (Ireland) Act 1898 gave county councils the power to acquire land compulsorily to enable the council to carry out or fulfil any of its powers and duties.

6–74   Section 77 of the Local Government (Planning and Development) Act 1963 authorised the planning authority to develop or secure the development of land. Section 74 of the Act also allows the planning authority to appropriate land for the purposes of the Planning Acts, while section 75 allows the planning authority to sell, lease or exchange land acquired for the planning purposes.[37]

6–75   A planning authority may develop or secure the development of land and, in particular may secure, facilitate and control the improvement of the frontage of any public road by widening, opening, enlarging or otherwise improving, or develop any land in the vicinity of any road or bridge which it is proposed to improve or construct, or provide areas with roads and such services and works as may be needed for development, or provide areas of convenient shape for development, or secure or carry out, as respects obsolete areas, the development or renewal thereof and the provision therein of open

---

[37]   A planning authority may exercise powers under s.10 of the Local Government (No. 2) Act 1960, regarding compulsory acquisition apply in relation to the purposes of any functions under the 1963 Act.

spaces.[38] The planning authority may also secure the preservation of any view or prospect, any structure or natural physical feature.

6–76 The Dublin Docklands Development Authority Act 1997[39] allows the Development Authority to acquire land compulsorily. Section 27 provides that the Authority may authorise the compulsorily acquisition of land situated in the Dublin Docklands Area for the purpose of performing any of the functions assigned to it by means of a compulsory purchase order made by the Authority and submitted to and confirmed by the Minister in accordance with section 76 of the Housing Act, 1966. The provisions of the Housing Act 1966 apply in relation to the compulsory acquisition of such land as if it were an acquisition by a housing authority within the meaning of the Housing Act 1966.

(ii) Housing Act 1966

6–77 Section 76 of the Housing Act 1966 allows a housing authority to acquire land compulsorily for any of the purposes of the Act through a compulsory purchase order which is made by the authority, which is submitted for confirmation to the Minister in accordance with the provisions contained in the Third Schedule. Section 77 allows the housing authority to acquire land through compulsory acquisition of land which is not immediately required by the housing authority, provided that the Minister is of opinion that there is a reasonable expectation that the land will be required by the authority in the future.

6–78 Section 79 provides that where a compulsory purchase order which is made and confirmed has become operative and the housing authority has decided to acquire the land, the authority shall serve a notice, referred to as a notice to treat, on every owner, lessee and occupier of the land, except tenants for a month or less period than a month, stating that they are willing to treat for the purchase of the interests in the land. The notice to treat requires each owner, lessee and occupier to state within a specified period, not being less than one month from the date of service of the notice to treat, the exact nature of the interest of which compensation is claimed and details of the compensation claimed. If the authority requires the person making a claim for compensation may be required to distinguish each of the separate amounts of the compensation and to show how each such amount is calculated.[40]

6–79 The housing authority are obliged to publish in a newspaper circulating within their functional area a notice in the prescribed form stating that the

---

[38] s. 77 of the 1963 Act.

[39] No. 7 of 1997.

[40] A notice to treat served is deemed to be a notice to treat for the purposes of the Acquisition of Land (Assessment of Compensation) Act, 1919.

compulsory purchase order has been confirmed in respect of land within their functional area, naming a place where a copy of the compulsory purchase order and any map may be inspected. The housing authority are obliged to serve a notice on every person having an interest in the relevant land which the compulsory purchase order has been confirmed who, having given notice to the Minister of his objection to the compulsory purchase order, appeared at the local public inquiry in support of his objection.[41] If any person is aggrieved by a compulsory purchase order, which has been confirmed by the Minister and wishes to question the validity of the order that person may, not later than three weeks after the publication of notice of the confirmation order, make an application for the purpose to the High Court. The High Court may, if satisfied that the compulsory purchase order is not within the powers of the Act or that the interests of the applicant have been substantially prejudiced by any requirement of the Act not having been complied with, quash the order as so confirmed either generally or in so far only as it affects any property of the applicant.[42] This is the only mechanism by which a compulsory purchase order can be challenged as section 78(4) provides that a person shall not question a compulsory purchase order by prohibition or certiorari or in any legal proceedings whatsoever.

6–80   A compulsory purchase order becomes operative after twenty-one days following the publication of the notice as required by section 78(1), or the withdrawal of the application, or following an appeal to the High Court on the date of the determination of the appeal.

6–81   Where a housing authority have entered into and taken possession of land in and after six months, and if the interests in the land have not been conveyed or transferred to the authority, and where the authority consider that it is urgently necessary, in connection with the purposes for which they have been authorised to acquire the land compulsorily, that the acquisition of the land should be completed, and the authority have made a proper offer in writing to each person having an interest in the land who has furnished sufficient particulars of his interest to enable the authority to make a proper offer for such interest the authority may by means of a vesting order acquire the land.[43]

6–82   Where a housing authority has made a vesting order the authority shall within seven days after making the order publish in one or more newspapers circulating within their functional area a notice stating that the order has been made, describing the land referred to therein and naming a place where a copy of the order may be seen at all reasonable times, and serve on every person

---

[41] s.78(1).
[42] s.78(2).
[43] s.81(1).

appearing to them to have an interest in the land to which the order relates a notice stating the fact of such an order having been made and the effect of the order.[44]

---

[44] s.81(3).

CHAPTER 7

Urban renewal relief

A. INTRODUCTION[1]

7–01 The 1985 Finance Act provides for income and corporation tax reliefs in connection with the redevelopment of the Custom House Docks in Dublin as well as in respect of certain designated areas in Cork, Dublin, Galway, Limerick, Waterford, Athlone, Castlebar, Dundalk, Letterkenny, Tralee, Kilkenny, Wexford, Tullamore, Sligo, Ballina, Bray, Carlow, Clonmel, Drogheda, Ennis, Portlaoise and Longford, as well as to the Temple Bar area in Dublin.[1]

7–02 The capital allowances allowed in respect of these designated areas are available against expenditure on the construction or refurbishment of commercial premises such as offices, shops, leisure and car parking facilities, cinemas, theatres and so on. In the areas outside of Dublin the allowances for owner/occupiers are up to 100 per cent for depreciation, and for lessors a 50 per cent initial allowance followed by a 4 per cent annual allowance. The relief applies to expenditure which as been incurred up to July 31, 1994 and in certain circumstances for expenditure incurred up to December 31, 1994.

B. CUSTOMS HOUSE DOCKS AREA AND TEMPLE BAR

7–03 For the Customs House Docks Area and for Tallaght the allowance periods are similar save that the allowances for Tallaght are for the same pe-

---

[1] Finance Act 1986, ss.41–45.

riod as allowances for areas outside of Dublin, while the Custom House Docks Area the time period for expenditure to be incurred is from January 25, 1988 to January 24, 1999, with the allowance allowed for expenditure incurred after January 25, 1998 reduced to 54 per cent. The allowable expenditure for free depreciation for owner/occupiers in Dublin is only 50 per cent while lessors have a 25 per cent initial allowance and a 25 per cent annual allowance.

7–04 The Dublin Docklands Area has the benefit of a scheme of incentives which operate from July 1, 1997 until June 30, 2000 and allow reliefs on expenditure incurred on respect of industrial and commercial buildings of up to 100 per cent in the first year and 50 per cent in the first year for lessors with a 4 per cent per year relief thereafter. An industrial building may be sold after twenty five years and commercial buildings may be sold after thirteen. A double rent allowance for ten years may be received against rents paid under a lease of a building which had the benefit of capital allowances. The reliefs in respect of hotels is 15 per cent per annum for six years and 10 per cent in the seventh year for any expenditure incurred during construction or refurbishment. However, only one type of allowance, capital or double rent allowance may be claimed for hotels. Owner/occupiers of residential accommodation are allowed to claim a deduction of 55 per annum for ten years for newly constructed residences and 10 per cent per annum for ten years for refurbished residences.[2]

7–05 The Temple Bar area in Dublin[3] has an allowable expenditure period of between January 31, 1991 until April 5, 1999. The reliefs available for expenditure on the construction of commercial buildings and industrial buildings are for owner/occupiers a 50 per cent free depreciation allowance or a 25 per cent initial allowance with a 2 per cent annual allowance, but subject to a maximum allowance of 50 per cent of total expenditure. For lessors the initial allowed is 25 per cent followed by an annual allowance of 2 per cent and a ceiling of 50 per cent of expenditure. In the case of multi-storey car parks and for certain refurbishment expenditure on existing buildings the allowance for owner/occupiers is a 100 per cent free depreciation allowance or a 50 per cent initial allowance followed by an annual allowance of 4 per cent with a maximum ceiling of 100 per cent of expenditure. Lessors have an initial allowance of 50 per cent followed by a 4 per cent allowance and again a ceiling of 100 per cent. For existing buildings which are refurbished the capital allowances are also given in respect of the purchase price of the property, but only if the amount of the refurbishment expenditure exceeds or equals the purchase price

---

[2] Finance Act 1997, Part One; see also Finance Act 1998.
[3] Area between Westmoreland St., Dame St., Lord Edward St., and the River Liffey, approval for building must be given by Temple Bar Renewal Ltd. as well as the usual planning requirements.

or the market value of the building on January 1, 1991 whichever is the lower. With all of the allowances, the commercial buildings must be retained for a period of 13 years so as to avoid a balancing charge being imposed (or clawback).[4]

7–06 Section 23 reliefs are available for expenditure incurred for the provision of rented accommodation within the designated areas for urban renewal. The qualifying conditions are similar to those for commercial premises except that the floor area in the case of flats or apartments in the Customs House Docks Area and the Temple Bar area is 125 square metres in respect to expenditure incurred after April 12, 1995. The qualifying expenditure will be allowed against the rental income from the property and from all other properties, and the reliefs are the same for all of the designated areas with the exception that the qualifying date for expenditure in the Temple Bar and Customs House Docks area is on or before July 31, 1994 and for the Custom House Docks area relief is available for expenditure incurred on or before January 24, 1999.[5]

7–07 Individuals who are owner occupiers are entitled to an annual deduction from their income of 5 per cent of the amount of expenditure incurred on the qualifying premises for a period of ten years. The qualifying premises must have been newly constructed or refurbished within the time allocated under the urban renewal scheme. For each year which the allowance is granted the premises must have been the individual's sole or main residence.[6]

7–08 A double rent allowance is allowed in respect of industrial buildings[7] in all of the designated areas and the Customs House Docks area. The double rent allowance is allowed against the trading profits of a trade or profession, and the building must be let under a bona fide commercial lease. The allowance is for a period of ten years starting on the date on which the rent for the premises is first payable.

7–09 Individuals may also claim relief for expenditure incurred on repairing, restoring or maintaining a building which is occupied by that person as their sole or main residence. The building must also be determined by the Commissioners for Public Works in Ireland as being a building which is of significant scientific, historical, architectural or aesthetic interest.[8] The relief is applied to expenditure which has been incurred between May 24, 1989 and

---

4   Finance Act 1993, s.30, in respect of disposals after May 6, 1993.
5   Finance Act 1995, s.32.
6   Finance Act 1993, s.30.
7   See s.42 of the Finance Act 1986.
8   Finance Act 1989, s.4, amended by Finance Act 1992, s.31 and Finance Act 1993, s.31.

July 31, 1994 and is composed of a 25 per cent relief on expenditure in the year of assessment in which the expenditure was incurred and a 5 per cent allowance per annum in the succeeding five years.

C. URBAN RENEWAL SCHEME FOR DESIGNATED STREETS AND AREAS

7–10   A separate scheme has been in operation for designated areas and streets in Dublin, Cork, Limerick, Waterford, Galway, Athlone, Ballina, Ballinasloe, Bray, Carlow, Castlebar, Clonmel, Drogheda, Dundalk, Dungarvan, Ennis, Enniscorthy, Kilkenny, Killarney, Letterkenny, Longford, Mallow, Monaghan, Mullingar, Navan, Nenagh, Newbridge, Portlaoise, Roscommon, Sligo, Tralee, Tullamore, Wexford and Wicklow. The qualifying period commended on August 1, 1994 and ended on July 31, 1997, however that date was extended to July 31, 1998 for projects in respect of which the relevant local authority was able to certify that at least 15 per cent of the total cost of the project had been incurred before July 31, 1997.

7–11   Within the designated areas, expenditure on the construction or refurbishment of a qualifying building qualified for free depreciation of up to 50 per cent of qualifying expenditure in the first year and 4 per cent annual allowance, with only a 25 per cent free depreciation rate allowed for lessors. A qualifying building was one for which was used for the purpose of a trade carried out in a factory, mill, or similar premises or which was let on a bona fide commercial basis.

7–12   For designated streets the allowances are similar to those for designated areas and may be claimed against expenditure spent on refurbishment on a building which was in existence on August 1, 1994 and which fronted onto a designated street. In order to qualify for the allowances, an amount equal to that allowed under the relief must have been spent on the conversion or refurbishment of residential premises in the building, but the annual allowance may be claimed on the excess of expenditure incurred on the industrial refurbishment rather than on the residential premises. Clawback of the allowances operate within a period of thirteen years from the time the premises were first used as an industrial building.

7–13   In the case of commercial buildings the qualifying expenditure has a free depreciation rate of up to 50 per cent in the first year for owner/occupiers, while lessors enjoy the rate of 25 per cent in the first year and a 2 per cent annual allowance. For commercial buildings to qualify it must be used for the purposes of a trade or let on a bona fide commercial basis (even if not used for the purposes of a trade).

7–14   Office accommodation within the county boroughs of Dublin, Cork, Limerick, Galway and Waterford are excluded from the relief for commercial buildings except where the capital expenditure is in relation to the development of office space which amounts to less than 10 per cent of the total capital expenditure of the entire premises, in all other areas office accommodation qualifies as commercial buildings. For designated streets, the qualification criteria includes a matching expenditure for residential accommodation, with a similar clawback as industrial buildings.

7–15   A double rent allowance was also allowed in respect of leases of certain industrial and commercial premises, similar to the double rent allowance under the previous urban renewal relief scheme, and was allowed only in respect of the designated areas.

7–16   In the case of rented residential accommodation expenditure incurred on the construction of rented accommodation in a designated area was allowed as a deduction against the rental income from the premises or other rental income received from other premises. However, there was a maximum floor size of ninety square metres allowed for a flat or maisonette of one hundred and twenty five square metres in respect of expenditure incurred after April 12, 1995 for a house. The relief is claimed over a ten year period and the property must be let for value at arms length and there is a clawback in operation for those who dispose of the property within the ten year period to another party, but the new owner may claim the original relief, provided the relief does not exceed the purchase price paid by the new owner.

7–17   Expenditure incurred on conversion and refurbishment on rented residential accommodation may also be allowed to be deducted against rental income, but only in so far as it relates to the residential premises, with a minimum of two residential units.

D.   OWNER/OCCUPIER RESIDENTIAL ACCOMMODATION

7–18   An annual deduction of 5 per cent in the case of construction expenditure and 10 per cent in the case of refurbishment expenditure is allowed in respect of the construction or refurbishment of residential accommodation in designated areas or refurbishment costs in designated streets in respect of owner/occupiers. The dwelling must be occupied as the sole or main residence of person claiming the relief, and the maximum floor size for a flat or maisonette was 90 square metres and 125 square metres for houses, while any properties being refurbished could have a maximum floor size of 125 square metres.[9]

---

[9]   Finance Act 1997, Finance Act 1995, s.35 and Finance Act 1997, s.26.

There is no clawback on the relief where the owner ceases to occupy or own the premises.

E. URBAN RENEWAL AND ENTERPRISE AREAS

7–19 The 1995 Finance Act[10] allowed for tax allowances for enterprise areas in Dublin, Cork, and Galway, while additional areas in Dublin and Wexford were allowed under the 1997 Finance Act as were areas adjacent to the seven regional airports at Cork, Donegal, Galway, Kerry, Knock, Sligo and Waterford.[11] The allowances are in relation to the construction or refurbishment of premises used by qualifying companies carrying on qualifying trading in these areas.[12]

7–20 Where the areas were designated under the 1995 Finance Act the qualifying period ended on July 31, 1995 but was extended to July 31, 1998 for projects which have been certified by the local authority as having had at least 15 per cent of the total cost of the project spent before July 31, 1997. In areas designated under the 1997 Act the period for relief is extended to June 30, 2000. The service activities which are eligible are data processing, software development, technical and consulting, commercial laboratory, healthcare, research and development, media recording, training, publishing, financial and administrative headquarters.

F. URBAN RENEWAL – RESORTS

7–21 The 1995 Finance Act provided for a scheme for tax reliefs which were aimed at the renewal and the improvement of resort areas in Achill, Arklow, Ballybunion, Bettystown/Laytown/Mosney, Bundoran, Clogherdeah, Clonakilty, Courtown, Enniscrone, Kilkee, Lahinch, Salthill, Tramore, Westport and Youghal. The qualifying period was for expenditure on construction or refurbishment on industrial and tourist buildings from July 1, 1995 until June 30, 1998.

7–22 Industrial buildings are buildings which are used for tourism such as hotels, holiday camps and holiday cottages registered with Bord Fáilte.[13] Other

---

[10] Finance Act 1995, s.35.
[11] Finance Act 1997, s.26.
[12] Certified by the Minister for Enterprise and Employment and either a manufacturing company or an internationally traded service industry approved by Forfas, Forbairt or the IDA.
[13] Finance Act 1995, s.47.

tourist building or facilities are structures in use in the operation of qualifying tourism facilities including accommodation registered or listed under Bord Failte, as well as hotels, guesthouses, caravan camping sites, holiday hostels, youth hostels, and so on.

7–23 Other facilities which do not involve accommodation and which are tourist facilities include leisure and sports facilities, marinas, amusement centres and parks, Irish language schools, tourist information centres interpretative centres and craft centres, restaurants and cafes, car hire centres, and existing enterprises which were listed under the Gaming and Lotteries Act 1956.

7–24 A clawback of the allowances can arise within eleven years after construction or refurbishment and the buildings must remain registered or listed during that period.[14] The reliefs or allowances allowable in the case of holiday cottages, apartments and self catering accommodation are restricted to the double rent allowance with the non application of capital allowances and capital allowances can only be set off against rental income or against income arising from the direct trade of operating the accommodation.[15] The tenants who carry out a trade or profession in a qualifying building will be entitled to a double rent allowance for a period of ten years.[16]

7–25 Allowances which are similar to the allowances allowed under section 23 of the Finance Act 1981 could also be claimed for expenditure which was incurred on the construction, conversion or refurbishment of certain rented residential accommodation. The accommodation had to have been within the resort area and had to have a total floor area of not less than 30 square metres and not more than 125 square metres where the property is a self contained flat, or not less than 35 square metres and not more than 125 square metres in any other case. In addition the premises had to be used primarily for the letting to and occupation by tourists with or without prior arrangement, and that the property is used and occupied for no other purpose during the months of April to October in each year.

7–26 Certain other conditions also apply in that the premises cannot be rented for more than three consecutive months to any one person, or more than six months in any one year to the same person and a register of the tenants must also be maintained. However, the allowances are an attractive 100 per cent of expenditure, exclusive of site costs, which can be offset against all rental income.[17]

---

[14] Finance Act 1995, s.48.
[15] Finance Act 1996, s.30, however, certain reliefs were allowed where certain work was carried out before April 5, 1996
[16] Finance Act 1995, s.49.
[17] Finance Act 1995, s.50–53.

G. URBAN RENEWAL – ISLANDS

7–27 The 1996 Finance Act provided for a scheme of incentives aimed at encouraging people to reside on a number of islands off the south and west coasts of Ireland, namely islands in the counties of Cork, Donegal, Galway, Limerick, Mayo and Sligo. The qualifying period for the reliefs was from August 1, 1996 until July 31, 1999 and were of the similar type as section 23 reliefs under the 1981 Finance Act, in that they allowed rented residential accommodation relief and owner/occupier residential accommodation relief.

7–28 For owner/occupiers the relief can be claimed in each of the first ten years following expenditure on construction or refurbishment but excluding site costs and any local authority grants. The deduction allowed against taxation is 5 per cent per annum of the costs of construction/refurbishment, but the floor area of the property cannot exceed 125 square metres and a certificate of reasonable cost was required from the Department for the Environment. The allowances cannot be carried over and no clawback operates where the owner ceases to occupy the dwelling after first occupation.

CHAPTER 8

Street trading, casual and occasional trading

A. ROLE OF LOCAL AUTHORITIES

8–01   The Occasional Trading Act of 1979,[1] the Casual Trading Act of 1980,[2] repealed by the Casual Trading Act 1995[3] gave the local authority a role in the regulation of occasional trading through the introduction of a system of licensing for casual traders. The Street Trading Act of 1926[4] and the Town Improvements (Ireland) Act of 1854[5] are still in force and have a role to play in the regulation or prescription of certain events and activities.

8–02   The Town Improvements (Ireland) Act of 1854 was introduced into Ireland in a bye gone age where cattle were frequently on the streets of towns and where waggons, carts, or carriages were commonplace. The Act covers a multitude of sins, from hanging clothes lines across streets, rolling casks or wheels upon footpaths to indecent exposure and prostitutes loitering and importuning passengers, and nowadays is rarely used, although children who ring doorbells should be aware that the Act provides for a fine of £2 for their prank.[6]

---

[1]   No. 35 of 1979.
[2]   No. 43 of 1980.
[3]   No. 19 of 1995, came into operation by the Casual Trading Act 1995 (Commencement) Order 1995, S.I. 267 of 1995 on October 16, 1995.
[4]   No. 15 of 1926.
[5]   17 & 18 Vic., c.103.
[6]   s.72.

B. STREET TRADING ACT

8–03 The Street Trading Act was enacted principally to regulate street trading in the County Borough of Dublin and in such other County Boroughs and Urban County Districts as may adopt the Act. Section 2 of the Act made it unlawful for any person to sell or offer, expose or carry for sale any goods of any description in any street in the City of Dublin without holding a street trader's certificate.

8–04 Street trading licences are not required for goods which are displayed or offered or exposed for sale immediately outside of the place at which the trader resides or where the shop is located or for traders at public markets or fairs.[7] Licenses were granted by the Garda Commissioner to persons whom the Commissioner feels is a fit and proper person, and are valid for one year. [8] A street traders stall licence is granted by the Corporation and specifies the place at which the stall is to be kept, and may either be granted in respect of any goods or may be granted for specific goods and at specific places or streets.[9] A stall licence cannot be issued to someone who does not first hold a street traders certificate from the Garda Commissioner, and the stall licence remains in force for so long as the street trader's certificate granted remains in force.

8–05 Whenever the holder of a street trader's certificate is convicted of an offence under the Street Trading Act or of an offence under any regulation or bye-law made under the Act or of another crime or other offence which, in the opinion of the court renders the holder unfit to hold the certificate, the Court may, when imposing sentence, revoke the certificate.[10]

8–06 Any member of the Garda Síochána may demand from any person, whom the member observes engaging in street trading, the production of a street trader's certificate. Any person who fails or refuses to produce the certificate or allow the Garda to read and examine the certificate may be guilty of an offence. A Garda may also demand from any person whom the member observes to be engaged or whom the member believes to be engaging in stall trading in the City of Dublin to produce a street trader's certificate, to produce a street trader's stall licence, the names and addresses and number of assistants, and failure to produce these details may result in the person being found guilty of an offence, unless the person of whom the Garda demanded the details was an assistant to a stall trader.[11] A person who claims to be merely an

---

[7] s.2(5).
[8] s.3.
[9] s.4(2).
[10] s.7(1).
[11] s.9(2).

assistant to a stall trader is obliged to furnish their name and address and the name and address of the stall holder.[12]

8–07   If a demand is made by a Garda of any person in relation to section 9 of the Act, and that person fails or refuses to comply with the demand, the Garda may arrest that person and may seize all of the goods together with any receptacle, vehicle, stand utensils, boxes, any draught animal and other articles, including money.[13] A Garda may without warrant arrest any person whom the member believes to be selling or offering, exposing or carrying for sale any goods, or who has a stall and is operating same in contravention of the Street Trading Act or of any regulation or bye-law made under the Act and may require the stall to be removed or may seize and remove any goods which that person was offering for sale, together with any other article which is being used.[14]

8–08   Whenever any goods are sized and removed under the Street Trading Act, the Commissioner may, in the case of perishable goods, in not less than twelve hours, and any other goods not less than three days after the seizure, cause the goods to be sold and out of the proceeds may take the expenses incurred in the seizure of the goods as well as the expenses incurred in the removal, storage and sale, and shall then pay the remainder to the owner of the goods.[15] Goods which are intended for human consumption and which in the opinion of the Commissioner are unfit for human consumption may have them destroyed.[16]

C.   OCCASIONAL TRADING ACT

8–09   The Occasional Trading Act of 1979 refers to occasional trading by selling goods by retail at a premises or place, not being a public road or an area to which the public have access as of right, and of which the person selling has been in occupation for a continuous period of less than three months.[17] The term occasional trading does not include selling by auction through an auctioneer, selling at a trade, commercial, agricultural or industrial fair or show which is held mainly or wholly for the purpose of other than selling goods, selling of agricultural or horticultural produce, including livestock, by the producer, selling, to a person or at a place which is adjacent to

---

[12] s.9(3).
[13] s.9(4).
[14] s.10.
[15] s.11(1).
[16] s.11(2).
[17] s.2(1).

the place where he resides or carries on business, or the selling by or on behalf of the State or a Minister of Government. Occasional trading also does not include the selling of ice cream, sweets, chocolate confectionery, cooked foods, other than those cooked at the place of sale, fruit or non-alcoholic beverages from a tray, basket, barrow, trolley or other similar device at an event to which the public are admitted, or on the day on which, and at or in the immediate vicinity of the place at which, there takes place, such an event, or the selling of ice-cream, with or without wafers, biscuits or cornets, newspapers, periodicals, magazines or other printed matter or pious or religious objects, or the selling of fish, or other types of trading the profits of which are used for charitable or other purposes from which no private profit is derived or intended to be derived, or the selling of hand-crafted goods by the maker thereof or the spouse or child of such maker.[18]

8–10 A person may also not engage in occasional trading unless he is, or is the servant or agent acting as such of, a person who holds an occasional trading permit and the occasional trading is in accordance with the permit, unless the occasional trading relates to occasional trading engaged in by a person within one month after the commencement of this Act at a premises or place of which the person has been in continuous occupation for a period of less than three months ending at the time of such trading.[19] A trader who intends to engage in occasional trading at a premises or place of which the trader has been in occupation for a period of less than three months, must if the trader intends to occupy the premises or place for more than three months and before commencing such trading makes and gives a declaration to the Minister, a statutory declaration stating that the trader wishes to trade for more than three months and remains in the premises or place for a continuous period of three months or more.[20]

8–11 An application is made, with a payment of a fee of £50, together with a further fee of £25 for each day or part of a day on which the person proposes to engage in occasional trading, and the application must be made not less than thirty days before the first day on which it is intended in occasional trading.[21]

8–12 Occasional trading permits can include conditions which must be complied with, otherwise the holder may be guilty of an offence. An occasional trading permit may be declined if a person has been convicted of an offence under section 3, and a permit may be revoked if a condition of a permit has

---

[18] s.2(2).
[19] s.3.
[20] s.3(3).
[21] s.4.

been or is being contravened or if the person is convicted of an offence under section 3. A permit cannot be granted to a person who was convicted more than once of an offence under section 3 of the Act if the latest conviction occurred less than five years before the first day of proposed trading.

8–13   A person who engages in occasional trading is obliged to display the occasional trading permit at or near the place where the trading is to be carried on and needs to be clearly visible and easily legible to members of the public, otherwise an offence is committed.[22]

8–14   Other offences under the Occasional Trading Act 1979 include giving false information in relation to an application for an occasional trading permit, intending to deceive by either altering or using an occasional trading permit, forging a document and purporting it to be an occasional trading permit.[23] Penalties for offences under the 1979 Act consist of, on indictment to a fine of not over £5,000 together with a fine of not over £250 for each day or part of a day on which the offence is continued, or to a term of imprisonment of not over six months or to both. On a summary conviction a defendant is liable to a fine of not over £500.[24]

8–15   Advertising relating to occasional trading may not be published unless the person intending to trade and has placed the advertisement has a valid occasional trading permit, and the advertisement must contain the number of the permit as well as the name and address of the trader who was granted the licence.[25]

D.   CASUAL TRADING

8–16   Casual trading refers to selling goods at a place, including a public road, to which the public have access as of right or at any other place that is a casual trading area. Casual trading does not include selling by auction, other than Dutch auction, by an auctioneer, or selling to a person at a place where the trader carries on business, or the selling where profits are for charitable purposes or for other purposes from which no private profit is made and that no remuneration, emolument, gain or profit is made by the seller or agents of

---

[22] s.5(1).
[23] s.6(1).
[24] The judge being satisfied that the offence constitutes a minor offence and the Director of Public Prosecutions and the defendant consent to the matter being handled summarily, s.9(2).
[25] s.7.

the seller. A local authority may add to the classes of selling which is not classified as casual trading in respect to their functional area.[26]

8–17 A person may not engage in casual trading unless that person holds a casual trading licence or is the servant or agent of a person who holds a casual trading licence. Where there is a casual trading area within the functional area of a local authority then a person may not engage in casual trading in that area other than in the casual trading area and that person holds a casual trading licence.[27] However, if a casual trading area has not been designated within a functional area of a local authority then casual trading may be permitted.[28]

8–18 Section 7 of the 1980 Act had allowed the local authority to designate areas as casual trading areas, section 7 also allowed local authorities to make bye laws. Kilkenny Corporation made such a set of bye laws but these were declared to be ultra vires in Lyons v. Kilkenny Corporation.[29] The Corporation had made a bye law stating that charges for rental bays would be determined from time to time by the County Manager under the Local Government (Financial Provisions) (No.2) Act 1983.[30] Charges were in fact made headed as "Casual Trading Act 1980" for the use of the trading bays. Barron J. in the High Court held that these charges were ultra vires the corporation because once the local authority had granted a permit to a trader under section 5 it could not then deny the trader the right to use the permit by imposing a charge under section 7 of the Act. The judge did however suggest that a charge could be levied for a ticket to be displayed in the causal trading bay since this could be regarded as a control or regulation of the trading bays.[31]

8–19 In a prosecution for the offence of trading in an area other than a casual trading area, it is presumed, until the contrary is shown that, at the time of the casual trading that the accused was not the holder of a casual trading licence., and that there was a casual trading area within the functional area of the local authority, that the casual trading was carried on in an area that was not a casual trading area.

8–20 Casual trading permits are granted under section 4 of the 1995 Act, and an application in writing is made together with the appropriate fee.[32] The application must be made not less than thirty days before the first day on which

---

[26] s.2.
[27] s.3(2).
[28] s.3(2)(b).
[29] unreported, High Court, February 13, 1987.
[30] See also *Comerford and Others v. O'Malley* [1987] I.L.R.M. 595.
[31] See Byrne and Binchy, *Annual Review of Irish Law 1987* (Round Hall, 1987), p. 7.
[32] s.4(1).

it is intended to engage in casual trading.[33] Conditions can be attached to the casual licence and these conditions are to be complied with, otherwise the holder may be guilty of an offence. A casual licence may not be gratned to a person who has been convicted of an offence under section 3 of the Act. A licence may also be revoked if a condition of the licence has been or is being contravened or if the trader has been convicted of an offence under section 3 of the Act. A casual trading permit cannot be granted to a person who has been convicted more than once of an offence under section 3 if the conviction occurred less than five years before the date of trading, and two of the convictions occurred after the expiration of the last period of disqualification which may have been imposed under any of the convictions.[34]

8–21 A causal trading licence shall not be granted unless the application for a casual trading licence contains the applicant's tax number. The local authority must, following the granting of a casual trading licence, notify the Revenue Commissioners in writing of the name, address and tax reference number of the applicant.[35]

8–22 A person who is engaged in casual trading is obliged to display the trading permit relating to that trading in a position which is at or near to the place where the trading is being carried on so that the permit is clearly visible and easily legible to members of the public. Otherwise the trader may be guilty of an offence under the Act.[36] Other offences under the Casual Trading Act include giving false information in respect to an application for the grant of a casual trading permit, intended to deceive by either altering or using a casual trading permit, forging a document purporting to be a casual trading permit.[37]

8–23 Persons who advertise without a casual trading permit may also be guilty of an offence as casual traders, who are not in possession of a casual trading permit may not advertise the trading, the advertising should also include the number of the permit as well as the name and address of the trader who was granted the licence.[38]

8–24 Authorised officers may be appointed under both under the Casual Trading Act and the Occasional Trading Act, and these officers may enter, inspect and examine any place or premises where casual trading is being engaged in. Authorised officers may require any person, whom the officer has

---

[33] s.4(2).
[34] s.4(6).
[35] s.2A(a), inserted by the Finance Act 1996.
[36] s.5.
[37] s.6.
[38] s.7(1), advertising includes a catalogue, a circular and a price list.

reasonable cause to believe to be engaging in casual trading to produce a casual trading permit, or to take the name of the trader as well as the servant or agent of a trader. The officer may also require a person to give particulars of the ownership of any goods which are being sold or used for the purpose of casual trading, and may require any person to produce documents, books or records relating to the trading, and the officer may examine, copy or take extracts from these documents.[39] Obstruction or interference of an authorised officer or the giving of false information is an offence, as is failing, refusing or neglecting to comply with a requirement of an authorised officer. However, a person who has failed to comply with a requirement of an authorised officer or has failed to produce a casual trading permit may instead give the authorised officer their name and address as well as the name and address of the trader of whom the person is the servant or agent of a trader.[40]

8–25   A person who has been found guilty of an offence under section 3 of the Casual Trading Act may be liable to a fine not exceeding £500 in the case of a summary offence and a fine of £5,000 on a conviction on indictment and in the case of a continuing offence to a fine of not over £250 for each day or part of a day on which the offence is continued, or to a term of imprisonment of not over six months or to both the fine and imprisonment.[41] A Judge of the District Court may have jurisdiction to try a prosecution under section 3 summarily if the Judge is of the opinion that the facts proved or alleged constitutes a minor offence which is fit to be tried summarily, and the Director of Public Prosecutions consents to the case being tried summarily and the defendant does not object to being tried summarily. A defendant has the right to have a prosecution dealt with before a jury.

8–26   A person who has being found guilty of an offence other than an offence under section 3 may be liable, on summary conviction, to a fine of not over £500.[42]

---

[39]   s.8(1).
[40]   s.8(4).
[41]   s.9(1).
[42]   s.9.

CHAPTER 9

Control of animals

A. CONTROL OF DOGS

9–01 Under the Control of Dogs Act 1986 to 1992[1] the local authorities[2] are given a role in the control and licensing of dogs. Section 2 of the Act makes it unlawful for any person to keep a dog unless that person holds a dog licence for that dog or holds a general dog licence. A general dog licence means a licence entitling a person to keep an unspecified number of dogs at a premises which is specified in the licence. Only one premises can be specified in a general dog licence.[3] Dog licences are issued by the local authority for the functional area in which the dog is kept at or is intended to be kept. General dog licences are also issued by the local authority and relate to all dogs kept at the premises specified in the licence.[4]

9–02 Licences cannot be issued to any person under the age of sixteen years or to a person who has been disqualified under the Act from keeping a dog.[5] Any person who has been convicted under the Protection of Animals Acts, 1911 and 1965, of the offence of cruelty to a dog may be disqualified from keeping a dog for such period as the Court sees fit.[6] A licence is not required for dogs in the custody of the local authority, the Irish Society for the Preven-

---

[1] No. 32 of 1986 and 13 of 1992.
[2] The term local authorities in these Acts does not include urban district council.
[3] s.1, as amended by s.2 of the 1992 Act.
[4] s.3, under s.3(3) allows the local authorities to issue the licences by arrangement with other parties, the current practice is to issue dog licences with An Post
[5] s.4.
[6] s.18(1).

tion of Cruelty to Animals,[7] or such other person who has entered into an agreement with the local authority, or by members of An Garda Síochána for dogs used in the course of duty, nor are licences required by a blind person whose eyesight is so defective as to require a guide dog.[8] Licences are also not required for dogs who are under the age of four months and are being kept with their dam or foster mother, nor for dogs in the possession of an inspector or other office of the Department of Agriculture for the purposes of the Diseases of Animals Act 1966, nor for dogs who are imported into the State for a period of not over thirty days, nor for a dog which is a greyhound who is purchased for export and which is then exported within thirty days from the State. Dog licences are issued for a period of twelve months and the current fee in respect of dog licences is £10, while the fee for a general dog licence is £200.[9]

9–03 Under section 9 the owners or any person in charge of a dog are obliged to ensure that the dog is not in any place other than the premises of the owner, or the premises of a person in charge of the dog unless the owner or other person accompanies the dog and keeps it under effectual control.[10] Section 10 obliges greyhounds to be led by means of a sufficiently strong chain or leash while they are in a public place, and a person may not lead more than four greyhounds at a time in a public place.

9–04 If a dog worries livestock, the owner or any other person in charge of the dog may be guilty of an offence, unless it can be established that at the time the dog worried the livestock for the purpose of removing trespassing livestock, and that having regard to all the circumstances it was a reasonable and necessary action.[11]

9–05 Section 15 gives local authorities the power, in fact they have a duty, to appoint dog wardens for the purposes of the Act, and dog wardens are obliged to carry a certificate of appointment for production on request. Local authorities are also obliged to establish and maintain one or more shelters for dogs who are seized, accepted or detained under any provision of the Control of Dogs Acts and can also enter into arrangements with other persons for the provision and maintenance of these shelters, as well as for the exercise of certain functions under the Act such as the disposal and destruction of stray and unwanted dogs.[12] The local authority may arrange for another local au-

---

[7] For a case involving the ISPCA see *Flannery v. Dean* [1995] 2 I.L.R.M. 393.
[8] s.5.
[9] Formerly £5 and £100 respectively.
[10] s.9(1), note the section does not say to keep the dog on a lead.
[11] s.9(2).
[12] s.15(2).

thority or the Irish Society for the Prevention of Cruelty to Animals to exercise all of their functions under the Act with the exception to the power to make bye laws and the role of prosecutor which the local authority has under section 30.[13]

9–06 With respect to dog wardens, a dog warden has the power to seize any dog and detain it in order to ascertain whether an offence under the Act has been committed and may enter any premises other than a dwelling, for such purposes.[14] A dog warden may request the name and address of a person whom the warden has reasonable grounds for believing has committed an offence under the Act.

9–07 Dog wardens may also enter any premises, other than a dwelling, for the purpose of preventing or ending an attack by a dog on any person, or the worrying of livestock and may also enter any premises (other than a dwelling) which are registered in accordance with regulations made under section 19 of this Act, or where he has reasonable grounds for believing that more than five dogs which are aged over four months are kept, and examine any dogs contained within the premises and may request any person who owns or is in charge of any kennels on the premises to produce a dog licence or a general dog licence within ten days for examination by the warden.[15] A dog warden is obliged to take all reasonable steps to seize and detain any dog that appears to be a stray dog and may enter any premises, other than a dwelling, for the purpose of seizing and detaining a stray dog.[16] The powers of the dog warden to enter any premises is therefore restricted to these categories and a dog warden does not have any authority to enter onto any dwelling for any purpose under the Act.

9–08 Any person who obstructs or impedes a dog warden in the exercise of his functions under this Act, or refuses to give his name and address to a dog warden when requested so to do, or who gives a name or address which is false or misleading when so requested shall be guilty of an offence.[17]

9–09 A dog warden is obliged to take all reasonable steps to seize and detain any dog that appears to be a stray dog and may enter any premises, other than a dwelling, for the purpose of seizing and detaining a stray dog. Stray dogs include any dog which appears to be unaccompanied by a person, unless the dog is on the premises of its owner or of some other person who has the

---

[13] s.15(3).
[14] s.16(1).
[15] s.16(1).
[16] s.11(1).
[17] s.16(3).

dog in their charge.[18] Gardai may also seize and detain a dog whom the member believes to be a stray and that member is then obliged to deliver the dog to the local authority in whose area the dog was found. Following the seizure and detention of a stray dog, notice is required to be given by the local authority or by the Superintendent of the Garda Síochána, to the owner of the dog of the fact that the dog has been seized and that the dog will be disposed of or destroyed after five days from the date of the giving of the notice, unless the dog is claimed and all expenses paid.[19]

9–10 Whenever a stray dog has been seized and detained the local authority or the Garda Superintendent are required to enter the fact into the register which they are obliged to keep under section 14 of the Act, and five days after making the entry into the register or after the service of the notice, the dog may be disposed of or destroyed in a humane manner.[20] The disposal of dogs under section 11, or of unwanted dogs under section 12, does not include the disposal of a dog for the purposes of animal experimentation,[21] although before disposing of a dog the local authority may arrange to have the dog sterilised.[22]

9–11 Any person who finds and takes possession of a stray dog is obliged to do one of three things, to return the dog to its owner, or to deliver the dog to a dog warden or to detain the dog and give notice in writing to the member in charge of the nearest Garda Station, giving a description of the dog, where it was found and the address of the place where it is now being kept.[23] After one year, the person who has found the dog, and if the dog has not been claimed by its owner, shall become its owner and the title of the former owner is ended.[24] Where a person believes that a dog has worried or is about to worry livestock, that person may seize the dog and deliver it to a dog warden.

9–12 The owner of a dog is liable in damages for any damage caused in an attack on any person by a dog and for any injury done to livestock. It is not necessary for the person seeking such damages to show a previous mischievous propensity in the dog, or to prove the owner's knowledge of such previous propensity, or to show that such injury or damage was attributable to neglect on the part of the owner.[25] Where livestock are injured by a dog on land onto

---

[18] s.11(11).
[19] s.11(4).
[20] s.11(6), (7).
[21] s.11(8).
[22] s.11(9).
[23] s.13(1), a dog licence need not be purchased by the person who has found the dog until the expiration of twenty eight days, s.13(5).
[24] s.13 (3).
[25] s.21(1).

which they had strayed, and the dog belonged to the occupier of the land, a person shall not be liable for damages in respect of injury done to the livestock, unless the person caused the dog to attack the livestock. Damages in relation to trespass of a dog onto property are restricted to the rules relating to liability for negligence and are not covered by section 21.

9–13   In the case of dangerous dogs a complaint can be made to the District Court by any interested person, including a local authority, that a dog is dangerous and not kept under proper control, and if it appears to the Court that the dog is dangerous and not kept under proper control, the Court may order that the dog be kept under proper control or be destroyed.[26] The expenses of the destruction of the dog may be directed to be paid by the owner of the dog, and the dog is then delivered to the dog warden for destruction, in a humane manner. Any sums payable by the owner of a dog pursuant to a direction of the Court may be recovered by a local authority as a simple contract debt. Where a dog is proved to have caused damage in an attack on any person, or to have injured livestock, the dog may be treated as a dangerous dog which has not been kept under proper control.

9–14   Where a person, such as a farmer shoots a dog the Act allows a defence to any action for damages, or to any charge arising out of the shooting of a dog, if the farmer, or other person proves that the dog was shot when it was worrying, or was about to worry, livestock and that there were no other reasonable means of ending or preventing the worrying, or the dog was a stray dog which was in the vicinity of a place where livestock had been injured or killed. The farmer or person must also have reasonably believed that the dog had been involved in the injury or killing, and that there were no practicable means of seizing the dog or ascertaining to whom the dog belonged, and that at the time of the shooting he was the person in charge of the livestock; and that the shooting was notified within forty-eight hours to the member in charge at the nearest Garda Station.[27]

9–15   In relation to nuisance caused by the excessive barking of dogs a complaint can be made to the District Court by any person, including a local authority. The District Court may order the occupier of the premises in which the dog is kept to abate the nuisance by exercising due control over the dog and/or make an order limiting for such period, as may be specified in the order, the

---

[26] s.22(1).
[27] s.23, the dog must have been about to worry or have worried livestock, and not have entered the lands for the purpose of gaining access to an unburied carcass, as allowing unburied carcass on land is an offence under s.24.
[28] s.25(1).
[29] s.27.

number of dogs to be kept by the respondent on his premises or direct that the dog be delivered to a dog warden to be dealt with by him in accordance with the provisions of this Act as if the dog were an unwanted dog.[28]

9–16 Offences under the Control of Dogs Acts bring with them a fine of not over £1,000 and a term of imprisonment of not over three months or both on summary prosecution,[29] and prosecution of offences may be pursued by the local authority in whose area the offence is alleged to have been committed, while search warrants for dangerous dogs or dogs who have worried livestock can only be obtained by members of the Garda Síochána on application to the District Court Judge or to a Peace Commissioner.[30]

B. CONTROL OF HORSES

9–17 The Control of Horses Act of 1996[31] came about in response to the then increasing numbers of horses being kept by people, especially young people in built up areas, and which are a danger to people and property or which create a nuisance. The Act provides for the appointment of persons appointed by the local authority to carry out the functions of the authority in respect of the Act, creates a number of new offences, provides for the disqualification of certain persons from keeping horses, and most importantly provides for a system of control and of the licensing of horses in certain "controlled" areas. Under the Act the term "horse" includes a donkey, mule and hinny.[32]

9–18 In respect to disqualification from keeping a horse, a person, who is convicted of an offence under section 45, or under section 46(3), dealing with bye laws[33] for the control and welfare of horses,[34] or section 47(3) dealing with bye laws for the exclusion of horses from certain areas, may also be disqualified from keeping, dealing in or having charge or control, directly or indirectly of a horse for such period as the court sees fit.[35] Section 45 states that the "owner, keeper or person in charge or control of a horse who wilfully or recklessly permits the horse to pose a danger to a person or property or to cause injury to a person or damage to any property shall be guilty of an offence". Section 45(2) provides that a person who wilfully or recklessly causes

---

[30] s.26.

[31] No. 37 of 1996.

[32] s.2(1).

[33] The making of bye laws under the Act is a reserved function, s.13(9).

[34] See *Flannery v. Dean* [1995] 2 I.L.R.M. 393.

[35] s.7(1), a person so disqualified may apply to have the disqualification lifted under s.7(2) after three months.

a horse to pose a danger to a person or to property or to injure a person or damage any property shall also be guilty of an offence.

9–19   On a conviction for an offence under the Control of Horses Act the court may order the forfeiture of the horse to the local authority, who may then seize and detain the horse and dispose of it. The local authority may also apply to the court to have the horse seized and detained where the owner of the horse is unknown or cannot be found and where it is considered necessary having regard to the welfare and interests of the horse and the fitness of the owner to own the horse.[36]

9–20   A local authority may decide to adopt bye laws in order to declare all or part of its functional area to be a control area and provide that horses within this controlled area should have licenses.[37] The decision to create a controlled area will be based on the fact that horses are straying or being allowed to stray in the area and are becoming a nuisance or danger to persons and property. Local authorities may decide to exclude horses from certain areas of its functional area by bye-law, without making the area a "controlled area", where it considers that in that place horses are causing or may cause a nuisance or danger to persons or property. The bye-laws may prohibit persons from having, keeping, riding or driving a horse in that area or place at any time or at specified times, and any contravention of these bye-laws would be an offence under the Act.[38]

9–21   Where a local authority has already declared part of its area to be a control area and horses are regularly straying or being brought into that control area from any area, or kept or straying into any area adjacent to the control area, which is part of the functional area of an adjoining local authority and which has not been declared a control area and these horses from the adjoining area are causing nuisance, annoyance or injury to persons or damage to property in the control area, the local authority affected may request the adjoining local authority to declare that part of its functional area to be a control area.[39] If it is the case that the adjoining local authority is unwilling to so declare, the local authority may request the Minister to make a direction that an area be declared a controlled area for the purposes of the Act.[40]

9–22   Once an area has been declared to be a controlled area under the Control of Horses Act a person who owns a horse, which is kept by them or on

---

[36] s.8(1).
[37] s.17(1).
[38] s.47.
[39] s.17(2).
[40] s.17(3).

their behalf in a control area shall, unless he or she holds a horse licence in respect of the horse entitling that owner to keep the horse in the control area, be guilty of an offence.[41]

9–23   A person who is not the owner of the horse and who keeps the horse in a controlled area or under their charge, to which there is no licence in force shall also be guilty of an offence.[42] Licences are not required by an authorised person or a member of the Garda Síochána acting in the course of his or her duty, a pound keeper who keeps a horse in a pound, a veterinary surgeon providing veterinary services for a horse, any person who keeps or has charge or control of a horse for the purpose of preventing it causing injury to persons or damage to property, and restoring the horse to its owner or keeper, or handing it over to an authorised person or a member of the Garda Síochána, or any person with whom a local authority or a Garda Superintendent has entered into an arrangement to hold horses under the Act.[43]

9–24   In a prosecution for not having a licence for a horse in a controlled area it is a defence for the accused to show that at the time of the alleged offence he or she had not given permission for the horse to be kept in the control area. Whereas in a prosecution for an offence of not having a licence for a horse in a controlled area, and not being the owner of the horse it is a defence for the accused who is not the keeper to show that at the time of the alleged offence he or she had no reason to believe that there was not a horse licence in force in respect of the horse entitling it to be kept in the control area.[44] It is also a defence to show that at the time of the alleged offence there was an application for a horse licence in respect of the horse being considered, provided the accused can produce a receipt of the application and accompanying fee issued by the relevant authority.[45]

9–25   Certain exemptions from holding a horse licence are allowed under section 19 of the Act. A horse licence is not required in respect of a horse which is kept by a local authority in respect of any of its functions, or for a horse which is kept by the Garda Síochána and used by a member of the Garda Síochána or for a horse which is kept by the Minister for Defence and used by a member of the Defence Forces in the execution of the member's duties, or for a horse which is in the possession of an authorised officer under the Diseases of Animals Act 1966. Horses imported into the State for a period of not over ninety days do not require a horse licence, nor for horses which have

---

[41] s.18(1).
[42] s.18(2).
[43] s.18(3).
[44] s.18(6), (7).
[45] s.18(8).

been brought into the controlled area for the purpose of participating in an event on a day or days allowed by bye-laws.[46] Licences are not required for foals, or for horses who are receiving veterinary treatment from a veterinary surgeon.

9–26 Horses which have been recently purchased or have come into the possession of the owner or keeper for the first time, for a period of one week from the date of the purchase or the coming into possession, or such other period as may be permitted by the local authority by their bye-laws are also not required to have a licence, nor do horses which are being transported through the controlled area for the purposes of export or for horses which have been imported and are being transported through the controlled area. No exemption has been specified in the Act for the transportation of horses within the State through the controlled area for the purposes of, for instance, selling the horse to another person. The Act clearly intends that in controlled areas even bringing a horse in a horse box through the area requires a licence, unless the horse has been recently purchased.

9–27 Horse licences are issued by the local authority for the area in which the horse is to be kept or brought into. The licence is issued in respect to a particular horse which is specified and identified in the licence.[47] Horse licences cannot be granted to persons under the age of sixteen or to a person who has been disqualified under the Act from keeping a horse, or to a person who is, in the opinion of the local authority, unfit to keep a horse or who fails to satisfy the local authority that the horse will be properly maintained.[48] It is also an offence for any person to sell or offer to sell a horse to a person who is apparently under the age of sixteen, where the word "sell" also includes barter, exchange and other types of transactions by which a horse is disposed of for value.[49]

9–28 A horse licence is valid for a period of twelve months, or less if provided for by the local authority bye-laws, or is valid until such time as the holder of the licence ceases to own the horse to which the licence relates. A local authority may revoke or suspend a horse licence if the holder of the licence is convicted of an offence in relation to the horse, or the horse is detained under the Act on two or more occasions while the licence is in force. The licence can also be revoked where there are reasonable grounds for believing that the holder of the licence is not complying with the terms of the licence, if any, or is abusing or not properly keeping, controlling or maintain-

---

[46] s.19(1), the making of bye laws is a reserved function, s.19(2).
[47] s.20(3).
[48] s.20(5).
[49] s.43.

ing or causing injury or harm to any horse, including the horse to which the licence relates, or where the holder of the licence has had another licence for a horse revoked, suspended or amended.[50]

9–29 With regard to the issue of horse licences local authorities may enter into arrangements with other local authorities whereby the other local authority would issue, amend or revoke licences, and such an arrangement is a reserved function.[51] Applications for horse licences are made by the owner of the horse in writing and accompanied by the relevant fee to the local authority in whose area the horse will be kept. Any person who knowingly and wilfully gives any false or misleading information in respect of an application for a licence may be guilty of an offence.[52] An offence is also committed by persons who forge, or fraudulently alter or use or permit the fraudulent alteration or use of a horse licence.[53] A local authority may examine the horse to which the application for a horse licence relates and, where appropriate, any premises where the horse is kept or intended to be kept.[54]

9–30 Whenever a local authority proposes to refuse to grant or decides to suspend or revoke, or amend the terms or conditions of, a horse licence the local authority are obliged to notify in writing the applicant or the holder of the licence of that fact and, if any representations are made to it in writing by such applicant or holder within fourteen days of the notification, the local authority are obliged to consider the representations.[55] Following the consideration of these representations, the local authority may then decide to grant, amend or revoke a licence, and the applicant has fourteen days, from the date of receipt of the decision, in which to appeal that decision to the District Court within whose district the horse was or is to be kept, otherwise the decision of the local authority shall take effect, shall stand suspended or the licence shall remain in force, whichever the case may be, until the appeal is heard.[56] Decisions of the District Court are final save on a specified question of law where an appeal shall lie to the High Court, by leave of the District Court.[57]

9–31 Each local authority is obliged to establish and maintain a register of all horse licences granted by it. Each register contains particulars regarding an identification reference, a description of the horse, the name and address of the owner of the horse, when the horse licence was granted, where the horse is

---

[50] s.21(8).
[51] s.20(10).
[52] s.22(1).
[53] s.21.
[54] s.22(4).
[55] s.23(1).
[56] s.23(2).
[57] s.23(7).

normally kept, the name and address of the keeper of the horse, where the horse is kept by a person other than the owner, the name and address of any person to whom ownership of the horse is transferee and any other relevant particulars.[58]

9–32   Where the holder of a horse licence disposes of the horse he shall within fourteen days inform the local authority of that fact and shall surrender the licence and give the name and address of the new owner, the same is the case where the horse dies.[59] A person who, without reasonable excuse, fails to comply with this section may be guilty of an offence.[60]

9–33   An authorised person appointed by the local authority or a member of the Garda Síochána may request any person whom the person or member reasonably suspects of being the owner of a horse which is being kept in a control area to state whether he or she is the holder of a horse licence in force in respect of the horse, and to produce the licence relating to the horse.[61] If the holder of the licence fails to produce the licence within ten days, they may be guilty of an offence.

9–34   Where an authorised person acting on behalf of the local authority or a member of the Garda Síochána finds a horse in a public place within a control area and the person or member has reasonable cause to suspect that there is no horse licence in force in respect of the horse or that the horse is not exempt under section 19 from being licensed in that control area, the authorised person or member may require any person apparently keeping or having charge or control of the horse to remove it immediately from that public place or the control area, and any person who, without reasonable excuse, fails to comply with such a requirement may be guilty of an offence.[62]

9–35   An authorised person or a member of the Garda Síochána may inspect and examine any horse and any person who is apparently in charge or control of a horse that is the subject of an inspection or examination are obliged to give to the authorised person or member of the Garda Síochána making the inspection or examination such reasonable assistance as the authorised person or member may request. A person who, again without reasonable excuse, fails to comply with such a request may be guilty of an offence.[63] Any person who keeps or has charge or control of a horse, or the owner or any person having

---

[58]   s.24(1).
[59]   s.25(1), (2).
[60]   s.25(3).
[61]   s.26(1).
[62]   s.27(1)
[63]   s.29.

the charge or management of any premises on which a horse is found, are obliged if requested by an authorised person or a member of the Garda Síochána, to give the name and address of the owner of the horse, as well as the name and address of a person to whom the member has reasonable grounds for suspecting has committed an offence under the Act and a person who fails to comply with such a request may be also guilty of an offence.[64]

9–36 An authorised person or a Garda who has reasonable cause to believe that a person is offending the provisions of section 45 of the Act, dealing with criminal liability for injury or damage caused by horses, or of any bye laws made under the Act, may direct that person to desist from offending, and any person who, without reasonable excuse, fails to comply with the order may be guilty of an offence.[65]

9–37 Where an authorised person or a member of the Garda Síochána has reasonable cause to suspect that a horse is in pain, or distress or in an acute state of neglect or is so severely injured or diseased as to be in need of veterinary attention, the authorised person or the Garda may require the owner or keeper of the horse, or the person in charge or control of the horse, to immediately obtain any necessary veterinary attention from a veterinary surgeon for the horse.[66] Any person who, without reasonable excuse, does not comply with this requirement may be guilty of an offence.

9–38 Where an authorised person or a member of the Garda Síochána has reason to suspect that an offence is being or has been committed under this Act in or on any premises or in any vehicle, or a person is causing harm to or mistreating a horse on any premises or in any vehicle, that authorised person or Garda may stop any such vehicle or enter, if necessary by the use of reasonable force, any premises or any vehicle, and there search for any horse, or search for and examine any document and take extracts from and copies of any such document and carry out any of the functions conferred on an authorised person or Garda under the Act. However, an authorised person or Garda may not enter a dwelling unless the occupier has consented to their entry or unless a search warrant has been obtained from the District Court authorising the entry.[67]

9–39 Search warrants are obtained by information supplied on oath of an authorised person or of a Garda that the person applying for the warrant has reasonable grounds for believing that there is evidence on any premises relat-

---

[64] s.30(1) and s.31(1).
[65] s.32.
[66] s.33.
[67] s.34.

ing to an offence under the Act or that a person is causing harm to or mistreating a horse on any premises. Applications for search warrants are made to the District Court in whose area the premises are situated. Search warrants are issued to a named member of the Garda Síochána accompanied by other Gardai or accompanied by an authorised person and with equipment which is necessary. The search warrant is valid for a period of one month and may be used on more than one occasion, and reasonable force may be used to gain entry to the premises detailed in the warrant.[68] Any person who obstructs or impedes an authorised person or a member of the Gardai while exercising any of the powers or functions under the Act may be guilty of an offence.[69]

9–40 An authorised person or a member of the Garda Síochána may seize and detain any horse that the person or member has reason to suspect is a stray horse, or which is causing a nuisance, or is not under adequate control, or is posing a danger to persons or property, or is posing a threat to the health and welfare of persons or other animals, or is being kept in a control area, without a horse licence in respect of it entitling the horse to be kept in that area, or is not identifiable, or is being kept or ridden or driven in an area contrary to any bye-laws made under the Act. An authorised person or a member of the Garda Síochána may seize and detain a horse in relation to which a requirement has been made under section 33, regarding the requirement that a horse receive veterinary treatment, and the person or member has reasonable cause to suspect that the necessary veterinary attention has not been or is not likely to be obtained.[70]

9–41 A horse which has been seized may be detained in a pound anywhere or in such other place as which may be specified by the local authority in whose functional area the horse was seized or by the Garda Superintendent. A person who without lawful authority removes a horse while it is being detained under this section shall be guilty of an offence.[71] Where a horse has been detained the local authority in whose functional area the horse is detained or the Garda Superintendent may cause to be attached to the horse an identification mark or device.[72]

9–42 Whenever a horse has been detained the local authority or the Garda Superintendent may continue to detain the horse for use in evidence in any criminal proceedings, for such period from the seizure or detention as is reasonable, or, if proceedings are commenced in which the horse is required for

---

[68] s.35.
[69] s.36.
[70] s.37.
[71] s.37(3), (4).
[72] s.38.

use in evidence, until the conclusion of the proceedings. The horse may also be continued to be detained where it is intended to make an application under section 8 for the forfeiture of the horse, and to continue to detain the horse until the conclusion of the proceedings, or where that horse has previously been detained on two or more occasions within a period of twelve months, and deal with the horse in accordance with section 40, regarding the power to dispose of horses detained on three or more occasions and in any other case, deal with the horse in accordance with any bye-laws made by the local authority. If a horse has to be destroyed the local authority are obliged to endeavour that the horse is destroyed humanely.[73]

9–43 Bye laws may be made regarding the detention of horses and may prescribe the notices to be given or displayed in connection with the detaining of such horses, the fees to be paid by the owner or keeper of such horses including fees in respect of their keep, any veterinary services and any transportation, the provision of veterinary services for such horses, the disposal of a horse where the owner or keeper is unknown or cannot be found and the time after which such disposal shall take place. Bye laws may also be made relating to the disposal of a horse where the owner or keeper fails to pay any fees specified in bye-laws made under this subsection, or fails to produce, where appropriate, a horse licence for the time being in force in respect of the horse granted by that local authority or another relevant local authority if the horse is kept in a control area declared by that authority or another authority, or fails to remove the horse, and for the disposal pursuant to a direction of the local authority in whose functional area a horse is detained or of the Superintendent.[74]

9–44 Even where the required fees are paid to the local authority or to the keeper of a pound, as the case may be, a local authority or a Superintendent or the keeper of the pound may refuse to release any horse detained where it or he or she, is not satisfied that adequate accommodation and sustenance, or that adequate veterinary attention, will be provided for the horse, or has reason to believe that the horse will be cruelly treated, following release.[75] Where a horse is to be disposed of, the local authority, or the Garda Superintendent may prevent the disposal of the horse to the previous owner or keeper of the horse from whom it was seized, or that the horse is disposed of to a person acting on the previous owners' or keepers' behalf.[76]

9–45 Where a horse which has been detained under section 37 and has pre-

---

[73] s.39(7).
[74] s.39(2).
[75] s.39(5).
[76] s.39(6).

viously been detained on two or more occasions within a period of twelve months, the horse may be disposed of by the local authority or by the Garda Superintendent, if they are of the opinion that the owner or keeper of the horse is not exercising adequate control over the horse so as to prevent it straying, causing a nuisance, or posing a danger to persons or property, or that the horse is likely to be in a public place while not under adequate control, or which is not identifiable or capable of identification as may be required by section 28 of the Act.[77] The fees which are specified by bye law for the disposal of the horse under section 40 may be recoverable from the owner or keeper of the horse which has been detained, and may be recovered as a simple debt by the local authority.[78]

9–46   Where it is proposed to dispose of a horse the authority or the Superintendent, are obliged to display publicly a notice to that effect at the place where the horse is detained and in such other places as it or he or she sees fit and shall send a notice in writing to the owner or keeper, whose whereabouts is known and can be readily found, of the horse, stating that at any time after the expiration of five days from the publication of the notice,[79] it is intended to dispose of the horse and the reasons for and the nature of the proposed disposal. The owner or keeper may within that period make representations, including representations to the effect that the owner of the horse was not the owner of the horse on any previous occasion when it was detained under section 37 during the aforesaid period of twelve months, to the local authority or the Superintendent, against the proposal.[80] Following consideration of the representations made the local authority or Garda Superintendent are obliged to notify the person who has made the representations of their decision on the disposal of the horse and an appeal may be made to the District Court within seven days.[81]

9–47   Section 41 of the Act makes provision for the destruction of detained horses which are in pain or distress or who are in an acute state of neglect. After a veterinary examination, if it is the opinion of the veterinary surgeon making the examination that the horse is in such pain or distress or state of acute neglect or so severely injured or diseased and that it would be in the interests of the welfare of the horse, or the safety, health or welfare of other animals or persons it may come into contact with, to have it humanely destroyed, the local or the Superintendent or a person authorised by the authority or Superintendent may direct that the horse be so destroyed.

---

[77] s.40(1).
[78] s.40(2).
[79] Or such longer period as may be stated in the notice.
[80] s.40(3).
[81] s.40(4).

9–48 Local authorities are obliged to establish and maintain a register of all horses seized and detained within its area, as do Garda Superintendents. Every register shall contain at least the following details, an identification reference, a description of the horse, the date of the seizure or detention of the horse, particulars of the manner in which the horse is dealt with, details of the person by whom a horse is reclaimed, and particulars of where the horse is detained.[82]

9–49 Lastly, the Control of Horses Act provided for an increase in the penalties which can be imposed for cruelty to animals. On a summary conviction a person may face a fine of not over £1,500 or a term of imprisonment of six months or both, and on indictment to a fine of not over £10,000 or two years imprisonment or both. Under the Protection of Animals Act 1911, an offence is committed if any person:

"(a) shall cruelly beat, kick, ill-treat, over-ride, over-drive, over-load, torture, infuriate, or terrify any animal, or shall cause or procure, or, being the owner, permit any animal to be so used, or shall, by wantonly or unreasonably doing or omitting to do any act, or causing or procuring the commission or omission of any act, cause any unnecessary suffering, or, being the owner, permit any unnecessary suffering to be so caused to any animal; or

(b) shall convey or carry, or cause or procure, or, being the owner, permit to be conveyed or carried, any animal in such manner or position as to cause that animal any unnecessary suffering; or

(c) shall cause, procure, or assist at the fighting or baiting of any animal; or shall keep, use, manage, or act or assist in the management of, any premises or place for the purpose, or partly for the purpose, of fighting or baiting any animal, or shall permit any premises or place to be so kept, managed, or used, or shall receive, or cause or procure any person to receive, money for the admission of any person to such premises or place; or

(d) shall wilfully, without any reasonable cause or excuse, administer, or cause or procure, or being the owner permit, such administration of, any poisonous or injurious drug or substance to any animal, or shall wilfully, without any reasonable cause or excuse, cause any such substance to be taken by any animal; or

(e) shall subject, or cause or procure, or being the owner permit, to be subjected, any animal to any operation which is performed without due care and humanity; or

(f) being the owner or having care or control of any animal shall without reasonable cause or excuse abandon it, whether permanently or not, in circumstances likely to cause it unnecessary suffering, or cause or procure or, being the owner, permit it to be so abandoned."[83]

---

[82] s.42.

[83] s.1 of the Protection of Animals Act 1911 as amended by the Control of Horses Act 1996.

CHAPTER 10

Pollution control

A. WATER POLLUTION

1. Introduction

10–01   The Local Government (Water Pollution) Acts 1977 to 1990[1] govern the control of water pollution and matters related to water pollution and build upon a base of previous legislation, including the Public Health (Ireland) Act of 1878. Section 3 of the 1977 Act forbids the entry of any polluting matter into waters, the term waters includes any river, stream, lake, canal, reservoir, aquifer, pond, watercourse, or other inland waters, whether it is natural or artificial, any tidal waters and any beach, river bank, and salt marsh or areas contiguous to any of these, as well as the channel or bed of any of the above, but the term does not include a sewer. The term sewer refers to the term of sewer in the Local Government (Sanitary Services) Acts 1878 to 1965 and includes sewage treatment or the disposal works of a sanitary authority.[2]

2. Waste licences

(a) Issuing of licences

10–02   With respect to licensing of trade and sewage effluents a licence to discharge trade effluent or sewage to waters in the functional area of a local

---

[1]   Nos. 21 of 1990 and 1 of 1977.
[2]   s.1. See also Public Health (Ireland) Act 1878 which established sanitary authorities and dealt with sewers.

authority is issued by that local authority and in any other case by a local authority in whose area the premises, works, apparatus, plant or drainage pipe from which the effluent is being discharged from is situated. Discharges to tidal waters from vessels or marine structures, or discharges from a sewer do not require a licence.

10–03 A local authority has a discretion to issue or not to issue a licence or it may grant a licence subject to conditions as it thinks appropriate.[3] Local authorities may require a licensee to contribute towards the costs incurred by the local authority in monitoring a discharge. In considering the application for a licence the local authority is bound to have regard to the water quality plan which it is obliged to make under section 15 of the Act. A licence does not allow a person to allow the discharge or permit the discharge of trade effluent or sewage effluent to waters solely by reason of holding a licence. Persons who have applied for a licence under section 4 of the Act are allowed a defence to a prosecution that they have not contravened section 4 by reason of having made the application and that the application was not granted or refused by the local authority before the prosecution was commenced.[4]

10–04 A local authority may review a licence granted under section 4 of the Act at intervals of not less than three years from the date of the licence of the last review, or at any time with the consent of the licence holder or of the person making the discharge. A licence may also be reviewed where the local authority has reasonable grounds for believing that the discharge which is authorised by the licence is or is likely to be injurious to public health or which may render the waters unfit for use for domestic, commercial, industrial, fishery, or fish farming, agricultural or recreational uses. Licences may also be reviewed by the local authority where there has been a material change in the nature or in the volume of discharges, or where there has been a material change in relation to the waters to which the discharge is made. A licence may also be reviewed where more information has become available since the granting of the licence or where there has been a development in the technology used or where the licensee applies to have the licence reviewed.[5]

(b) Appeals

10–05 Where an application has been refused, the applicant or any person may appeal to An Bord Pleanála in relation to the grant, refusal or revocation of the licence, to the attachment of conditions or additional conditions attached to the licence or to the amendment or to the deletion of any condition

---

[3] Some conditions are listed in ss.4(5) but the authority is not restricted to these conditions only.
[4] s.5(1).
[5] s.7(2).

attached to the licence. Licences from the sanitary authority can also be granted to persons who wish to discharge trade effluent or other matters, other than domestic sewage or storm waters, into sewers.[6] Conditions may also be attached to the licence regarding the nature, composition, and so on of the discharges, however, regard is to be made to quality plans made under the Act and no authority may grant a licence if the discharges contravene these standards. These licences may also be reviewed under section 16 of the Act.[7]

(c) Register

10–06   Each local and sanitary authority is obliged to keep a register of all licences granted under the Act as well as a register of abstractions from waters in its functional area. Each register is to be kept at the offices of the authority and shall be open to inspection by any person at all reasonable times, and copies may be obtained on payment of a fee.

10–07   Local authorities have the power to serve a notice in writing to any person having the custody or control of any polluting matter on premises within its area where it is necessary to prevent or control pollution of waters. The notice specifies the measures which are necessary to prevent polluting matter from entering waters and direct the person on whom the notice is served to take measures specified in the notice within a certain period.[8] A person who has been served with a notice may make representations to the local authority regarding the terms of the notice, but following a consideration of these representations, and once the local authority has made a final decision, the notice must be complied with, otherwise an offence may be committed.[9] Where a notice is not complied with and a prosecution is successful a person may face a fine of not over £1,000 and a further fine of not over £100 in the case of a continuing offence, in addition to which the local authority may take such steps to comply with the notice as may be necessary and may recover the costs of these steps from the person on whom the notice was served.[10]

3. Prosecutions

(a) Complaints

10–08   Where a sanitary authority receives a complaint from any person that water in a well, tank or a cistern within its area is polluted and is likely to be used for drinking or for domestic purposes and is therefore liable to be injuri-

---

[6]   s.16(1).
[7]   s.17.
[8]   s.12(1).
[9]   s.12.
[10]   s.12(5).

ous to public health, the authority may apply for a court order to close the well or tank.[11] The court may make an order directing that the well or cistern be permanently or temporarily closed or the water to be used for certain purposes only.

10–09 Persons who contravene the provisions of section 3 of the Local Government (Water Pollution) Acts 1977 to 1990 are liable to a fine of not over £1,000, and to an additional fine of £100 for every day on which the contravention continues, or to a term of imprisonment of six months or to both on summary conviction. On indictment the fine is up to £25,000, together with a fine of not over £500 for every day on which the contravention continues or to a term of imprisonment of not over two years or both, at the discretion of the court.

(b) Defences

10–10 A defence, to a charge of committing an offence under section 3, is allowed provided the accused proves that all reasonable care was taken to prevent the entry to waters to which the charge relates by providing, maintaining, using, operating and supervising facilities, or by employing practices or methods of operation, that were suitable for the purpose of such prevention.[12] A defence is also available of allowing the entry to waters of matter which arose from an activity carried on in accordance with a nutrient management plan approved under section 21A.[13] Prosecutions under section 3 may be taken by a local authority or by any person affected by the pollution.[14] No prosecution may be taken in respect to a discharge of a trade effluent or a sewage effluent which is made under and in accordance with a licence or for a discharge of a sewage effluent from a sewer or to a discharge of a trade effluent or sewage effluent to which regulations under the Acts apply.

10–11 Prosecutions under the Act are taken by the local or sanitary authority, and can be taken for offences which occurred outside of their functional area,[15] except in the case of section 10 where it is the person who applied to a court for the order to which the offence relates. Prosecutions may be taken at any time within six months from the date on which evidence sufficient, in the opinion of the person by whom the proceedings are initiated, to justify the proceedings comes to that person's knowledge, which varies the provisions of the Petty Sessions (Ireland) Act, 1851 where summary proceedings are to be taken within six months of the occurrence of the offence. However, no pro-

---

[11] s.79 of the Public Health (Ireland) Act 1878.
[12] s.3(3).
[13] Inserted by s.66 of the Waste Management Act 1996.
[14] s.3(4).
[15] s.31.

ceedings are to be initiated later than five years from the date on which the
offence was committed.[16] The costs of prosecutions may be ordered to be
paid by the person found guilty of the offence, unless the court is satisfied that
there are special and substantial reasons for not so doing.[17] Fines which are
imposed under the Act, on the application of the local or sanitary authority,
are paid to the local or sanitary authority.[18]

(c) Preventative action

10–12   Where it appears necessary to the local or sanitary authority to prevent the entry of polluting matter into any waters or sewers or drains provided
for storm waters, or for removing polluting matter from waters, drains or sewers, or it is necessary to prevent polluting matter in waters outside of its functional area or on any seashore adjoining their area or for mitigating or remedying
damage to any seashore, the local authority may take whatever measures are
appropriate and may dispose of any polluting matter in whatever manner it
thinks fit.[19] If any measures are taken by the authority these measures must
have been necessitated by the acts or by the omissions of a person, which were
acts or omissions that the person ought reasonably to have foreseen would or
might necessitate the taking of the measures by the authority, then the expenditure which was incurred by the authority may be recovered from the
person responsible as a simple contract debt.[20]

(d) Order of prohibition

10–13   Any person may apply to the High Court for an order prohibiting the
entry of polluting matter to waters or allowing the discharge of trade effluent
or sewage effluent to waters, or for an order requiring the carrying out of
remedial measures to prevent the entry of polluting matter into waters. An
order may also be sought for the purpose of preventing, or preventing the
continuance or the recurrence of an entry or discharge or of avoiding any risk
that a person having custody or the control of polluting matter or trade or
sewage effluents requiring that person to refrain from or cease from doing any
specified act or to refrain from or cease from making any omission. Orders
may also be sought from the High Court preventing the escape of the continuance or the recurrence of an escape, requiring the carrying out of measures by
the occupier of the premises. Before granting any orders it must be shown to
the Court that polluting matter is being, has been or is likely to be caused or
permitted to enter waters and that the entry not allowed under section 3 or 4 of

---

[16] s.27 of the 1990 Act.
[17] s.28 of the 1990 Act.
[18] s.26 of the 1990 Act.
[19] s.13(1).
[20] s.13(2).

the Act or is not covered by a licence, or that polluting matter has escaped or is escaping or is likely to escape accidentally from premises to waters.

4. Quality managment plans

10–14 Water quality management plans may be made by local authorities regarding waters which are situated in its functional area or which adjoin their area. The plan is to contain the objectives for the prevention and abatement of pollution of the waters and may contain other particulars which the authority consider are necessary.[21] Two or more local authorities may jointly make a water quality management plan in relation to waters which are adjoining their functional area. Copies of the plans, or revised plans are to be forwarded to the Minister and the Minister for the Defence and Marine and to any local, sanitary or regional authority whose functional area either adjoins the waters to which the plan relates.[22]

10–15 A nutrient management plan may be adopted by a local authority where it considers that it is necessary for the purposes of preventing, eliminating or minimising the entry of polluting to waters from an activity.[23] The local authority may serve a notice on the owner of the land on which the activity is carried on or on the person who is in occupation of the land, requiring the person to prepare and furnish a plan which includes the particulars detailed in section 21A(4) including providing the particulars of the activity carried on specifying the quantities of such nutrients in animal and other waste as are specified in the notice which it is estimated will be used in each year, providing the types and concentrations of the nutrients in the soil of the land and so on.

10–16 Once a plan has been submitted to the local authority, the authority has two months in which to make a decision as to whether or not to accept the plan or to vary or modify it.[24] Persons who fail to comply with the notice will be liable on summary conviction to a fine not over £1,000 or to a term of imprisonment of not over six months or both.[25]

10–17 Finally with regard to civil liability for pollution section 20 of the 1990 Act provides that where trade sewage effluent, or other polluting matters

---

[21] s.15(1).
[22] s.15(6).
[23] The activity relates to the application to land or the growing of crops or the injection into land of any silage effluent, animal slurry, manure, fertiliser, pesticide or other polluting matter, s.21(1)(b) of the 1990 Act.
[24] s.21A(9).
[25] s.21A(11).

enters waters and causes injury, loss or damage to a person or to the property, the person may, without prejudice to any other cause of action which may arise in respect of the injury, loss or damage, recover damages from the occupier of the premises from which the effluent or matter originated unless the entry to the waters was caused by an act of God or an act or omission of a third party over whose conduct such occupier had no control, being an act or omission that such occupier could not reasonably have foreseen and guarded against. Liability also arises in relation to entry to waters that was caused by an act of omission of any person which contravened a provision of the Local Government (Water Pollution) Acts. However, liability does not arise in respect of effluent or other polluting matter arising from anything allowed under section 3 of the Act or in accordance with a licence issued under section 4.

B. AIR POLLUTION

1. Introduction

10–18   Under the Air Pollution Act of 1987 air pollution is deemed to be a condition of the atmosphere in which a pollutant[26] is present in such a quantity as to be liable to be injurious to public health, or have a deleterious effect on flora or fauna or damage property, or impair or interfere with amenities or with the environment.[27] Under this Act the term local authority refers to the county councils and corporations of boroughs, and does not include urban district councils.

2. Best practicable means

10–19   The 1987 Act obliged the occupier of any premises, other than the occupier of a private dwelling, to use the best practicable means to limit and, if possible, to prevent an emission from the premises. The occupiers of any premises shall not cause or permit an emission from premises in such a quantity as to be a nuisance.[28]

10–20   The term "best practicable means" refers to the provision and proper maintenance, use, operation and supervision of facilities which, having regard to all the circumstances, are the most suitable for such prevention or limitation. In considering whether facilities are the most suitable for the prevention

---

[26] The definition of pollutant means any substance specified in the First Schedule or other substance or energy which may cause air pollution, s.7(1) as amended by the Third Schedule of the Environmental Protection Agency Act 1992.

[27] s.4.

[28] s.24.

or limitation of an emission regard is to be made to the current state of technical knowledge and the requirements of the environment and the costs which would be incurred in providing, maintaining, using, operating and supervising the facilities concerned. Regard is also to be made as to the age of the existing industrial plant or other premises, the nature of the facilities installed and the costs which would be incurred in renovating the plant or premises or of renovating or replacing the facilities.[29]

3. Prosecutions

10–21 Local authorities have a role, under the Act, in the prosecution of offences by summary prosecution, instituted at any time within twelve months from the date on which the offence was committed or at any time within three months from the date on which evidence sufficient to justify a prosecution, whichever is the later, provided no proceedings are initiated later than five years from the date on which the offence was committed.[30] Summary proceedings for an offence under the Act may be brought by any person.[31]

10–22 In any prosecution for a contravention of section 24 of the Act it is a good defence to establish that the best practicable means was used to prevent or limit the emission or that the emission concerned was in accordance with a licence issued under the Act, now issued under the Environmental Protection Agency Act 1992, or that the emission concerned was in accordance with an emission limit value or that the emission was in accordance with a special control area in operation in relation to the area concerned, or in the case of an emission of smoke the emission concerned was in accordance with regulations made under the 1987 Act or that the emission did not cause air pollution.

10–23 Offences under the Act may be prosecuted summarily by the local authority in whose functional area the offence is committed, or by the local authority who has served any notice under the Act.[32] Where a local authority is of the opinion that an emission from any premises may cause air pollution which may affect part of their functional area, the local authority may initiate summary proceedings for an offence under the Act.

4. Prevention and service of notices

10–24 Where it appears to a local authority that it is necessary so to do in

---

[29] s.5.
[30] s.13.
[31] Art. 4, Waste Management (Miscellaneous Provisions) Regulations, 1998, SI No. 164 of 1998.
[32] s.13(1)(a).

order to prevent or to limit air pollution, the local authority may serve a notice on the occupier of any premises from which there is an emission.[33] In considering whether a notice should be served, the local authority is obliged to have regard to any air quality management plan in relation to the area in which the premises are situate, to any special control area order in operation in relation to the area in which the premises are situate. Regard is also to be made to any relevant emission limit value, any relevant air quality standard, the availability of the means necessary for compliance with the notice and the expense which would be incurred in complying with the notice.[34]

10–25 The notice which is served under section 26 specifies the measures which appear to be necessary in order to prevent or to limit air pollution, it shall also direct the person on whom the notice is served to take such measures as may be specified to prevent or limit air pollution and shall specify a period, being not less than fourteen days commencing on the date of the service of the notice, within which such measures are to be taken.[35] A person who is served with a notice has the right to make representations to the local authority.[36]

10–26 If the person upon whom the notice has been served fails to comply with the terms of the notice, the local authority may carry out such necessary works or steps as are necessary to carry out the requirements of the notice and may recover any expense incurred as a simple contract debt against that person.[37]

5. Licences

10–27 Applications for licences under the Act are made to the relevant local authority, and in considering an application the local authority shall have regard to any air quality management plan in force, and to any special control order in operation.[38] A local authority cannot grant a licence in relation to industrial plant unless it is satisfied that the best practicable means will be used to prevent or limit any emissions from the plant, and any emissions from the plant will comply with any relevant emission limit value and that any emissions from the plant will not result in the contravention of any relevant air quality standard, and that any emissions from the plant will not cause signifi-

---

[33] s.26.
[34] s.26(2).
[35] s.26(3).
[36] s.26(5).
[37] s.26(7).
[38] s.32(1).

cant air pollution.[39] Where appropriate the local authority shall attach conditions relating to the use of best practicable means, to emission limits values and to the air quality standard. Conditions may also be attached relating to the nature, temperature, volume, rate and location of an emission, specify the periods during which the emission may be made, specify a concentration of a pollutant which shall not be exceeded. Amongst other conditions which may be attached are conditions relating to the means to be used for controlling an emission, conditions specifying the type of fuel to be, or not to be, used, as well as the measures which are to be taken if there is a breakdown in plant.[40]

6. Urgent measures

10–28 Section 27 allows the local authority to carry out urgent measures necessary to prevent or limit air pollution affecting any part of their functional areas or any adjoining area. Where the local authority carries out such works or operations, the costs of such operations may be recovered against the person whom the local authority can satisfy the court is the person whose act or omission necessitated such steps, operations or assistance. Section 28 allows any person or local authority to apply to the High Court to make an order prohibiting or restricting an emission from any premises, provided the High Court is satisfied that the continuance of the emission would give rise to a serious risk of air pollution or that the emission is an emission from an industrial plant in contravention of the terms of a licence under the Act or that the emission is an emission from industrial plant for which a licence under the Act is required and in relation to which no such licence has been granted.

10–29 Section 28A[41] provides for remedies for unauthorised emissions by allowing any person to make an application to the appropriate court for an order requiring the occupier of the premises to terminate the emission, to mitigate or remedy any effects of the emission or to pay to the applicant or other person a specified amount to defray all or part of any costs incurred by the applicant or such order as the court may see fit.

10–30 If the resulting order of the court is not carried out by the respondent, then the local authority may step in and carry out such works as are required to comply with the order and may recoup the costs from the person responsible.

10–31 Section 28B, which was inserted by the Environmental Protection Agency Act 1992, establishes civil liability for the creation of pollution. The

---

[39] s.32(3) as inserted by the third schedule of the Environmental Protection Agency Act 1992 (the 1992 Act).

[40] s.32(4).

[41] As inserted by the 1992 Act.

section states that where an emission causes injury, loss or damage to a person or to property of a person, that person may claim damages for injury, loss or damage from the occupier of the premises from which the emission originated. The section allows a defence of an act of God or an act or omission of a third party over whose conduct the occupier had no control, being an act or omission that the occupier could not have reasonably foreseen and guarded against. It the emission was occasioned by an act or omission of any person, which in the opinion of the court, constitutes a contravention by the person of a provision of the Act, then damages may also arise. However, damages may not arise from an emission arising from a licence granted under the Act or an emission in compliance with an emission limit value allowed under section 51 of the Act or an emission which is in accordance with directions specifying best practicable means issued by the Minister.[42]

10–32 Section 29 requires the occupier of any premises, other than a private dwelling, to, as soon as practicable after the occurrence of any incident which may cause air pollution, notify the relevant local authority of the incident, including an accidental emission.

7. Special control areas

(a) Special control orders

10–33 Where it appears to a local authority that part, or the entire, functional area under their control that a special control area is required in order to prevent or limit air pollution, that local authority may make an order known as a special control area order.[43] In making the order the local authority is to have regard to the incidence and cause of the air pollution, to any air quality management plan in force for the area, to any relevant air quality standard, the availability of the means necessary to comply with the order and the expense which would be incurred in complying with the order.[44] The special control area is required to specify the area to which it relates, the pollutant with which it is concerned and the measures to be taken and the requirements which shall have effect in the area.[45] The Minister for the Environment may also direct a local authority to make a special control order and may further specify that particular measures are taken by the local authority.[46]

10–34 Local authorities who make special control area orders are obliged to

---

[42] s.28B(2).
[43] s.39(1).
[44] s.39(2).
[45] s.39(3).
[46] s.39(4).

review every special control area order made by it for the purpose of deciding whether it is necessary, or desirable, to revoke or amend the order. Local authorities may also make a special control area order in relation to an area which is outside of its functional area, however, such an order is to be made with the consent of the local authority in whose functional area the special control order is to have effect.

10–35 A special control area order may prohibit the emission of a specified pollutant from specified classes or premises. The order may also prohibit the burning of fuel other than the burning of an authorised fuel. The local authority may also prohibit the burning of straw, waste or any other substance which may cause air pollution.[47]

10–36 The local authority can exempt certain premises and fireplaces from the prohibitions included in the special control area. The authority may also, in order to enforce the order, prohibit or restrict the sale of delivery of specified fuels or classes of fuels in the area.[48] As soon as the local authority makes a special control order, the local authority is obliged to publish in one or more newspapers circulating in the area to which the order relates, a notice stating that the order has been made and specifying the area to which the order relates, naming a place where a copy of the order and any map or plan which was included in the order and where it can be inspected free of charge by any person, specifying the times and periods, being not less than one month, during which the order and the map or plan can be inspected, specifying the period, being not less than one month within which a person affected by the order may make objections to the making of the order. The notice should also include that the order will not come into operation until it has been confirmed by the Minister, and stating that if objections are made and are not withdrawn that the Minister before confirming or refusing the order, will cause an oral hearing to be held at which any person who has made an objection may attend for the purpose of being heard.[49]

10–37 As soon as the period during which objections can be made has elapsed, the local authority is obliged to forward the special control area order to the Minister for confirmation of the making of an order, and shall include any objections which the local authority would have received. Where no objections have been made to the making of the special control order, or the objections have been withdrawn, the Minister may confirm the special control order with or without making modifications. The Minister may also refuse to confirm the order or may cause an oral hearing to be first heard before making

---

[47] s.40(1).
[48] s.40(1)(j).
[49] s.41(1).

a decision, however, if objections have been made and not withdrawn then the Minister is obliged to cause an oral hearing to be held.[50]

10–38   The Minister ultimately decides whether to confirm the order, or may modify the order or may refuse to confirm it. Every order made by the Minister shall include the date on which the order is to come into effect, and this date should not be less than six months after the date of the making of the confirming order. The notice of the making of an order confirming a special control area order and the date on which it is to come into effect shall be published, given or served by the local authority concerned in such manner as the Minister may direct.[51]

(b) Prosecution and offences

10–39   Any person who contravenes the provisions of a special control order which is in operation may be found guilty of an offence under the Act. The penalties under the Act include, on summary conviction, a fine of not over £1,000, together with an additional fine of £100 for every day on which the offence is continued, subject to an overall maximum of £1,000, or to a term of imprisonment of a term of not over six months, or to the term of imprisonment and a fine. A conviction on indictment, attracts a fine of not over £10,000, together with an additional fine of £1,000 for every day on which the offence is continued, or to a term of imprisonment of not over two years or to the term of imprisonment and the fine. There is no maximum set for the fines which can be imposed in respect of the continuation of an offence, whereas there is a limit on summary conviction.[52]

10–40   In the prosecution for offences under the Act, it is a good defence to show that the emission of the pollutant was not caused by the use of a fuel other than an authorised fuel, and that the emission of the pollutant was caused by the burning of a fuel other than an authorised fuel in an authorised fireplace in accordance with the conditions subject to which the fireplace was declared to be an authorised fireplace.[53]

(c) Service of notices

10–41   Section 44 of the Act allows a local authority to serve a notice in writing on a person who appears to be the owner or occupier of premises which is within a special control area or will be when the order is confirmed

---

[50] s.41(4), oral hearings are conducted under the rules contained in s.42.
[51] s.41(8).
[52] s.12, although it is submitted that a continuation of an offence would need to be proved in the same manner as the offence itself.
[53] s.40(5).

by the Minister, requiring the owner or occupier to carry out such alterations to the premises as may be specified.[54] The notice shall specify the works which are necessary, directing the person to cause to be carried out the specified works, specifying the period, being not less than twenty eight days beginning on the date of service of the notice and ending not sooner than the date on which the special control area order comes into operation, within which the works are to be completed, and specifying that representations in writing in relation to the terms of the notice may be made by the person who has been served.[55]

10–42 Representations may be made by the person upon whom the notice has been served to the local authority in relation to the contents of the notice, and the local authority may, after considering these representations, revoke or amend the notice as it sees fit.[56] Where the terms of the notice have not been complied with, the local authority may take such steps as it considers reasonable and necessary in order to secure compliance and may recover the costs incurred as a simple debt from the person upon whom the notice was served.[57]

(d) Air quality management plans

10–43 A local authority may make an air quality management plan in relation to their functional area, or to a part of their functional area. The air management plan relates to the preservation or the improvement of the air quality of the functional area, and the local authority is bound to review the plan at least once every five years.[58] Two or more local authorities may jointly make an air quality management plan. The making, review, variation or replacement of an air quality management plan is a reserved function.[59]

10–44 The Minister may direct a local authority, or two or more local authorities to jointly make, an air quality management plan, and may require a local authority to vary the plan or may order the replacement of the plan, and may require a plan to be co-ordinated between the local authorities.[60]

10–45 When a local authority plans to make, vary or replace an air quality management plan, the local authority is obliged to publish in at least one newspaper circulating in their area a notice of the proposal. Representations may be made to the local authority upon the publication of the notice, regarding the

---

[54] s.44(1).
[55] s.44(2).
[56] s.44(3).
[57] s.44(5), (6).
[58] s.46(2).
[59] s.46(5).
[60] s.47.

proposed plan or variation.[61] As soon as the local authority has made, varied or replaced an air quality management plan, the local authority are obliged to forward a copy of the plan to the Minister and to other persons as provided for under regulations or by statute, such as the Environmental Protection Agency.

10–46 A local authority is obliged under section 54 to carry out monitoring of air quality and the nature, extent and effects of emissions as the local authority considers necessary for the performance of their functions under the Act. A local authority is also obliged to keep and maintain records of this monitoring and the local authority may require the occupier of any premises, other than a private dwelling, from which there is an emission to carry out monitoring and to forward these records to the local authority.[62]

10–47 Section 55 of the Act allows the District Court to order works to be carried out if the occupier, without the consent of another person, of any premises is unable to carry out works which are required under the provisions of the Act. If the occupier of a premises is obliged to carry out works under the provisions of the Act and the costs of these works should be borne by any person, such as a lessor, then an application can be made to a court of competent jurisdiction for an order directing that the whole or part of the costs of the works be borne by that other person.

(e) Licences

10–48 Licences are issued under section 30 to operators of industrial plant by local authorities, who are obliged to have regard to any air quality management plan in force and to any special control area orders. A local authority is not able to grant licences in relation to industrial plant unless it is satisfied that the best practicable means will be used to prevent or limit any emissions from the plant, or that any emissions from the plant will comply with any relevant emission limit value or that any emissions from the plant will not result in the contravention of any relevant air quality standard.[63]

10–49 Local authorities may attach conditions to a licence for example conditions relating to the nature and composition of an emission, specifying the periods during which an emission may, or may not, be made. Local authorities may review a licence with the consent of the licence holder, or at a time not less than three years from the date on which the licence was granted, and may issue a revised licence in substitution for the licence reviewed.[64] Where an

---

[61] s.48(2).
[62] ss.54(2), (3).
[63] s.32(3).
[64] s.33(1).

industrial plant to which a licence relates has not commenced operations within three years after the date on which the licence was granted or has ceased operations for a period of not less than three years, the licence granted shall cease to have effect.[65]

10–50   Local authorities are obliged to review a licence which it has granted if it has reasonable grounds for believing that any emission from the industrial plant to which the licence relates constitutes a serious risk of air pollution. Local authorities are also obliged to review the licence if there has been a material change in the nature or the extent of the emission, or there has been a material change, which could not have been reasonably have been foreseen when the licence was granted, in the air quality in the area where the industrial premises is situated, or where further and better evidence has now become available relating to a pollutant present in the emission covered by the licence or regarding the effects of the pollutant concerned.[66] The licensee may also apply to the local authority for a review of the licence under section 36(3)(v). In reviewing a licence a local authority shall have regard to any change in air quality in the functional area and to the development of technical knowledge in relation to air pollution and the effect of and extent of the constructions works and any other relevant consideration. The local authority is also obliged to be satisfied that the licence should continue in force for such period as the local authority considers reasonable having regard to all the circumstances.[67]

10–51   The local authority is also bound to review the licence, or licences granted in their functional area, if a relevant emission limit value is specified under regulations made under the Act, or a relevant air quality standard is specified, or a special control area order, or directions are issued by the Minister specifying the best practicable means for the prevention or limitation of an emission.[68]

10–52   Where there is an alteration in an industrial plant which has a licence, the occupier is obliged to give notice in writing to the local authority in whose functional area the industrial plant is situate. Such notice should be given prior to any alteration, or reconstruction of the plant if such change or alteration would or would be likely to materially increase the emissions from the plant or which may cause new emissions.[69]

---

[65] s.36.
[66] s.36(3).
[67] s.36(5).
[68] s.36(3)(b).
[69] s.38, although failure to inform the local authority was not created an offence under the Act.

10–53   Where a local authority receives such a notice the local authority can either review the licence or direct the occupier to apply for a new licence or if there is no such licence in force, may direct the occupier to apply for a licence. The occupier may not affect the alteration or reconstruction until the review has been completed or the new licence has been granted.[70] Changes in ownership of premises which have the benefit of a licence must also be notified to the local authority giving notice of the name of the person to whom interest in the plant has been transferred.[71]

C. WASTE MANAGEMENT ACT 1996[72]

1. Introduction

10–54   The Waste Management Act of 1996 brings into Irish law several European Council directives which deal with the disposal of waste and waste by products as well as on packaging and packaging waste.[73] The Act does not apply to emissions into the atmosphere, or of sewage and sewage effluent, or of the dumping of waste at sea[74] or radioactive substances.[75] Instead the Act concentrates on the holding, recovery and the disposal of waste.

10–55   Within the Act reference is made to the use of the best technology not entailing excessive costs to prevent or eliminate or reduce emissions from activities, and regard should be made to the provision and proper maintenance, use, operation and supervision of facilities which are the most suitable for the purpose. Regard also is made to the current state of technical knowledge, the requirements of environmental protection and the application of measures not entailing excessive costs having regard to the risk of environmental pollution that the Agency or local authority concerned believes exists. Therefore the Act places the Environmental Agency and the local authorities to the forefront of environmental protection.

2. Monitoring

(a) Duties and powers

10–56   Each local authority together with the Environmental Protection

---

[70] s.38.
[71] s.37(2).
[72] No. 10 of 1996.
[73] See table to s.2.
[74] See Dumping at Sea Act 1981.
[75] See Radiological Protection Act 1991.

Agency,[76] is obliged to carry out, or cause to be carried out, monitoring of the effects, nature and extent of emissions into the environment arising from the holding, recovery or disposal of waste as the local authority considers necessary. Each local authority, or the Agency, are also obliged to carry out periodic inspection of facilities for the holding, recovery or disposal of waste and premises where hazardous waste is produced. Following monitoring and inspection the local authority and Agency also keep and maintain records of the inspections and monitoring.[77]

10–57 To assist the local authority in keeping records, the Act provides that persons who are in control of the recovery or disposal of waste can be obliged to keep and to supply records of monitoring as the local authority or Agency may specify.[78] However, the local authority are obliged to double check the veracity of the records presented to them,[79] and charges may be made by the local authority to defray the cost of monitoring.

(b) Authorised officers

10–58 Section 16 of the Act allows authorised persons, appointed by the local authority or the Minister, to enter any premises or board any vehicle and may make such plans or take photographs, make tests and take samples or carry out surveys[80]. However, an authorised person may not enter into a private dwelling unless permission has been obtained or the authorised person has given twenty four hours notice in writing of the intention to inspect the premises.[81]

10–59 An authorised person may also require that the premises or the vehicle remain left undisturbed, or require that the occupier of a premises or the occupant of a vehicle provide such information as may be needed and may also require the production of and inspect any records and documents and to take any copies from same, and if necessary to take such records away for inspection.[82]

10–60 Where an authorised person considers that waste in any premises or contained in any vehicle is being handled or transported in such a manner as to constitute a risk of environmental pollution, they may direct the holder of

---

[76] Established under the Environmental Protection Agency Act 1992.

[77] s.15.

[78] s.15(3), and a person who fails to comply may be guilty of an offence, s.15(3)(b).

[79] s.15(5).

[80] Any prescribed test, examination or analysis of any sample shall be evidence, without proof of the result until the contrary is shown.

[81] s.14(2), authorised persons are also obliged to carry a certificate of appointment and to produce same on demand.

[82] s.16(4).

such waste to take any and all measures which are considered to be necessary to remove the risk, including the proper disposal of the waste.[83] If the holder of the waste fails to comply with the directions of the authorised person, then the authorised official may do all things necessary to ensure that the waste is secured properly and any consequential costs shall be borne as a simple contract debt against the person who failed to comply with the direction of the authorised person.[84] Any person who refuses to allow an authorised person to enter any premises or to board any vehicle for the purposes of the Act, or obstructs or impedes the authorised person, or gives misleading or false information, or fails to comply with any requirement of a direction from an authorised person shall be guilty of an offence.

10–61   Where an authorised person, during the exercise of their powers, is prevented from entering any premises or the authorised person believes that evidence relating to a suspected offence may be present in any premises and that the evidence may be removed or destroyed, the authorised person may apply to a judge of the District Court for a warrant authorising entry by the authorised person into the premises. The judge may issue a warrant and may direct that members of the Garda Síochána accompany the authorised person, and the warrant may be used at any time or times within one month from the date of issue of the warrant. The warrant allows the authorised person to enter the premises, by force if necessary in order to carry out the appropriate functions under the Act. The authorised person may also request the assistance of the Gardaí if the authorised person believes or anticipates any obstruction in the exercise of any power under the Act.[85]

(c) Offences

10–62   A person who has been found guilty of an offence under the Act is liable, on summary conviction to a fine not exceeding £ 1,500 or to imprisonment for a term of not over twelve months, or both, and on indictment to a fine not over £10,000,000 or to a term of imprisonment not exceeding ten years or both, with the exception of an offence under section 16(5)[86] and section 32(6),[87] section 33(8),[88] section 38(7)[89] or section 40(13)[90] where the penalty shall, on summary conviction, be a fine of not over £1,500 or twelve months or both.

---

[83] s.16(5)(a).

[84] s.16(5)(b).

[85] s.14(8).

[86] Offences relating to removing, damaging or defacing a notice.

[87] Offences relating to general duties of holding waste.

[88] Offences relating to interfering, disturbing or removing waste from an appropriate area.

[89] Failing to comply with a requirement of a local authority.

[90] A holder of a waste licence shall, within a period of one month after the cesser of the activity to which the licence relates, give notice in writing of that fact to the Agency.

If the contravention of the offence under the Act is continued after the conviction, the person shall be guilty of a further offence on every day on which the contraventions continues and for each such offence the person shall be liable to a fine, on summary conviction, of a fine not exceeding £200 or on indictment to a fine not exceeding £100,000.[91] In imposing any penalty the court may have regard to the risk or extent of environmental pollution from the act or omission constituting the offence.[92]

3. Keeping of records

10–63 The Minister, the Agency or a local authority may for any purpose under the Act require any holder or waste or any person engaged in the importation, exportation, production, collection, recovery or disposal of waste or any person acting as a waste broker or dealer or the occupier or person in charge of any waste facility to maintain records and to furnish, in writing particulars of any activity or process or the importation or exportation, collection, recovery or disposal of waste material.[93] Any person who fails to comply with a notice under section 18 or gives false or misleading information may be found guilty of an offence under the Act.

10–64 Each local authority is obliged to establish and maintain a register for the purposes of the Act and are obliged to make the necessary entries and additions in the register.[94] The register is to be kept at the principal office of the local authority and shall make the register available for inspection during office hours.[95] The local authority shall also give copies, at a reasonable cost, to any person who requests.[96]

4. Waste management planning

10–65 Each local authority, or jointly with another local authority, is obliged under section 22 of the Act to make a plan concerning the prevention, minimisation, collection, recovery and disposal of nonhazardous waste within its functional area. The waste management plan also must include information as respects the implementation of measures relating to the provisions of hazardous waste management or any recommendations which may be made by the Agency.

---

[91] s.10.
[92] s.10(4).
[93] s.18.
[94] s.19.
[95] s.19(1) and (2).
[96] s.19(3).

10–66   Before the local authority commences the preparation of the waste management plan, the local authority shall publish a notice in a newspaper circulating in its functional area and the notice shall state that written representations in relation to the plan may be made to the local authority within a specified period, such period being not less than two months from the date of publication of the notice.[97] The local authority is also required to publish a notice when the waste management plan has plans to vary or review the plan, and shall also make a copy of the proposed plan available for inspection and purchase, and shall also include in the notice the fact that written representations may be made to the authority on the plan.[98]

10–67   A local authority is also required to review a waste management plan from time to time as occasion may require and at least once every five years after making the plan, and may make any alterations required.[99]

10–68   In respect of a nonhazardous waste, the waste management plan should contain objectives to prevent or minimise the production of harmful waste, to encourage and support the recovery of waste, to ensure that hazardous waste does not cause environmental pollution, and to ensure that in the context of the disposal of hazardous waste to give effect to the principle of the polluter pays.[100] The polluter pays principle refers the principle set out in Council Recommendation 75/436[101] regarding the allocation of cost and action by public authorities on environmental matters. The plan should also address the type, quantity and origin of waste which may be in or carried through the functional area of the local authority. The making, review, variation or replacement of a waste management is a reserved function,[102] and in making the plan the local authority should also have regard to the proper planning and development of the functional area, in particular to the development plan of the local authority and to the provision of any special amenity area made under the planning acts. Regard should also be made to the water quality management plan under the Local Government (Water Pollution) Acts, 1977 and 1990[103] and to air quality management plan made under the Air Pollution Act, 1987[104] which may be in force for the area.

10–69   The local authority is obliged to take such steps as is necessary to attain, in relation to the functional area under the control of the local authority,

---

[97] s.22(5).
[98] s.23.
[99] s.22(4).
[100] s.22(6).
[101] Euratom, ECSC, EEC of March 3, 1975, 1975 1(20).
[102] s.22(10).
[103] Nos. 21 of 1990 and 1 of 1977.
[104] No. 6 of 1987.

the objectives contained in the waste management plan.[105] In the case of a corporation of a borough or the council of an urban district, such council or corporation shall have regard to the provisions of the waste management plan of the county in whose functional area the borough or urban district is situate.[106]

10–70 Following the making of a waste management plan, the local authority is required to forward a copy to the Minister and the Agency and to other persons who may be prescribed.[107] The Minister may also require that two or more local authorities jointly make a waste management plan and that the making of a plan be co-ordinated between the local authorities.[108]

5. Waste prevention and minimisation

(a) Recovery of waste

10–71 Under section 28(1) for the purpose of promoting, supporting or facilitating the prevention or minimisation of waste and under section 29 the recovery of waste, any Minister of the Government or a local authority may provide such support or assistance, including the provision of finance, as he or she or the local authority considers appropriate in relation to research and development projects being carried out, or proposed to be carried out, by any person in respect of the prevention or minimisation of waste, and for the purposes aforesaid may establish programmes and specify criteria and objectives governing the availability and provision of such assistance and support.

(b) Recovery of waste by local authorities

10–72 Under section 31(1) a local authority may engage or participate in the recovery of waste, and for that purpose may enter into one or more agreements with any other local authority or other person, buy or otherwise acquire waste for the purpose of recovering it, and use, sell or otherwise dispose of any material or thing, including energy, recovered from waste.

10–73 Under Section 32 of the Act a person is not permitted to hold, transport, recover or dispose of waste in a manner that causes or is likely to cause environmental pollution. The holder of waste is obliged to inform the local authority, without delay, of any loss or spillage or accident which is likely to cause environmental pollution, and in the case of hazardous waste both the local authority and the Agency.

---

[105] s.22(12).
[106] s.22(13).
[107] s.25.
[108] s.24.

10–74   Section 52 of the Public Health (Ireland) Act 1878 also empowered sanitary authorities to undertake the removal of house refuse from premises or to contract for its removal, while section 54 allowed the authority to enact bye-laws imposing the duty of removing household refuse on the occupiers of premises. However, the power which was conferred by section 52 of the 1878 Act was discretionary and did not impose a statutory duty upon sanitary authorities.[109]

6. Collection of waste

(a) Domestic waste

10–75   In relation to the collection of household waste within the functional area of a local authority, the local authority is obliged to collect or to arrange the collection of such waste.[110] The Public Health (Ireland) Act 1878 permitted the provision of private systems for the removal of domestic waste by agreement with the sanitary authority.[111] Section 48 of the 1878 Act allows the sanitary authority to require the construction of domestic waste disposal facilities serving any premises which is used as a factory or for any trade or business.

10–76   The corporation of a borough or the council of an urban district may collect, or arrange to collect household waste, that is household waste outside of its functional area.[112] However, the local authority need not arrange for the collection of household waste if an adequate waste collection service is available in the part concerned of the local authority's functional area, or the estimated costs of the collection of the waste concerned by the local authority would, in the opinion of the authority, be unreasonably high, or the local authority is satisfied that adequate arrangements for the disposal of the waste concerned can reasonably be made by the holder of the waste.[113] A local authority may also refuse to collect waste from any person who has not complied with the regulations made under the Act and if the waste contains any product or substance or packaging in contravention of regulations made under the Act.

(b) Other waste

10–77   A local authority may collect, or arrange for the collection of waste, other than household waste.[114] A local authority may also enter into arrange-

---

[109] *Bradley v. Meath Co. Co.* [1991] I.L.R.M. 179.
[110] s.33.
[111] s.48.
[112] s.33(1).
[113] s.33(3).
[114] s.33(4).

ments with one or more other local authorities, or with one or more other persons, for the collection on its behalf of waste.[115]

10–78   Waste collected or recovered by a local authority shall become the property of the local authority who has collected it.[116] Under section 33(8) a person may not interfere with, disturb, or remove anything held in a facility owned by a local authority or of an authorised waste collector for the storage or deposit of waste. Nor may any person disturb, interfere with or remove anything deposited in a receptacle for waste, whether used by members of the public or not, nor shall a person obstruct or interfere with the collection of waste by a local authority or an authorised waste collector. Any person contravening this section shall be guilty of an offence.

(c) Collection by other persons and permits

10–79   Persons other than local authorities are not able to collect, for reward or with a view to profit or otherwise in the course of a business collect waste except where that person holds a waste collection permit.

(i) Waste collection permit

10–80   A local authority cannot grant a waste collection permit unless it is satisfied that the activity in question would not cause environmental pollution and that the grant of a permit is in accordance with the relevant provisions of the local authority's waste management plan and the hazardous waste management plan of the Agency. The local authorities may attach conditions to the granting of permits as it may deem necessary. An application permit may be refused or revoked if the permit holder or the applicant has been convicted of an offence under the Act or of an offence under any other enactment or instrument under an enactment which may be prescribed by regulation.[117] A local authority may at any time review and decide to amend the conditions attached to the permit, or revoke the permit, which has been granted.[118]

(ii) Conditions

10–81   Conditions attached to a permit shall specify the requirements which need to be complied with in respect to the activities which the permit relates and may include requirements in relation to the types and quantities of waste which may be collected. Conditions may also be attached relating to the place or places to which waste may or shall be delivered for recovery or disposal, the methods, vehicles and receptacles used for the disposal of waste, the iden-

---

[115] s.33(5).
[116] s.33(7).
[117] s.34(5).
[118] s.34(6).

tifying marks which are to be placed on vehicles used, the technical, environmental or safety standards to be complied with, the documentation which needs to accompany each consignment of waste and the keeping and preservation of records and the information to be supplied to the local authority, as well as the holding of a policy of insurance regarding liability to pay damages or costs which may arise from the activities carried out.[119]

(iii) Contraventions and Bye-Laws

10–82   Any contravention of the provisions of sections 32 or 39 of the Act or of any conditions attached to a waste collection permit by any person employed by or on behalf of the holder of the permit is deemed to be also a contravention of the provision or conditions by the holder.[120]

10–83   Local authorities have the power to make bye laws under section 35 of the Act to require a holder of household or commercial waste to present household waste for collection in a certain manner and to require the waste to be collected by authorised persons, who are the holders of permits.[121] The local authority can therefore decide as to what type of waste bin is used, the amount of waste which can be collected, the times during which the waste is to be made available for collection, and for commercial waste the mixtures of waste which are allowed and whether any particular precautions or measures are to be taken with the waste prior to collection.[122] The local authority can also, of course, levy a charge for the provision of receptacles which are used for the collection of waste.[123]

(d) Provision of waste recovery facilities

10–84   Local authorities are required to provide and operate, or arrange for the provision and operation of, facilities necessary for the recovery and disposal of household waste which originates from its functional area.[124] In fact local authorities are responsible for the supervision of, and the enforcement of the relevant provisions of the Act in relation to the holding, recovery and disposal of waste within its functional area.[125] Local authorities may also provide or arrange civic waste facilities at which waste may be deposited by members of the public as well as other facilities for the segregation, storage and

---

[119] s.34(7) a right of appeal against conditions which may be imposed exists to the District Court under subs.9.
[120] s.34(10).
[121] s.35(1).
[122] s.35(3).
[123] s.35(4).
[124] s.38(1).
[125] s.59.

treatment of waste prior to recovery or disposal, together with the recovery and disposal of waste, other than household waste.[126] Section 38 of the Act allows local authorities to arrange for the provision of facilities at which vehicles may be discarded.[127] Section 38 makes provision for local authorities to enter into contracts with other authorities or other persons for the recovery and disposal of waste or by joint operation of any facility.

10–85 Where it appears to the Agency or the local authority that it is necessary for the purpose of the effective and orderly disposal of waste, it may require the holder or a producer of any class of waste, other than household waste, to dispose, or arrange for the disposal of the waste under such conditions and at such appropriate waste disposal facility as may be specified.[128] A person who fails to comply with a requirement under section 38(7) may be guilty of an offence under the Act. A person also commits an offence under this section if waste is deposited or discarded otherwise than in accordance with conditions for its use set down by the local authority.

10–86 Any waste deposited or discarded at a facility provided by a local authority becomes the property of the local authority, however, the waste which is deposited or discarded in contravention of section 38(11) does not become the property of the local authority unless the local authority decides to assume ownership of the waste, and any expenses incurred by the local authority in recovering or disposing or arranging for the recovery or disposal is recoverable by the local authority, from the person who discarded same, as a simple debt.

7. Waste licences

(a) Framework

10–87 Under section 39 no person can dispose or undertake to recover waste at a facility without the benefit of a waste licence which is in force in relation to the carrying on of the waste activity at that facility. However, waste disposal carried out in accordance with a permit issued under the E.C. (Waste) Regulations, 1979 or the E.C. (Toxic and Dangerous Waste) Regulations, 1982[129] does not contravene the provisions of section 39, that is the requirement to hold a licence. Section 39 allows the Minister to make further regula-

---

[126] s.38(2), in this sub section local authority includes a corporation of a borough and a council of an urban district, except with the disposal of waste other than waste from their own functional area, as with subs.3.

[127] s.38(3).

[128] s.38(7).

[129] Now replaced by the Waste Management (Permit) Regulations 1998, SI No. 165 of 1998.

tions allowing the disposal in a specified manner of a specified class of waste at its place of production, or the recovery in a specified manner of a specified class of waste without the need of a waste licence.[130] The Minister may also make regulations regarding the quantity of waste which may be recovered or disposed during a set period of time, and to the use of the best available technology not entailing excessive cost to prevent or eliminate or limit an emission from the recovery or disposal of waste or other matters which the Minister considers appropriate to ensure that the recovery or disposal of waste will not cause environmental pollution, including the requirement that the local authority's written consent be required prior to the creation of certain types of waste.[131] A waste licence is not required for the recovery[132] of sludge from a facility operated by a local authority for the treatment of water, of waste water, or for the blood of animal or poultry origin, or faecal matter of animals or poultry in the form of manure or slurry, or other natural agricultural waste.[133]

(b) Applications and conditions

10–88 The Minister may, also by regulations, require the producer of a class of waste, other than household waste, to comply with specified conditions in relation to the treatment or temporary storage of the waste at the premises which the waste is produced, including obtaining the written permission of the local authority to the treatment and storage of the waste. Regulations may also be made in relation to the making of a plan with respect to the taking of measures preventing or minimising the risk of environmental pollution from an accident or other incident.[134] Waste producers may also be required, by regulation, to hold a policy of insurance against any liability which may arise on account of injury to persons or property which may arise from the production or the holding of waste. Local authorities may also be given powers to attach specific conditions, one of which may be specifying a maximum period for which the waste may be held, to a consent granted by it and also to revoke the consent where any of the conditions are not complied with.[135]

10–89 The recovery or disposal of waste at a facility by the holder of a licence or revised licence under the Environmental Protection Agency Act 1992 is an exempted activity from the requirement to hold a waste licence. Household waste produced and disposed of within the curtilage of the same dwell-

---

[130] Waste Management (Licensing) (Amendment) Regulations 1998, SI 162 of 1998. See also SI. Nos. 163 to 168 of 1998 for Regulations made in respect of permits, collection of waste and so on.
[131] s.39(5).
[132] The term "recovery" includes the injection of waste into land.
[133] s.51 (2).
[134] s.39(6).
[135] s.39 (6)(b).

ing, the deposit of litter in a litter bin, the deposit of waste at a civic waste facility, the transfer of waste to a local authority under the 1992 Act, the disposal of animal by-products,[136] and other activities which may be prescribed, are also exempted from the requirement to hold a waste licence.[137]

10–90 Applications for waste licences[138] are made to the Environmental Protection Agency and the Agency may grant a waste licence, subject to conditions as it may deem necessary, or refuse to grant a licence.[139] In considering the application for a waste licence, the Agency is obliged to carry out such investigations as it deems necessary and also to have regard to any relevant air quality management plan or water quality management plan or waste management plan or hazardous waste management plan. The Agency must also have regard to any environmental impact statement in respect of the proposed development, as well as to any submissions or observations made to the Agency in relation to the environmental impact statement, and any supplementary information relating to such statement as may have been furnished to the Agency by the applicant or licence holder. Where appropriate the Agency may also take into account the views of other Member States of the E.U. particularly in relation to the effects on the environment of the proposed activity, and to such other matters related to the prevention, limitation, elimination, abatement or reduction of environmental pollution from the activity the subject matter of the application.[140]

10–91 The Agency shall not grant a waste licence unless it is satisfied that any emissions from the recovery or disposal activity in question will not result in the contravention of any relevant standard, including any standard for an environmental medium,[141] the activity concerned, carried on in accordance with such conditions as may be attached to the licence, will not cause environmental pollution, the best available technology not entailing excessive costs will be used to prevent or eliminate or, where that is not practical, to limit, abate or reduce an emission from the activity concerned.[142] The Agency may also attach to the licence conditions listed in section 41(2) of the Act and include specifying the waste recovery or disposal activity to which the licence may relate and the types, nature, composition and quantity of waste permitted to be recovered or disposed of during specified periods. The Agency may also

---

[136] Within the meaning of the E.C. (Disposal, Processing and Placing on the Market of Animal By-Products) Regulations 1994.
[137] s.39(7).
[138] A notice of intention to apply for a licence must be published in the prescribed form under s.42.
[139] s.40(1).
[140] s.40(2).
[141] Or any relevant emission limit value, prescribed under any other enactment.
[142] s.40(4).

require that certain requirements relating to the design, construction, provision, operation or maintenance of the facility be undertaken and may also require the carrying out of specified procedures or codes of practice in relation to employees.[143]

10–92　Other conditions which may be attached to licences are specifying procedures or methods which need to be followed or employed, having regard to the nature and composition of the waste, and in particular to the proximity to the facility of waste catchment areas as well as the general surrounding environment, and may require certain specified measures to be taken in order to prevent the entry to waters of pollution from the facility. The condition that records of the quantity, nature and origin of waste be kept may also be attached to the licence, as well as particulars of the nature, destination, frequency of collection and mode of transport of the waste leaving the facility concerned.[144]

10–93　If the applicant is not a local authority, the Agency must also be satisfied that he or she is a fit and proper person to hold a waste licence, and that the applicant has complied with any requirements under section 53 of the Act. A person shall be regarded as a fit and proper person if, neither that person nor any other relevant person has been convicted of an offence under this Act prescribed, in the opinion of the Agency, that person or, any person or persons employed by him or her to direct or control the carrying on of the activity to which the waste licence will relate have the requisite technical knowledge or qualifications to carry on that activity in accordance with the licence. The Agency must also be satisfied that person is likely to be in a position to meet any financial commitments or liabilities that the Agency reasonably considers will be entered into in carrying on the activity to which the waste licence will relate in accordance with the terms thereof or in consequence of ceasing to carry on that activity.[145] The Agency may, if it considers it appropriate, regard the applicant as a fit and proper person even though that person may have been convicted of an offence under the Act.[146]

10–94　A waste licence may not be transferred to another person other than allowed under section 47 of the Act.[147] Section 47 allows the transfer of a

---

[143] s.41(2).
[144] s.41(2)(vii).
[145] s.40 (7).
[146] s.40(8).
[147] Waste licences may also be surrendered under s.48, but the Agency are obliged to inspect the facility and may require certain information to be tendered and certain works to be carried out. The lifetime of a licence is restricted to three years, or longer should the Agency decide, s.49.

waste licence by the making of an application to the Agency. Before allowing the transfer of the licence the Agency may require the provision of information from the holder of the licence and the proposed transferee as may be appropriate for the application. The transferee should be a fit and proper person and the proposed transferee is also obliged to have complied with the financial requirements of section 53 of the Act, as indeed does an applicant. The transferee is deemed to have assumed and accepted all liabilities, requirements and obligations provided for or arising under the licence, regardless of how and in what period they may arise.[148]

10–95 Section 53 allows the Agency to require an applicant for a waste licence to furnish proof that the applicant can meet the financial commitments or liabilities which the Agency reasonably considers will be entered into or incurred as a result of carrying on the activity to which the licence may relate, and furnish a bond or other form of security as will, in the opinion of the Agency, be adequate to discharge the financial commitments or liabilities. A person who knowingly furnishes to the Agency any particulars or evidence which they know to be false or misleading in a material respect may be guilty of an offence.[149]

(c) Objections

10–96 Objections to the issuing of a waste licence are obliged to be made in writing, and they must state the name and address of the objector, the subject matter of the objection, the full grounds of the objection and the reasons, considerations and arguments on which they are based, as well as being accompanied with the relevant fee.[150] An objection may be accompanied with such documents, particulars or other information relating to the objection as may be appropriate. An objector is not entitled to elaborate in writing upon the grounds of objection which have been already stated.[151]

10–97 A decision of the Agency in connection with the granting of a waste licence may be challenged by way of judicial review, provided the application for judicial review is made within two months from the date upon which the decision is given.[152] Notice for judicial review is made to the Agency, to the holder or applicant of the licence, to any person which has made an objection to the granting of the licence, and to any person to whom the High Court may direct, and leave to challenge the decision of the granting of a licence shall not

---

[148] s.47(6).
[149] s.53(2).
[150] s.42 (4), an objection which does not comply with subsection 4 is declared to be invalid under subs.5, an oral hearing may be requested by the objector, s.42(9).
[151] s.42(7).
[152] s.43(5).

be granted unless the High Court is satisfied that there are substantial grounds for believing that the decision is invalid or ought to be quashed.[153]

8. Planning permissions and waste licences

10–98   Section 54 provides that where a waste licence has been granted in connection with an activity to which a planning permission has issued under the Local Government (Planning and Development) Act 1963, the conditions contained in the planning permission cease to have an affect where the conditions contained in the waste licence relate to the prevention, limitation, elimination, abatement or reduction of environmental pollution. The granting of a permission under the 1963 Act in relation to any development which comprises of waste recovery or disposal activity does not prejudice, affect or restrict in any way the application of any provision of the Waste Management Act.[154]

10–99   Where a waste licence has been granted or will be granted, a planning authority or An Bord Pleanála shall not, in respect of any development comprising or for the purposes of the activity, decide to refuse a permission or an approval under the 1963 Act for the reason that the development would cause environmental pollution or cannot decide to grant a permission subject to conditions which are for the purposes of prevention, limitation, elimination, abatement or reduction of environmental pollution. Therefore, a planning authority in dealing with an application for a permission or for an approval for any development, shall not consider any matter relating to the risk of environmental pollution from the activity which has the benefit of a waste licence.

10–100   An Bord Pleanála shall not consider any appeal which is made to it against a decision of a planning authority in relation to an application in so far as it relates to the risk of environmental pollution from the activity carried out by the holder of a waste licence.[155]

10–101   Where an application has been made for permission or a permission has been granted for a development which includes waste recovery or a disposal activity, the carrying on of which requires a waste licence, the Agency is obliged to consult with the planning authority in whose area the activity is or will be carried on in relation to any development which is necessary to give effect to any conditions to be attached to a waste licence. The Agency may then attach to the waste licence such conditions related to the development as may be specified by the planning authority for the purposes of the proper

---

[153] The decision of the High Court is final and no appeal is allowable to the Supreme Court unless it involves a point of law.
[154] s.54(2).
[155] s.54(3)(ii).

planning and development of its functional area, and the Agency may impose more stringent conditions as the Agency may consider necessary for the prevention, limitation, elimination, abatement or reduction of environmental pollution from the activity.[156]

10–102 Works which are of an incidental nature to the carrying out of development and the provision of waste collection are deemed to be exempted development within the meaning of the planning legislation and a condition attached to a planning permission does not prejudice, affect or restrict in any way the provision of waste collection.[157] Where development is proposed to be carried out by or on behalf of a local authority in its own functional area, being a development which includes or is comprised of waste recovery or disposal requiring a waste licence from the Agency, the Minister may instead by order grant an exemption in respect of that development from the requirement to hold or apply for a waste licence.[158]

9. General provisions for environmental protection

10–103 When it appears to a local authority that it is necessary to prevent or limit environmental pollution which has been caused or is likely to be caused by the holding, recovery or disposal of waste, the local authority may serve a notice on a person who holds, recovers or is disposing of waste, unless that person holds a waste licence granted.[159]

10–104 This notice may require a person to take specific measures necessary to prevent of limit the environmental pollution caused or to prevent a recurrence. The notice could also demand the end to the holding, recovery or disposal of waste and, or, the mitigation or remedying of any effects of such activity, all within a specified period, not being less than fourteen days commencing on the date of the service of the notice.[160] A notice may be served whether or not there has been a prosecution for an offence under the Waste Management Act and shall not prejudice the initiation of a prosecution for an offence under the Act in relation to the holding, recovery or disposal of waste.

10–105 A person upon whom the notice has been served may make representations to the local authority concerning the terms of the notice and the local authority may take such representations in account and may amend, con-

---

[156] s.54(4).
[157] s.54(5).
[158] The Minister must comply with Council Directive 85/337/EEC of June 27, 1985 when making such an order.
[159] s.55(1).
[160] s.55(2).

firm or revoke the notice as it sees fit.[161] However, if the person on whom the notice has been served does not, within the specified period, comply with the terms of the notice, the local authority may take such steps as it considers reasonable and necessary to secure compliance with the notice, and may recover any expense incurred as a simple contract debt.[162] A person who fails to comply with the notice may be found guilty of an offence.[163]

10–106 The local authority may include in the notice a requirement to remove the waste from a location to a specified facility, or the taking of measures to prevent the continuance of the activity causing the waste. The authority may also include in the notice a requirement regarding the treatment of affected lands or waters so as to mitigate or remedy the effects of the waste and the taking of such other action as may be necessary in order to counteract any risk of environmental pollution.

10–107 In the case of where a notice will not be an effective step to take, as in the case where measures are needed to be taken in order to prevent or limit environmental pollution, the local authority may carry out operations to recover or dispose of waste or arrange to recover or dispose of waste or give assistance as it considers necessary in order to prevent or limit pollution.[164] The local authority may recover the costs of such operations or assistance as a simple contract debt in the relevant court from such person as the local authority satisfies the court is a person whose act or omission required the taking of those operations or required the giving of assistance.

10–108 An application can also be made to the High Court, by any person, requesting an order requiring the person holding, recovering or disposing of waste to carry out specified steps or prevent or limit, or prevent a recurrence of pollution within a specified period, or an order requiring the person holding, recovering or disposing of waste to do, refrain from or cease doing any specified act or to refrain from or cease from making an omission, or make such other provision, including the payment of costs as the Court may consider appropriate.[165] An interim or interlocutory order may also be granted by the High Court if it deems it necessary, and an application for an order may be made regardless of whether or not a prosecution has been made under the Act in relation to the activity concerned.[166]

---

[161] s.55(4).
[162] s.55(6).
[163] s.55(8).
[164] s.56(1).
[165] s.57.
[166] s.57 (4) states that a person failing to comply with an order shall be guilty of an offence, however, that person may also be guilty of failing to comply with an order of the High Court.

10–109 An application, by any person, may also be made in relation to the holding, recovery or disposal of waste in a manner that is causing, or has caused environmental pollution. The relevant court may make an order requiring the discontinuance of the holding, recovery or disposal of waste within a specified period, or the mitigation or the remedying of any effects of the said holding, recovery or disposal of waste in a specified manner and within a specified period. The appropriate court refers to the estimated cost of complying with the order to which the application relates, that is if the estimated costs does not exceed £5,000 the District Court, where the estimated costs does not exceed £30,000 the Circuit Court, an in any other case the High Court.[167] Where a person does not comply with a court order, a local authority may take steps specified in the order to mitigate or remedy any effects of the activity concerned, and the cost of same can be recovered by the local authority as a simple contract debt.

10–110 Local authorities, and the Agency, are immune from action in respect of the recovery of damages in respect to any injury to persons, damage to property or other loss alleged to have been caused or contributed to by a failure to exercise any power or carry out any duty conferred or imposed by the Agency or the local authority. Authorised persons appointed by the local authority and the Agency, or any officer or employee of the local authority or the Agency, in the carrying out of their duties in relation to the performance of functions under the Act are indemnified by the local authorities or the Agency as the case may be, against all actions or claims however arising in respect of the carrying out of their duties.[168]

D. LITTER

1. Litter Acts

10–111 The Litter Act of 1997[169] repealed the Litter Act of 1982[170] which gave local authorities a role in the prevention and regulation of the creation of litter in public places. In the 1997 Act the term "litter" means a substance or object, whether or not intended as waste, other than waste within the meaning of the Waste Management Act, 1996 and which is properly consigned for disposal, that when deposited in a place other than a litter receptacle or other place lawfully designated for the deposit, is or is likely to become unsightly, deleterious, nauseous or unsanitary, whether by itself or with any other such

---

[167] s.58(1)(b).
[168] s.67.
[169] No. 12 of 1997.
[170] No. 11 of 1982.

substance or object, and regardless of its size or volume or the extent of the deposit. Obviously an attempt has been made in the making of the Act to include all possible permutations of litter, except that the term waste was not defined.

2. Prevention

10–112   Local authorities are obliged to take measures for the prevention of the creation of litter as well as for the prevention and overcoming of the harmful effects, and for the disposal of litter.[171] A local authority may enter into arrangements with or may assist other persons, including other local authorities, to assist in this duty. Measures which may be taken include the collection and disposal of litter, the encouragement of public use of the collection and disposal of litter and to prevent the harmful effects of litter. Local authorities may also facilitate and encourage the recycling of waste and may undertake works including the provision of facilities and services including advisory and educational services as well as running advertising campaigns.

3. Offences

10–113   Section 3 of the Litter Act provides that a person shall not deposit any substance or object so as to create litter in a public place or in any place that is visible to any extent from a public place. No person shall deposit any thing that is commercial, household, industrial or municipal waste in any place for collection by or on behalf of a local authority or by another person. No person may also load, transport, unload or otherwise handle or process any thing or carry on a business, trade or activity in such circumstances as to create litter or lead to litter in any public place or any place that is visible to any extent from a public place.[172] It is also prohibited for persons to place municipal waste[173] into or near a litter receptacle, or move or interfere with a litter receptacle that has been provided for by a local authority or other person.[174]

10–114   A person who is the registered owner, or is in charge of a vehicle being used to transport goods or materials shall take measures to prevent the creation of litter from the vehicle on a public road or in a public place, as does the person who is the owner or is in charge of a skip designed or used for carriage on a vehicle and that is parked or situated in a public place so as to prevent the creation of litter in the vicinity of the skip.[175] The registered own-

---

[171] Litter Act 1982, s.2.
[172] s.3(2).
[173] Municipal waste has the meaning assigned by s.5 of the Waste Management Act 1996.
[174] s.3(3), (4).
[175] s.4.

ers of vehicles, other than a large public service vehicle within the meaning of the Road Traffic Act, 1961, or the hirer of vehicles under a hire drive agreement which is used in the commission of an offence under the Litter Pollution Act may be also found guilty of an offence, whether or not any of them is prosecuted and convicted of the offence.[176] It is a defence to show that the registered owner of the vehicle is not guilty of an offence by showing that at the time of the commission of an offence the vehicle was being used by another person and that this use was unauthorised or was subject to a hire drive agreement.[177]

10–115 A good defence against a prosecution under section 4 is that as soon as practicable after the occurrence of litter that the litter was removed. Section 5 allows the deposit of waste in a place or in a receptacle provided for that purpose, the deposit in any place of a receptacle containing any commercial, household, municipal or industrial waste for collection by the local authority (or other authorised person) or the deposit of waste at a civic waste facility, provided that reasonable care is taken to prevent the creation of litter.[178]

10–116 The occupier of a public place, not being a public road or a building or other structure, is obliged to keep the place free of litter, as does the occupier of any land which is not a public place and which is visible from a public place.[179] The owner of any land which adjoins a residence that is let in two or more dwelling units is also obliged to keep the land free of litter that is to any extent visible from a public place.[180] Every occupier of land which adjoins a public road in respect of which a built up area speed limit or special speed limit has been established is also obliged to keep free from litter, any footpath or any area of land forming part of a public road.[181]

4. Public roads

10–117 Local authorities are obliged to ensure that each public road within its functional area is, so far as practicable, kept free of litter, and under section 8 are obliged to take all practicable measures to prevent the creation of litter. Section 8 also allows local authorities to enter into arrangements with, or assist other persons, including other local authorities to take measures to prevent or remove litter. Local authorities may also take measures for the collection and disposal of litter, to promote awareness of the polluting effects of litter, to

---

[176] s.27(1).
[177] s.27(2).
[178] s.5.
[179] s.6.
[180] s.6(3).
[181] s.6(4).

encourage the public to keep public areas free of litter, and to undertake works and the provision of facilities and services in relation to litter, including publicity.

10–118 Local authorities are under a duty to ensure that where litter receptacles are provided, that these receptacles do not become a nuisance or be the cause of litter.[182] Local authorities may make regulations in relation to the use of skips on public roads under section 72 of the Roads Act 1993.[183]

5. Notices

10–119 Local authorities may serve a notice requiring the removal of litter on a person whom it believes is contravening the provisions of section 6, or where the local authority believes that the service of a notice is required as a precautionary measure to prevent the creation of litter.[184] The notice may require a person to remove the litter and may require the taking of other precautionary measures to ensure that the creation of litter is prevented. The notice shall identify the place or land to which it relates and state the grounds on which it was issued, and shall specify the time within which it is to be complied with. A person upon whom a notice is served may make submissions in writing to the local authority, and the authority may revoke or amend the notice following these representations. Where a person fails to comply with the notice, the local authority may give effect to the notice by, if necessary, entering into the place or the land concerned and remove the litter or take the appropriate steps.[185] The local authority may recover the costs of this intervention from the person who failed to comply with the notice as a simple contract debt. Any person who obstructs or impedes a local authority or who fails to comply with the notice shall be guilty of an offence.

10–120 Section 14 provides that no action or other proceeding shall lie or be maintained against a local authority, a litter warden or any other office or employee of a local authority or against a member of the Garda Síochána for the recovery of any damages in respect to an injury to any person, or for damage to property or other loss which is alleged to have been caused or contributed to by those persons in respect to the exercise of any function under the Act.

10–121 In respect to the owners, occupiers or persons in charge of a mobile outlet which is used for the sale of produce, food or drink are obliged to at all

---

[182] s.7(3).
[183] No. 14 of 1993.
[184] s.9.
[185] s.9(5).

times, when open to customers, to provide and maintain adequate litter receptacles in the vicinity of the outlet while it is in operation, and to ensure that any litter arising from the operation of the outlet is removed from the vicinity within a reasonable distance, not exceeding 100 metres from the outlet.[186] A local authority may by notice require the owner, occupier or person in charge of a mobile outlet to comply with additional measures in order to prevent or remove litter at or in the vicinity of the outlet.[187] Failing to comply with the terms of section 15 may result in a prosecution for an offence under the Act.

10–122 Where it appears to a local authority that special measures are required to be taken by an occupier or any premises in order to prevent or limit the creation of litter at a premises or on land or in its vicinity, the local authority may serve a notice requiring the taking of such measures to prevent the creation of litter and may also provide for the removal of litter so created.[188] In lieu of the taking of measures such as removing litter, the local authority may require the making of a financial contribution to the authority towards the estimated cost to the local authority of collecting and removing the litter caused or likely to be caused by the operation of a business or undertaking. The section relates to certain businesses or premises, and although certain premises are specified in subsection 9, such as premises which sell confectionery, food or drink, a cinema, theatre, concert hall or leisure centre, an amusement arcade or an area for other indoor or outdoor sport or recreation, a financial institution, having automated equipment for withdrawals, deposits or payments located on an outside location at the premises (ATMs) a bookmaking (gaming) business, a bus or rail station, airport or seaport, a public car park, a retail shopping centre, the list is not exhaustive and merely outlines certain businesses which are clearly within the terms of the section.

10–123 When determining the measures which are required to be taken a local authority shall, in addition to other factors as may be relevant in the circumstances, have due regard to, the nature and quantity of litter caused or likely to be caused at or on land in the vicinity of the premises, or both, which exceeds the nature or quantity that would ordinarily be caused if the occupier's business or undertaking was not being operated at those premises, and the duties of the local authority in respect of the land in the vicinity of the premises.[189] Before a local authority exercises its powers under section 16 to serve a notice on the occupier or owner of a business or undertaking it shall advise the occupier of the nature and extent of the measures that the local authority proposes to specify and to provide the occupier with an opportunity

---

[186] s.15(1).
[187] s.15(2).
[188] s.16.
[189] s.16(3).

to make submissions in writing to the local authority in relation to the proposed measures. The local authority, having considered any such submissions, may amend the proposed measures or confirm or revoke the proposed measures, and shall inform the occupier of such amendment, confirmation or revocation as soon as possible thereafter.[190]

10–124   Under section 17 if it appears to a local authority that measures are required to be taken in order to prevent or limit the creation of litter in a public place or in a place that is visible from a public place caused by the holding of an event at which large numbers of persons are likely to be present, the local authority may serve a notice on the person who is the promoter or organiser of the event or events or on such other person as appears to the local authority to be associated with the organisation of the event or events, requiring the person to take such measures as the local authority considers necessary to prevent the creation of litter and provide for the removal of the litter.[191] Notices under section 17 shall specify the measures which are to be taken before, during and after the event or in their vicinity, and may require the person upon whom the notice is served to deposit an amount specified as security which can be realised by the local authority in the event that the measures specified are not done to the satisfaction of the local authority. The notice may also specify that a financial contribution, independent of the security, be paid to the local authority as contribution to the costs of collecting and removing litter following the event or events.[192] As with a notice under section 16, a local authority is obliged to give the person upon whom the notice is to be served an opportunity to make representations or submissions in writing prior to the service of a notice.[193]

10–125   A person on whom a notice has been served who fails to comply with a requirement referred to in a notice and has not made to the local authority the specified financial contribution may be guilty of an offence. A local authority may take such steps as it considers reasonable and necessary in order to remedy any failure to comply with a notice and may recover the reasonable costs incurred from the person as a simple contract debt in any court of relevant jurisdiction.[194]

6. Appeals

10–126   An occupier of premises who is dissatisfied with any of the terms of

---

[190] s.16(4).
[191] s.17.
[192] s.17(2).
[193] s.17(3).
[194] s.17(5).

a notice may, within twenty one days after receipt of the notice, appeal to the District Court and the District Court may confirm or annul the notice, or may confirm or vary any of the terms thereof or provide such other relief or may impose such other requirement or requirements in relation to the notice and the occupier as the Court deems appropriate in the circumstances.[195] An occupier on whom a notice has been served who fails to comply with the measures specified in the notice and who is not relieved from the obligation to comply by virtue of having made to the local authority a financial contribution referred to in section 16(2)(c) may be guilty of an offence under the Act. Any financial contribution made to a local authority shall be used by the local authority solely for the prevention and limitation of the creation of litter and the removal of litter in respect of the premises or land in relation to which the financial contribution is made.[196]

7. Action by local authorities

(a) Limiting litter in public places

10–127   Where it appears to a local authority that measures are required to be taken in order to prevent or limit the creation of litter in a public place or in a place that is visible from a public place caused by the holding of an event or series of events at which large numbers of persons are likely to be present, and either in the absence of steps being taken or operations being carried out by the local authority under this subsection, the creation of the litter will not be prevented or limited, or due to the timing of the event or series of events, it is not practicable for the local authority to exercise its powers under section 17 the local authority may take such steps as it considers necessary to prevent or limit the creation of the litter.

10–128   Where a local authority takes such steps it may recover the reasonable costs of such steps or operations as a simple contract debt from such person as the local authority satisfies the court is a person whose promotion of the event or series of events, as the case may be, necessitated such steps or operations.[197]

(b) Advertisements

10–129   Advertisements or articles which tend to deface any structure or door, gate, window, tree, pole or post which is visible from a public place may not be placed other than by the owner of the property.[198] Advertisements may not

---

[195] s.16(5).
[196] s.16(8).
[197] s.18(2).
[198] s.19(1).

also be placed on vehicles which are in public places without the prior consent of the owner, and in the case of an advertisement which relates to a meeting or other event, the person who is promoting or arranging the meeting or event or any other advertisement, the person on whose behalf the advertisement is exhibited shall be deemed also to have contravened section 19. A local authority may remove or obliterate an article or advertisement or remedy a defacement and may, by its employees or agents, enter onto the structure or land concerned to carry out the removal or remedy the defacement. A person who obstructs or impedes a local authority or who contravenes section 19 may be guilty of an offence. Advertisements which have the benefit of planning permission, or which advertises a public meeting, other than an auction, or an advertisement relating to a presidential election or elections for local authorities, Dáil Eireann or for the European Parliament do not contravene section 19, unless the advertisements remain in position for seven days longer after the holding of the election or elections.[199]

10–130   Local authorities may require the occupiers of property to remove any article or advertisement if the advertisement is visible from a public place and that its removal is in the interests of amenity or of the environment. The notice may require the occupier to remove the advertisement or article and to take other measures in order to prevent a recurrence of the advertisement or defacement.[200] If the occupiers fails to comply with the terms of the notice employees or agents of the local authority may give effect to the terms of the notice and where necessary enter onto land or structure, the local authority may recover the costs of carrying out the terms of the notice. An occupier who fails to comply with the terms of a notice, or who impedes or obstructs a local authority or its employees or agents may be guilty of an offence.[201]

10–131   Local authorities may by bye-law prohibit or regulate the distribution to the public of advertising material or certain specified categories of advertising material, but these bye-laws shall not apply to advertisements which are delivered by direct delivery or election material relating to presidential, Dáil, local, or European elections.

8. Obstructing Litter Wardens

10–132   A person who obstructs or impedes a litter warden or a member of the Garda Síochána who is exercising functions under the Litter Pollution Act shall be guilty of an offence. A litter warden[202] or a member of the Garda

---

[199] s.19(7).
[200] s.20(1).
[201] s.20(7).
[202] Litter wardens are obliged to produce a copy of their certification to any person who requests same, s.23(4).

Síochána who has reasonable grounds for believing that a person is committing or has committed an offence under this Act, may request the person to give his or her name and address, and may request that the information given be verified, and if dissatisfied with the verification provided pursuant to a request, may request that the person accompany the warden or member to a local authority office or Garda station for the purpose of the verification. A person who fails to give his or her name and address when requested to do so or gives a name or address that is false or misleading, or fails to comply with a request made by a warden or a Garda may be guilty of an offence.

10–133 A litter warden who in the course of his duty believes that the assistance of a member of the Garda Síochána is required in any particular instance to prevent the obstruction of the litter warden in exercising the litter warden's functions may request the Garda to assist the litter warden to prevent the obstruction and the Garda is obliged to comply with the request from the litter warden.[203] A member of the Garda Síochána who is of the opinion that a person is committing or has committed an offence under this section may arrest the person without warrant.

10–134 If a litter warden or a member of the Garda Síochána has reasonable grounds for believing that a person is committing or has committed a prescribed offence under this Act, or a dog warden, appointed under the Control of Dogs Act, 1986, or a member of the Garda Síochána has reasonable grounds for believing that a person is committing or has committed an offence under section 22 relating to the deposit of dog faeces in a public place or land forming part of a retail shopping centre, or school or sports grounds or a beach, the warden or member may give to the person a notice in prescribed form stating that the person is alleged to have committed the offence, and that the person may during the period of 21 days beginning on the date of the notice, make to the local authority specified in the notice a payment of £25 accompanied by the notice, on the spot notice, and that accompanied by the notice. If the fine has not been paid within twenty one days a prosecution in respect of the alleged offence may be instituted.[204]

10–135 Litter wardens may be appointed by the local authority, after consultation with the Commissioner of the Garda Síochána, and may carry out functions in respect of offences under the Road Traffic Acts, 1961 to 1973 which relate to the prohibition or restriction relating to the stopping or parking of vehicles, as well as functions relating to offences under regulations made under the Roads Act 1920 regarding licences issued under the Act.[205] Traffic

---

[203] s.20(5).
[204] s.28(1).
[205] Local Authorities (Traffic Wardens) Act 1975, s.2.

wardens who have reasonable grounds for believing that a person has committed an offence may deliver a notice, in the prescribed form, stating the offence and that the person may pay the fine within a period of twenty one days beginning on the date of the notice, and that a prosecution will not be instituted during that period.

10–136   A person who obstructs a traffic warden acting in the course of his duty may be found guilty of an offence and shall be liable on summary conviction to a fine. A traffic warden who has reasonable grounds for believing that a person has committed an offence to which the 1975 Act relates may request or demand the person's name and address, and if the person refuses to give their name can be liable to a further offence and a fine on summary conviction.[206]

10–137   Offences under the Litter Pollution Act are punishable by a fine on summary conviction of £1,500, and if after the conviction the contravention is continued the person may be found guilty of a further offence and be liable to a further fine of £100 for each day during which the additional contravention continues.[207] Offences under the Litter Pollution Act may be prosecuted by the local authority in whose functional area the offence was committed, and in addition to any penalty the convicted person may be ordered to pay to the local authority or to a person who has suffered loss the costs incurred by the local authority or person for the repair or replacement of the receptacle. The court may order that payment of costs of the prosecution of offences in proceedings brought under the Litter Pollution Act, unless there are special and substantial reasons for not doing so.[208] Offences committed by a body corporate the director, manager, secretary or other similar officer of the corporate body may also be found guilty of a similar offence.[209] Fines imposed under the Act are to be paid to the local authority and the payment of the fine may be enforced by the local authority as if it were due to the authority by way of a decree made by a court in civil proceedings.[210]

10–138   Under section 27, where the contents of litter that has been deposited in contravention of the Act or of municipal waste that has been placed in contravention of section 3(3) of the Act, gives rise to a reasonable suspicion as to the identity of the person from whom the litter or waste emanated, the contents are allowed to be given as evidence. In the absence of evidence to the

---

[206] Prosecutions may be taken by the local authority for offences under the 1975 Act.
[207] s.24.
[208] s.25(4).
[209] s.25(3).
[210] s.25(5).

contrary, it may be held that the litter or waste emanated from the person before the deposit or placement and that the person made the contravening deposit or placement. Items such as envelopes with addresses on them, or invoices or statements are often used as evidence in court proceedings.

9. Litter management plans

10–139 Section 11 of the Litter Pollution Act require local authorities to create a litter management plan specifying the objectives of the local authority for the prevention and control of litter, specifying the measures to encourage public awareness with a view to eliminate litter pollution, specify the measures or arrangements that are to be undertaken by the local authority. The plan should also include information on an appraisal of all existing litter prevention and control programmes operated by the local authorities, the policies and objectives of the local authority in relation to the prevention and control of litter and the facilities at which waste may be deposited by members of the public for the recovery or disposal within the meaning of the Waste Management Act 1996.

10–140 In making or reviewing a litter management plan the local authority shall have regard to the proper planning and development of its functional area. Where the authority intends to make a litter management plan it is obliged to publish in one or more newspapers circulating in its functional area a notice of their proposal and arrange for the notice of their intention to make a litter management plan at least once on three successive days on one or more local radio stations broadcasting in the functional area.[211] The local authority shall also consult with such voluntary and representative bodies as the local authority may deem appropriate concerning the steps which the local authority need to take. Written submissions may be made to local authorities in relation to the proposed plan and such submissions are to be considered by the authority. Copies of the proposed litter management plan are to be made available free of charge.

10–141 As soon as the local authority makes, replaces or amends a management litter plan the local authority shall publish and distribute the plan as widely as possible in its functional area and shall give adequate publicity to the plan.[212] The making, review, amendment or replacement of a litter management plan is a reserved function.[213]

---

[211] s.12(1).
[212] s.12(5).
[213] s.13.

E. NOISE

1. Definition

10–142   Noise is included in the definition of emission under section 3 of the Environmental Protection Act of 1992,[214] and the definition of noise also includes vibration. In the 1992 Act environmental "pollution" means, amongst other things, the disposal of waste in a manner which would endanger human health or harm the environment and cause a nuisance through noise or odours.

2. Notice

10–143   The Environmental Protection Agency Act provides that a local authority may when it so appears, in relation to any premises, processes or works, other than an activity for which a licence is required under the Act or that a licence has not been issued by the Agency and that it is necessary to do so for the prevention or limitation of noise, the local authority or the Agency, may serve a notice on the person in charge of the premises. The notice shall indicate the requirements for the prevention or limitation of the noise and may specify the measures which appear to the local authority or the Agency, to be necessary in order to prevent or limit the noise and direct the person on whom the notice is served to take such measures as may be specified in the notice to prevent or limit the noise.[215] The notice may specify a period, which the local authority or the Agency, considers reasonable in all the circumstances of the case, within which such measures are to be taken.[216]

10–144   A person on whom a notice has been served may, within the period specified in the notice, make representations in writing to the local authority or the Agency, concerning the terms of the notice. The local authority or the Agency, having considered any such representations, may amend a provision of the notice, or may confirm or revoke the notice, and shall inform the person, upon whom the notice was served and who made representations of the amendment, confirmation or revocation.[217] A person on whom a notice under this section has been served shall, within the period specified in the notice, comply with the requirements of the notice.

10–145   If the person does not, within the period specified in the notice,

---

[214] No. 7 of 1992.
[215] See *Budd v. Colchester Borough Council*, Court of Appeal, *The Times*, April 14, 1999, for the discussion of the contents of a noise notice. Relevant legislation in England is the Environmental Protection Act of 1990.
[216] s.107(2).
[217] s.107(3).

comply with the requirements of the notice, the local authority or the Agency, may take steps as it considers reasonable and necessary to secure compliance with the notice. The local authority or the Agency may recover any costs and expenses thereby incurred from the person on whom the notice was served as a simple contract debt.[218]

10–146 A defence is allowed, in a prosecution for a contravention of section 107 in the case of noise caused in the course of a trade or business, for the person accused of a contravention of section 107 to prove that the person took all reasonable care to prevent or limit the noise by providing, maintaining, using, operating and supervising facilities, or by employing practices or methods of operation, that, having regard to all the circumstances, were suitable for the purposes of such prevention or limitation, or the noise is in accordance with the terms of a licence under this Act, or regulations under section 106:[219]

> "Where any noise which is so loud, so continuous, so repeated, of such duration or pitch or occurring at such times as to give reasonable cause for annoyance to a person in any premises in the neighbourhood or to a person lawfully using any public place, a local authority, the Agency or any such person may complain to the District Court and the Court may order the person or body making, causing or responsible for the noise to take the measures necessary to reduce the noise to a specified level or to take specified measures for the prevention or limitation of the noise and the person or body concerned shall comply with such order."[220]

3. Court application

10–147 Section 108 of the 1992 Act therefore allows any person, as well as the local authority, to make an application to the District Court for an order to prevent or limit noise which has become a nuisance. It is provided that it shall be a good defence, in the case of proceedings under section 108, in the case of noise caused in the course of a trade or business, for the accused to prove that all reasonable care was taken to prevent or limit the noise by providing, maintaining, using, operating and supervising facilities, or by employing practices or methods of operation, that, having regard to all the circumstances, were suitable for the purposes of such prevention or limitation, or that the noise is in accordance with the terms of a licence under the Environmental Protection Agency Act, or by regulations under section 106 of that Act.[221]

---

[218] s.107(4).
[219] s.107(5).
[220] s.108.
[221] s.108(2).

4. Noise and planning

10–148   Under section 51 of the Local Government (Planning and Development) Act 1963[222] a person cannot, in any public place or in connection with any premises which adjoins any public place or in connection with any premises which adjoins any public place and to which the public are admitted, or upon any other premises, either by operating, or causing or suffering to be operated any wireless, loudspeaker, television, gramophone, amplifier, or similar instrument, or any machine or other appliance, or by any other means cause, any noise or vibration which "is so loud or so continuous or so repeated or of such duration or pitch or at such times as to give reasonable cause for annoyance to persons in any premises in the neighbourhood or to persons lawfully using any public place."[223]

5. Proceedings

10–149   Proceedings cannot be taken unless the annoyance is continued after the end of seven days from the date of the service of a notice alleging annoyance, and which was signed by not less than three persons residing or carrying on a business within the area in which the noise is heard or the vibration is felt.[224]   Section 51 of the Local Government (Planning and Development) Act 1963 does not apply to noise or vibration caused by aircraft, or by any statutory bodies who act in the course of powers conferred on them by any statute or order or other instrument made under statute. In proceedings relating to noise or vibration caused in the course of a trade or business or in performing any statutory functions, it shall be a good defence for the defendant to prove that the best practicable means have been used for preventing, and for counteracting the effect of the noise or vibration.[225]

---

[222] No. 28 of 1963.
[223] Does not apply to a public meeting.
[224] s.51(3) a person who contravenes this section shall be guilty of an offence and shall be liable on summary conviction to a fine not exceeding ten pound.
[225] s.51(6).

CHAPTER 11

Local elections

A. INTRODUCTION

1. Constitutional review

11–01 Following a recommendation from the Constitution Review Group in 1996[1] not to give local authorities the benefit of a constitutional amendment which could give rise to new separation of powers between the government and regions, and which could invalidate a whole range of central government controls. An All-Party Oireachtas Committee on the Constitution concluded that while there ought to be general constitutional recognition that it would not be appropriate to insert specific provisions into the Constitution.[2] A majority of the Constitution Review Group concluded that a form of recognition in principle of local government should be inserted into the Constitution, that is a general recognition.

11–02 The All Party Committee felt that because local authorities were creatures of legislation it was possible to defer elections for local authorities for so prolonged a period that their representational character was affected. In order to assert, or perhaps reassert, the democratic value of local authorities the Committee believed that there should be a constitutional provision for elections to local authorities. The All Party Committee, from individual submissions, recognised that there was widespread dissatisfaction with the structures which exist, the financing of local government, their relationship with central

---

[1] Report of Constitution Review Group (1996, Pn. 2632).
[2] See Morgan and Hogan (Dublin, 1998), p.252.

government and the relationship between local government and the community. Functions were removed from the local authorities and given to other institutions, while the establishment of city and county management from 1929 onwards was seen as diminishment of the role of elected councillors while the abolition of rates on domestic property was seen as a reduction in the autonomy of local authorities.[3]

11–03 The Committee recommended that the Constitution should be amended by the insertion of a provision stating that local authorities be empowered to carry out functions which the Oireachtas may from time to time devolve upon them by law, and that elections were to be held every five years. The Committee felt that constitutional recognition of local government would strengthen the democratic system and would thereby counteract the perceived dependency syndrome system in local government.[4]

11–04 Following the adoption of the Twentieth Amendment of the Constitution Act 1999 local authorities were given a constitutional base. The Amendment provides that elections for members of local authorities are now held not later that the end of the fifth year after the year in which they were last held.[5] Every citizen who has the right to vote at an election for members of Dáil Éireann, and other persons as may be determined by law, have the right to vote at an election for members of local authorities.[6] There are a total of 114 local authorities with 1,627 elected members. County councils are elected in 29 administrative counties, 5 county borough corporations, 5 borough corporations, 49 urban district councils, and 26 town commissioners.

2. Right to vote

11–05 Under section 23 of the Local Government Act 1994 every person whose name is on the register of local government electors which has been prepared under the Electoral Act of 1992 which is in force for the local electoral area is entitled to vote at the poll at a local election.[7] Voting is done in secret[8] and no person is obliged to state for whom he or she has voted.[9] A person who is registered in the register but is not entitled to be registered or who is not registered in the register is not able to vote at the poll at a local election in the relevant area.[10] Article 10 of the Local Elections Regulations

---

[3] All Party Committee on the Constitution April 1997, p.70.
[4] p.69.
[5] Art. 28A.3, Constitution of Ireland.
[6] Art. 28A.4.
[7] Local Government Act 1994, s.23(1).
[8] Breach of secrecy is an offence under Art. 98, Local Elections Regs. 1995.
[9] s. 23(3).
[10] s.23(4).

1995[11] provides for the manner of voting at local elections, and provides that every elector whose name is, at the time of an election, entitled to vote at an election is entitled to vote in person only and at the polling station allotted.

11–06 A person may not vote or apply for a ballot paper more than once at an election for members of local authorities. This applies to an election of the members of more than one local authority of the same class held at the same local elections or at both an election of the members of the corporation of a county borough and an election of the members of a corporation of a borough which is not a county borough, or of an urban district council or the council of commissioners of a town.[12] A person who does vote or who applies for a ballot paper may be guilty of an offence and may be liable on summary conviction to a term of imprisonment not exceeding six months or to a fine not exceeding £1,000 or to both the term of imprisonment and the fine.

3. Register of electors

(a) Register

11–07 A register of electors is to be prepared for each administrative county and county boroughs and published each year.[13] Each register is to contain the names of the persons who are entitled to be registered as electors on the qualifying date, 1st of September. Each register is in fact divided into separate registers, a register of Presidential Electors, a register of Dáil electors, a register of European electors and a register of local government electors. In practice, the register contains a list of names under the headings of each street or town land followed by a reference to which register, Presidential, Dáil, local government and European, the voter is included in, are arranged under polling districts or by reference to the general character of any part of the area, arrangement in street order or in any other order is possible and convenient.[14]

(b) Postal list

11–08 The postal voters list contains electors who qualify under section 14 as of right, namely a member of the Garda Síochána, or a whole time member of the Defence Forces as well as persons who are deemed to be ordinarily resident in the State under section 12. Section 12 deems persons in the service of the State to be ordinarily resident in the State namely citizens over the age of eighteen who are civil servants and members of a mission outside of the State together with their spouses, but not their children.

---

[11] S.I. No. 297 of 1995.
[12] Local Government Act 1991, s.10.
[13] According to the Second Schedule to the Act.
[14] Second Schedule to the Act.

11–09   Section 10 of the Electoral Act of 1992[15] specifies that local authority electors are required to be over the age of eighteen and that the elector was on the qualifying date, ordinarily resident in the local electoral area. The electors age is taken as the age of the elector on the qualifying date, not at the time of the election.[16]

11–10   The qualifying date is specified in the second schedule to the Act and refers to September 1 in the year preceding the year in which the register comes into force. Section 11 of the Act prevents voters from being registered in more than one constituency, the section also prevents double registration in the same constituency or electoral area. If it is the case that a person seems to be eligible for registration in respect of two or more premises, the question of which premises the voter should be registered of shall be determined by the registration authority, unless the voter express a choice. This is distinct from being eligible for registration in two or more electoral areas, in that case the elector must chose which area he or she wishes to be registered in, and in fact the registration authorities are bound to ensure that the elector is not registered in two areas.[17]

11–11   Section 11 was enacted following the Supreme Court decision in *Quinn v. Waterford Corporation*[18] where the court found that section 5 of the 1963 Act did not prevent an individual from being ordinarily resident in more than one electoral area and that it was not proper for a county registrar to enquire into an individual's possible registration in another constituency.[19]

(c) Supplement to the register

11–12   Section 15 of the Act specifies that persons who were entitled on the qualifying date to be on a register, may apply to the registration authority to have their name entered in a supplement to the register. The second schedule to the Act details the procedure which is to be taken in regard to the preparation and contents of the register. On receipt of an application to be included in the supplement to the register of electors, the registration authority are obliged to make inquiries in order to consider the application and Rule 5 shall apply in relation to the consideration of such application. An application by a person to be entered in the supplement to the register, if received on or after the twelfth

---

[15] No. 23 of 1992.
[16] s.11(2)(b).
[17] s.1(1)(c).
[18] [1991] I.L.R.M. 433.
[19] In so finding the Court approved *Fox v. Stirk and Bristol Electoral Registration Office* [1970] 2 Q.B. 463.

day before the polling day of an election or referendum does not have effect in relation to that election or referendum.[20]

11–13 Rule 5 states that the registration authorities may make house to house or other such inquiries in their registration area and for this purpose may require a person to give any information which the registration authority may require, or to produce a certificate of birth or make a statutory declaration of age, or to provide documentary evidence or make a statutory declaration that the person is entitled to be registered as a Dáil elector or as a national of a Member State of the European Union.

11–14 The registration authority are obliged to ensure that the register is correct and free from errors of a clerical or typographical nature or because of misnomers of inaccurate descriptions. If there are any such errors the registration authority is obliged to publish a list of these corrections and this list becomes part of the supplemental list.[21] Once the supplement to the register has been published the supplement becomes part of the register of electors.[22]

11–15 Special voters lists are prepared by the registration authority and refers to persons who are unable to vote at the polling place in the polling district due to physical illness or physical disability.[23] The voter must satisfy the registration authority that the physical illness or physical disability is likely to continue for the period the then current register of electors in respect of which the application to be entered as a special voter is made.[24] At the time of elections special presiding officers are appointed to deal with the votes of special voters, and these special presiding officers have the same role and powers as the usual presiding officers at elections.[25]

11–16 A supplement to the postal voters list may be made under section 15A of the 1992 Act[26] which provides that an elector who is not entered in the postal voters list of the special voters list may apply to the registration authority to have their name entered in a supplement to the postal voters list. An elector who is not entered in the special voters list or the postal voters list may apply to the registration authority to have their name entered in a supplement to the special voters list which the registration authority is empowered to prepare and publish under section 15B of the 1997 Act.

---

[20] s.15(5).
[21] s.15(3).
[22] s.15(4).
[23] See *Draper v. Attorney General* [1984] I.L.R.M. 643.
[24] s.17(2).
[25] s.80.
[26] As inserted by s. 76 of the Electoral Act 1997, No. 25 of 1997.

11–17 At a Dáil election, a special presiding officer, in the presence of a member of the Garda Síochána, delivers to the special voter a form of declaration of identity and no person other than the special presiding officer and the member of the Garda Síochána can be present when the special voter is voting. The special voter is obliged to complete the declaration of identity and shall sign it or, if he is unable to write, place his mark thereon and the said signature, or as the case may be mark, is witnessed by the special presiding officer.[27] Following the casting of the special votes the special presiding officer returns the votes to the returning officer before the time fixed for the close of the poll at the Dáil election.[28]

4. Polling districts and polling places

11–18 Each local authority is obliged at least once in every ten years, following consultation with the returning officer for Dáil elections in respect of the county or county borough and in accordance with regulations,[29] to make a scheme bearing in mind that each polling place must have reasonable facilities for voting, dividing the county or county borough into polling districts for the purposes of Dáil elections, European elections and local elections and appointing a polling place for each polling district.[30] Each local authority is also required to endeavour to appoint as polling places only such areas as may allow the returning officer to provide at least one polling station at each polling place which is accessible to wheelchair users.[31] Polls for local elections are to be held for a period of not less than twelve hours, between the hours of 8.00 a.m. and 10.30 p.m., and as may be fixed by the Minister by order, and that the polling day for local elections is to be fixed during the month of June.[32]

B. LOCAL AUTHORITY MEMBERSHIP

1. Right to become a member

11–19 Every person who is a citizen of Ireland or who is ordinarily resident in the State and who has reached the age of eighteen years and is not subject to any of the disqualifications is eligible for election or for co-option to and membership of a local authority.[33] Previously a person could not be elected or be a

---

[27] s.82.
[28] s. 83(1).
[29] See Art. 49, Local Elections Regulations 1995.
[30] s.28(1) the making of a scheme is a reserved function.
[31] s.28(1A) inserted by the Electoral (Amendment) Act 1996.
[32] s. 21(1).
[33] Local Government Act 1994, s.5.

councillor of a county council unless that person was not only a local government elector for the district but also was during the whole of the twelve months before the election resided in and continued to reside in the district.[34]

2. Disqualification

11–20 A person is disqualified from being elected, or being co-opted, or from being a member of a local authority if that person is a member of the Commission of the European Communities or a representative in the European Parliament, or is a Judge, Advocate General or Registrar of the Court of Justice of the European Communities. Other office holders are also prevented from being members of local authorities, such as if that person is a member of the Court of Auditors of the European Communities, or is a Minister of the Government or a Minister of State, or is the chairman of Dáil Éireann or of Seanad Éireann, or is the chairman of a select committee of either House of the Oireachtas (or of a joint committee of both Houses), a Judge or the Comptroller and Auditor General. Members of the Garda Síochána or a wholetime member of the Defence Forces, or a civil servant who is not by terms of employment expressly permitted to be a member of a local authority, or persons who are undergoing a sentence of imprisonment for any term exceeding six months, imposed by a court of competent jurisdiction in the State are also disqualified from being members of local authorities.

11–21 Persons who fail to pay any portion of any sum which is charged or surcharged by an auditor of the accounts of any local authority are also disqualified from being members of local authorities.[35] This disqualification comes into effect on the expiration of the time limit for an appeal, or on the expiration of one month from the date of an order confirming the charge or surcharge, where an appeal is taken to the Minister or the High Court and the disqualification applies and the disqualification has effect for a period of five years from the date of its coming into effect. Persons who also fail to comply with a final judgement, order or decree of a court of competent jurisdiction, for payment of money due to a local authority,[36] or is convicted of, or has had a conviction confirmed on appeal for, an offence relating to fraudulent or dishonest dealings affecting a local authority, or corrupt practice, or acting when disqualified are also disqualified.[37]

---

[34] Local Government (Ireland) Act 1898, s.23(4).

[35] Other charges are also required to be paid, see *The Munster Express*, March 17, 2000, p.1.

[36] A disqualification from such a decree comes into effect on the seventh day following the last day for compliance with the relevant final judgement, order or decree and the disqualification shall apply and have effect for a period of five years from such last day.

[37] Local Government Act 1994, s.6, No. 8 of 1994.

11–22   If a person knowingly acts as a member of a local authority when that person is disqualified or votes while prohibited from doing so, then that person commits an offence and may be liable to a fine of not over £1,000 for each offence, and a prosecution for an offence of this type may be taken at the suit of a local government elector, by the local authority or by the Minister for the Environment and Local Government.[38]

11–23   Where a member of a local authority becomes disqualified from membership of a local authority, that person shall immediately cease to be a member and a vacancy then exists in the membership of the local authority. A person who ceases to be a member of a local authority also ceases to be a member of any body to which that person was elected, or nominated or appointed by a local authority, or of which the person is a member by virtue of being a member of a local authority.[39]

11–24   A person who is a Minister of the Government or a Minister of State is disqualified from being elected, chosen or appointed as a member of a local authority.[40] Where a person, who is a member of a local authority, is appointed to hold office as a Minister of the Government or as a Minister of State, that person then ceases to be a member of a local authority.[41]

3. Term of office

11–25   Terms of office for members of local authorities continue until the ordinary day of retirement of members of the local authority, that is until the seventh day after the polling day of the next election, or the day after the date on which the poll is completed if a fresh poll is held.[42]

4. Vacancies and resignation

11–26   A member of a local authority may, at any time, resign from membership by notice in writing, signed by the member and delivered to the principal offices of the local authority, and that member shall cease to be a member of the local authority on the day of receipt of the notice.[43] A person who resigns from the membership of a local authority shall on their resignation also cease to be a member of any body to which that person was elected, nominated or

---

[38] s.7(1).
[39] s.8.
[40] Local Government Act 1991, s.13.
[41] Local Government Act 1991, s.13(2).
[42] s.9.
[43] s.10(1).

appointed by the local authority, or of which that person is a member by virtue of being a member of that local authority.[44]

11–27 Vacancies, referred to as casual vacancies, may arise in the membership of a local authority by virtue of the death, resignation, or disqualification of a member.[45] It is the duty of the secretary or clerk to notify the members of the local authority in writing on becoming aware that a casual vacancy has or may have occurred. Casual vacancies are filled by the co-option by the local authority of a person to fill the vacancy.[46] Co-options are made, after due notice, at the next meeting of the local authority following the passing of fourteen days from the date of the vacancy or as soon as circumstances permit. Due notice is a period of not less than three clear days notice in writing given to every member of the local authority.[47]

11–28 A person who is co-opted onto a local authority holds office until the next ordinary day of retirement of the members of the local authority.[48] Persons who are co-opted onto the council of a county or other borough holds office as a councillor as opposed to an alderman.[49] If a casual vacancy occurs by reason of an alderman ceasing to hold office, the number of aldermen for the county or county borough is reduced by one in respect of each vacancy.[50] In the case of a vacancy or vacancies arising from resignation, disqualification or death, no act, decision or proceeding of the local authority can be invalidated by reason only of the vacancy.[51]

C.   LOCAL ELECTORAL AREAS

1. Boundaries

11–29 The Minister for the Environment and Local Government may by order divide a county, county or other borough or urban district into local electoral areas, and may also decide by order regarding the members of the council, fix the number of such members to be elected for each electoral area

---

[44] s.10(2).
[45] A casual vacancy also exists under the Local Elections Regulations 1965 or where a court declares that a person was not duly elected as a member of a local authority or was not qualified for membership of a local authority under s.15 of the Local Elections (Petitions and Disqualifications) Act 1974. See also Art. 28A.5 of the Constitution.
[46] s.11(4).
[47] s.11(5).
[48] s.11(7).
[49] s.11(8).
[50] s.11(9).
[51] s.12.

and in the case of a county or other borough, the numbers of those members who are to be aldermen. This provision remains in line with the Twentieth Amendment of the Constitution Act, in that Article 28A, s.2 in that it confirms that there shall be such directly local authorities as may be determined by law, and that their powers and functions shall be determined and exercised and performed in accordance with law.

11–30   The Minister for the Environment and Local Government has by the Local Government (Boundary Alteration) Regulations, 1996[52] dealt with procedural matters in relation to local authority boundary alterations under Part V of the Local Government Act 1991, and provides for the procedure which is to be gone through in connection with boundary alteration, including publication in a newspaper circulating in the area the subject of the proposal.

11–31   Where a proposed boundary alteration is shown on a map which has been submitted and which would involve the inclusion in a borough or urban district of an area which is located in a county other than the county in which the said borough or urban district is situated, regulations may provide for the simultaneous alteration of the boundary between the two counties in question so as to correspond with the boundary of the borough or urban district which are proposed to be altered.[53]

11–32   Regulations for the alteration of a boundary may not be made in respect of a borough, urban district or town unless either a reorganisation report has been submitted,[54] and the Minister has considered any proposals contained within the reorganisation report which may have a bearing on matters which are the subject of the proposed regulation, or there are in the opinion of the Minister in a particular case exceptional circumstances for altering the relevant boundary for purposes specified in the regulations in advance of such submission and agreement has been reached and satisfactory arrangements have been made by the local authorities concerned as respects all matters related to or connected with the proposed boundary alteration.

11–33   Once a boundary has been altered, the Commissioner for Valuation prepares for each county, borough, urban district and town the boundary of which has been altered a map drawn to convenient scale showing the boundaries of the county or counties, borough, urban district or town, who then transmits a copy of the map to the Minister, and to each of the relevant local authorities.[55] Maps prepared by the Commissioner for Valuation may be in-

---

[52] S.I. No. 217 of 1996.
[53] s.17.
[54] Made under s. 56 of the Act.
[55] s.17(5).

spected free of charge at any of the offices to which the Commissioner has forwarded a copy of the map, and copies may be obtained for a reasonable fee.

D. CONDUCT OF ELECTIONS

1. Local election regulations

11–34 The conduct of local elections is regulated under section 22 and by way of the Local Elections Regulations 1995 and which include nominations,[56] deposits by candidates,[57] deaths of candidates,[58] duties of returning officers,[59] staff of returning officers, taking of polls[60] and counting of votes,[61] arrangements for postal voting,[62] arrangements for special voting,[63] polling on islands,[64] as well as other matters relating to local elections.[65]

11–35 Part XV of the Local Elections Regulations 1995 deals with offences in relation to local elections under the Electoral Act of 1992 and the penalties for these offences. Article 95 deals with the offence of personation and provides that a person who applies for a ballot paper in the name of some other person, whether that name be the name of a living person or of a dead person or of a fictitious person, or having obtained a ballot paper once at an election applies at the same election for a ballot paper in that person's own name.

2. Undue influence

11–36 Undue influence is outlawed under article 97 and states that a person who, in relation to an election, directly or indirectly makes use of or threatens to make use of any force, violence or restraint against or inflicts or causes or threatens to inflict or cause any temporal or spiritual injury or loss on or to any person, or attempts by abduction, duress, or fraud, to induce or compel any person to vote or refrain from voting, or to vote or refrain from voting for a particular person or in a particular way, or to induce or compel any person to withdraw, or to refrain from withdrawing, from being a candidate, or to induce or compel any person to be a candidate or to impede or prevent any

---

[56] Art.17.
[57] Art.15.
[58] Art.28.
[59] Part II, see also *Boyle v. Allen* [1979] I.L.R.M. 281.
[60] Part X.
[61] Part XII and XIII.
[62] Part VII.
[63] Part VIII.
[64] Part IX.
[65] s.22(2).

person from being a candidate, or to impede or prevent the free exercise of the franchise by any elector, may be guilty of an offence.

3. Ballot boxes

11–37   Articles 98 to 100 deal extensively with offences relating to ballot boxes, ballot papers, nomination papers, disorderly conduct at election meetings, and breach of secrecy at elections. Article 121 provides that a person who is present at the issue of ballot papers to postal voters, or present while a special voter is voting, or present at the opening of postal ballot boxes, or admitted to a polling station in any capacity, or who is present in any capacity at the counting of the votes, is obliged and in fact shall maintain and aid in maintaining the secrecy of the ballot.

4. Electoral offences

11–38   Articles 101 to 119 deal with the remaining electoral offences including obstruction of nomination or poll,[66] interference or destruction of postal ballot papers,[67] and so on. Article 117 provides that where a person is guilty of an offence under the Regulations that person may be liable on summary conviction to a fine not exceeding £1,000 or, at the discretion of the court, to imprisonment for a period not exceeding six months or to both such fine and such imprisonment, or on conviction on indictment to a fine not exceeding £2,500 or, at the discretion of the court, to imprisonment for a period not exceeding two years or to both a fine and a term of imprisonment. Offences under Article 101,[68] Article 109[69] or Article 114,[70] such person shall be liable on summary conviction to a fine of not over £500 or, at the discretion of the court, to imprisonment of a maximum of three months or a fine and imprisonment.

11–39   However, it is important to note that a local election cannot be declared to be invalid by reason of the non-compliance with any regulation made regarding the conduct of elections, or by reason of any mistake in the use of forms, if it appears to a court that the election was conducted in accordance with the principles laid down within the regulations which were made, and that the non-compliance or mistake did not affect the material result of the election.[71]

---

[66] Art.106.
[67] Art.107.
[68] Omission of name and address of printer and publisher from election documents.
[69] Personation agent leaving polling station without permission.
[70] Handling of ballot papers by candidate or agent.
[71] s.22(6).

E. CHAIR AND VICE CHAIR OF LOCAL AUTHORITIES

11–40 Within each local authority there shall be a Chairman and a Vice Chairman known in the legislation as a Cathaoirleach and Leas-Chathaoirleach who are elected from among the members of the local authority.[72] The Chairman and Vice Chairman are elected at every annual meeting, except that members of either Houses of the Oireachtas are disqualified from being elected as Cathaoirleach or Leas-Chathaoirleach. The Cathaoirleach and Leas-Chathaoirleach of Dublin City Council and Cork City Council are each known as the Lord Mayor and Deputy Lord Mayor and of any other city council they are known as the Mayor or the Deputy Mayor of the city or of the borough.[73]

11–41 Where a casual vacancy occurs in the office of Cathaoirleach of a local authority the Leas-Cathaoirleach assumes the responsibilities of the office until the members of the local authority elect a replacement Cathaoirleach.[74] The Cathaoirleach may nominate another member of the local authority, including the Leas-Cathaoirleach to represent the Cathaoirleach at any ceremony or event.[75] A member who holds the office of Cathaoirleach or Leas-Chathaoirleach shall, unless he or she becomes disqualified or resigns, hold office from election until a successor is elected at the annual meeting of the local authority next after that member's election to office except in an election year. In an election year a Cathaoirleach continues to hold office during the period between the retirement, following the local elections, of the outgoing members and the commencement of the meeting at which a successor is elected to the office of Cathaoirleach unless he or she sooner dies or resigns from the office or becomes disqualified from local authority membership.[76] At every annual meeting, an outgoing Cathaoirleach or Leas-Cathaoirleach are eligible for re-election.

11–42 If a Cathaoirleach or Leas-Cathaoirleach ceases to be a member of a local authority then they shall also cease to be Cathaoirleach or Leas-Cathaoirleach. A Cathaoirleach or Leas-Cathaoirleach may resign from office by delivering a notice in writing to the principal offices of the local authority and the vacancy is deemed to occur on the day of the receipt of the written notice.[77] Where a casual vacancy occurs in the office of Cathaoirleach or Leas-Cathaoirleach the members of the local authority who are present at the

---

[72] s.25(1).
[73] s.25(3).
[74] s.25(7).
[75] s.25(6).
[76] s.27(3).
[77] s.28.

meeting of the local authority following the vacancy , or if that meeting is held within fourteen days of the vacancy, at the next meeting of the local authority, elect one of them to be Cathaoirleach or Leas-Cathaoirleach. However, not less than three clear days' notice is to be given to each member of the local authority of a meeting to fill a casual vacancy. A person who is elected to fill a casual vacancy in the office of Cathaoirleach or Leas-Cathaoirleach is elected for the remainder of the term of office of their predecessor.[78]

F. DISCLOSURE OF DONATIONS AND EXPENDITURE

1. Local Elections (Disclosure of Donations and Expenditure) Act 1999

11–43   The Local Elections (Disclosure of Donations and Expenditure) Act 1999[79] was passed in order to provide for the disclosure of donations and expenditure in respect of local elections and to amend the law in relation to local elections.[80] Within the Act the word "donation" refers to any contribution given for political purposes by any person, whether or not a member of a political party to a candidate at an election which is accepted in whole or in part by or on behalf of that person and includes, any donation of money, any donation of property or goods, or the conferring of the right to use, without payment or other consideration, indefinitely or for a specified period of any property or goods. Donation includes any supply of services without payment or other consideration or where there is a difference between the commercial price and the price charged for the purchase, acquisition or use of property or goods or the supply of any service where the price, fee or other consideration is less than the commercial price. Where a contribution is made by a person in connection with an event organised for the purpose of raising funds for a candidate at an election, any proportion which is attributable to that contribution of the net profit, if any which is derived from the event is also classed as a "donation" within the meaning of the Act.[81] Before a political party may incur any election expenses at an election the party must appoint a national agent. Each political party, not later than the last day for receiving nominations for an election, must notify the specified local authority in writing of the name and address of the national agent.[82]

---

[78] s.29(3).

[79] No. 7 of 1999.

[80] The Act also provides for research into electronic methods of recording and counting of votes.

[81] s.2.

[82] s.7, a candidate at an election may be appointed national agent of a party.

2. Designated persons – national agents

11–44   Designated persons are appointed by the relevant political party who shall be responsible for submitting a statement of election expenses.[83] A political party is obliged to notify the local authority of the designated person not later than the last day for receiving nominations for an election. The national agent of a political party and a designated person who are appointed under the provisions of the Act are obliged to have in the State an office or place to which claims, notices, writs, summonses and other documents may be sent.[84] The effect of this is that any claim, notice, writ, summons or document which is delivered at the office or place of the national agent of a political party or designated person is deemed to have been served.

11–45   Under section 13 of the Act the national agent of a political party or a person who incurs election expenses at a national level are obliged to, within ninety days following the polling day at an election, furnish in person to the specified local authority a statement in writing of all election expenses incurred by the agent or person in relation to the election and the matters to which the expenses relate. The same is the case of political expenses in respect of a local electoral area. Candidates are obliged to within ninety days following the polling date at an election to furnish in person to the local authority concerned a statement in writing of all election expenses incurred by the candidate in relation to the election.

3. Statement of donations and expenses

11–46   The national agent of a political party or a designated person is obliged to include in the statement of election expenses which is furnished details of the election expenses incurred.[85] The statement is made in the prescribed form and is accompanied by a statutory declaration made by the national agent or designated person to the effect that the statement is made to the best of knowledge and belief that the statement is correct in every material respect and that he or she has taken all reasonable action to ensure that the statement is accurate. National agents, candidates or designated person are obliged to maintain such records as are necessary for the purpose of furnishing the relevant statement to the local authority and for making the statutory declaration.[86] Where a candidate at an election dies before or after the close of the poll of the election and before a statement has been furnished to the local authority the statement is not required to be made.[87]

---

[83] s.8(1).
[84] s.9(1).
[85] s.13(1)(b).
[86] s.13(3).
[87] s.3(4).

11–47   A candidate at an election must include in the statement of donations and election expenses furnished details of the election expenses incurred and the source of the income, including details of each donation over £500, which cover the election expenses. Where a person makes more than one donation to a candidate in relation to the same election all donations are treated as a single donation and as such are aggregated. Each statement which is furnished must also include particulars of all disputed claims, if any together with all claims, if any, which are received after the period which is set for the making of claims in relation to election expenses.

11–48   Section 6 of the Act provides that election expenses refer to all expenditure for electoral purposes which have been incurred in the provision of property, goods, or services for use at an election. This use includes the promotion or opposition, directly or indirectly of the interests of a political party, or which are used to present the policies or a particular policy of a political party or used to make a comment on policies, or to solicit votes for or against a candidate or which are used to influence the outcome of an election.[88] Expenditure used to take an opinion poll or other similar survey relating to an election by or on behalf of a political party or on behalf of one or more than one candidate within a period of sixty days before an election is also classed as "election expenses" within the provisions of the Act.

11–49   However the payment by or on behalf of a candidate of a deposit under the Local Elections Regulations of 1995,[89] or the expenditure on the purchase of copies of the register of electors, the reasonable living expenses of a candidate or of any persons working on their behalf on a voluntary basis, or any sum which any individual paid out of their own resources for any minor expenses, or any payment, or service or facility which was provided by any institution of the EU or other intergovernmental organisation to which the State is a party, or benefits which are derived from a service rendered by an individual, including the use of a motor vehicle, on behalf of a political party or a candidate where the service is gratuitous are not regarded as "election expenses". The publication in a newspaper, magazine or other periodical publication or a broadcast on radio or television of news, reports, articles, features, editorial or other comments broadcasted or published in the same manner as that of any other material which is of public interest or concern as well as the transmission on radio or television of a broadcast on behalf of a political party or a candidate is also not classed as "election expenses". There is also no need to declare as election expenses any sums expended on property, goods or services which were previously bought or used in a previous election pro-

---

[88] s.6(1).
[89] S.I. No. 297 of 1995.

vided that expenditure has already been included in a statement of election expenses.

11–50 Where any property, goods or services are provided to a political party or to a candidate without any payment or other consideration or for a price which is less than the commercial price, then such property, goods or services are deemed to be an election expense at the usual commercial price and should be included at the commercial price in the statements which are furnished to the local authority.[90]

11–51 All election expenses which are incurred by or on behalf of a political party or on behalf of a candidate at any time during the period starting with the date of the order which is made under section 21 of the Local Government Act 1994 appointing the polling day and ending on the polling day are to be included in the statement of election expenses.[91] All election expenses which have been incurred by or on behalf of a political party or a candidate at any time before the commencement of the period between the order made under the Local Government Act of 1994 and the polling day relating to the provision of property, goods or services for use at the election are also to be included in the statement of election expenses.[92]

11–52 Election expenses may be only included at an election and any payment, advance or deposit shall only be made on behalf of a political party by the national agent of the party or by a designated person or on behalf of a candidate.[93] Section 6(7) obliges the national agent of a political party or designated person or the candidate, before incurring election expenses, to furnish in writing to the local authority the name, address and description of the person proposing to incur the expenses, a statement of the nature, purpose and estimated amount of the expenses, and an indication of the person's connection with the party or candidate.[94]

11–53 Section 11 provides that every claim in respect of election expenses against a national agent of a political party, or against a designated person or a candidate or other person under the Act, which is not delivered on or before the forty-fifth day after the polling day of the election shall not be paid and shall not be enforceable against the national agent, designated person, candidate or other person. If an order for payment has been made by a court the national agent, candidate or designated person is obliged to furnish, within

---

[90] s.6(2).
[91] s.6(3).
[92] s.6(3)(a), (b).
[93] s.6(5).
[94] s.6(7).

seven days after the court order, a copy of the order together with a statement of the sum which is to be paid under the order.[95]

4. Copy statements

11–54   As soon as the clerk or secretary of the relevant local authority receives the statements and declarations he or she must furnish a copy of the statement and declaration, together with a copy of any relevant court orders, to the members of the local authority.[96] Where a fresh election is held in a local electoral area the original election and the fresh election are deemed to be an election under the 1999 Act and statements and statutory declarations are to be furnished as required.[97]

11–55   The clerk or secretary of a local authority is obliged to register every statement which is furnished to a local authority and is obliged to give notice in writing, by post or otherwise, of the receipt of the statement to the person who furnished it.[98] Where a local authority finds a minor error or omission in the statement, the local authority is obliged to furnish the unsuccessful candidate, elected member, designated person, national agent or other person with details of the error or omission and that the person may correct the error or make good the omission within the period of fourteen days from the date of the notification.

5. Complaints and offences

11–56   If the local authority receives a complaint or report in writing in relation to a statement and the authority is of the opinion that there may have been a contravention of the provisions of the Act, the clerk or secretary of the local authority furnishes to the person who submitted the statement notice that comments on the complaint may be made to the local authority within fourteen days from the date on which the notification was issued to that person and that any comments will be considered by the local authority before considering the matter any further.[99] Following receipt of any comments the local authority are to have regard to these comments, and if the authority continues to be of the belief that a contravention of the provisions of the Act has been committed the local authority may either initiate summary proceedings against the person concerned or furnish a written report to the Director of Public Prosecutions.[100]

---

[95] s.13(2).
[96] s.14(1).
[97] s.17.
[98] s.18(1).
[99] s.18(3)(a).
[100] s.18(3)(b).

Summary proceedings for an offence under the Act may be commenced at any time within twelve months from the date on which the offence was committed and at any time within six months from the date on which the sufficient evidence to justify the proceedings comes to the authority's knowledge, whichever is the later but no proceedings are to be initiated later than five years from the date on which the offence was committed.[101]

11–57   In any proceedings where a statement has not been made or submitted to the local authority or the statement contains an error, omission or a false or misleading statement, and where it is shown to the Circuit Court that the failure arose due to the illness of the relevant party or due to the death, illness, absence or misconduct of any employee or former employee and not due to any lack of bona fides on the part of such party to the proceedings the Circuit Court may make an order granting relief as it considers necessary. The Circuit Court must be satisfied that the party to the proceedings took all reasonable action to prevent misconduct on the part of any employee or former employee.[102] A Circuit Court order granting relief may relieve the agent, designated person, candidate or other person from any liability or consequences under the Act. The Court may make the granting of relief conditional on the furnishing of a statement in a modified form or within an extended period of time and subject to compliance with other conditions as the Court deems necessary. The relevant Circuit Court is the court which sits in respect of the county where the principal office of the local authority is situated.[103]

11–58   Where it appears to the Circuit Court that any person who is or has been a national agent of a political party, or a designated person or a candidate at an election and has refused or has failed to furnish a statement or has failed to furnish the particulars required under the Act the Circuit Court has the power to order that person to come before it.[104] The Circuit Court may then order that person to furnish the statement to the local authority or to furnish the necessary particulars as may be required for the purpose of furnishing the statement, within a specified period of time and in such a manner as the Court may direct.

11–59   If a national agent of a political party or a designated person or a person to whom section 6 applies, fails to furnish within the specified period a statement of election expenses or the statutory declaration or furnishes a false or misleading statement or fails to comply with the provisions of section 13 that person may be guilty of an offence.[105] A person to whom section 6 ap-

---

[101] s.18(4).
[102] s.15(2).
[103] s.15(4).
[104] s.16(1).
[105] s.21.

plies who fails to notify the local authority of their intention to incur election expenses may also be guilty of an offence.

11–60   A person who publishes in a newspaper, magazine or other periodical publication of which he or she is publisher, an advertisement or notice in relation to an election which supports or promotes or opposes the interest of a political party or a candidate at the election at the request of a person other than the national agent or the designated person of a political party or a person authorised in writing by such a person or candidate may be guilty of an offence, unless the person who wishes to place a notice or advertisement produces a certificate from a local authority as provided for in section 6(9). This subsection provides that the local authority issues a certificate to confirm that a person has complied without the requirements of section 6 in that a person, before incurring any expenses at an election writes to the local authority giving the details of the name and address and description of the person who proposes to incur the election expenses, a statement of the nature, purpose and estimated amount of these expenses and an indication of the person's connection, if any, with any party or candidate at the election.

11–61   If a person is found guilty of an offence that person may be liable on summary conviction to a fine of not over £1,500. On indictment the penalty is increased to a maximum of £20,000 or to a period of imprisonment of not over three years or to both the fine and term of imprisonment.[106] Where a person is convicted of failing to furnish a statement of election expenses under section 13 that person may also be found guilty of another offence if that person continues to fail to comply with the provisions of section 13 and is liable to a further fine of £100 for each every day which the failure continues. All proceedings for offences under section 22 are to be instituted only with the consent of the Director of Public Prosecutions.[107]

11–62   Where a person is convicted of an offence in proceedings which have been brought by a local authority the court shall order the person to pay the costs and expenses of the investigation, detection and prosecution of the offence, including the remuneration and other expenses of employees, consultants and advisers. The court may not order the person to pay these expenses and costs if it is satisfied that there are special and substantial reasons for not so doing.[108]

---

[106] s. 21(5).
[107] s.21(6).
[108] s.22.

6. Further information

11–63   Local authorities may make whatever inquiries as it considers appropriate and may require any person to furnish any information, document or thing in the possession of the person which the local authority may require for the purposes of the authority's duties under the Act.[109] A local authority is obliged to, from time to time, draw up and publish to persons to whom the Act applies guidelines concerning the steps which are to be taken to comply with the provisions of the Act. The local authority may give advice to a person (on their request) in relation to any provision of the Act or regarding the application or any of the provisions of the Act. Where such a request is made the provisions of section 13 does not apply in relation to that case during the period of the making of the request and the furnishing of advice by the local authority, and the authority is obliged to furnish the relevant advice within twenty one days or to inform the person of its decision to decline to give advice.

7. Retention of statements

11–64   A local authority is obliged to retain, for at least three years from the latest date for the furnishing statements, every statement and declaration, copies of any court order, and a copy of any notice which has been published.[110] Local authorities are obliged to, within fourteen days after the latest date for receipt of the statements, publish a notice in a newspaper circulating in the functional area of the local authority giving the time and place at which the statements can be inspected and the names of unsuccessful candidates, elected members, designated persons, national agents and other persons referred to in the Act who have not furnished statements in accordance with the Act. The local authority are to permit any person to inspect any document free of charge and to give a copy or an extract of any document on payment of a fee not over the reasonable cost of copying.[111]

8. Disqualification under Local Elections (Disclosure of Donations and Expenditure) Act 1999

11–65   Where an unsuccessful candidate at an election fails to furnish a statement of donations and election expenses or the statutory declaration, that person is disqualified from the membership of any local authority for the remainder of the term of office of the members of the local authority.[112] Where a member

---

[109] s.18(5).
[110] s.19(1).
[111] s.19(3).
[112] s.20(1).

of a local authority is elected and fails to furnish a statement of donations and election expenses, or a statutory declaration, the member is suspended from the membership of the authority for a period of seven days commencing on the expiry of the time specified for that purpose or a lessor period ending with the compliance by the member of the provisions of the Act. If at the end of that seven day period the member still has failed to comply with the provisions of the Act, that member is then disqualified from the membership of any local authority.[113]

11–66   A disqualification arising from the failure to furnish the statement or the statutory declaration comes into effect on the eighth day following the last day scheduled for compliance with the provisions of section 13 of the Act and the disqualification applies and has effect for the remainder of the term of office of the members of the local authority.

11–67   Where an unsuccessful candidate makes and furnishes a statement which is false or misleading in a material respect and this is known to the person who has made the statement, then that person may be prosecuted by the local authority for making a false or misleading statutory declaration under the Statutory Declarations Act 1938.[114] The local authority may also institute proceedings against an elected member of a local authority where the elected member has made a false or misleading declaration or statement.[115] If a person is convicted by a court of an offence under the 1938 Act the person so convicted is also disqualified from the membership of any local authority and the disqualification applies and has effect for the remainder of the term in office of the members of the local authority. Where a member of a local authority becomes disqualified from a local authority that person ceases to be a member and a vacancy then exists and the former member also ceases to be a member of any body or authority to which that person was elected, nominated or appointed by the local authority. However, any act done previously by the person who is now disqualified while a member of any authority or the body does not become invalid solely as a result of that member's disqualification.[116]

9. Procedures at meetings of local authorities

11–68   The Minister is entitled to make regulations in respect of meetings and procedures or any ancillary matters which are held by local authorities. Regulations may be made in relation to the holding of annual meetings, estimates meetings, ordinary meetings, special or other specified meetings, busi-

---

[113] s.20(2).
[114] No. 37 of 1938.
[115] s.20(4).
[116] s.20(7).

ness of meetings, place, date and time of meetings, notice of meetings, summons and agenda, quorum, failure to hold a meeting, commencement and termination of meetings, the appointment of a chairman of meeting. Regulations may also be made regarding the doing of acts by local authorities, deciding of questions and methods and procedures for voting generally or in respect of specified matters, disclosure of specified interests, consideration of motions generally or motions under specified enactments or in respect of specified matters, adjournment, disorderly conduct, record of attendance, minutes, attendance of persons other than members of the relevant local authority, as well as regarding the making of standing orders.[117] To date very few such regulations have been made.

G. LOCAL AUTHORITY MEETINGS

1. Introduction

11–69 Like the administration of national government, local authorities must observe the fundamental rules of natural justice as well as uphold constitutional rights. Local authority meetings in particular should be conducted accordingly to the principles of natural justice and it is incumbent on the chairman in particular to ensure that meetings are run correctly. Every party to an argument should be afforded the right to attend and the right of reply. Failure to conduct a meeting properly, or legally, may invalidate the proceedings.

2. Notice of meetings and business

11–70 At least three clear days notice must be given for any meeting of the council,[118] which must also specify the time and place of the intended meeting and must be signed by the chairperson of the authority. If the meeting is called by one of the members of the authority the notice must be signed by the members who requisitioned the meeting and a notice to this effect should be fixed at the place where the council normally meets. In all other cases the notice should state the business which is to be dealt with and be signed by the secretary. The notice is sent to every member of the authority, but the validity of a meeting is not affected by a failure to serve the notice.

11–71 No business other than that specified in the summons is allowed to be transacted at the meeting, except in the case of an annual meeting involving the election of a chairperson. The first business which is to be transacted at an

---

[117] s.30(2), see *McNelis v. Donegal Co. Co.* [1978] I.L.R.M. 230.
[118] Local Government Act 1994, s.11(5).

annual meeting of a county council is the election of the chairperson and vice-chairperson.

3. Election of chairman

11–72 The procedure for the election of the chairperson and vice-chairperson is set out in section 43(1) of the Local Government Act 1941. The proceedings are begun by the proposal and secondment of one of the authority's members to the chair, where there is only one candidate the candidate is deemed elected, and where there are more than two candidates a poll is taken, election being by a majority of the members present. If at the poll no candidate receives a majority of the votes the candidate receiving the least number of votes is eliminated and one or more further polls are taken and so on until one member are elected.

11–73 The chairperson chairs every meeting of the council and in the absence of the chairperson the vice-chairperson chairs the meeting. Where the chairperson dies the vice-chairperson sits as chairperson, but does not have a casting vote.[119] If the chairperson committees an illegal act the members of the authority may elect another member as chairperson.

4. Quorum

11–74 The quorum required for meetings of a local authority is ordinarily one quarter of the whole number of the authority.[120] A meeting of the authority may be abandoned due to the lack of quorum, and if it is so abandoned the names of the members attending is recorded so as to act as a record should any question arise relating to disqualification for non-attendance. With respect to quorums, the quorum for county councils is a quarter of its members.[121] The quorum for the county borough of Galway is set at four,[122] for Cork the quorum is ten,[123] Waterford and Limerick county boroughs have a quorum of seven, while the remaining county boroughs may fix their quorum by standing orders.

5. Venue and number of meetings

11–75 Meetings of local authorities may be held within or outside the func-

---

[119] *R. (Curran) v. Brennan* [1916] I.L.T.R. 68.
[120] Schedule to the Application of Enactments Order 1898.
[121] Local Government (Ireland) Act 1898, s.23(2).
[122] Local Government (Reorganisation) Act 1985, s.25.
[123] Contained in the Cork City Management Act 1929 which was repealed by the Local government Act 1994, no regulation has been made replacing this provision.

tional area of the authority. A meeting of a local authority shall not be held in a licensed premises except where no other suitable room is available.[124]

11–76   A county borough should hold at least four quarterly meetings as well as an estimate meeting. The mayor or lord mayor has the power to call a meeting of the borough council as often as is necessary, while any five members of the borough council may call a meeting of the council if the mayor or lord mayor fails to do so.

11–77   The public has not got a general right to attend meetings of a borough council, and there is a limited right to attend meetings of other local authorities.

6. Committees of local authorities

11–78   A local authority may delegate matters relating to some of their functions to committees. Committees can either deal with general issues, dealing with a wide range of matters relating to the whole of the functional area of the authority, or dealing only with part of the functional area. Committees must have at least three members and may include both members and non-members of the authority. The local authority may make regulations for the conduct and procedure of committee meetings, however, a local authority may not delegate powers to a committee where it is prohibited by law or statute or where the functions relate to functions of an executive nature and which are carried out by the county manager.[125]

H.   ETHICS AND LOCAL ELECTIONS

11–79   The Ethics in Public Office Act of 1995[126] provides for the disclosure of interest of holders of certain public offices, as well as designated directors and person employed in certain designated positions in certain public bodies. The Act also established a commission to investigate contraventions of the act and to establish guidelines to ensure compliance with the provisions of the Act.

11–80   The first schedule to the Act designates the public bodies which come within the terms of the Act, and includes local authorities as well as health boards. Section 18 of the Act provides that a person who occupies or has occupied a designated position in a public body shall in each year during any

---

[124]Maloney and Spellman, *The Law of Local Government*, Round Hall, 1999.
[125]See Part VI of the Local Government Act 1991.
[126]No. 22 of 1995.

part of which he or she occupies or has occupied the position, prepare and furnish to the relevant authority for the position a statement in writing of the interests of the person. The person who occupies or has occupied a designated position in a public body must also furnish details of interests of which he or she has actual knowledge of his or her spouse or a child of the person or of his or her spouse, which could materially influence the person in or in relation to the performance of the functions of the position by reason of the fact that such performance could so affect those interests as to confer on or withhold from the person or the spouse or child a substantial benefit.

11–81   Where the person who must make a statement has actual knowledge that he or she or a connected person has a material interest in a matter to which the function relates shall, as soon as possible, prepare and furnish to the relevant authority[127] a statement in writing of those facts, and the person shall not perform the relevant function unless there are compelling reasons, and shall, if the function requires to be done, prepare and furnish to the relevant authority, before or, if that is not reasonably practicable, as soon as may be after such performance, a statement in writing of the compelling reason.[128]

11–82   Complaints can be made to the Commission by any person regarding another person who may have contravened the provisions of the Act at a time when that person was an office holder, or that the office holder may have contravened part two of the Act, relating to members of the Oireachtas, before becoming an office holder such a complaint is to be made in writing to the Clerk of the Commission.[129]

11–83   The Commission may, at the request of a person to whom a provision of the Act applies, give advice to the person in relation to any provision of the Act or as to the application, in any particular case, of any provision of the Act. When a person seeks such advice, the requirement to make a statement the provisions of parts two to four shall not apply in relation to that case during the period from the making of the request to the time when advice is given by the Commission in relation to the case or it declines to give such advice.[130] The Commission is obliged to, within twenty one days of the receipt of a request for advice, furnish the advice to the person concerned or notify him or her of its decision to decline to do so. A person, who has requested the advice, shall act in accordance with guidelines or advice published or given to the

---

[127] The relevant authority names such person or persons who has been appointed by the Minister for Finance.
[128] s.18(2)(b).
[129] s.22(1).
[130] s.25(2).

person under this section unless, by so doing, the act concerned would constitute a contravention of another provision of the Act.[131]

11–84 The interests which may be registered as interests are detailed in the second schedule to the act and include a remunerated trade, profession, employment, vocation or other occupation of the person concerned at any time during the appropriate period, the remuneration which the person concerned during that period exceeded £2,000. Also included as interests are the holding of shares in, or bonds or debentures of, or other like investments in, a particular company or other enterprise or undertaking if the aggregate value of the holding exceeded £10,000, as well as the holding of a directorship or the holding of a shadow directorship of any company, any interest in land valued at over £10,000, but excluding the value of the family home. Gifts given to the person, who is required to make a statement, by any person, except by relatives or friends of that person, their spouse, or their children unless such a gift could have materially influenced that person in the exercise of their office, are also registrable except which the gifts which have a value of less than £500.

11–85 Travel facilities, living accommodation, meals which were provided free of charge or at a price that was less than the commercial price or prices, but not such matters which were supplied within the State or during the performance of the functions of the person as an office holder or in the course of their trade, profession, employment, vocation or other occupation are also registrable as well as travel facilitates, living accommodation and meals which were supplied to the person by a relative or friend of the person, their spouse, or child, or their childs' spouse, which were given in the nature of a gift, unless same did not exceed £500.

11–86 A remunerated position held by the person as a political or public affairs lobbyist, consultant or adviser as well as any contract to which the person concerned was a party to or was in any other way, directly or indirectly, interested for the supply of goods or services to a Minister of the Government or a public body exceeding £5,000 are also registrable interests.[132]

---

[131] s.25(4), see also s.29(1)(c).
[132] Or where there is more than one contract on aggregation exceeded £5,000.

CHAPTER 12

Freedom of information

A. FREEDOM OF INFORMATION ACT 1997[1]

1. Introduction

12–01   The Freedom of Information Act was enacted to enable members of the public to obtain access to information which is in the possession of public bodies and to enable persons to have personal information relating to them which is in the possession of public bodies corrected. The Act also provides for an independent review of decisions made by public bodies in relation to allowing access to records held by them and regarding the operation of the Act generally.

2. Information Commissioner

12–02   The independent review under the Act is carried out by the Information Commissioner who is an independent person appointed by the President on the advice of the Government following a resolution passed by the Dáil and Seanad.[2]

12–03   The Information Commissioner holds office for a term of six years and may be re-appointed for a second or subsequent term and can only be removed from office by the President for stated misbehaviour, incapacity or

---

[1]   See generally McDonagh, *Freedom of Information Law in Ireland* (Dublin, 1998).
[2]   s.33.

bankruptcy and then only upon resolutions passed by the Dáil and Seanad. The Information Commissioner may, following an application made in writing, review a decision by the head of a public body regarding access to records held by that body or regarding other matters under the Act, and the Information Commissioner may affirm or vary any decision made or may annual a decision and make a decision in relation to the matter concerned as the Commissioner considers proper. A right of appeal exists to the High Court from a decision of the Commissioner on a point of law but must be made within four weeks after the making of a decision. The Information Commissioner may also decide to refer any question of law to the High Court for determination and may postpone a decision pending the outcome that referral.[3]

12–04 The Commissioner is bound to make a decision within four months during the first three years following the commencement of the Act and within three months thereafter. An application can only be made to the Information Commissioner within two weeks after the notification of the relevant decision by the public body, but this time period can be extended where the Information Commissioner believes that there are reasonable grounds for extending that period.[4]

12–05 The Information Commissioner may refuse to grant an application to review any decision if the Commissioner is of the opinion that the application is frivolous or vexatious or that the application does not relate to a decision which can be reviewed by the Commissioner[5] or that the application relates to a matter which is, has been or will be the subject of another review by the Commissioner. The Information Commissioner, under section 37 is given extensive powers to require any person to attend before the Commissioner and examine and take copies of records which in the opinion of the Commissioner is relevant to a review or investigation. Any person who is required to give information to the Commissioner or who makes records available to the Commissioner is entitled to the same immunities and privileges as a witness in a court.[6]

3. Application

12–06 The Act does not does not apply to a record held by the courts, a tribunal to which the Tribunals of Inquiry (Evidence) Act 1921, is applied, a record relating to the general administration of the courts or the offices of the courts or such a tribunal or any offices of such a tribunal, a record held or

---

[3] s.42.
[4] s.34(5).
[5] See s.34(1).
[6] s.37(4).

created by the Attorney General or the Director of Public Prosecutions or the Office of the Attorney General or the Director of Public Prosecutions, other than a record concerning the general administration of either of those Offices, or to records relating to an audit, inspection or examination carried out by the Comptroller and Auditor or an investigation or examination carried out by the Ombudsman under the Ombudsman Act 1980. The act also does not apply to a record relating to the President, records relating to any of the private papers of a member of either House of the Oireachtas or an official document of either or both of such Houses that is required by the rules or standing orders of either or both of such Houses to be treated as confidential.

12–07   The Act also does not apply to a record relating to information whose disclosure could reasonably be expected to reveal or lead to the revelation of the identity of a person who has provided information to a public body in confidence in relation to the enforcement of the criminal law, or any other source of such information provided in confidence to a public body.[7] Persons who hinder or who obstructs the Commissioner may be guilty of an offence and may be liable on summary conviction to a fine of not over £1,500 or to a term of imprisonment of not over six months or to both.

4. Right to information

12–08   Section 6 of the Act provides that every person has a right access to any record which is held by a public body. To enforce this right each public body has a duty to give reasonable assistance to a person who is seeking a record and if the person has a disability, to give reasonable assistance to that person in order to facilitate the exercise by the person of his or her rights under the Act. The records which are referred to in the Act are records which have come into existence after enactment or records created during a period before the commencement of the Act, as well as records created before the passing of the Act and relating to such particular matters, and records created during a specific period and relating to particular matters as may be prescribed, after consultation with such Ministers of the Government as the Minister for Finance considers appropriate.[8]

12–09   However, certain records which did not come into existence since the commencement of the Act or which are not included in documents prescribed by the Minister may be released where access to records created before the commencement of the Act is necessary or expedient in order to understand records created after the commencement, or the records created before such commencement relate to personal information about the person seeking ac-

---

[7]   s.46.

[8]   See Freedom of Information Act 1997 Regulations, 1998, S.I. Nos. 516–524/1998.

cess to them.[9] This provision does not apply in relation to an individual who is a member of the staff of a public body, the right of access to a record held by a public body that is a personnel record, that is a record which relates wholly or mainly to the competence or ability of the individual in his or her capacity as a member of the staff of a public body or his or her employment or employment history or an evaluation of the performance of his or her functions generally or a particular function. The right of access to records created before the commencement of the Act does not apply to records which were created more than three years before the commencement of the Act, and is not being used or proposed to be used in a manner or for a purpose that affects, or will or may affect, adversely the interests of the person.

5. Request for information

12–10 A request for access to records is made under section 7 of the Act which provides that a person who wishes to exercise the right of access makes a request, in writing, addressed to the head of the public body concerned for access to the record concerned stating that the request is made under the Act. The request must contain sufficient particulars in relation to the information concerned to enable the record to be identified by the taking of reasonable steps, and if the person requires such access to be given in a particular form or manner, specifying the form or manner of access. The request is formally acknowledged by the head of the public body, or a person designated by the head of that body, and the acknowledgement is to be made as soon as possible but not later than two weeks after receipt. The notification is also to include a summary of the provisions of section 41 of the Act and particulars of the rights of review, the procedure governing the exercise of those rights, and the time limits governing such exercise, in a case to which that section applies.

12–11 Section 41 provides that where a decision refusing to grant the request under section 7 or the application under section 17 is be deemed to have been made upon the expiration of the two week period and to have been made by a person to whom the relevant functions were delegated to or which that person were responsible for. In deciding whether to grant or refuse to grant a request under section 7 any reason that the requester gives for the request, and any belief or opinion of the head of the public body as to what are the reasons of the requester for the request, is disregarded.

12–12 If the head of a public body and the record or records which are requested are not held by the body but, to the knowledge of the head, is or are held by one or more other public bodies, the head shall, within two weeks, after the receipt of the request, forward a copy of the request to the head of the

---

[9] s.6(5).

other body or bodies and inform the requester concerned, by notice in writing. The head to whom the copy is furnished is be deemed, for the purposes of the Act, to have received the request and therefore becomes the person responsible under the Act.

12–13   The head shall, as soon as may be, but not later than four weeks, after the receipt of a request decide whether to grant or refuse to grant the request or to grant it in part, if a decision is made to grant the request, whether wholly or in part, the head shall determine the form and manner in which the right of access will be exercised, and forward a notice, in writing, of the decision and determination to be given to the requester. The notice which is sent to the requester includes a note of the decision made and the day on which it was made, and, unless the head concerned reasonably believes that their disclosure could prejudice the safety or well-being of the person concerned, the name and designation of the person in the public body concerned who is dealing with the request, the day on which, and the form and manner in which, access to the record concerned will be offered to the requester and the period during which the record will be kept available for the purpose of such access, and the amount of any fee.

6. Deferring or refusing a request

(i) Deferring a request for information

12–14   If, instead of refusing or granting access to records the head of the public body decides to defer the giving of access to the record under section 11, the reasons for the deferral and the period of the deferral, and the particulars of rights of review and appeal under the Act in relation to the decision under and any other decision referred must be included in the notice, as well as the procedure governing the exercise of those rights and the time limits involved.

12–15   Access to certain records may be deferred if they relate to records which were prepared solely for the information of either or the Houses of the Oireachtas or a committee of the Oireachtas, or information which comes under the provisions of section 20(2) and the giving of access before the specified day would be contrary to the public interest. A record which is held by a public body which is a Department of State or the Office of the Tanaiste or Minister for Government and that the record relates to a matter of public interest and that the record or the contents or the record, or part of it, will be published or will be revealed in either or both of the Houses of the Oireachtas within one week, the release of those records may be deferred.[10]

---

[10] s.8(3) applies in this case, *i.e.* expiration period of four weeks.

(ii) Refusing a request for information

12–16   If the request is refused, whether wholly or partly the notice given by the head of the body to the requester must include the reasons for the refusal, and unless the refusal is pursuant to sections 19 (5), 22 (2), 23 (2) or 24 (3), to the provision of the Act under which the request was refused and the findings of any material issues relevant to the decision and particulars of any matter relating to the public interest taken into consideration for the purposes of the decision.

12–17   The head of a public body may refuse to grant a request for access to records if the record concerned does not exist or cannot be found after all reasonable steps have been taken in order to ascertain its whereabouts. The head may also refuse to grant a request if the request does not comply with section 7(1)(b), in relation to the requirement that a request contains sufficient particulars in relation to the information concerned to enable the record to be identified by the taking of reasonable steps. The head may also refuse to grant access to records if in the opinion of the head, granting the request would, by reason of the number or nature of the records concerned or the nature of the information concerned, require the retrieval and examination of such a number of records or an examination of such kind of the records concerned as to cause a substantial and unreasonable interference with or disruption of the other work of the public body concerned.[11] A head have assisted, or offered to assist the requester so as to amend the request so that the records can be more readily identified or located or the request is amended in order to comply with the provisions of section 7(1)(b).

12–18   A head may also refuse to grant access to records if publication of the record is required by law and is intended to be published within twelve weeks after the receipt of the request. A request which is, in the opinion of the head, frivolous or vexatious may also be refused, as may a request not accompanied by the relevant fees. For the relevant fees see section 47 together with Freedom of Information Act 1997, (Section 47(3)) Regulations 1998[12] which sets the amount of £16.50 per hour, 3 pence per sheet in relation to a photocopy, the amount of 40 pence in relation to a 3½" computer diskette, and the amount of £8 in relation to a CD-ROM as the relevant charges and £5 in relation to a radiograph.

12–19   Part three of the Act exempts records from a request for access, including records relating to meetings of the Government, certain deliberations of public bodies, records which affect the functions and the negotiation capa-

---

[11] s.10(1).
[12] S.I. No. 522 of 1998.

bility of public bodies, certain records relating to parliamentary and court records, as well as records relating to law enforcement and public safety.

12–20   In relation to records of the meetings of the Government the head of a public body *may* refuse to grant a request if the record concerned has been, or is proposed to be, submitted to the Government for consideration by a Minister of the Government or by the Attorney General and was created for that purpose, or is a record of the Government,[13] or the record contains information (including advice) for a member of the Government, the Attorney General, a Minister of State, the Secretary to the Government or the Assistant Secretary to the Government for use solely for the purpose of the transaction of any business of the Government at a meeting of the Government.[14] This exemption does not apply to a record if it contains factual information relating to a decision of the Government which has been published to the general public, or if the record relates to a decision of the Government that was made more than five years before.[15]

12–21   Before making a decision the head must have consulted the leader of each political party to which belonged a member of the Government that made any decision to which the record relates, and any member of the Government aforesaid who was not a member of a political party. Where a request relates to a record and the head concerned is satisfied that the disclosure of the existence or non-existence of the record would be contrary to the public interest, he or she shall refuse to grant the request and shall not disclose to the requester concerned whether or not the record exists.

12–22   A head *shall* refuse to grant a request if the relevant records or record contains the whole or part of a statement made at a meeting of the Government or information that reveals, or from which it may be inferred, the substance of the whole or part of a statement made at a meeting of a Government, but may release the record if it relates to a decision of the Government is published to the general public by or on behalf of the Government.[16] The term "government" includes a committee of the Government such as a committee appointed by the Government whose membership consists of members of the Government, or one or more members of the Government together with either or both of the following, one or more Ministers of State,the Attorney General.[17]

---

[13] Except a record by which a decision of the Government is published to the general public by or on behalf of the Government.
[14] s.19(1).
[15] s.19(3).
[16] s.19(2).
[17] s.19(6).

12–23 A head *may* refuse to grant a request for access to a record,if the record contains matters relating to the deliberative processes of a public body, including opinions, advice, recommendations, and the results of consultations, considered by the body, and the granting of the request would be contrary to the public interest, and, the head shall, in deciding whether to grant or refuse to grant the request, and shall consider whether allowing access would be contrary to the public interest by reason of the fact that the requester would become aware of a significant decision that the body proposes to make.[18] This does not apply to records if the records contain matters used, or which were intended to be used, by a public body for the purpose of making decisions, determinations or recommendations which are published or factual, including statistical information and any analyses made and the reasons for the making of a decision by a public body, or a report of an investigation or analysis of the performance, efficiency or effectiveness of a public body in relation to the functions generally or a particular function of the body, a report, study or analysis of a scientific or technical expert relating to the subject of expertise or a report containing opinions or advice of such an expert and not being a report used or commissioned for the purposes of a decision of a public body made pursuant to any enactment or scheme.[19]

(iii) Confidential information and privileged information

12–24 The head of a public body may refuse to grant a request if access to the records could, in the opinion of the head, be reasonably be expected to prejudice the effectiveness of tests, examinations, investigations, inquiries or audits conducted by or on behalf of the public body concerned or the procedures or methods employed for the conduct thereof, have a significant, adverse effect on the performance by the body of any of its functions relating to management, including industrial relations and management of its staff. Records which could disclose positions taken, or to be taken, or plans, procedures, criteria or instructions used or followed, or to be used or followed, for the purpose of any negotiations carried on or being, or to be, carried on by or on behalf of the Government or a public body, may also be refused to be released by the head of a public body.[20] In making a decision the head of the public body must decide as to whether the public interest would, on balance, be better served by granting than by refusing to grant the request, where the documents are of the nature just described.

12–25 The head of a public body is obliged to refuse to grant a request for access to records if the record concernedwould be exempt from production in

---

[18] s.20(1).
[19] s.20(2).
[20] s.21(1).

proceedings in a court on the ground of legal professional privilege, or is such that its disclosure would constitute contempt of court, or consists of the private papers of a representative in the European Parliament or a member of a local authority or a health board. Records relating toopinions, advice, recommendations, or the results of consultations, considered by either House of the Oireachtas or the Chairman or Deputy Chairman or any other member of either such House or a member of the staff of the Office of the Houses of the Oireachtas for the purposes of the proceedings, or an Oireachtas committee, are also not allowed to be disclosed under the Act. In the case of these records if the head concerned is satisfied that the disclosure of the existence or non-existence of the record would be contrary to the public interest, he or she shall refuse to grant the request and shall not disclose to the requester concerned whether or not the record exists.[21]

12–26 Access to records is not allowed in relation to records the disclosure of the record concerned is prohibited by any enactment, or the non-disclosure of the record is authorised by any such enactment in certain circumstances and the case is one in which the head would, pursuant to the enactment, refuse to disclose the record.[22]

12–27 Access to records is not allowed when such access may be reasonably be expected toprejudice or impair the prevention, detection or investigation of offences, the apprehension or prosecution of offenders or the effectiveness of lawful methods, systems, plans or procedures employed for the purposes of the matters aforesaid, the enforcement of, compliance with or administration of any law, or any lawful methods, systems, plans or procedures for ensuring the safety of the public and the safety or security of persons and property. Access to records which relate to the fairness of criminal proceedings in a court or of civil proceedings in a court or other tribunal, the security of a penal institution, the security of the Central Mental Hospital, the security of a building or other structure or a vehicle, ship, boat or aircraft, the security of any system of communications, whether internal or external, of the Garda Síochána, the Defence Forces, the Revenue Commissioners or a penal institution, or which reveal or lead to the revelation of the identity of a person who has given information to a public body in confidence in relation to the enforcement or administration of the civil law or any other source of such information given in confidence may also be refused following a request under section 7. The head of a public body may, in the opinion of the head, refuse access to records which may facilitate the commission of an offence. The head of a public body can refuse disclose to the requester concerned whether or not any of the above records exists or not.

---

[21] s.22.
[22] s.32.

12–28 Where, in the opinion of the head concerned, the public interest would, on balance, be better served by granting than by refusing to grant a request to access records if those records relate to or disclose that an investigation for the purpose of the enforcement of any law, or anything done in the course of an investigation or for the purposes of the prevention or detection of offences or the apprehension or prosecution of offenders, is not authorised by law or contravenes any law, or relates to the performance of the functions of a public body whose functions include functions relating to the enforcement of law or the ensuring of the safety of the public or relate to the merits or otherwise or the success or otherwise of any programme, scheme or policy of a public body for preventing, detecting or investigating contraventions of the law or the effectiveness or efficiency of the implementation of any such programme, scheme or policy by a public body.[23]

12–29 The head of a public body may refuse to grant a request in relation to a record if, in the opinion of the head, access to it could reasonably be expected to affect adversely the security of the State, the defence of the State, the international relations of the State, or in relation to matters regarding Northern Ireland. This applies to a record that contains information that was obtained or prepared for the purpose of intelligence in respect of the security or defence of the State, or that relates to the tactics, strategy or operations of the Defence Forces in or outside the State, or the detection, prevention, or suppression of activities calculated or tending to undermine the public order or the authority of the State or contains a communication between a Minister of the Government and a diplomatic mission or contains a communication between a Minister of the Government and a diplomatic mission or consular post of the State, or relates to the protection of human rights and expressed by the latter person to be confidential or to be communicated in confidence, or contains information communicated in confidence from, to or within an international organisation of states or to the European Union or relates to negotiations between the State.[24]

12–30 The head of a public body *shall* refuse to grant a request if the records contain information given to the public body in confidence and on the understanding that it would be treated by it as confidential and, in the opinion of the head, the disclosure of the records would be likely to prejudice the provision of further similar information from the same person or from other persons and it is of importance to the body that such further similar information should continue to be given to the body.[25] However, in a case in which, in the opinion of the head concerned, the public interest would, on balance, be better served

---

[23] s.23.
[24] s.24.
[25] s.26(1).

by granting than by refusing to grant the request the head may release the records.[26] Access to records must also be refused if it would involve the disclosure of the information which would constitute a breach of a duty of confidence provided for by a provision of an agreement or enactment or otherwise by law.

12–31 Access to records may be given in the case where a record, which is prepared by a head or any other person during the course of the performance of their functions, unless disclosure of the information concerned would constitute a breach of a duty of confidence that is provided for by an agreement or by law and is owed to a person other than a public body or head or a director, or member of the staff of, a public body or a person who is providing or provided a service for a public body under a contract for services.

12–32 In the case of commercially sensitive information a head *shall* refuse to grant a request if the records concerned contain trade secrets of a person other than the person making the request, or financial, commercial, scientific or technical or other information whose disclosure could reasonably be expected to result in a material financial loss or gain. A request can also be refused if the release of the information could prejudice the competitive position of that person in the conduct of their profession, business occupation, or information whose disclosure could prejudice the conduct or outcome of contractual or other negotiations of the person to whom the information relates, however, access to such records may be allowed if in the opinion of the head concerned, the public interest would, on balance, be better served by granting than by refusing to grant the request.[27]

12–33 A head shall grant a request for access to records relating to what could be viewed as commercially sensitive information if the person to whom the record concerned relates consents, to access to the record being granted to the requester concerned, information of the same kind as that contained in the record in respect of persons generally or a class of persons that is, having regard to all the circumstances, of significant size, is available to the general public, the record relates only to the requester, information contained in the record was given to the public body concerned by the person to whom it relates and the person was informed on behalf of the body, before its being so given, that the information belongs to a class of information that would or might be made available to the general public, or disclosure of the information concerned is necessary in order to avoid a serious and imminent danger to the life or health of an individual or to the environment.[28]

---

[26] s.26(3).
[27] s.27(1).
[28] s.27(2).

(iv) Personal information

12–34   In relation to records which could contain personal information, if, in the opinion of the head, access to the record concerned would involve the disclosure of such personal information a head may refuse to grant access to those records. If in the opinion of the head that it a release of the records would on balance be in the public interest and that the release of the records outweighs the public interest that the right to privacy of the individual, or that the grant of the request would benefit the individual aforesaid, the head may grant the request.[29]

12–35   However, records containing personal information relating to the requester may be granted, as well as records which any individual to whom the information relates consents to its disclosure to the requester. Information that is, having regard to all the circumstances, of such a significant size, and which is available to the general public, or where the information was given to the public body concerned by the individual to whom it relates and the individual was informed on behalf of the body, before its being so given, that the information belongs to a class of information that would or might be made available to the general public. Records may be made available, which if released would involve the disclosure of the information that is necessary in order to avoid a serious and imminent danger to the life or health of an individual, but, the head shall ensure that, before the request is granted, that the identity of the requester or the consent of the individual is established to the satisfaction of the head.[30]

12–36   Where a request relates to a record which is of a medical or psychiatric nature relating to the requester concerned, or a records kept or obtained in the course of the carrying out of, social work in relation to the requester, and, in the opinion of the head concerned, disclosure of the information concerned to the requester might be prejudicial to his or her physical or mental health, well-being or emotional condition, the head may decide to refuse to release the records. If the head decides to grant access to these records the head is obliged to include in the notice to the requester a statement to the effect that, if the requester requests the head to do so, the head will offer access to the record concerned, and keep the records available for that purpose to a health professional having expertise in relation to the subject-matter of the record as the requester may specify.[31]

---

[29] s.28(5).
[30] s.28(2).
[31] "Health professional" refers to a medical practitioner, a registered dentist, or a member of any other class of health worker or social worker standing prescribed.

(v) Information concerning financial interest

12–37 With respect to research and natural resources, a head may refuse to grant a request for access to a record if, in the opinion of the head, and after taking the public interest into account, that record contains information in relation to research being carried out by or on behalf of a public body and the disclosure of that information or the release of any information before the completion of the research would be likely to expose the body or of the research to serious disadvantage, or that the disclosure of information could reasonably be expected to prejudice the well-being of a cultural, heritage or natural resource or a species, or the habitat of a species, of flora or fauna.[32]

12–38 Records which relate to the financial and economic interests of the State and pubic bodies may also not be released to a requester if, in the opinion of the head access to the record could reasonably be expected to have a serious adverse affect on the financial interests of the State or on the ability of the Government to manage the national economy, unless it would be in the public interest to release those records. Access to records can also be refused if, in the opinion of the head, the premature disclosure of information contained in the record could reasonably be expected to result in undue disturbance of the ordinary course of business generally, or any particular class of business, in the State and access to the record would involve disclosure of the information that would, in all the circumstances, be premature, or that access to the record could reasonably be expected to result in an unwarranted benefit or loss to a person or class of persons.[33]

12–39 Section 31 specifically mentions that certain records are included within its terms including records relating to rates of exchange or the currency of the State, taxes, revenue duties or other sources of income for the State, a local authority or any other public body, interest rates, borrowing by or on behalf of the State or a public body. It also mentions records relating to the regulation or supervision by or on behalf of the State or a public body of the business of banking or insurance or the lending of money or of other financial business or of institutions or other persons carrying on any of the businesses aforesaid, dealings in securities or foreign currency, the regulation or control by or on behalf of the State or a public body of wages, salaries or prices, proposals in relation to expenditure by or on behalf of the State or a public body including the control, restriction or prohibition of any such expenditure. Records relating to property held by, or on behalf of the State or a public body and transactions or proposed or contemplated transactions involving such property, foreign investment in enterprises in the State, industrial development in

---

[32] s.30(1).
[33] s.31(1).

the State, trade between persons in the State and persons outside the State, trade secrets or financial, commercial, industrial, scientific or technical information belonging to the State or a public body and is of substantial value or is reasonably likely to be of substantial value, information the disclosure of which could reasonably be expected to affect adversely the competitive position of a public body in relation to activities carried on by it on a commercial basis, or the economic or financial circumstances of a public body. However, in making a decision as to whether or not to release any of these types of records the head of the relevant public body must take into account whether the release of the records would be in the public interest, and it is envisaged that while it may not be in the public interest at a particular point in time it could be the case that the records could be released, safely, following the passage of in some cases a quite short period of time.

B. ACCESS TO INFORMATION ON THE ENVIRONMENT

12–40 Article 6 of the European Communities Act 1972 (Access to Information on the Environment) Regulations 1998[34] provides that public authorities[35] shall make available any information relating to the environment to any person who requests it. A request for information must be made in writing, state the name and address of the person making the request, and state, in terms which are as specific as possible, the information which is the subject of the request.

12–41 A public authority is obliged to respond as soon as possible to a request for information and in any case not later than one month from the date on which such request is received.[36] If a public authority cannot respond within one month from the date on which such request is received, that authority shall give notice in writing to the person making the request of the reasons why it is not possible to do so and shall specify the date, not later than two months before which the response shall be made.[37] The public authority may make a charge for the making available of information, but the charge cannot exceed an amount which is reasonable having regard to the cost of making available the information.[38]

---

[34] S.I. No. 124 of 1998, the Regulation implements the provisions of Council Directive of June, 1990, No. 90/313/EEC (O.J. No. L158/56 of June 23, 1990) on the Freedom of Access to Information on the Environment.

[35] For definition of "public authorities" see Art. 4(2), and includes local authorities.

[36] Art. 10.

[37] Art. 10(2).

[38] Art. 11.

12–42   However, under Article 7 public authorities cannot make available information which relates to personal information held in relation to an individual who has not given consent to the disclosure of the information, or material supplied to the public authority by a third party where that third party was not, or is not capable of being put, under a legal obligation to supply the material, or where the disclosure of the information would make it more likely that the environment to which such information relates will be damaged. A public authority may refuse to make available information where the information requested affects international relations, national defence or public security, matters which are *sub judice*, or which are under inquiry (including disciplinary inquiries), or which are the subject of preliminary investigation proceedings, or commercial or industrial confidentiality, or intellectual property, or where the information requested relates to internal communications of the public authority or to material which is still in the course of completion. A public authority may refuse to make available information where the request is manifestly unreasonable having regard to the volume or range of information sought.

CHAPTER 13

Health boards

A. INTRODUCTION

13–01 The administration of the health services in the State, the Minister by regulation established health boards, such number of health boards as may appear to be appropriate, and by regulation specify the title and define the functional area of each health board and specifies the membership of each health board.[1] Each of the health boards are given a wide variety of functions which have the origin in the provision of health care by private institutions and the provision of public health care which went under a revolution with the introduction of the Health Act of 1947, which was introduced by the then Minister for Health, Dr F.C. Ward and finally passed through Dr Jim Ryan in 1947. The provisions relating to the provision of free voluntary ante- and post-natal care for mothers and free medical care for all children under sixteen was activated by Dr Noel Browne in 1950.[2] Modern health authorities provide not only the basics in health care but also act as a second welfare agency implementing the supplementary welfare allowance,[3] and have been given an extremely important role in the care of children through the Child Care Act of 1991.

---

[1] s.4(1).
[2] See, Lee, *Ireland 1912-1985: Politics and Society* (Cambridge, 1989), p. 315.
[3] Social Welfare (Consolidation) Act 1993, s.170.

B. HEALTH SERVICES

1. Health Act 1970

13–02   The law relating to health authorities was revised in 1970 with the introduction of the Health Act of 1970 and replaced the then existing public health structures through the establishment of regionally based health boards.

13–03   Health boards are empowered by section 38 of the Health Act 1970[4] to provide and maintain any hospital, sanatorium, home, laboratory, clinic, health centre or similar premises required for the provision of services under the Health Acts. Section 45 provides that the Health Boards provide services for person who meet the requirements of eligibility, that is adult persons, and their dependants who are unable without undue hardship to arrange general practitioner medical and surgical services for themselves. Section 46 allows the health boards to provide limited eligibility for persons who are of limited means.

2. In patient services

13–04   In patient services which refers to the institutional services provided for persons while maintained in a hospital, convalescent home or home for persons suffering from physical or mental disability are provided by health boards under section 51. Section 56 of the Act makes provision for "out-patient services," which refers to the provision of services other than in-patient services provided at, or by persons attached to, a hospital or home and institutional services provided at a laboratory, clinic, health centre or similar premises, but does not include the giving of any drug, medicine or other preparation, except where it is administered to the patient direct by a person providing the service or is for psychiatric treatment, or dental, ophthalmic or aural services.[5]

3. Infectious diseases

13–05   The Health Act of 1947[6] still regulates the control and treatment of infectious diseases,[7] as well as the prevention of danger to the public health arising from the manufacture, preparation, importation, storage, distribution or exposure for sale of food intended for sale for human consumption and the

---

[4] No. 1 of 1970.
[5] Dental, ophthalmic and aural services are provided under s.57.
[6] No. 28 of 1947.
[7] Part IV.

prevention of contamination of food intended for sale for human consumption. The 1947 Act also allowed the Minister for Health to introduce regulations regarding the prohibition and prevention of the sale or offering or keeping for sale of articles of food intended f or human consumption, or of animals intended for such food, or materials or articles used or intended for use in the preparation or manufacture of such food, which are diseased, contaminated or otherwise unfit for human consumption.[8]

4. Food

13–06 The Minister was also empowered to introduce regulations to provide for provisions in relation to the nature, quality or amount of any substance to be contained in the food to which the regulations relate, or specifying any substance which is not to be contained in such food, or limiting the amount of any substance to be contained in such food, or in relation to the methods used or the time taken in the manufacture, preparation or distribution of such food, as well as introducing provisions in relation to the labelling or description of such food, and providing for connected offences.[9]

5. Emergency and other services

13–07 Other services which are specifically provided for in the 1970 Act include the provision of ambulance services,[10] general practitioner medical and surgical service,[11] supply without charge of drugs, medicines and medical and surgical appliances to persons with full eligibility,[12] home nursing,[13] home help service,[14] medical and midwifery care for mothers,[15] together with medical care for infants,[16] and health examination and treatment service for children under the age of six years.[17]

13–08 Health boards are obliged, under section 68, to make available a service for the training of disabled persons for employment suitable to their condition of health, and for the making of arrangements with employers for placing disabled persons in suitable employment. A health board may also provide

---

[8] s.54.
[9] s.56(3).
[10] s.57.
[11] s.58.
[12] s.59(1).
[13] s.60.
[14] s.61.
[15] s.62.
[16] s.63.
[17] s.66.

equipment, or materials for disabled adult persons where neither the person nor the person's spouse is able to provide for his maintenance.[18] Section 70 provides that health boards are obliged to make arrangements for carrying out tests on persons, without charge, for the purpose of screening in order to detect the presence of a particular disease, defect or condition that may be prescribed.

13–09 The remaining functions which are provided for under the 1970 Act include arranging for the dissemination of information and advice on matters relating to health and health services, and the removal of the body of a deceased person to appropriate premises which is found within the boards' functional area.[19] The Social Welfare (Consolidation) Act of 1981[20] provides that a health board is to provide for the burial of a person who dies within their functional area and in respect of which no suitable burial arrangements were made, or of a person who has been drowned and cast ashore within its functional area or who was otherwise found perished or has been found dead within their area and whose body has not been claimed for burial.[21] Health boards have also be given a role in assisting courts regarding the preparation of a medical report in writing on a person convicted of offences under the Misuse of Drugs Acts 1977 to 1984, and the board may be requested to include recommendations as to medical treatment appropriate to the needs of the convicted person.[22]

C. HEALTH BOARDS

1. Membership

13–10 The membership of a health board consists of persons appointed by the relevant local authorities, and persons appointed by election by registered medical practitioners and by election by members of ancillary professions as are specified in appropriate regulations and persons appointed by the Minister. However, the number of local authority appointees cannot exceed the total number of the other members of the health board. The local authorities which may appoint nominees to the health board are the councils of a county or corporations of a county boroughs the functional area of which, or part of the functional area of which, is included in the functional area of the relevant health board.

---

[18] s.68.
[19] s.77.
[20] No. 1 of 1981.
[21] s.216.
[22] Misuse of Drugs Act 1984, s.8.

13–11 Each health board are the board bodies corporate with perpetual succession. A health board may sue and be sued in its corporate name and may hold and dispose of land, a health board shall provide and have a common seal and all courts of justice shall take judicial notice of the seal. The members of the board who are appointed by the council of a county are required to be members of that council and the members of the board who are appointed by the corporation of a county or other borough shall be members of the city or borough council for that borough.[23]

13–12 Health boards perform the functions conferred on it under the Act and other functions which, before the enactment of the Act, were performed by a local authority, other than sanitary functions, in the functional area of the health board in relation to the operation of services provided under, or in connection with the administration of, the Health Acts 1947 to 1966, the Mental Treatment Acts 1945 to 1966, the Births and Deaths Registration Acts 1863 to 1952, the Notification of Births Acts 1907 and 1915, the Acts relating to the registration of marriages, the Sale of Food and Drugs Acts 1875 to 1936, part I of the Children Act 1908, and sections 2 and 3 of the Children (Amendment) Act 1957, the Rats and Mice (Destruction) Act 1919, the Blind Persons Act 1920, the State Lands (Workhouses) Act 1930 and the State Lands (Workhouses) Act 1962, the Registration of Maternity Homes Act 1934, the Midwives Act 1944, as amended by the Nurses Act 1950, the Adoption Acts 1952 and 1964, the Poisons Act 1961.

13–13 A health board may establish such committees as it thinks fit and may, subject to this Act, define the functions and procedure of any such committee and, subject to any limitations specified by the Minister, may delegate specified functions to any such committee.[24] The membership of a health board committee which is appointed or organised by a health board, with the consent of the Minister for Health, include persons who are not members of the health board.

2. Expenses and allowances

13–14 Health boards may make payments to members of a health boards or of committees which are established, relating to travelling and subsistence expenses which are incurred in attending a meeting of the board or of the committee or otherwise in the pursuance of the business of the board, and may make allowances in favour of the chairman and vice chairman in respect of

---

[23] s.5.
[24] s.8(1).

expenses, and all such payments are made in accordance with a scale which is determined by the Minister.[25]

3. Appointment of health board members

13–15 The second schedule of the 1970 Act provide the framework for the rules in relation to the membership of health boards and for the meetings of the board. The members of the board which are appointed by the council of a county, or the corporation of a county borough, are appointed at the annual meeting of the council or corporation which is held after every election of the members of the Council.[26]

13–16 The members of the board who are appointed by the Minister are appointed from time to time for a term of office not exceeding five years as may be specified by the Minister at the time of appointment. Every member of the board holds office, unless that member dies, resigns or becomes disqualified or membership of the health board is terminated under Rule 11, until the day after a successor has been appointed or elected. Rule 11 provides that where a member of a health board who was appointed by the council of a county has not, for a consecutive period of six months, attended a meeting of the board, that members membership of the board is terminated and the council shall, at its next meeting after the expiration of that period, appoint one of its members to fill the vacancy.

13–17 Any officer or servant of a health board cannot be appointed to the board but the Minister may by order specify a class of officer or servant to which this rule does not apply. Where a member of the health board was appointed by the council of a county or borough council, and that member ceases to be or has become disqualified from being a member of the council, that member also ceases to be a member of the health board.

13–18 A member of a health board may resign from a health board by giving notice in writing to the secretary of the health board, but the resignation does not become effective until the next meeting of the board held after the receipt of the notice. A person shall cease to be a member of a health board if that person ceases to have a qualification which entitled him to be a candidate for election under section 4 of the Act. With regard to ministerial appointments, the Minister may at any time terminate such an appointment.

13–19 Casual vacancies which occur in the membership of the board appointed by the local authorities is to be filled by the council or corporation

---

[25] s.9(1).
[26] With regard to nomination and election of members see rr. 2 and 3 of the Schedule Two.

within one month or as the Minister may allow. A casual vacancy occurring among the other members of the board shall be filled by appointment by the Minister.

13–20 A quorum of a health board is, where the total number of the members of the board is a number divisible by four without a remainder either one-fourth of the total number of the members of the board, or five, whichever is the greater, and where the total number of the members of the board is a number which is not divisible by four without a remainder one-fourth of the next higher number which is divisible by four without a remainder or five, whichever is the greater.

13–21 The proceedings of a health board cannot be invalidated by reason of any vacancy among the boards' members or due to any defect in the appointments to the board or regarding the qualification of any member of the board. The chairman or in his absence, the vice-chairman of the board may call a meeting of the board, and the board must hold at least twelve meetings in each year, and as many other meetings as are required. If the chairman or vice-chairman of the board refuses to call a meeting of the board after a request signed by three members of the board, any three members of the board may call a meeting, firstly giving the chairman or vice-chairman seven days to call a meeting, after which any three members of the board may call a meeting of the board. At least three clear days notice of the time and place of the intended meeting is required, if the meeting is called by members of the board, the notice, is to specify the business which is to be proposed to be dealt with. The secretary of the health board is to give each member a summons to attend a meeting together with a copy of the agenda of the meeting at least three clear days before the meeting, but failure so to leave or deliver the summons shall not affect the validity of a meeting. The importance of the summons and detailing of the agenda is that no business can be transacted at a meeting of the board other than that specified in the summons.

13–22 Minutes of the proceedings of a meeting of the board are drawn up and entered in a book and are signed by the chairman of the meeting or at the next meeting. The names of the members present at a meeting of the board are also recorded in the minutes of the proceedings of the meeting. The names of the members voting on any question arising at a meeting of the board are also recorded in the minutes of the proceedings of the meeting and the record also shows which members voted for and which against any question. With regard to tied votes the chairman of the meeting has a second or casting vote. All acts of the board and all questions coming or arising before the board may be done and decided by the majority of the members of the board present and vote at a meeting of the board held according to law.

13–23   Members of the health board who has any interest in any company or concern with which the board proposes to make any contract, or any interest in any contract which the board proposes to make is obliged to disclose this interest, and shall take no part in any deliberation or decision of the board relating to the contract, and any disclosure shall be recorded in the minutes of the board.

13–24   The board may make standing orders for the regulation of its own proceedings, other than proceedings the regulation of which is already provided for by or under statute and may amend or revoke their standing orders. With regard to the seal of the board, the seal is to be authenticated by the signature of the chairman, or other member authorised by the board, and the signature of an officer of the board authorised to act in that behalf.

4. Officers and employees of health boards

13–25   Each health board appoints a person who acts as the chief executive officer of the board, and where a chief executive officer, other than suspension from performance of his duties, is temporarily unable to act, the chief executive, may after consultation with the chairman of the health board, appoint one of the other officers of that board to act as deputy chief executive officer. If the chief executive is unable to appoint a deputy, the chairman of the board may appoint one of the other officers of the board to act as deputy chief executive officer.[27] An appointment as deputy chief executive officer may at any time be terminated by the chairman of the health board with the consent of the Minister. A temporary appointment of a chief executive officer may be made by the Minister after consultation with the chairman of the board or, in his absence the vice-chairman of the board.[28]

13–26   The chief executive may delegate any function which is preferable by the chief executive to another officer of the board. Where a delegation to an officer is made the officer shall perform the delegated function under the general direction and control of the chief executive officer, and the officer shall also perform the delegated function in accordance with any limitations which are specified by the chief executive.[29] At any stage the chief executive officer may decide to perform any delegated function, and if the officer to whom functions have been delegated feels that because of the importance of the decision involved or because of any other reasonable consideration, a decision should be made by the chief executive, the officer may refer the matter to the chief executive. A chief executive officer is obliged to give notification

---

[27]   s.13.
[28]   s.13(9).
[29]   s.16.

of any delegation or a revocation of a delegation to the Minister and to the health board at its next meeting.

13–27 A chief executive officer, after the enactment of section 14 of the 1996 Act, provides that, unless the chief executive dies, resigns or is removed from office, holds office during either a period of such length, not exceeding seven years, as the Minister prescribes by order, or the period from the date of the appointment to the date on which he or she attains such age as the Minister prescribes by order. A person who is appointed as chief executive officer holds office under a contract of service in writing with the health board.[30] A chief executive officer who has agreed a contract with the health board may be removed from office by the health board with the consent of the Minister in accordance with the terms and conditions of his or her contract of service. The effect of a contract having been concluded between the chief executive and the health board is that the provisions of section 21 of the Health Act 1970, dealing with the suspension and removal of chief executive officers, does not apply to that chief executive officer. It is envisaged by the 1996 Act that all chief executive officers will have agreed a service contract with their health boards before taking office and that the terms and conditions contained in the contract will include the ways and means whereby a chief executive officer may be suspended or removed from office, although the consent of the Minister will still be required under section 14(3) of the 1996 Act. The appointment, and removal, of a chief executive officer is a reserved function made following a recommendation from the Local Appointments Commissioners.[31]

13–28 The appointment of officers or servants of a health board is a function of the chief executive officer. An officer or servant of a health board who is appointed by the chief executive holds their office or employment on such terms and conditions and shall perform such duties as the chief executive officer from time to time determines.[32]

13–29 Section 17 of the Act provides that certain functions are to be performed by the chief executive officer, and as such cannot be performed by the health board. These functions relate to any function specified by any enactment to be a function of the chief executive officer of the board, any function with respect to a decision as to whether or not any particular person shall be eligible to avail himself of a service, any function with respect to a decision as to the making or recovery of a charge, or the amount of any charge for a service for a particular person, and any function with respect to the control, supervision, service, remuneration, privileges or superannuation of officers

---

[30] s.14(2) of the 1996 Act.
[31] s.14(5) of the 1996 Act.
[32] s.14.

and servants of the board. Any disputes as to whether or not a particular function is a function of the chief executive officer, or whether a particular function is a function of an officer of a health board other than the chief executive officer, is resolved or determined by the Minister.

13–30   Section 4 of the Health (Amendment) (No. 3) Act 1996 provides that a function of a health board that is not a reserved function is regarded as a function of the chief executive officer unless otherwise provided for, and a function that is required to be so carried out shall be an executive function and "executive function" shall be construed as such.[33] The first schedule to the 1996 Act contains a list of the functions which are specifically mentioned as being reserved functions under that Act.

13–31   A chief executive officer may be suspended from the performance of his duties by the Minister, or by the board through a resolution passed by the board of which not less than two-thirds of the members of the board voted, of which not less than seven days notice was given to every person who was a member of the board when the notice was given.[34] The suspension of a chief executive officer may be ended by the Minister. However, the Minister may remove a chief executive officer where the Minister is satisfied, following a local inquiry, that the chief executive officer has become incapable of performing the duties of chief executive officer, that the person is unfit to be a chief executive officer or is guilty of misconduct. The chief executive officer may suspend any officer of the heath board where the chief executive is of the opinion that the officer may be guilty of misconduct in relation to the officer held or is otherwise unfit to hold office. The chief executive officer must first have a consultation with the chairman of the board before suspending the officer, and an inquiry into the alleged misconduct or unfitness must be held and any disciplinary action to be taken.[35] An officer of the health board may be removed by a chief executive following an inquiry and following a direction from the Minister or on the recommendation of a committee appointed by the Minister to inquire into any allegations of misconduct or unfitness to hold office. A permanent officer cannot be removed for a reason other than misconduct or unfitness except with the approval of the health board.[36]

5. Removal of health board members

13–32   The Minister can, by order, remove from office the members of a health board if and whenever the Minister is satisfied, after holding a public

---

[33]   See, for example, s.72 of the Child Care Act 1991.
[34]   s.21.
[35]   s.22(1).
[36]   s.23(4).

local inquiry into the performance of its boards duties, and that the duties are not being duly and effectually performed, and the board has refused or neglected to comply with a judgement, order or decree of any court, the board has refused, after due notice, to allow its accounts to be audited by the auditor appointed under the Act, or the members of the board capable of acting are less in number than the quorum for meetings of the board.[37] The Minister is obliged to inform the persons who have been removed from office as members of the board of the making of the order and of the reasons for their removal. The Minister is obliged to within two years of the removal from office of the members of a health board provide for the appointment of members to the board.[38]

D. HEALTH BOARD AREAS AND ADMINISTRATION

1. Board areas

13–33   The Eastern Health Board comprised the county boroughs of Dublin and the administrative counties of Dublin, Kildare and Wicklow and is now called the Eastern Regional Health Authority with three sub regional authorities.[39] The Midland Health Board comprises the administratives counties of Laois, Longford, Offaly and Westmeath, the Mid-Western Health Board contains the county borough of Limerick and the administrative counties of Clare, Limerick and Tipperary North Riding. The North-Eastern Health Board comprises the administrative counties of Cavan, Meath and Monaghan, while the North-Western Health Board contains the administrative counties of Donegal, Leitrim and Sligo, the Southern Health Board contains the county borough of Cork and the administrative counties of Cork and Kerry while the remaining health board, the Western Health Board contains the administrative counties of Galway, Mayo and Roscommon.

2. Finance

13–34   Each health board, in addition to the chief executive officer is obliged to furnish to the Minister any information which the Minister requires in relation to the proposed spending of the health board. A health board cannot, except with the Minister's consent, incur any expenditure for any service or purpose in excess of a sum as may be specified by the Minister. The Minister is obliged under section 5(10) of the Health (Amendment) (No. 3) Act 1996

---

[37] s.12(1).
[38] s.12(4).
[39] Health (Eastern Regional Health Authority) Act 1999.

to, in respect of a financial year of a health board, determine the maximum amount of net expenditure that may be incurred by the board for that financial year and to notify the health board in writing of the amount which has been so determined not more than twenty one days after the publication by the Government of the Estimates for Supply Services. The Minister may, however, amend a determination of the expenditure ceiling by varying the maximum amount of net expenditure that a health board may incur for a particular financial year.

13–35 Following a determination of the maximum amount of expenditure each health board are required to submit a service plan which is to include a statement of the services to be provided by the health board and estimates of the income and expenditure of the board for the period to which the plan relates.[40] A service plan which is submitted by the chief executive officer is deemed to have been adopted and submitted by the chief executives' health board. The service plan is designed to ensure that each health board remains within the financial limits set down in the plan and each health board is obliged to supervise the implementation of its service plan during its financial year. A service plan may be amended by a health board but the health board are obliged to ensure that expenditure does not exceed the net expenditure which has already been determined.[41] Section 8 of the 1996 Act ensures that each health board does not exceed the amount of debt which has been determined by the Minister for the financial year. The chief executive officer implements the service plan on behalf of the health board. If the chief executive officer is of opinion that a decision of the health board will result in overspending or increase the amount of indebtedness of the board, the chief executive is under a duty to inform the Minister.

13–36 A health board may borrow money which may be done in any manner which the health board considers suitable including, by obtaining a mortgage, the issue of stock or bonds, temporary loan or overdraft. A loan, interest or dividends may be secured on the revenues, funds or property of the health board.[42] A health board shall not borrow money without the prior consent of the Minister with the agreement of the Minister for Finance, and the borrowing of any money by a health board is subject to terms and conditions as may be specified by the Minister for Health and the Minister for Finance.[43]

---

[40] s.6 of the 1996 Act.
[41] s.7(4).
[42] s.33.
[43] s.17 of the 1996 Act.

3. Reserved functions

13–37 A health board, in performing the functions conferred on it, are to have regard to the resources, wherever originating, that are available to the board for the purpose of such performance and the need to secure the most beneficial, effective and efficient use of such resources, the need for co-operation with voluntary bodies providing services, similar or ancillary to services which the health board may provide, to people residing in the functional area of the health board, as well as to the need for co-operation with, and the co-ordination of its activities with those of, other health boards, local authorities and public authorities, the performance of whose functions affect or may affect the health of the population of the functional area of the health board, together with the policies and objectives of the Government or any Minister of the Government in so far as they may affect or relate to the functions of the health board.[44]

13–38 A health board is also obliged to comply with a direction given to it by the Minister as well as to furnish the Minister with such information as the Minister may reasonably require for the purpose of satisfying himself or herself that any such direction has been complied with by the board.[45]

4. Annual reports

13–39 Each health board is obliged to, not later than the 30th day of June in each year, prepare and adopt a report in relation to the performance of its functions during the preceding year, and the annual report is to include a statement of the services provided by the board in the preceding year. The adoption by a health board of its annual report is a reserved function, and the health board is obliged to forward a copy of the report to the Minister.[46] Copies of the annual report of a health board are to be made available at the principal office of the board during normal office hours for inspection and purchase by any member of the public and a health board is obliged to give public notice of the date on and from and the place at which the annual report will be made available.

5. Transfer of functions of health board

13–40 Where the Minister after considering a report prepared is satisfied that a health board is not performing any one or more of its functions in an effective manner or has failed to comply with any direction given by the Min-

---

[44] Health (Amendment) (No. 3) Act 1996, s.2.
[45] s.13(3) of the 1996 Act.
[46] s.15 of the 1996 Act.

ister, the Minister may by order transfer any of the reserved functions of the board to either the chief executive officer, or to another person as the Minister may specify for a specified period of not over two years. Where the Minister proposes to make such an order the Minister is obliged to give notice in writing to the health board giving the terms of the order which is proposed. A health board may make representations in writing with regard to the proposed order to the Minister, within fourteen days.[47]

E.   DUTIES OF HEALTH BOARDS TOWARDS CHILDREN

1. Introduction

13–41   Section 4 of the Children Act 1989 provides that where a child is in the care of a health board, the health board is obliged to provide whatever care for that child, subject to its control and supervision, by placing the child in foster care, or by placing the child in a suitable home, school, certified industrial school or other place of residence, or in the case of a child who may be eligible for adoption under the Adoption Acts 1952 to 1988, by placing the child with a suitable person with a view to his adoption, or by making such other suitable arrangements as the health board thinks proper.

13–42   A health board may send a child in its care to any hospital or to any institution which provides nursing or care for persons suffering from physical or mental disability.[48] Section 4 also allows a health board to place a child in its care under the charge and control of a parent or other suitable person for either a fixed period or until the health board otherwise determines.

2. Child Care Act 1991

(i) Functions of health board

13–43   It is the function of every health board to promote the welfare of children in its area who are not receiving adequate care and protection. In the performance of this function, a health board are obliged to take whatever steps as the health board considers are required to identify children who are not receiving adequate care and protection. The health board is also obliged to co-ordinate information from all relevant sources relating to children in its area, having regard to the rights and duties of parents, regard the welfare of the child being regarded as the first and paramount consideration, and in so far as

---

[47] s.12 of the 1996 Act.
[48] s.4(2).

is practicable, give due consideration, having regard to his age and understanding, to the wishes of the child, as well as to the principle that it is generally in the best interests of a child to be brought up in the childs' own family.[49]

13–44 Health Boards are classified as being "fit persons" under section 1 of the Children Act of 1989 for the purposes of section 38 of the Children Act of 1908 which enabled health boards to take children into care. Under the Child Care Act of 1991 all persons under the age of eighteen are regard as children, which replaced the previous categorisation of children and young persons.

13–45 Health boards are also obliged to provide child care and family support services and the boards retain a discretion in how the board provides such services.[50] It should be noted that while the health boards are obliged to carry out certain statutory functions it has been held that a breach of any of the provisions of the Child Care Act give rise to damages for a failure on the part of the health board to carry out a statutory duty.[51] However, such is not the case in an action for damages on foot of negligence in the exercise of a statutory function.[52] A health board in the carrying out of its functions under section 3 of the Child Care Act maybe vicariously liable for the negligent acts, omissions or statements of its servants and agents as was held in the case of *E. V. Dorset County Council*[53] where the House of Lords held that there was a case for damages for negligent advice which had been given concerning the special educational needs of the plaintiff. The Child Care Act sets out the parameters in which the health boards are to carry out their powers and duties. A health board must operate within the powers and duties which are conferred under the Act but may in exceptional circumstances may perform a certain function which vindicates the constitutional rights of children.[54]

13–46 Section 4 of the Act provides that where it appears to a health board that a child who resides or is found in its area requires care or protection which the child is unlikely to receive unless the child is taken into its care, it is the duty of the health board to take the child into its care. However, a health board cannot take a child into its care against the wishes of a parent having custody of the child or of any person acting *in loco parentis* or to maintain the child in its care if the parent or any such person wishes to resume care of the child. Where a health board has taken a child into its care the health board are under duty of the board to maintain the child in its care so long as the child's

---

[49] s.3.
[50] s.3(3).
[51] *Paul Stephens v. Eastern Health Board*, unreported, High Court, Geoghegan J.).
[52] See *Ward v. McMaster* [1988] I.R. 337.
[53] [1995] 1 All E.R. 35.
[54] See Ward, *The Child Care Act 1991* (Dublin, 1997), p. 9.

welfare appears to the board to require it while the child in question remains a child. The health board is also to have regard to the wishes of a parent having custody of the child or of any person acting *in loco parentis* in the provision of such care.[55] Where a health board takes a child into its care because it appears that the child is lost or that a parent having custody of the child is missing or that the child has been deserted or abandoned, the health board are obliged to endeavour to reunite the child with its parent where this appears to the board to be in the child's best interests.[56]

(ii) Refugee and homeless children

13–47   Section 5 of the Child Care Act of 1991[57] imposes upon health boards the obligation to accommodate homeless children where the child has not been brought into care under the provisions of the Act and following an assessment of the child's circumstances. Where there is no accommodation available or the accommodation is the type which the child cannot be reasonably expected to live in. Health boards are obliged to include the needs of homeless children in their annual report which they are required to complete under section 8 of the Act.

13–48   Under the Refugee Act of 1996[58] where it appears to an immigration officer that a child under the age of eighteen years who has arrived at an entry point of the State is not in the custody of any person, the immigration officer is obliged to, as soon as practicable, to inform the health board in whose functional area the place of arrival is situated following notification the provisions of the Child Care Act 1991, shall apply in relation to the child.[59]

13–49   Where it appears to the health board, on the basis of information available to the health board, that an application for a declaration that a person is a refugee should be made by or on behalf of a child, the health board shall arrange for the appointment of an officer of the health board or such other person to make an application on behalf of the child.

(iii) Adoption

13–50   Each health board, under the section 6 of the Child Care Act of 1991 are obliged to provide or ensure the provision within its functional area a service for the adoption of children in accordance with the provisions of the Adoption Acts 1952 to 1988. A health board may enter into an arrangement with

---

[55] s.4(3).
[56] s.4(4).
[57] No. 17 of 1991.
[58] No. 17 of 1996.
[59] s.8(5).

any adoption society which are registered in the Adoption Societies Register which is maintained by An Bord Uchtála.[60] A health board may take a child into its care with a view to adoption and in the interim may maintain the child under the provisions of the Act. However, the health board cannot take a child into its care for the purposes of adoption against the wishes to a parent having custody of the child or of any person acting *in loco parentis* or to maintain the child in its care.

13–51   In relation to foreign adoptions, section 5 of the Adoption Act 1991 gives a role to the health boards by providing that the health board compiles a report regarding an assessment as respects the matters referred to in section 13 of the 1952 Act, which relates to an investigation as to whether the applicant, or applicants, is of good moral character, has sufficient means to support the child and is a suitable person to have parental rights and duties in respect of the child.

13–52   Health boards may be called upon by the High Court where an order by the High Court authorising adoption of children whose parents have failed in their duty towards them has been applied for.[61] In fact where such proceedings are initiated the health board are joined as parties to the action and their role is to assist the court in deciding what is in the best interests of the child, and a health board itself may make an application to the High Court for an order. In such proceedings the health board are obliged to pay the costs of the parents of the child concerned which are incurred by the parents of the child in relation to the action or an appeal to the Supreme Court. The health board are also responsible for costs which are not paid by another party to the proceedings, andin relation to which legal aid under any scheme for the provision of legal aid operated by or on behalf of the State has been refused.[62]

(iv) Child care advisory committees

13–53   Each health board was obliged by section 7 of the Child Care Act to establish within their functional area a child care advisory committee to advise the health board on the performance of its functions under the Act. A health board is obliged to consider and have regard to any advice given by the committee. The child care advisory committee is composed of persons with a special interest or expertise in matters which affect the welfare of children, and includes representatives of voluntary bodies which provide child care and family support services. Each child care advisory committee is allowed to have access to non-personal information in relation to child care and family support

---

[60] s.6.
[61] Adoption Act 1988, s.3.
[62] s.5.

services, and to consult with voluntary bodies providing child care and family support services in its area. The committee reports on child care and family support services in its area, either on its own initiative or when so requested by the health board, and reviews the needs of children in its area who are not receiving adequate care and protection.[63]

(v) Emergency, interim and care orders

13–54   Section 12 of the Child Care Act allows a member of the Gardaí who has reasonable grounds for believing that there is an immediate and serious risk to the health or welfare of a child, and that it would not be sufficient for the protection of the child from such immediate and serious risk to await the making of an application for an emergency care order by a health board. The Garda may be accompanied by such other persons as may be necessary, may, without warrant, enter, if need be by force, any house or other place and re-move the child to safety. Where a child is removed by a member of the Garda Síochána the child has to be delivered up to the custody of the health board, after which the health board shall, unless it returns the child to the parent having custody of him or a person acting *in loco parentis*, make application for an emergency care order at the next sitting of the District Court.

13–55   A judge of the District Court, on the application of a health board may make an emergency care order where there is reasonable cause to believe that there is an immediate and serious risk to the health or welfare of a child which necessitates his being placed in the care of a health board, or there is likely to be such a risk if the child is removed from the place where he is for the time being. An emergency care order places the child under the care of the health board for the area in which the child is for the time being for a period of eight days or such shorter period as may be specified in the order.[64]

13–56   Where a child is delivered up to or is placed in the custody of a health board the board is obliged to as soon as possible inform a parent having cus-tody of the child or a person acting *in loco parentis* unless that parent or per-son is missing and cannot be found.[65] A health board is in fact under a duty to apply for a a care order or a supervision order with respect to a child who resides or is found in its area that the child requires care or protection which the child is unlikely to receive unless a court makes a care order or a supervi-sion order.[66]

---

[63]   s.7(7).

[64]   s.13, an application be made *ex parte* and *in camera*. The constitutionality of s.13, and of s.17 was upheld by *A. v. Eastern Health Board*, unreported, High Court, Geoghegan J., November 28, 1997).

[65]   s.14(1).

[66]   s.16.

13–57 An interim care order may be made on the application of a health board where an application for a care order in respect of the child has been or is about to be made and there is reasonable cause to believe that the child has been or is being assaulted, ill-treated, neglected or sexually abused, or the child's health, development or welfare has been or is being avoidably impaired or neglected, or the child's health, development or welfare is likely to be avoidably impaired or neglected, exists or has existed with respect to the child and that it is necessary for the protection of the child's health or welfare that he be placed or maintained in the care of the health board pending the determination of the application for the care order.

13–58 An interim care order, which is temporary in nature, requires that the child named in the order be placed or maintained in the care of the health board for a period not exceeding eight days. Where the health board and the parent having custody of the child or person acting *in loco parentis* consent an extension may be granted.[67]

13–59 A health board may apply to the District Court for a care order in respect of a child within its functional area where the board believes that the child has been or is being assaulted, ill-treated, neglected or sexually abused, or the child's health, development or welfare has been or is being avoidably impaired or neglected, or the child's health, development or welfare is likely to be avoidably impaired or neglected, and that the child requires care or protection which he is unlikely to receive unless the court makes an order under this section, the court may make an order.[68]

13–60 A care order commits the child to the care of the health board for so long as the child remains under the age of eighteen or for such shorter period as the court may determine and, the court may, of its own motion or on the application of any person, extend the operation of the order if the court is satisfied that grounds for the making of a care order continue to exist. The health board so long as the care order is in force has the like control over the child as if it were his parent and may do what is reasonable in all the circumstances of the case for the purpose of safeguarding or promoting the child's health, development or welfare. In particular the health board has the authority to decide the type of care to be provided for the child under section 36, give consent to any necessary medical or psychiatric examination, treatment or assessment with respect to the child, and give consent to the issue of a passport to the child, or to the provision of passport facilities for him, to enable him to travel abroad for a limited period.

---

[67] s.17(2).
[68] s.18(1).

13–61   The health board has sufficient authority to authorise the carrying out of a medical or psychiatric examination or assessment, the provision of medical or psychiatric treatment, the issue of a passport or the provision of passport facilities.

13–62   Section 36 provides that where a child is in the care of a health board, the health board shall provide such care for him, subject to its control and supervision, in such of the following ways as it considers to be in his best interests either by placing him with a foster parent, or by placing him in residential care, or in the case of a child who may be eligible for adoption under the Adoption Acts 1952 to 1988, by placing him with a suitable person with a view to his adoption, or by making such other suitable arrangements, including the placing the child with a relative, as the health board thinks proper.

13–63   Where a child is in the care of a health board the health board is to facilitate reasonable access to the child by his parents, or any person acting *in loco parentis*, or any other person who has a bona fide interest in the child and such access may include allowing the child to reside temporarily with any such person.[69]

13–64   On the application of a health board and where there are reasonable grounds for believing that the child has been or is being assaulted, ill-treated, neglected or sexually abused, or the child's health, development or welfare has been or is being avoidably impaired or neglected, or the child's health, development or welfare is likely to be avoidably impaired or neglected, and it is found desirable, by the court, that the child be visited from time to time by or on behalf of the health board, the court may make a "supervision order" in respect of the child.[70] A supervision order remains in force for a period of twelve months or a shorter period as may be specified by the court and, in any event, shall cease to have effect when the person in respect of whom the order is made reaches the age of eighteen. Further supervision orders may be made in respect of the child.

13–65   A supervision order authorises a health board to visit the child from time to time as the board may consider necessary in order to satisfy itself as to the welfare of the child. The supervision order is also designed to allow the health board to give to the childs' parents or to a person acting *in loco parentis* any necessary advice as to the care of the child.

13–66   Any person who fails to comply with the terms of a supervision order or with any directions given by a court regarding the supervision order or who

---

[69] s.37(1).
[70] s.19(1).

prevents a person from visiting a child on behalf of the health board or who obstructs or impedes any such person visiting a child in pursuance of such an order may be guilty of an offence. Any person found guilty of this office may be liable on summary conviction to a fine not exceeding £500 or, at the discretion of the court, to imprisonment for a term not exceeding six months or both the fine and imprisonment.[71]

13–67   In any proceedings under the Child Care Act in relation to the care and protection of a child, the court, having regard to the rights and duties of parents, regard the welfare of the child as the first and paramount consideration, and in so far as is practicable, give due consideration, having regard to his age and understanding, to the wishes of the child, it should also be noted that it is not be necessary for the child to whom the proceedings relate to be brought before the court or to be present for all or any part of the hearing unless the court directs otherwise.[72] In any proceedings the court or any party to the proceedings, may procure a report from any person as the court may nominate on any question affecting the welfare of the child.[73]

13–68   Where a child leaves the care of a health board, the health board may, assist the child for so long as the board is satisfied as to the childs' need for assistance up to the age of twenty one. Where a health board is assisting a person, the board may continue to provide such assistance until the completion of the course of education in which the child is engaged.[74] This assistance can take the form of either by visiting the child, or by arranging for the completion of the childs' education and by contributing towards the childs' maintenance while completing their education, or by placing the child in a suitable trade, calling or business and paying such fee or sum as may be requisite for that purpose, by arranging hostel or other forms of accommodation for the child, or by co-operating with housing authorities in planning accommodation for children leaving care on reaching the age of eighteen years.

F.   ANNUAL REPORT OF SERVICES

13–69   Each health board are required to complete an annual report on its activities carried out under the Child Care Act, as well as regarding other enactments involving the provision of family support services, as well as on the adequacy of the child care. The health board in preparing a report under are to have regard to the needs of children who are not receiving adequate care

---

[71] s.19(5).
[72] s.24.
[73] s.27(1).
[74] s.45.

and protection and, in particular regarding children whose parents are dead or missing, children whose parents have deserted or abandoned them, children who are in the care of the board, children who are homeless, children who are at risk of being neglected or ill-treated, and children whose parents are unable to care for them due to ill-health or for any other reason. The health boards ave powers, in fact duties, under such acts as the Domestic Violence Act 1996.[75]

13–70   A health board are obliged to give notice of the preparation of their report to any child care advisory committee within its area, together with other bodies which the board believes have as one of their purposes include the provision of child care and family support services. The health board are obliged to give due regard to any views or information furnished by these committee or bodies in the preparation of the report, the health board is also required to give a copy of their report to those bodies as well as to the Minister for Health.[76]

G.   DOMESTIC VIOLENCE ACT

13–71   Under section 6 a health board may apply for a safety or barring order, where it becomes aware of an alleged incident or series of incidents which in its opinion puts into doubt the safety or welfare of a person, has reasonable cause to believe that the aggrieved person has been subjected to molestation, violence or threatened violence or otherwise put in fear of his or her safety or welfare, and the health board is of the opinion that there are reasonable grounds for believing that, where appropriate in the circumstances, a person would be deterred or prevented as a consequence of molestation, violence or threatened violence by the respondent or fear of the respondent from pursuing an application for a safety order or a barring order. A court cannot make a safety or an interim barring order where the person on whose behalf the health board are applying for an order, is a dependent person unless the health board satisfies the court that is willing and able to provide reasonable care for such dependent person.

13–72   Section 7 of the Domestic Violence Act provides that if it appears to the court that it may be appropriate for a care order or a supervision order to be made under the Child Care Act 1991, with respect to a dependent person concerned in the proceedings, the court may, of its own motion or on the application of any person concerned with the proceedings, adjourn the proceedings and direct the health board for the area in which the dependent person resides or is for the time being to undertake an investigation or, request further investigations of such dependent person's circumstances. Following an order of the

---

[75] No. 1 of 1996.
[76] s.3(3).

court for a health board to undertake an investigation of a dependent person's circumstances and the health board are obliged to consider if it should apply for a care order or a supervision order under the Child Care Act 1991, provide services or assistance for such dependent person's family, or take any other action.[77]

13–73 Where a health board undertakes an investigation and decides not to apply for a care order or supervision order under the Child Care Act 1991, the health board are obliged to inform the court of its reasons for so deciding, of any service or assistance it has provided, or intends to provide, for such dependent person and his or her family, and any other action which it has taken, or proposes to take.[78]

H. FAMILY LAW ACT 1995

13–74 In certain family law proceedings a court may, of its own motion or on application to it, by order give such directions as it thinks proper for the purpose of obtaining a report in writing on any question which affects the welfare of a party to the proceedings or other person to whom the proceedings relate from a person nominated by a health board specified in the order as the board may nominate, who in the opinion of that board, is suitably qualified.[79]

I. DENTAL SERVICES FOR CHILDREN

13–75 Health boards are obliged under the Health Amendment Act of 1994[80] make available without charge, for children who have attended a national school or a school standing specified in an order under section 66 (3) of the Health Act 1970, dental health services as are specified by regulations made by the Minister.

J. AUDIT OF ACCOUNTS

13–76 The Comptroller and Auditor General (Amendment) Act of 1993[81] provides that the accounts of health boards are audited by the Comptroller and Auditor General.[82] In the course of the auditing of health board accounts, the

---

[77] s.7(3).
[78] s.7(4).
[79] Family Law Act 1995, s.47.
[80] No. 11 of 1994.
[81] No. 8 of 1993.
[82] s.6.

Comptroller and Auditor General is obliged to carry out whatever audit tests as may be appropriate in order to ascertain whether the income and expenditure recorded within the accounts of the board are supported by substantiating documentation, and whether the health board has applied expenditure for the purpose or purposes for which sums were originally paid to the board. The Comptroller and Auditor General must also be satisfied that the transactions of the health board conform with the authority under are supposed to have been carried out.[83]

13–77   The Comptroller and Auditor General attaches to the accounts a certificate stating whether, the accounts properly present the income and expenditure of the board, the balance sheet properly presents the state of affairs of the board at the end of the financial year concerned, and that the accounts are in accordance with any accounting policies laid down by the Minister for Health. The Comptroller and Auditor General may, in the report, make reference to any material case in which the board has failed to apply expenditure recorded in the accounts for a purpose for which the sums paid to the board and out of which the expenditure was made, or to transactions recorded in the accounts do not conform to the authority under which they purport to have been carried out. Upon the completion of the audit of the accounts of a health board, the Comptroller and Auditor General also draws up a report on other matters which may have arose during the carrying out of the audit as he considers it appropriate to report on, and such matters as the Comptroller and Auditor General considers appropriate to report regarding internal controls which are operated by the health board to ensure the regularity of its financial transactions, the correctness of its income and expenditure, the reliability and completeness of its accounting records, and the safeguarding of the assets owned or controlled by it.

K.   REGISTRATION OF NURSING HOMES

13–78   Under the Health (Nursing Homes) Act 1990[84] a health board is obliged to establish and maintain a register of nursing homes of nursing homes within the functional area of the board. Details which are entered in a register in respect of each nursing home registered include the name of the person by whom the nursing home is owned, the name of the person who is in charge of it, the address of the premises in which it is carried on, a statement of the number of patients who can be accommodated in the home, the date on which the registration is to take effect.[85] The period of registration is fixed at three

---

[83] s.6(2).
[84] No. 23 of 1990.
[85] s.4(1).

years after which the nursing home must be reregistered, and the health board issues a certificate of registration to each of the nursing homes registered within their functional area. Applications for re-registration are required to be made within two months of the expiry of the previous registration.[86] Where the nursing home is not being managed by the registered proprietor, the registration of the nursing home ceases to be registered and a new application must be made. if the application aforesaid is duly made, and is not refused then, during the period from the commencement aforesaid until the home is registered it shall be deemed to be registered and there shall be deemed to be attached to the registration any conditions attached to the previous registration[87]. The register which is kept by the health board is to be made available for inspection free of charge by members of the public at all reasonable times.

13–79 Persons who wish to apply for registration under the Act are firstly required to apply to the health board for a declaration that the applicant is a suitable person to carry on a nursing home. On payment of the prescribed fee to the board, the board shall, unless the person has been convicted of an offence under this Act or the Health (Homes for Incapacitated Persons) Act of 1964[88] or of any other offence that is such as to render the person unfit to carry on a nursing home, give to the person a statement by it in writing declaring that the applicant is a suitable person to carry on a nursing home. A health board may refuse to give a declaration to a person who fails or refuses to furnish the health board with information requested by in relation to the application for the declaration and may refuse to give a declaration, or may revoke a declaration given, to a person who has furnished the board with information that is false or misleading in a material way.[89]

13–80 A nursing home may be removed from the register by a health board or the health board may refuse to register a nursing home, but the health board cannot remove the home, or reject the application, unless it is first satisfied the premises to which the application the registration relates do not comply with the regulations, or the carrying on of the home will not be or is not in compliance with the regulations. A health board may refuse to issue a declaration or remove a nursing home from the register if the applicant or the registered proprietor, or the person in charge or, proposed to be in charge of the home has been convicted of an offence under this Act or the Act of 1964 or of any other offence that is such as to render the person unfit to carry on or, as the case may be, to be in charge of the home, or where the applicant or the registered proprietor has failed or refused to furnish to the health board with in-

---

[86] s.4(11).
[87] s.4(12).
[88] No. 8 of 1964.
[89] s.4(4).

formation requested or has furnished the board with information that is false or misleading in a material way, or where the registered proprietor has within the past year failed to comply with conditions previously attached to the registration by the health board.[90]

13–81   In respect of the registration of a nursing home a health board may at the time of registration, or subsequently, attach to the registration, conditions in relation to the carrying on of the nursing home, the health board may attach different conditions to the registration of different nursing homes, and may amend or revoke a condition of registration.[91] Conditions which are imposed upon registration or amendments and revocations made by the health board are stated in the certificate of registration or are notified in writing to the registered proprietor of the nursing home.[92]

13–82   Where a health board proposes to refuse to register a nursing home, or to refuse to give a declaration or intends to revoke a declaration, or to remove a nursing home from the register, or attach a condition to, or amend or revoke a condition attached to, a registration, the health board are obliged to notify in writing the applicant or the registered proprietor of its proposal and of the reasons for it.[93] A person who has been so notified may, within twenty one days of the receipt of the notification, make representations in writing to the health board. The board are obliged to before deciding the matter, take into consideration any representations duly made to it and shall notify the person in writing of its decision and of the reasons for it.[94] An appeal against a decision of the health board may be made to the District Court in which the nursing home concerned is situated within twenty one days from the receipt of the notification, a decision of the District Court on a question of fact is final. On the hearing of an appeal a health board is entitled to appear, be heard and adduce evidence on the hearing of the appeal.[95]

L.   REGULATIONS

13–83   Regulations under this section may prescribe requirements as to the maintenance, care, welfare and well-being of dependent persons while being maintained in nursing homes, prescribe requirements as to the numbers, qualifications and availability of members of the staffs, including the medical staffs,

---

[90] s.4(7).
[91] s.4(8).
[92] s.4(8)(b).
[93] s.4(13).
[94] s.4(13).
[95] s.5(5).

of nursing homes, prescribe requirements as to the design, maintenance, repair, cleaning and cleanliness, ventilation, heating and lighting of nursing homes, prescribe requirements as to the accommodation, including the amount of space in bedrooms and wards, the washing facilities and the sanitary conveniences, provided in nursing homes, prescribe requirements as to the food provided for dependent persons while being maintained in nursing homes, prescribe requirements as to the description of nursing homes in written communications by or on behalf of the registered proprietors or the persons in charge of the homes and the display in nursing homes of specified notices, prescribe requirements as to the records to be kept in nursing homes and for the examination and copying of any such records or of extracts therefrom by officers of health boards, provide for the effecting by the registered proprietors of nursing homes of contracts of insurance against injury to dependent persons being maintained in the homes while in the homes.

13–84 Regulations may also be made in relation to provide for the holding and conduct of interviews and examinations of dependent persons while being maintained in nursing homes, and interviews of persons employed in nursing homes, where the health board concerned has reasonable cause to believe that such dependent persons are not receiving proper maintenance or care or medical or other treatment. The Minister may provide for the inspection of premises in which nursing homes are being carried on or are proposed to be carried. The regulations may authorise a health board to train members of the staffs of nursing homes upon such terms and conditions and to such extent as the health boards may determine.

13–85 A health board may under regulations regarding the consideration and investigation by the health board concerned of a complaint made to it in writing by, or on behalf of, a dependent person who is being maintained in a nursing home in relation to any matter regarding the home or the maintenance, care, welfare or well-being of the person while being so maintained or any specified related matter. Where the complaint is upheld by the health board in case a complaint and if the board considers it appropriate to do so, may issue a direction requiring that the proprietor of the nursing home take such specified action as the board may decide in relation to the complaint.

13–86 Where, there is a contravention of a provision of the regulations in relation to a nursing home the registered proprietor and the person in charge of the home shall be guilty of an offence, additionally a person who fails or refuses to comply with a requirement of a direction under the regulations shall be guilty of an offence.[96] Following a conviction for offences under the Act, the Circuit Court may, on the application of the health board, which is brought

---

[96] s.6(3).

not more than six months after the conviction, by order declare that the person who has been convicted is disqualified during whatever period as may be specified in the order for carrying on, being in charge, or concerned with the management, of the nursing home to which the conviction related or, at the discretion of that Court, any nursing home.[97]

M. MAINTENANCE CONTRIBUTIONS

13–87　Under section 7 of the 1990 Act a health board may, following an assessment of the dependency of a person, their circumstances and the costs of maintenance, if the person enters or is in a nursing home, and subject to compliance by the home with any requirements which made be made by the board, pay to the nursing home a contribution in respect of the maintenance as the board considers appropriate having regard to the degree of the dependency and to the means and circumstances of the person.

13–88　Section 9 of the Act allows a health board to take charge of and manage a nursing home where it is of the opinion that there is a failure to comply with the regulations and may, for that purpose appoint a person to take charge of and manage the home on its behalf during such period as the health board or the District Court may determine, or with the consent of the registered proprietor. The amount paid in respect of the salary by a health board to a person appointed by it may be recovered by the health board from the registered proprietor of the nursing home as a simple contract debt in any court of competent jurisdiction.[98]

13–89　On application, by a health board, and where the District Court is satisfied that there is a failure by a nursing home to comply with any regulations made under the Act, the Court may make a management order authorising the health board to take charge of and manage the home, and to appoint such person as the board may decide to manage and take charge of the home on behalf of the board, for a period, not exceeding three months, as may be specified in the order.[99]

N. SUPERVISION OF PRE-SCHOOL SERVICES

13–90　Section 51 of the Child Care Act provides that a person carrying on a

---

[97] s.6(4).
[98] s.9(1).
[99] s.9(2).

pre-school service or who proposes to carry on a pre-school service is obliged to give notice to the relevant health board. Section 52 of the Act provides that it is the duty of every person carrying on a pre-school service to take all reasonable measures to safeguard the health, safety and welfare of pre-school children attending the service and to comply with any regulations made under the Act. A health board may itself provide pre-school services in its area and provide and maintain premises for that purpose.

13–91 Health boards are obliged to visit each pre-school service within its functional area in order to ensure that the person who is carrying on the service is fulfilling the duties which are imposed under section 52. The provisions of the Child Care Act in relation to the supervision of pre-school services does not apply to the care of one or more pre-school children undertaken by a relative of the child or children or the spouse of a relative, a person taking care of one or more pre-school children of the same family and no other such children, other than that person's own such children, in that person's home, or a person taking care of not more than three pre-school children of different families, other than that person's own such children, in that person's home.[100]

13–92 Each health board is obliged under section 61 of the Act to establish and maintain a register of children's residential centres in its functional area. Furthermore no person may carry on a children's residential centre unless the centre is registered and the person is the registered proprietor, a person cannot be in charge of a centre unless the centre is registered.

O. TOBACCO (HEALTH PROMOTION AND PROTECTION) ACT 1988[101]

13–93 In relation to summary proceedings under this Act, proceedings may be brought and prosecuted by the health board. These offences include the selling or the offering for sale of the making available any tobacco product to a person under the age of sixteen years, whether for that persons' own use or otherwise, or who sells to any person, acting on behalf of a person under the age of sixteen years, any tobacco products.[102] An offence is also committed under section 3(2) of the Act where the owner, or person in charge, of any machine for the sale of tobacco products permits the machine to be used for the sale of such products to a person under the age of sixteen.

13–94 An offence is also committed where any person who sells, offers to

---

[100] s.58(1).
[101] No. 24 of 1988.
[102] s.3(1).

sell or makes available in relation to the sale of any other product, cigarettes to a person otherwise than in packets of ten or more cigarettes.[103] Section 5(1) of the Act provides that persons engaged in the manufacture of tobacco products or in the importation of tobacco products, are obliged to notify the Minister for Health, when requested by the Minister, of any constituent of the tobacco product, other than tobacco, water or reconstituted sheet made wholly from tobacco, and of the amount of the constituent, used in the manufacture of such products, and an offence is committed where that person fails to comply with a request under section 5 from the Minister.

13–95 An offence is also committed by any person who imports, manufactures, sells or otherwise disposes of, or offers for sale or other disposal, or advertises, an oral smokeless tobacco product, otherwise known as chewing tobacco.[104] A health board may also prosecute offences committed under the Tobacco Products (Control of Advertising, Sponsorship and Sales Promotion) Act 1978.[105]

P.   HEALTH BOARD CHARGES

13–96 Health boards make out-patient services available for persons with full eligibility and persons with limited eligibility. Health boards are obliged to make out-patient services available, without charge, for children in respect of diseases and disabilities of a permanent or of a long term nature which are prescribed by the Minister for Health. Health boards are obliged to make out-patient services available without charge for children in respect of defects which are noticed at a health examination provided under the Health Act 1970.[106]

13–97 Health boards may provide for the imposition of charges for out patient services including the drugs, medicines or other preparations in specified circumstances for persons who are not persons entitled to full eligibility and are not children. Where injury is caused to a person by the negligent use of a mechanically propelled vehicle in a public place, and in-patient services or out-patient services have been, are being or will be provided by or on behalf of a health board in respect of the injury, the person who was injured of that person's dependants, has received, or is entitled to receive damages or compensation the health board are entitled, in fact obliged, to make a charge upon the person who has received or is entitled to receive damages or compensation in respect of in-patient services or out-patient services.[107]

---

[103] s.4.
[104] s.6(1).
[105] No. 27 of 1978.
[106] Health (Amendment) Act 1986.
[107] Health (Amendment) Act 1986, s.2.

13–98 A health board may waive the charge or part of a charge if the health board considers it proper to do so. The health board in making a decision to waive the charge are to having had regard to the amount of damages or compensation, and interest, received by the person who is liable to pay the charge in respect of the injury to which the charge relates, and in a case where there was contributory negligence on the part of the person to whose injury the charge relates or of one for whose acts he is responsible, having had regard to any reduction in the amount which would have been received but for the contributory negligence.[108]

13–99 Any sums due to a health board in respect of these charges following a road traffic accident may be recovered by the health board from the person as a simple contract debt in any court of competent jurisdiction, and a cause of action against a person in respect of a charge is deemed to accrue on the date on which damages or compensation are paid by the person liable to pay such damages or compensation or on the date on which the services to which the charge relates are provided, whichever is the later.[109]

Q. MIDWIVES

13–100 Where a midwife, who is not employed by a health board, or by a hospital authority providing maternity services or by a maternity home authority, is practising or proposes to practise midwifery, that person is obliged to notify the health board, or health boards, in whose functional area that person practises or intends to practise. It is the duty of a health board, in accordance with regulations made by the Minister, to exercise supervision and control over a midwife practising in their functional area.[110] No person can attend a woman in childbirth unless that person is a midwife, or a registered medical practitioner, or is undergoing training to be a registered medical practitioner or a midwife and gives such attention as part of a course of professional training, or is undergoing experience and training in obstetrics in the course of professional training, unless such attention is given, otherwise than for reward, in any case of sudden or urgent necessity where neither a midwife nor a registered medical practitioner is immediately available.[111]

---

[108] s.2(2).
[109] s.3, which amends the provisions of Part III the Statute of Limitations 1957.
[110] Nurses Act 1985, s.57.
[11] s.58(1). Any person who acts in contravention of s.58(1) may be guilty of an offence and liable on summary conviction to a fine not exceeding £1,000.

R . MENTAL HEALTH

13–101   The Health (Mental Service) Act of 1981 provides that no person other than a health board may operate any premises for the detention of persons requiring care and treatment for mental disorder or to describe or hold out any place a place of detention for persons having metal disorders, unless it is approved and registered by the Minister.[112] A registered psychiatric centre may be a separate hospital or a unit in any hospital.

13–102   It is also not lawful for any person other than a health board to carry a psychiatric home for the care and treatment of persons suffering from mental disorder which is not a psychiatric centre. It is also unlawful to describe or hold out any such place as such a psychiatric home unless it is approved and registered by the health board in accordance with regulations made by the Minister. A health board may refuse to register or may cancel the registration of a psychiatric home.[113] Where a health board refuses to register or cancels the registration of a psychiatric home it is obliged to give a reason for the refusal to register or for the cancellation of registration in writing to the person who is maintaining the home, and an appeal from that decision is allowed to the Minister, and an appeal from the decision of the Minister may be made to the High Court.[114] Any person who maintains a psychiatric home are to allow it to be inspected by a designated officer of the health board and to allow the officer such facilities and information as are required.[115]

---

[112] s.10.
[113] s.12.
[114] ss.2(4), 12(7).
[115] s.12(5).

CHAPTER 14

Local Government Bill 2000

A. INTRODUCTION

14–01 The Local Government Bill 2000 aims to provide a modern statutory basis for the work of local authorities, repealing outdated legislation and replacing older terminology with simpler language. One of the stated aims of the Bill is to provide a single common legislative code which will apply to all local authorities.[1] The Bill follows on the proposals set out in various studies and government papers such as the Task Force on Integration of Local Government and Local Development Systems[2] and Real Local Government of 1997.

14–02 The central aims of the Bill are to enhance the role of the elected members of the local authorities, to support community involvement with local authorities through a more better participation in local government, and the modernising of local government legislation. The Bill also follows on from the recent amendment to the Constitution in the TwentiethAmendment of the Constitution which gave recognition to local government and the holding of elections at least every five years. The Bill contains a general statement of the functions of local authorities, a code on local authority membership, and provision for the office of Cathaoirleach for all local authorities. The Bill also deals with the holding of local elections, the filling of casual vacancies, and provides for the continued co-operation between local authorities. The Bill

---

[1] See explanatory memorandum of the bill.
[2] Report of the Task Force on Integration of Local Government and Local Development Systems (1998)

also introduces new financial management and accounting systems as well as local government audit. A separate bill will deal with the issue of local government rates and this will in time also mean in changes in the Local Government Bill.

B. LOCAL GOVERNMENT AREAS AND LOCAL AUTHORITIES

14–03 Part I of the Bill goes through the various definitions and interpretations to be used throughout the Bill, and refers to the "administrative area" as being an area, in the case of a county, a county council, a city will have a city council and a town will have a town council. Section 11 deals with these areas and in the case of the city, city councils will be established in Cork, Dublin, Galway, Limerick and Waterford.[3] County councils will be established in the present counties plus the county of Dun Laoghaire-Rathdown, Tipperary North Riding will become North Tipperary and Tipperary South Riding will become South Tipperary, while South Dublin and Fingal will also be counties for the purposes of local government, giving a total of twenty nine counties.

14–04 The former boroughs of Clonmel, Drogheda, Kilkenny, Sligo and Wexford will simply become towns under the Bill and will lose their city designation. Areas having urban districts, and town commissioners will also become towns and their councils will be known as Town Councils.[4] Each member of the Town Council will be known as councillors and each local authority shall have a Cathaoirleach and Leas-Chathaoirleach elected in accordance with Part 5 of the Bill.[5]

14–05 The County Councils will have jurisdiction throughout its administrative areas except for the area under the control and management of a town council, although a county council may carry out the functions of a town council within its area either separately or jointly with the town council.[6] City Councils have jurisdiction throughout its administrative area as do town councils within their own areas, subject to the provisions of section 69 regarding the carrying out of functions by county councils.

14–06 Section 11 of the Bill also deals with the provision of seals for the local authorities, and allows one authentication signature by either the Cathaoirleach or of an employee of the authority nominated in writing for that

---

[3] Listed in Sched. 5, Pt 2.
[4] See Sched. 6.
[5] s.5.
[6] s.11(6) and s.69.

purpose by the manager following consultation with the Cathaoirleach. Previously three signatures would have been required, a nominated member of the elected members of the authority together with the manager or town clerk and the county secretary. Section 11(16) provides that all royal charters and letters patent relating to local authorities will cease to have effect except for ceremonial or related purposes, however, the property rights of the authority will remain unaffected under section 11(15) which is important for such cities as Waterford whose founding charter under Charles II also gave Waterford Corporation lands and estates in Waterford.

C. LOCAL AUTHORITY MEMBERSHIP

14–07   Part three of the Bill deals with local authority membership and section 12 sets down the eligibility criteria for membership of local authorities. Disqualification from membership are set down in sections 13 and 14. Any person who is a citizen of Ireland or is a person who is ordinarily resident in the State and has or will be eighteen years of age on or before polling day at a local election,[7] are eligible for membership of a local authority.[8]

14–08   A person is disqualified from being a member of a local authority or from being co-opted onto a local authority if that person is a member of any EU body such as the Parliament or Commission, or is a member of the Government of Ceann Comhairle of Dáil Éireann or chairman of Seanad Éireann. Members of the Defence Forces or the Garda Síochána may not be members of a local authority, nor civil servants who are not expressly permitted to be a member of a local authority, or judges appointed under the Constitution or persons employed by a local authority and not allowed under section 160(1)(b) may not be members of a local authority. Also persons who are undergoing a sentence of imprisonment for any term of over six months or a person who has failed to pay any sum charged or surcharge by a local government auditor, or a person who has failed to discharge a final judgement or decree for payment of money due to any local authority may not be members of a local authority. Persons who have been convicted of an offence relating to fraudulent or dishonest dealings affecting a local authority or of acting as a member of a local authority while disqualified cannot be members of a local authority. This disqualification lasts for a period of five years from the date of conviction.

14–09   An important development is contained in section 14 in that members of Dáil Éireann and Seanad Éireann are disqualified from being members

---

[7]   Or the latest day for receiving nominations if there is no poll.
[8]   s.12.

of a local authority and will come into effect from the local elections to be held in 2004. Therefore members of the Oireachtas and members of the European Parliament may not be councillors of local authorities from 2004.

14–10   Casual vacancies in the membership of local authorities are dealt with in section 19 of the Bill and arise on a member becoming disqualified or upon the death of a member. The meetings administrator, which is a new post established under section 46 and has general responsibility as regards meetings of the authority, records decisions and carries additional functions under the bill and is a person appointed by the manager, notifies the members of the local authority in writing. The casual vacancy is then filled by co-opting persons to fill the vacancy by the political party to whom the previous councillor belonged nominating a person to fill the vacancy. Where the former councillor was not a party candidate the vacancy is filled by the co-option under the standing orders of the local authority which are to be made by the local authority under section 19(3)(c).

14–11   The number of councillors of each of the local authorities is set down in section 21 and listed in Schedule 7. The County Councils have between 20, for Co. Monaghan, and 48 members, for Co. Cork. The Cork City Council will have 31 members, Dublin will have 52, Galway will have 15, Limerick will have 17, and Waterford will have 15 councillors. The Town Councils of Bray, Clonmel, Drogheda, Dundalk, Kilkenny, Sligo, Tralee, and Wexford will each have twelve councillors. All other towns will have nine councillors. However, each of the county councils, or city councils may apply to have the number of councillors changed under section 22. The vote to change the number of councillors must be supported by more than half of the existing councillors, the proposal must have been placed as a public notice and public submissions must be sought, with the final hurdle being the Ministers' consent. The Local Government Commission may also make recommendations to the Minister regarding the proposal to change the number of councillors.

D. REMUNERATION

14–12   The Minister may, by regulation, provide for the payment by a local authority of allowances for expenses which are incurred by elected members for attending meetings of the authority, or for attending committee meetings or meetings of a joint body.[9] Members may also be paid for attending conferences, seminars, training courses or other events. The post of chair of a strate-

---

[9]   s.141(1).

gic policy committee may also be a remunerated post. Provision may also be made for the remunerating the Cathaoirleach or certain local authorities.[10]

14–13   Local authorities are allowed under section 142 to pay an allowance, as distinct from a salary or other remuneration, to its Cathaoirleach and Leas Cathaoirleach in order for the Cathaoirleach and Leas Cathaoirleach to pay reasonable expenses.

E. THE LOCAL GOVERNMENT COMMISSION

14–14   The Local Government Commission is a body set up under part eleven of the Bill and its functions include preparing and furnishing reports to the Minister. The Commission will furnish reports on the alteration of local authority boundaries under part eight of the Bill, the alteration of local electoral areas and the number of members of the authority assigned to those areas, the alteration of the number of members of a local authority, the establishment of a town council, an application by a town council under section 185 to dissolve the council.

14–15   The Commission is an independent organ and its members are appointed by the Minister and number not more than five and not less than three. The members are required to have knowledge or experience of local government affairs, or knowledge or experience of business, commerce, administration or community development or officer of the Minister. Each of the members of the Commission holds office for a period of three years or a lesser period as determined by the Minister. Members of the Oireachtas, local authorities or members of the European Parliament may not be members of the Commission.

14–16   The Commission as soon as practicable must give public notice of its intention to prepare a report, and any person may make a submission to the Commission in relation to the report which is to be prepared. Submissions received by the Commission are to be made available for public inspection.[11] During the preparation of a report the Commission may request from a local authority information and particulars which it may reasonably require. A local authority is obliged to comply with such a request within the period specified in the request from the Commission.[12]

---

[10] s.141(2).
[11] s.94.
[12] s.94(5).

F. LOCAL GOVERNMENT SERVICE

14–17   The elected council of a local authority are to directly exercise and perform every reserved function. Reserved functions are those designated in Schedule 13 or which have been so designated under any act or which was expressly made exercisable by resolution by a local authority after the 13th of June 1940.

14–18   Schedule 13 states that the procedure at any meeting of a local authority or of a joint body is a reserved function, as is the appointment of a person to be a member of a public authority, the election of the Cathaoirleach and Leas-Cathaoirleach and the chairpersons of a joint body, the determination of the annual rate of valuation, the making, amending or revoking of any bye-law. The making or revoking of an order or the passing or rescinding of a resolution whereby an enactment is brought into effect, the application of such an order to any Minister, and the demanding of the expenses of a local authority or of a joint body from any other local authority are all reserved functions.

14–19   The Minister may also designate specified functions of local authorities or joint bodies to be a reserved function. Section 144 makes the appointment of the manager a reserved function as well as the suspension or the removal of the manager by the local authority.

G. THE MANAGER

1. Position of Manager

14–20   Section 143 states that for every county and city there shall be a manager who shall hold employment under that county council or city council. Any function of the town clerk of a city now becomes vested in the manager of the local authority. The county manager shall also be the manager for every town council within the county's administrative area and for every joint body whose functional area is wholly situated within the county, with the Minister deciding who shall be the manager for joint bodies which are situated in more than one county.[13] The appointment of the manager is a reserved function under section 144 as is the suspension or removal of the manager.

14–21   A person who is appointed a manager holds office until that person either dies, retires or resigns or is removed. The Minister will set down the relevant retirement age for managers and the Minister may also specify the

---

[13] s.143(4).

period which a manager may hold office. Section 147 allows for the appointment of deputy managers. A manager may following consultation with the Cathaoirleach of the county or city council appoint an employee of the local authority to be a deputy manager, and that appointment may be terminated at any time. The appointment of a deputy manager may be made for specified duration. The deputy manager acts in the place of the manager where the manager is temporarily unable to act. If the manager has become temporarily unable to act, and a deputy manager has not been appointed, or the deputy manager is also unable to act, then the Cathaoirleach may appoint an employee of the local authority to be deputy manager. The manager has a general power under section 153 to delegate functions to an employee of the local authority as the manager sees fit.

14–22 In carrying out the executive functions of the local authority the manager may act by written order signed and dated by that person.[14] Schedule 14 sets out executive functions which are to be carried out by manager's order. These are decisions regarding applications for the grant of a permission, approval, permit, consent, certificate, licence or other form of statutory authorisation, the service of a statutory notice requiring compliance with a statutory enactment, any decision to take legal proceedings, the acquisition or the disposal of land or the entering into an agreement relating to land, the allocation of a house, the acceptance of a tender, the award of grants, loans or other financial assistance, the appointment of staff, and section 150 also relates to anything required to be done by any enactment by the order of the manager.

14–23 Every manager is obliged to keep a register in respect of all orders made by the manager and the register is to be made available at every meeting of the local authority.[15] The manager has the right to attend and to speak at meetings of the local authority and to take part in discussions. However, the manager does not have a vote on the local authority.[16]

14–24 It is the duty of the manager to carry into effect all of the lawful directions of the elected council, as well as to advise and assist the elected council generally as regards the exercise or performance by the council of its reserved functions and any particular matter or thing which the council requests.[17] The manager must give the local authority or one of its committees such advice and assistance as shall be reasonably be required, and the manager must also arrange for the attendance of any employee of the local authority whose presence if appropriate having regard to the business of the

---

[14] s.150.
[15] s.150(4).
[16] s.151.
[17] s.131(2).

meeting.[18] The council must also have regard to the advice or the assistance given by the manager.

14–25 The manager of a local authority acts for and on behalf of the local authority in every action or other legal proceeding whether civil or criminal which is instituted by or against the local authority.[19]

14–26 The manager is also obliged, under section 133(3) to prepare the corporate plan for the authority, in consultation with the policy group formed under section 132, and to ensure that the corporate plan is submitted to the elected council for their consideration. The corporate plan is a statement of strategy for the local authority. The strategy is to be submitted within a period of not longer than six months from the date of the annual meeting or in the case of a review from the date of the request for a review of the plan. The corporate plan will set out the principal activities of the local authority as well as its objectives and priorities, and any proposals for the improvement of service. An annual progress report is prepared by the manager and submitted to the council at the same time as the annual draft budget.

14–27 At the start of each local financial year the manager is obliged to prepare and submit a report indicating the capital projects proposed by the local authority including the capital projects for the following two years.

14–28 The manager must furnish information, whenever requested by the elected council or by the Cathaoirleach, which may be in the managers possession or procurement in relation to any business or transaction of the local authority.[20] The elected council may also require the manager to prepare and submit plans and specifications for the execution of any particular work, and an estimate of the probable cost of that work.[21] The manager must inform the elected council before any works, other than maintenance or repair, are undertaken, or before committing the authority to any expenditure in connection with proposed works.[22] The elected council may also by resolution direct the manager to inform the council of the manner in which the manager proposes to perform an executive function and the manager must comply with that direction. However, this does not prevent the manager from dealing with an immediate situation which is an emergency. An emergency is deemed to include of works which are urgent and necessary having regard to personal health,

---

18 s.151(3).
19 s.152.
20 s.135.
21 s.136.
22 s.137.

public health or safety in order to provide a reasonable standard of accommodation for any person.[23]

2. Direction to Managers - Works

14–29 The elected council may by resolution direct particular works shall
not proceed. However, the elected council cannot prevent the carrying out of
any works which the local authority is required to carry out under statute or by
an order of court, and the manager is obliged to comply with such a resolution.[24] An elected council may also require a particular thing or act be done by
the authority. The elected council must give notice of the intention to propose
a resolution by giving notice in writing to the manager, signed by at least five
members, and containing the text of the resolution. The resolution that a particular act be done must be considered at a special meeting of the local authority being not less than seven days after the date of the service of the notice,
unless an ordinary meeting of the authority is to be held within fourteen days
after the day on which the manager receives the notice. The resolution must
then receive the support of at least one third of the total number of members of
the local authority. Once the resolution has been passed, and when the money
for its purpose has been provided, the manager is to carry out that act, matter
or thing.[25] The resolution may not relate to the performance of any function of
the local authority generally, or if the resolution prevents the performance of
any function of the local authority which it is obliged to carry out by law. The
elected council may not also pass resolutions under section 139 which apply
to or extend to every case or the performance of a function or to the performance of a function within a particular area or substantially so.

H. LOCAL ELECTIONS

14–30 Each town, city or county may be divided by the Minister into local
electoral areas and the Minister may fix the number of councillors which are
elected for each of these areas.[26] Where the relevant area is not divided into
local electoral areas that area is regarded as one electoral area with all of the
councillors being elected from that one area.

14–31 Every person whose name is on the register of local government electors which is prepared under the Electoral Act of 1992 for the relevant local

---

[23] s.137(5).
[24] s.138.
[25] s.139.
[26] s.23.

electoral area is entitled to vote at the local election.[27] Voting in local government elections remains by secret ballot.[28]

14–32   Voters may not vote or apply for a ballot paper more than once at an election of the members of a local authority, or more than once at an election for a directly elected Cathaoirleach of a local authority, or for a Cathaoirleach of more than one local authority for the same class held in conjunction with local elections, or at both an election of the members of a city council and an election of the members of a local authority of a town council. Local authorities are broken into two classes, with county councils and city councils being in one class, and town councils in the other class, and a person may not vote for more than one authority in the same class.[29]

14–33   Elections are to be held in the year 2004 and every five years thereafter, with the poll held during either the months of May or June from the hours of 7.00 a.m. and 10.30 p.m. and not less than twelve hours. However, new elections can be held under part 21 of the Bill following a failure on the part of a local authority to carry out its functions. The poll is taken by the system of proportional representative, each local government elector having one transferable vote within the meaning of the Electoral Act of 1992. Regulations may be made dealing with the nomination of candidates, the relevant deposit to be paid, the duties of returning officers, the taking of polls and the counting of votes, the use, free of charge, of schools and public rooms, arrangements for postal and special voting, voting on islands and by persons who are ill or physically disabled and so on. In the meantime regulations made under section 22 of the Local Government Act 1994 will continue to have effect until amended or revoked.

I. CATHAOIRLEACH AND LEAS-CHATHAOIRLEACH

1. Introduction

14–34   Section 31 of the Bill introduces the offices of Cathaoirleach and Leas-Chathaoirleach to every local authority. The Cathaoirleach shall take precedence at all meetings of the local authority and all proceedings of the elected council. The Cathaoirleach may nominate from among the other members of

---

[27] s.24(1).
[28] s.24(2).
[29] s.25(1), penalties are contained in s.25(3), being a fine of not over £1,500 or to a term of imprisonment of not over six months.

the local authority a member for the purpose of representing the Cathaoirleach at any ceremony or event.

14–35 The use of the tiles "Lord Mayor" and "Deputy Lord Mayor" for Cork and Dublin can continue and any other city or town council may continue to use the titles of "Mayor" and "Deputy Mayor," provided same were used prior to the commencement of the bill. Any other local authority may give the alternative titles of Mayor and Deputy Mayor to the Cathaoirleach or Leas-Cathaoirleach.

14–36 Following a local election the Cathaoirleach continues to hold office until the commencement of the annual meeting at which the successor is elected unless that person dies or resigns from office or becomes disqualified from local authority membership.[30]

14–37 A local authority may by resolution remove from office the Cathaoirleach or Leas-Cathaoirleach of the local authority for stated misbehaviour or if that persons removal appears to the authority to be necessary for the effective performance by the local authority of its functions.[31] The notice of the intention to remove a Cathaoirleach or Leas-Cathaoirleach must be signed by at least one third of the total number of members of the local authority, it must contain a statement of the reasons for the removal, it must specify the day for the holding of the special meeting being not less than twenty one days after the date on which the notice is delivered to the meetings administrator, and is delivered or sent to the Cathaoirleach or Leas-Cathaoirleach. Once the meetings administrator receives the resolution a copy must be sent to every member of the local authority and shall convene a special meeting for the date specified in the proposal.

14–38 The meeting will be chaired by a person other than that proposed to be removed, and shall be chosen by the members present at the meeting. The person who is proposed to be removed must be afforded an opportunity to make a statement of response in relation to the proposal.[32] For the proposal to pass it must achieve the support of at least three-quarters of the total number of members of the local authority.[33] It would seem that the figure of three-quarters is of all of the members of the local authority and not just those who attend the meeting.

---

[30] s.36(4).
[31] s.34(1).
[32] s.34(4).
[33] s.34(5).

2. Election of the Cathaoirleach

14–39   At the annual meeting of the local authority following the local elections, the meetings administrator is obliged to firstly read out the members who have been elected. Following which the first item of business is the election of the Cathaoirleach, unless that person has already been directly elected in which case the Leas-Cathaoirleach is elected. Section 37 provides the method by which the Cathaoirleach is elected, which is by poll if there are more than two candidates, and by lot if two or more candidates receive equal votes in order to exclude one member from the subsequent voting or to elect the member.[34]

3. Direct Election

14–40   Chapter three of part five of the Bill makes provision for the direct election of the Cathaoirleach of a local authority. The chapter applies to county councils and city councils and will come into effect from 2004, therefore there is no provision for the direct election of the Cathaoirleach for towns.[35]

14–41   For the purposes of the election of the Cathaoirleach the entire county or city is classed as one electoral area. Regulations are to be made by the Minister for the holding of the direct elections for the office of Cathaoirleach. The regulations are to provide that the direct elections are to be held on the same day and at the same time as local elections, except for bye-elections.

14–42   If the direct election is contested then a poll is taken and each elector has one transferable vote. Any person who is a local government elector and who is not made ineligible for election to a local authority or who is disqualified under the Bill or under section 20 of the Local Elections (Disclosure of Donations and Expenditure) Act 1999 may vote. A person cannot hold office for two consecutive terms, excluding any period taken up following a bye election to fill a casual vacancy, and shall be disqualified from election if election would provide a third consecutive term of office.

14–43   If the person elected is not also elected a member of the local authority, then that person is deemed to be a member of the local authority, so long as that person holds office, and the number of the members of the local authority is increased by one during that period of office.[36] If the person holding office as a Cathaoirleach for any reason ceases to be a member of the local authority that person shall also cease to be the Cathaoirleach.

---

[34] s.37(h) and (k), there is no mention as to who draws the lots, but it could be suggested that the meetings administrator would be an appropriate person.

[35] s.39.

[36] s.40(7).

14-44   Where there is a casual vacancy in the office of Cathaoirleach, then provided there is more than twelve months remaining in the term of office, a bye-election shall be held to fill the vacancy by direct election. Where there is less than twelve months left then the council shall elect the Cathaoirleach a person from among the members of the authority.[37]

J. ETHICAL FRAMEWORK FOR LOCAL GOVERNMENT SERVICE

14-45   Section 167 states that in carrying out their functions it is the duty of every member and every employee of a local authority and every member of a local authority committee to maintain proper standards of integrity, conduct and concern for the public interest. Following consultation with the Public Offices Commission and the Government, codes of conduct for the guidance of members of the local authorities and of employees of local authorities may be issued. Every member is to have regard to and be guided by the relevant code of conduct in the exercise of their functions.

14-46   An employee or a member of a local authority or a committee of a local authority may not seek, exact or accept from any person any remuneration, fee, reward or other favour for anything done or not done by virtue of their employment or office. It is an offence for a person to offer, give or promise to give any such remuneration, fee, reward or other favour to an employee or member of a local authority.[38] A person contravening the provisions of section 169 may face a fine of £1,500 and a term of imprisonment of six months on summary conviction, and on indictment could face a fine of not over £100,000 or a term of imprisonment of three years or both.[39]

K. ANNUAL DECLARATIONS

14-47   Every member and employee of a local authority is obliged to furnish to the ethics registrar an annual written declaration containing details of any declarable interests and give an undertaking to have regard to and be guided by the relevant code of conduct. Each member of a local authority will be obliged to furnish an annual declaration and a statement that none of the grounds of disqualification referred to in the Bill or in the Local Elections (Disclosure of Donations and Expenditure) Act 1999 apply.

---

[37] s.41.

[38] s.169.

[39] Proceedings under s.169 are to be brought by the Director of Public Prosecutions.

14–48   The ethics registrar is a person or persons who are assigned by order of the manager of a local authority to perform the duties of the ethics registrar, and no person may serve as the ethics registrar for a continuous period of over two years.[40] The ethics registrar is obliged to keep on behalf of the local authority a public register composed of two parts, one containing the members' interests and the other the interests of the employees and other persons. Any declarations or disclosures must also be entered into the register of interests. Copies of the register of interest or any entry may be obtained by any person, on the payment of a reasonable fee. The entries last in the register for fifteen years following that person being either an employee or a member.[41] The ethics registrar is obliged to issue to each member of the local authority a signed and dated notice informing the member of the requirements of the legalisation. Similar notices must be given to employees of the local authority every January.

14–49   The declarable interests which have to be entered in the register of interests are referred to in section 174. These include any profession, business or occupation, the development of land, any remunerated trade, profession, employment, vocation, any estate or interest in land, or as a nominee of an interest in land, any holding of shares or bonds or debentures, any directorship or shadow directorship of any company, any gift, including foreign travel facilities (excluding gifts from relatives or personal friends for purely personal reasons, and gifts not over £500) and so on.[42]

14–50   Section 175 deals with the definition of beneficial interest and relates to any beneficial interest which may arise from the adoption of a resolution, motion, question or other matter, and includes an interest in respect of which that person is a member of a company or any other body which has a beneficial interest in the matter or of a connected person. A person is deemed to have a beneficial interest under section 175(2) if that person has actual knowledge that that person or a connected person has a declarable interest in or which is material to a resolution, motion, question or other matter being proposed, or which arises from the performance by the authority of any of its functions. A connected person means a brother, a sister, a parent or spouse of the person or a child of the person or of the spouse.[43]

14–51   The manager may not seek to influence nor seek to influence a decision of a local authority and the manager must disclose, in writing, to the Cathaoirleach the nature of any interest or the fact that a connected person to

---

[40] s.172.
[41] s.171(4).
[42] s.174.
[43] s.165.

the manager has an interest in any particular matter.[44] This disclosure is also entered into the ethics register. Where a function would normally be dealt with by the manager the function must be delegated once the manager has made a disclosure under section 177.

14–52 Section 178 provides that an employee of the local authority and any other person whose services are being availed of by the local authority, having actual knowledge that person or a connected person, has a pecuniary or other beneficial interest in any proposed matter, shall not seek to influence the decision of the local authority. That person must disclose the fact of the interest to the manager, and must carry out any directions which the manager may give. Any such disclosure must also be forwarded by the manager to the ethics registrar for inclusion in the ethics register.

14–53 Section 180 provides for various offences and related penalties, including fines of not over £10,000 or two years imprisonment or both in respect of a conviction on indictment for the offence of failing to comply with the requirements of section 170, or for the offence of giving false or misleading particulars. A person found guilty of an offence under section 180 will become disqualified from being elected or co-opted to or from being a member of a local authority, the disqualification lasts for five years.

L . MEETINGS AND PROCEEDINGS OF LOCAL AUTHORITIES

14–54 Part six together with schedule nine of the Bill regulate the holding of meetings and the proceedings of local authorities in place of existing legislation and the rules adopted by local authorities currently. Meetings can be held in either of the national languages, but the use of Irish is encouraged.

14–55 Members of the public and representatives of the media are entitled to be present at a meeting of a local authority, at present this is not the case, although members of the media are generally allowed into meetings of local authorities.[45] However, where a local authority is of the opinion that the public and the media should be excluded from a meeting or part of a meeting because of the special nature of the meeting or an item of business or for other special reasons, the authority may by resolution decide to meet in committee, provided the authority considers that it is in the public interest.[46] The author-

---

[44] s.177.
[45] s.45.
[46] s.45(3).

ity must pass the required resolution by at least a vote of one half of the total number of members of the authority.

14–56 The local authority can by standing order regulate the right of members of the public and representatives of the media to be present at meetings. The authority may make standing orders in relation to the number attending by taking into account the available space. The authority may make rules governing the conduct of persons present at meetings of the authority, and may provide for the removal of members of the public who interrupt the proceedings or who misconduct themselves. The local authority may also make rules relating to the taking of photographs or the use of recording equipment. However, the local authority may not limit the attendance of representatives of the media, nor may the authority limit the space to be made available to representatives of the media.

M. COMMITTEES AND JOINT COMMITTEES

14–57 County councils and city councils are obliged to establish committees to be known as strategic policy committees to consider matters connected with the formulation, development, monitoring and review of policy relating to the functions of local authority and to advise the local authority on those matters.[47]

14–58 Strategic policy committee is to contain not only members of the local authority but also persons who are not members of the local authority but the chairperson of each of the committees must be a member of the local authority. Guidelines will be issued by the Minister for regarding the representation of sectoral interests, the term of office of members of the committees and that of the chairpersons, and the procedures which are to be applied to ensure fairness and equity in the appointment of the chairpersons.

14–59 A town council may establish by resolution a committee called a municipal policy committee to consider matters connected with the formulation, development, monitoring and review of policy which relate to the functions of the town council and to advise the town council on those matters.[48] Again members of the municipal policy committee may be persons who are not members of the local authority, but the chairperson of the committee must be a member of the local authority. Guidelines will also be issued by the Minister with regard to workings of the municipal policy committee.

---

[47] s.48(1).
[48] s.49.

14–60   Area committees may be established with regard to a local electoral area or two or more adjoining electoral areas, and the Cathaoirleach of a town council who is not a member of an area committee will, by virtue of their office also be members of the area committee.[49]

14–61   A local authority may by resolution establish committees to consider matters connected with the functions of the authority and to assist and advise the local authority on those matters, and committees may also perform delegated functions, however, the local authority may not delegate generally all of its functions to a committee.[50]

14–62   The local authority may not delegate to a committee any of its functions relating to the power to adopt the local authority budget, the power to determine an annual rate on valuation or borrow money or any other functions as may be prescribed by the Minister. Prior to delegating any of its functions to a committee, the resolution must be supported by at least one-half of the total number of members of the local authority. The local authority may, by resolution, dissolve a committee but this is one without prejudice to anything which had been done previously by the committee.[51]

14–63   Members of committees are appointed by resolution and each committee shall consist of three or more members, and again may be contained of both members of the authority and persons who are not members of the local authority. Persons who are not members of the local authority must, in the opinion of the local authority, have the relevant knowledge, qualifications and experience which are relevant to the functions of the committee.[52] Each of the committees will be dissolved on the ordinary day of retirement of the members of the local authority.

14–64   Joint committees may be established between local authorities to consider matters connected with the functions of the local authorities and these joint committees may also perform functions delegated to it by the local authorities. Joint committees may be established which give it the status of a body corporate with perpetual succession and may by sue and be sued in its corporate name. The joint committee may also have the power to acquire, hold, manage, maintain and dispose of land or an interest in land, and shall have a common seal authenticated by the chairpersons or an employee nominated in writing. A local authority may by resolution, and with the consent of the other local authorities involved, delegate with or without restrictions any

---

[49] s.50.
[50] s.51(1).
[51] s.51(3).
[52] s.51(4).

of its functions which may be performed by resolution. However, the local authority budget, the determination of the annual rate on valuation or other functions prescribed by regulations made by the Minister, must remain with the local authority. The Minister may direct a local authority to establish a joint committee and may specify the conditions or restrictions regarding the delegation of functions.

14–65   Joint committees may be dissolved by resolution of any one of the local authorities which established the joint committee, the consent of the Minister being required where the Minister had previously ordered the formation of the joint committee.

14–66   The executive functions of the joint committee, where given, are to be carried out by the manager for that joint committee. The members of the local authority are appointed by the local authorities, the number having been agreed by them. A joint committee must be composed of at least six persons as agreed by the local authorities, and the committee may be composed of persons who are not members of the local authorities concerned, but that person must have the relevant knowledge, qualifications or experience which are relevant to the functions of the joint committee.[53]

N. LOCAL AUTHORITY BOUNDARY ALTERATION

14–67   A county council, city or town council may be resolution adopt a proposal that its boundary should be altered. A county council may also adopt a resolution that the boundary of any town which is situated in its area should have its boundaries changed. A county council and a town council may jointly make a proposal to alter the boundary of a county so as to incorporate an area in an adjoining county while at the same time altering the boundary of the town to coincide with the county boundary once altered.

14–68   The proposing local authority must furnish a copy of the proposal to each of the local authorities whose boundaries will be affected and whatever other local authorities which may be prescribed under regulations which may be made by the Minister. The local authority must also publish a notice giving details of the proposal and inviting submissions from any person concerned with the boundary alteration. Each local authority who have been informed of the proposal must within six months from the receipt of the proposal, or a longer period if agreed, furnish a statement responding to the proposal and

---

[53] s.52(10).

forward it to the proposing local authority. The making of a statement of response is a reserved function of the local authority. Following receipt and consideration of the statement of response the local authority may make an amendment to the proposal, and the amended proposal, the proposal, and the statement of response or responses must be forwarded to the Local Government Commission in order for the Commission to prepare a report.[54]

14–69 The proposal and the statement of response must set out the financial and other implications of the proposal and the adjustments to be made in relation to the financial, administrative or other matters between the various local authorities. Following the consideration of a report by the Local Government Commission the Minister may by order alter the boundary of the county, city or the town, however, the order must be passed by a resolution of each of the Houses of the Oireachtas. If the Local Government Commission make recommendations regarding the alteration of the boundary of a local authority, the Minister may require the local authorities to carry out those recommendations by issuing a direction in writing to the local authorities concerned.[55]

14–70 Schedule ten contains a list of matters for which provision may be made by the Minister, or other Government Minister, in a supplementary order under section 62(2). The supplementary orders may deal with the functions of any authority concerned, the inclusion of a relevant area into any local electoral area or any administrative or geographical district, the application or any enactment to a relevant area, the adjustment between the local authorities concerned regarding revenue by either a lump sum or by instalments, the transfer of employees, and so on. The supplementary orders may also alter the number of members of a local authority, the alteration of the local electoral areas and the number of members assigned to those areas.

O. ESTABLISHMENT OF NEW TOWN COUNCILS

14–71 Sections 183 to 185 deal with the procedure for the establishment of a new town council and for the dissolution of a town council. A proposal for the establishment of a new town council may be made in respect of towns which have a population of at least 7,500, according to the last preceding census. The proposal must be made in writing and submitted to the county council in whose county the town is situated. The proposal must be signed by at least one hundred qualified electors,[56] the proposal must also include a map

---

[54] s.57.
[55] s.61(4), each local authority must comply with the direction, s.61(5).
[56] Qualified electors are registered local government electors or rated occupiers of premises

showing the built up area and the boundaries proposed for the town. The proposal must also set out an indication of the likely costs of the town council and the likely financial implications for both the town and county council. A fee of £1,000 must also accompany the application. Following receipt of the proposal, the county council must publish a public notice and make the proposal available for inspection and must state in the notice that submissions or observations may be made to the county council within a stated period.

14–72   The county council then makes a decision on the proposal and sends it, together with the proposal, and any submissions or observations made, to the Local Government Commission, who shall then prepare a report for the Minister, who makes the final decision.

14–73   A town council may apply to the Minister, under section 185, to have the council dissolved and its functions and so forth transferred to a county council.

P. CHANGING OF NAMES AND DISPLAY OF STREET NAMES

14–74   A town council may by resolution, and supported by at least one-half of the total number of members of the council, change the name of the town.[57] The town council must notify the persons to be prescribed by regulation, and publish a public notice of the proposal inviting submissions from any person within a period of two months. Following this the proposal must again be voted upon by the town council and must again receive the support of more than half of the members. Following this the matter is to receive the consent of the majority of the qualified electors in the concerned town.

14–75   The procedure to change the name of a townland or a non-municipal town is the same as the procedure to change the name of a town, except that the matter is to be put to the qualified electors residing in the relevant townland or non municipal town.[58]

14–76   Changing the name of a street also requires the consent of the majority of the qualified electors in the street, and where the street is in more than one local authority area, must also be supported by the other local authorities.

---

not having full abatement of rates under the Local Government (Financial Provisions) Act 1978.
[57] s.187.
[58] s.188.

Q. FUNCTIONS OF LOCAL AUTHORITIES

14–77   Part nine of the Bill outlines the functions of a local authority as including the provision of a forum for the democratic representation of the local community and to provide civic leadership for that community. This representative role is further advanced by the carrying out of whatever functions as may at any material time be conferred on the local authority by an Act. A local authority may take such action as it considers necessary or desirable to promote the community interest, as expressed under section 66. Local authorities are stated as being independent in the performance of its functions, subject to law.[59] The functions of a local authority shall be performed for or on behalf of the local authority by the elected council or by the manager as may be appropriate, and as provided for by law.[60]

14–78   Local authorities are expressed to have ancillary functions under section 65. The local authority may do anything which is ancillary, supplementary or incidental to or consequential on or necessary to give full effect to a function of the authority or which will facilitate the performance by the local authority of its functions. This includes the ability of a local authority to provide offices, equipment, or the carrying out of any act which is necessary for or related to the general operation, organisation or administration of the authority.[61] The local authority may, under section 66, give assistance in money or in kind, and in accordance with law, to promote the interests of the local community, either directly or indirectly, whether the social, economic, environmental, recreational, cultural, community or general development of the administrative area of any part of the area of the local authority or of the local community.

14–79   A local authority may not undertake or provide assistance in money or in kind for any activity which would prejudice or unnecessarily duplicate an activity arising from the performance of an existing statutory duty by any person in the administrative area of the authority or having regard to the activities of that person would involve wasteful or unnecessary expenditure by the local authority.[62] The Minister may regulate the matters which a local authority may not exercise any assistance either in money or in kind, and the Minister may also, by regulation, set down the maximum amount which a local authority may spend on activities which are classed as the promotion of interest of the local community. To defray any costs, the local authority may

---

[59] s.63(3).
[60] s.63(4).
[61] s.65 (2).
[62] s.66(6).

charge for the use of, or the admission to any amenities, facilities, and services which it provides.[63]

14–80   Section 67 allows a local authority to take measures which it considers necessary or desirable to promote the interests of the local community. These matters are listed in sub section 2 as being general recreational and leisure activities, sports, games and similar activities, artistic, linguistic and cultural activities, civic improvements, general environmental and heritage protection and improvement, allotments, fairs and markets, and related amenities, facilities and services, the public use of amenities, and the promotion of public safety. Schedule twelve of the Bill lists under each of these headings matters which are included under those headings.

14–81   In performing their functions local authorities are to have regard to the resources which are available to it and the need to secure the most beneficial, effective and efficient use of those resources. The local authority must also have regard to the need to maintain those services provided by it and which it considers to be essential, and to ensure, as far as practicable, that a reasonable balance is achieved. Local authorities must also be aware of the need of co-operation with, and the co-ordination of activities with other local authorities, public authorities and other bodies, so as to ensure efficiency and economy. Local authorities are also obliged to have regard to the policies and objectives of the government of a Minister of the Government and the need for consultation with other local authorities and public bodies. The need for a high standard of environmental and heritage protection and the need to promote sustainable development must also be considered.[64] Every enactment which relates to a function of a local authority is now to be read as having these considerations contained in them. However, section 68 is not meant to give a local authority a role which it is prohibited from enjoying or performing by any enactment.

14–82   The functions of a local authority under sections 64 to 67 may be performed by any local authority with regard to its administrative area and may be exercised jointly by a town and county council.[65] With respect to county councils and town councils contained within the area of a county council, section 70 lays down certain provisions relating to the objective of unified service to the public. The town and county councils are to take such steps as may be practicable for the purpose of promoting the objective that the public have a unified local government service provided to them, and to improve

---

[63] s.66(10).
[64] s.68.
[65] s.69.

customer service to the public generally. The local authorities must endeavour to seek proper integration and co-ordination of their organisational arrangements, systems and procedures, including the provision of shared office accommodation and shared locations for public contact, including electronic locations. Section 70(4) states that it is the duty of these local authorities to co-operate to ensure that the services for which they are responsible are organised and delivered in the most efficient and effective manner.

14–83   The Government may, from time to time, transfer a function of the Government or Minister, by resolution passed by both Houses of the Oireachtas, which in the opinion of the Government may be performed effectively by local authorities.

R. MAKING OF BYE LAWS

14–84   Section 197 provides for the general power to make bye-laws for the regulation of facilities, services the management of land or any other matter provided by or which is under the control or management of the local authority. Bye laws may also be made to regulate matters of local concern or nuisance in the interest of the common good. Bye laws cannot be made under section 197 if those matters have been specifically provided for in other legislation.

14–85   Section 198 sets out the procedures to be followed in the making of bye laws, including public notice, and the consideration of any submissions made in relation to the proposed bye laws. The local authority must publish at least two months before making a bye law a notice in one or more newspapers circulating in the area.

14–86   Fixed penalty notices are dealt with under section 204 of the Bill, and allow local authorities to provide for fixed penalties in bye laws as an alternative to a prosecution, and where the fixed payment is paid no proceedings must be instituted.

S. CEREMONIAL FUNCTIONS

14–87   Local authorities may, under section 73, confer a civic honour on a distinguished person, including the admission of a person to the honorary freedom of its administrative area. A decision taken by a local authority to confer a civic honour on a person is a reserved function.[66]

---

[66] s.73(3).

14–88   Local authorities may enter into arrangements for the twinning of its administrative area or establish links with any other area inside or outside the State.[67] Local authorities may not enter into any twinning arrangements unless it has considered that there will be benefits likely to accrue to the administrative area and the local community, or that there will be benefits to the social, cultural and general interests of the administrative area and local community. Regard must also be had to the total costs involved.

14–89   Local authorities may also incur reasonable expenditure for the provision of receptions and entertainment for and the making of presentations to distinguished persons and in connection with the holding of special events.[68]

14–90   Chapter three of part nine deals with the library and archival functions of local authorities, and provides that county councils and city councils are library authorities. The functions of library authorities are listed in section 77 as being the provision of library services as the local authority considers necessary or desirable, including the provision of premises and facilities for the borrowing of books, and other printed matter, as well as tapes and discs, slides and so on. The library authority may also provide services involving activities and events of artistic, linguistic, educational, cultural, recreational, community or other similar interests, as well as the provision of information services involving computers and information technologies.

14–91   Section 79 places on a statutory footing the present policy undertaken by most local authorities of establishing local archives. A local authority is now under a duty to make arrangements for the proper management, custody, care and conservation of local records and local archives, and for the inspection by the public of those local archives. A local authority may acquire either by purchase, donation, bequest or loan, and undertake the care and conservation or archival material of local interest which is in the possession of any person or body.[69] Section 79(9) creates the offence of removing, concealing, damaging or destroying archives held by a local authority, and a fine of not over £1,500 on summary conviction.

14–92   Section 80 deals with the power of local authorities to give assistance towards non-public roads, that is roads which are not already in the charge of the local authority. The non-public road must provide access to parcels of land of which at least two are owned or occupied by different persons, or provides access for harvesting purposes, including turf and sea weed, for two or more persons, or which in the opinion of the local authority is used by the public.

---

[67] s.74, and such a decision is a reserved function.
[68] s.75, also a reserved function.
[69] s.79(3).

The assistance given by a local authority may be made conditional on a prior written agreement by the relevant parties and a financial contribution by those parties. The provision of assistance by a road authority under this section does not make the authority liable for the maintenance of the non-public road nor does it impose any other duties or liabilities on the authority in respect to that road.[70] A local authority may receive, after consultation with the Minister and the Minister for Finance, a grant from central funds, in relation to the construction or improvement of non-public roads.

T. SANITARY SERVICES

14–93 Section 82 transfers the water functions of a town sanitary authority to the county council and the county shall then be classed as a single sanitary district. However, the three sanitary divisions of Cork remain until Cork County Council pass a resolution altering the boundaries. Sanitary authorities may make arrangements with any other local authority in relation to the carrying out of its water functions. In this case the term "water functions" means the functions of a town sanitary authority under the Local Government (Sanitary Services) Acts 1878 to 1995 and Parts IV to VI of the Local Government (Sanitary Services) (Joint Burial Boards) Act 1952, the Local Government (Sanitary Services) Act 1964.[71]

U. AGREEMENTS WITH OTHER BODIES

14–94 Local authorities may make arrangements or agreements with other local authorities, if it is in the opinion of the local authority advantageous to do so. However, the other authority must be able and willing to perform that function. The agreement must contain terms and conditions relating to the performance of the function, for a specified period, the arrangements concerning payments or transfers, and any other relevant matters. The making of this type of arrangement or agreement is a reserved function of the local authority.

14–95 Two or more local authorities may make arrangements for the joint discharge of any of their functions, and may relate to all or only a part of their functional area. Local authorities may also, by agreement, provide staff or

---

[70] s.80(5).
[71] Except s.4 of that Act. Part II of the Public Health Acts Amendment Act 1907, ss.34 to 37 and Part IV of the Public Health Acts Amendment Act 1890, and functions under the Public Health (Ireland) Act 1878 and the Public Health (Ireland) Act 1896 provided they do not relate to sewerage and drainage or the supply of water.

other services, or avail of the services of any person other than a local authority.[72] The Minister may under section 86 direct that an agreement should be
made between local authorities for the carrying out of any of their functions.

V. FINANCIAL PROCEDURES

14–96   Each "local financial year" will now mean a calendar year, but this
may change as the Minister is empowered to make regulations prescribing
another period. Every local authority is to maintain a fund to be known as the
local fund and which will consist of accounts being the usual accounts of
moneys received or spent by the local authority, including an income and expenditure account and a balance sheet. Every local authority and joint body is
obliged to maintain financial systems, accounts, reporting and record keeping
procedures, including the preparation of an annual financial statement which
are consistent with an accounting code of practice which is approved by the
Minister.[73]

14–97   The local fund will replace the existing funds which are already in
existence in county councils, borough corporations, urban district councils
and town commissioners. All monies received by a local authority are to be
kept in the local fund, except for funds which are received under section 108
which establishes a community fund. The community fund is established so as
to fund community initiatives through the community initiative scheme. A
community initiative refers to any project or programme which is in the opinion of the local authority, beneficial to the local community and includes the
provision of improvement of an amenity or of recreational, cultural or heritage facilities. It also includes the protection or enhancement of the environment and programmes to promote community development.

14–98   Each local authority may, by resolution, establish a community fund
for the purposes of supporting community initiatives and may accept contributions from any voluntary, business or community group. The local authority
may also contribute from its funds to the community fund. Two or more local
authorities may establish a community fund for the purposes of a community
initiative.

14–99   Section 109 empowers a local authority to collect an annual contribution from the occupier of each dwelling within its area towards particular community initiatives which are specified in a community initiative scheme.

---

[72] s.85.
[73] s.106(2).

However, before making such a scheme the local authority must publish a notice in at least one newspaper which circulates in its administrative area indicating that a draft scheme has been prepared, and the notice shall describe the initiative, the amount of the proposed annual contribution, where a copy of the scheme can be inspected, and confirming that any person can make submissions or observations in writing to the local authority before a specified date.[74] A local authority can also decide to hold a plebiscite regarding a draft scheme in the part of its administrative area in which the proposed scheme relates.

14–100 To adopt the proposed scheme the local authority must pass the resolution by at least one half of its members voting in favour. Once the scheme has been adopted each occupier becomes liable to pay the annual contribution which is classed as an ordinary contract debt recoverable from the occupier.[75]

14–101 Section 99 provides for the payment by town councils to the county council for activities which are carried out by the county council in the town or in connection with the town. In determining the county charge which a town is liable to pay, the county council must prepare a statement of estimated costs which are expected to arise during a period ending on the 31st of December, allowing for any income accruing to the county council with respect to the provision of town services.

14–102 Where a town council is not a rating authority, the town council shall be provided with the necessary money to meet its expenses by the county council. The town council must prepare a demand in the prescribed way. The expenses of the county council which are incurred in meeting a town council demand are chargeable on the area of the town and are known as town charges. However, this provision does not prevent a non rating town council from collecting annual contributions to a community fund established by it.

14–103 A rating authority is defined in section 2 of the Bill as being a county council, a city council, and a town council referred to in Part I of Schedule 6, that is the former urban districts of Arklow, Athlone, Athy, Ballina, Ballinasloe, Birr, Bray, Buncrana, Bundoran, Carlow, Carrickmacross, Carrick on Suir, Cashel, Castlebar, Castleblayney, Cavan, Clonakility, Clones, Cobh, Dundalk, Dungarvan, Ennis, Enniscorthy, Fermoy, Kells, Killarney, Kilrush, Kinsale, Letterkenny, Listowel, Longford, Macroom, Mallow, Midleton, Monaghan, Naas, Navan, Nenagh, New Ross, Skibbereen, Templemore, Thurles, Tipperary, Tralee, Trim, Tullamore, Westport, Wicklow, and Youghal.

---

[74] s.109(6).
[75] Therefore, it is submitted, not a charge on the dwelling itself.

W. LOCAL AUTHORITY BUDGETS

1. Budget

14–104 Section 101 provides that in each financial year a local authority must prepare a draft budget, formerly known as the local authority estimates. The draft budget must set out the estimated expenditure necessary to carry out its functions as well as the income which is estimated will arise. The draft budget is prepared under the direction of the manager showing the amounts necessary for the functional programmes of the local authority. In preparing the estimates the manager must consult with the corporate policy group, which is a committee of a county council or of a city council and consists of the Cathaoirleach and the chairpersons of the strategic policy committees, and may be assisted by no more than three additional persons who are not elected members.

14–105 The draft local authority budget must be considered by the local authority at a meeting at which the manager is present and which is held during the prescribed period, and of which not less than seven days notice has been given to every member of the local authority. The manager must, not less than seven days before the budget meeting, place a copy of the draft budget in the principal offices of the local authority, and send a copy of the budget together with a report outlining the provisions of the draft budget to every member of the local authority. The manager must also give public notice of the fact that the draft budget has been prepared and that a copy of it has been placed in the principal offices as well as the date and time of the local authority budget meeting.[76] A copy of the draft budget must be made available at the principal offices of the local authority, and may be inspected by any member of the public during normal opening hours, and that copies may be purchased at a price not exceeding the reasonable cost of reproduction.

14–106 The local authority budget meeting may, by resolution, adjourn the meeting from time to time but each adjournment must be within a period of twenty one days beginning on the day on which the first meeting is held.[77] The local authority may at their budget meeting decide to amend the draft budget, or adopt the draft budget without amendment. Where the local authority is also a rating authority, the authority must adopt the annual rate on valuation which is to be levied. Town councils who are not rating authorities must adopt the annual demand which is made to the county council in respect of money needed by the town council for the year. Once adopted a copy of the annual budget must be made available at the principal offices which may be

---

[76] s.102(4).
[77] s.102(6).

inspected by any member of the public and copies must be made available at not over the reasonable cost of reproduction.

14–107   Where the local authority does not adopt a budget for the financial year it may continue to use money and incur liability. The local authority may not exceed one third of the amount previously used in the preceding local financial year.

14–108   At any time after the adoption of the local authority budget the local authority may authorise additional expenditure, but the expenditure may not exceed the total expenditure of the budget except where allowed by regulation. The manager may incur additional expenditure if the manager is of the opinion that the additional expenditure is necessary to avert or minimise a threat to public health, public safety, property or the environment or where there will be additional funding made available by the Minister or by any public authority.

14–109   The manager must inform the Cathaoirleach of the fact that additional expenditure has been incurred as soon as possible and the manager must also inform the other members of the local authority at the next practicable meeting of the local authority.

2. Illegal payments and deficiencies

14–110   Where a proposal is made at a meeting of a local authority or of a joint body which involves the carrying out of any act, matter or thing which is a reserved function and which will involve an illegal payment out of the funds of the authority, the manager, or other employee, must object. The manager must state the grounds of the objection and if a decision is taken the names of the members present and voting for and against the proposal and those abstaining from voting must be recorded in the minutes of the meeting.[78] The persons voting in favour of such a decision shall be surcharged and no other person is to be surcharged.[79]

3. Local Government Audit[80]

14–111   Section 115 of the Bill provides for the establishment of the Local Government Audit Service which will be staffed with suitably qualified per-

---

[78] s.111.
[79] The term "meeting" is not specified but since the proposal must relate to a reserved function it obviously refers to a meeting of the elected members of the local authority and not a committee composed partly of elected members and non elected members.
[80] Chap. 2 of Pt 12.

sons known as local government auditors. These auditors will carry out or assist in the carrying out of audits of the accounts of local authorities and of other prescribed bodies. The Local Government Audit Service is to be an independent body in the exercise of their professional functions. The existing local government auditors will be reassigned to the Service.

14–112   The Service is to be headed by a Director of Audit whose functions will include the organisation, direction and the allocating of resources within the audit service. The Director will also be responsible for the assigning of audits of particular local authorities and to arrange for auditors to certify claims or returns in respect of grants, subsidies or other money due to a local authority by a Government department, a public authority or a local authority. The Director will also, from time to time, report to the Minister with respect to audits carried out and generally on the performance of the Service. The Director of Audit will also be responsible for the Local Government (Value for Money) Unit which was established in the Local Government (Financial Provisions) Act 1997.

14–113   Section 118 establishes the right of local government auditors to obtain information, inspect documents, and be given access to and allowed to inspect all books, contracts, accounts, maps, plans, deeds and any other information, materials or things as the auditor may reasonably require. The local government auditor is also allowed to enter and inspect at all reasonable times any land or premises or structure, but not a dwelling, which is owned, used, controlled or managed by a local authority. Any person who obstructs or impedes or refuses to comply with a request of a local government auditor and acting in the exercise of any of the functions of an auditor, may be guilty of an offence and may be liable to a fine of not over £1,500 or to a term of imprisonment of six months or both.

14–114   The local government auditors report, once completed, is forwarded to the local authority and to both the Director and the Minister. The manager of the local authority must submit the report of the local government auditor to the elected body and the auditor may within three months of the report speak to the local authority. A local government auditor will be entitled to qualified privilege in relation to any statements made to an audit committee or a local authority meeting.

14–115   The Minister may direct that an extraordinary audit of the accounts of a local authority or on a particular aspect of the local government audits report if it appears to the Minister that it is appropriate to do so either by the information contained in the report or following a special auditor's report or for any other reason.[81]

---

[81] s.122.

4. Local Authorities and the Local Community

14–116   The need for local authorities to maintain contact and to consult with the local community and to promote local involvement in local government is dealt with part 13. Local authorities will be allowed to provide assistance to recognised bodies, that is bodies which the local authority are of the opinion promote the interests of the local community. Section 128 provides a statuary basis for the establishment of the county or City Development Boards, and these boards will now operate under the aegis of the relevant county or city council. The functions of these boards include the taking of steps to promote the economic, social or cultural development of the county or city, and to draw up strategies.

X. PUBLIC LOCAL INQUIRIES

14–117   The Bill has introduced the holding of public local inquiries by an inspector appointed by the Minister. The Minister may hold public local inquiries in relation to the performance of the functions of the local authority.[82] The inspector appointed by the Minister has the power to take evidence on oath and any person giving evidence has the same immunities and privileges as if that person was a witness before the High Court.[83] Furthermore any statements or admissions made by a person before the inspector at a public inquiry is not admissible in evidence against that person in any criminal proceedings other than proceedings which relate to an offence under sub section 4 or 5 of section 211. Section 211(4) and (5) creates the offence of wilfully refusing to attend the public inquiry following service of a notice under section 211(3), and the offence of wilfully altering, suppressing, concealing or destroying any document or other information relating to the notice served. Section 211(4) also creates the offence of refusing to give evidence at the inquiry, and refusing or wilfully failing to produce any document or other information. Anyone found guilty of an offence under section 211(4) may face a fine of not over £1,500 or a term of imprisonment of not over six months or both.

14–118   Section 211(5) creates the offence of wilfully giving false evidence at an inquiry, or by an act or omission, obstructing or hindering the inspector conducting the inquiry, as well as the offences of refusing to take an oath or affirmation, refusing to answer any question made by the inspector lawfully, omitting or doing any thing which would constitute a contempt of the High Court. Any person found guilty of an offence under section 211(5) faces simi-

---

[82]   s.210.
[83]   s.211(1)(b).

lar treatment as under section 211(4). Obstructing or impeding or assisting a person to obstruct or impede an inspector may also face a prosecution under section 211(9), and faces similar punishment as under sections 211(4) and (5). All summary proceedings are brought by the Minister.[84]

14–119   Section 212 provides that a local authority or another party may be directed by the Minister to pay costs to another party or to the Minister arising from the holding of a local public inquiry.

Y. PROVISIONS RELATING TO FAILURE TO PERFORM FUNCTIONS

14–120   Part twenty one deals with the power of the Minster to remove from office the members of a local authority. The Minister may, after holding a public local inquiry into the performance by a local authority of its functions, by order remove from office the members of a local authority if the Minister is satisfied that local authority functions are not being duly and effectually performed. The Minister may also remove the members of a local authority if the local authority refuses or neglects to comply with a judgement, order, or decree of any court, or the authority fails to comply with a requirement under section 10A(1) of the City and County Management (Amendment) Act 1955, relating to the adoption of expenses and revised estimates which are insufficient. The Minister may also remove members of a local authority, again following a local public inquiry, where the local authority refuses or wilfully neglects to comply with any express requirement imposed on the authority by any enactment. The members could also be removed where the members of a local authority are less in number than the quorum for meetings of the authority.

14–121   Following the removal of the members of the local authority, elections are held to replace the authority, and in the interim the Minister may appoint Commissioners to carry out the functions of the local authority.[85]

---

[84]   s.211(10).
[85]   s.216.

Index

References are to paragraph numbers.
References to Acts/Bills are when they appear as a heading in the text.
Otherwise, see the Table of Statutes.